SURREALISM

AND THE

BOOK

FRONTISPIECE: Collage by Max Ernst from *Une Semaine de bonté*
(Goodness Week). Paris: Pauvert, 1963. © SPADEM, Paris; VAGA, New York, 1985.

SURREALISM
AND THE
BOOK

RENÉE RIESE HUBERT

UNIVERSITY OF CALIFORNIA PRESS

BERKELEY   LOS ANGELES   OXFORD

The publishers wish to acknowledge with gratitude the contribution provided from the Art Book Fund of the Associates of the University of California Press, which is supported by a major gift of the Ahmanson Foundation.

The following sections of this work have been published previously: "Patch and Paradox in Joseph Cornell's Art" appeared in *Collage*, edited by Jeanine Parisier Plottel, *New York Literary Forum* 10 and 11 (1983); "The Illustrated Book, Text, and Image," in *Intertextuality*, edited by Jeanine Parisier Plottel and Hanna Charney, *New York Literary Forum* 2 (1978); "Max Ernst, the Displacement of the Visual and Verbal," in *New Literary History* (Spring 1984); "Max Ernst and Romanticism," in *Dada/Surrealism* 9 (1979): 48–62.

University of California Press
Berkeley and Los Angeles, California

University of California Press, Ltd.
Oxford, England

© 1988 by
The Regents of the University of California
First Paperback Printing 1992

LIBRARY OF CONGRESS CATALOGING-IN-PUBLICATION DATA

Hubert, Renée Riese, 1916–
Surrealism and the book.

Bibliography: p.
Includes index.
1. Surrealism—Themes, motives. 2. Illustration of books—20th century—Themes, motives. 3. Narrative art—Themes, motives. I. Title.
NC963.S87H8   1987   741.64′09′04   86-16099
ISBN 0-520-08089-0

Printed in the United States of America
1   2   3   4   5   6   7   8   9

TO JUDD D. HUBERT

Contents

List of Illustrations

FIGURES

PLATES

(following page 188)

Acknowledgments

A generous fellowship from the National Endowment for the Humanities enabled me to complete a year of indispensable research in Paris. The Humanities Committee on Research and Travel, and Dean Terence Parsons, provided necessary funds for typing and photographs.

I wish to express my gratitude to Ralph Cohen, whose *Art of Discrimination* revealed the importance of book illustration as a critical tool; to Marjorie Perloff, who so often provided sorely needed stimulation, encouragement, and advice; to Anna Balakian, Mary Ann Caws, and Jacqueline Chénieux, whose surrealistic support proved to be invaluable; to Nicole Boulestreau, Anne-Marie Christin, Anne Hyde Greet, and Eric Haskell, whose work on book illustration helped me put my own study in proper perspective; and to Robert W. Greene and Roger Shattuck, both of whom read and discussed my work in progress. I also wish to thank Beatrice Riese, for her professional interest as an artist and for her help in contacting New York galleries, and Julian Palley, for useful information concerning Benjamin Péret and Aztec culture. I am grateful for the essential aid provided by scholarly librarians, notably Antoine Caron, Curator of the Réserve at the Bibliothèque Nationale, François Chapon, Curator of the Fond Doucet, and Roger Berry, Director of Special Collections at U.C.I. I also wish to thank Inge Ruttman, for making an unruly manuscript presentable; Jane-Ellen Long, for her excellent editorial assistance; and Hazel Warlaumont and Molly Rothenberg, for their very special help in enabling me to overcome a multiplicity of obstacles.

Unless otherwise indicated, all translations are by my husband, Judd D. Hubert, who participated in all phases of the project.

SURREALISM

AND THE

BOOK

INTRODUCTION
MIMESIS AND THE BOOK

W ITH FEW EXCEPTIONS, book illustrations until the mid-nineteenth century are based on mimetic relations between text and image. In almost all cases the picture follows the text as a graphic paraphrase. The artist who shows in his own medium the salient features of the text usually aims to emphasize the textual description and narrativity. When the painter does his best to bring these textual qualities to immediate view, he functions as a penetrating reader, transferring the progression of the text into his own language. But, like most translators, he must for the sake of legibility in his own medium sacrifice ambiguities and enigmas in the original. Until the late nineteenth century, illustrations highlighted eminently recognizable moments, even when they were attempting to provide a reasonably complete running commentary. Under this system, pauses and disruptions occur when artists try to reproduce the illusion of diachronic continuity. The graphic artist, in selecting "moments" or "metaphors" according to consciously or unconsciously derived criteria, performed as a perceptive but submissive critic. He felt compelled to articulate the hidden laws of textual creation in his corresponding graphic series.

Throughout the nineteenth century graphic artists illustrated, in addition to writers of their own day, masterpieces of world literature such as the works of Dante, the Bible, *Don Quixote*, *La Nouvelle Héloïse*, and *Gulliver's Travels*. By the turn of the century, however, most artists were showing a marked preference for the texts of their contemporaries: Maurice Denis chose André Gide's *Le Voyage d'Urien*; Louis Marcoussis, Guillaume Apollinaire's *Alcools*; Raoul Dufy, Apollinaire's *Bestiaire*; Pierre Bonnard, Paul Verlaine's *Parallèlement*.[1] They became advocates of the literary avant-garde while de-

[1]André Gide and Maurice Denis, *Le Voyage d'Urien* (Paris: Librairie de l'Art Indépendant, 1893); Guillaume Apollinaire, *Alcools*, etchings by Louis Marcoussis (Paris: Presses de l'Académie Moderne, 1934), and his *Le Bestiaire*, woodcuts by Raoul Dufy (Paris: La Sirène,

veloping a new "poetics," a new approach to creativity in what had been up to that time an ancillary field. Starting with Manet's rendering of Stéphane Mallarmé's *L'Après-midi d'un faune*, book illustration inevitably underwent transformations corresponding to the revolutionary changes in the other arts.[2] *Les Fleurs du mal* and *Madame Bovary* had introduced an era of sophistication and acute self-consciousness in literature, characterized by an overdetermination of the medium of language at the expense of a confessional approach. Readers of Arthur Rimbaud and Stéphane Mallarmé had to become accomplices in deciphering and taking responsibility for the text.

A similar overdetermination of the medium was manifested in painting, notably in the works of Paul Cézanne. As a result, a new concept of representation in the arts was formulated, and it led to a drastic revision of traditional approaches to book illustrations. Charles Baudelaire, Stéphane Mallarmé, and Arthur Rimbaud, by breaking down the barriers between outside phenomena and inner experience, between event and ornamentation, had indeed brought into question the very idea of a model and hence of a mimetic approach. The point of view adopted by earlier illustrators had to give way to a new conception of graphic space as generated rather than imposed by the page. Moreover, avant-garde poetry, with its paucity of anecdotal and descriptive passages, could hardly be illustrated in the usual manner. This situation forced the painter to discover or, rather, to invent new relationships between text and image while relying on the principles of representation he had already made his own. The painter implemented a vision metaphorically based on, but not overtly or metonymically inscribed in, the text. Indeed, a literal interpretation would have cheapened the poem, in the manner of a prose paraphrase. For instance, Odilon Redon's illustrations of *Les Fleurs du mal* provide purely interiorized visions.[3] He does not copy the Baudelairean decor or his "creatures." The analogy of his lithographs to the text remains hermetic and has to be deciphered. One could say, rather, that he evokes the poet's thrust into the unknown.[4]

1919); Paul Verlaine, *Parallèlement*, with lithographs by Pierre Bonnard (Paris: Ambroise Vollard, 1900).

[2]Stéphane Mallarmé, *L'Après-midi d'un faune* (Afternoon of a Faun), frontispiece, fleurons, and cul-de-lampe by Edouard Manet (Paris: Vanier, 1887).

[3]Charles Baudelaire, *Les Fleurs du mal*, interpreted by Odilon Redon (Brussels: Deman, 1890).

[4]We have of course simplified and dramatized the changes that took place in book illustration. Rodin, a close contemporary of Redon's, also tried his hand at illustrating *Les Fleurs du mal*. In following his usual approach, that is, endowing the illustrations with the solidity and theatricality of his sculptures, he emphasized the anecdotal residue of Baudelaire's poetry. A more

It remained for the cubists to effect the first significant break with what was left of nineteenth-century traditions, mainly by their refusal to represent objects in isolation, their peculiar representation of distance and proximity, their subordination of perspective. By interrelating lettering, often "handwritten," with figurative shapes, they developed in their graphics a new rapport between text and page. The cubist illustrated book, so aptly described by Gérard Bertrand, juxtaposes the many-faceted poems of Guillaume Apollinaire, Pierre Reverdy, or Max Jacob and the multi-planed images of Pablo Picasso, André Derain, Georges Braque, and Juan Gris.[5] This entails a transposition that stresses differences rather than simple equivalence. The cubist writer and painter move beyond the surface of a single object to attain a new kind of simultaneity, best embodied in Sonia Delaunay and Blaise Cendrars's *Prose du transsibérien*.[6]

After the close of the nineteenth century, avant-garde book artists favored literary works that challenged a mimetic approach. The dadaists in particular—Hans Arp in *Die Wolkenpumpe*, or Francis Picabia in *Poèmes et dessins de la fille née sans mère*, Cendrars and Fernand Léger in *La Fin du monde*—sought to break down the order of textual space, the conventions of lettering, and whatever might smack of literary conformism.[7] Pages in their books defied and challenged the reader mainly through the elimination of descriptive and narrative elements that might provide a stable identity for the author or his subject matter. Breon Mitchell, whose significant title for his catalog on the *livre d'artiste* was *Beyond Illustration*, commented: "In part the very rev-

---

recent sculptor, Jacob Epstein, has betrayed the poet in much the same manner. Charles Baudelaire, *Les Fleurs du mal*, illustrated by Auguste Rodin (Paris: The Limited Editions Club, 1940). Charles Baudelaire, *The Flowers of Evil*, illustrated with drawings by Jacob Epstein (London: Fanfare Press, 1940).

[5]Gérard Bertrand, *L'Illustration de la poésie à l'époque du Cubisme* (The Illustration of Poetry during the Cubist Epoch) (Paris: Klincksieck, 1971). Max Jacob, *Saint-Matorel*, with etchings by Pablo Picasso (Paris: Galerie Simon, 1911). Guillaume Apollinaire, *L'Enchanteur pourrissant* (The Rotting Enchanter), with woodcuts by André Derain (Paris: Galerie Simon, 1909). Erik Satie, *Le Piège de Méduse* (Medusa's Trap), ornée de gravures sur bois par M. Georges Braque (Paris: Ed. Galerie Simon, 1921). Max Jacob, *Ne coupez pas Mademoiselle* (Operator, Don't cut me off), with lithographs by Juan Gris (Paris: Galerie Simon, 1921). Pierre Reverdy, *La Guitare endormie* (The Sleeping Guitar), drawings by Juan Gris (Paris: Birault, 1919).

[6]Blaise Cendrars and Sonia Delaunay, *La Prose du Transsibérien* (Prose of the Transsiberian Railroad), pochoir illustrations (Paris: Editions des Hommes Nouveaux, 1913).

[7]Hans Arp, *Die Wolkenpumpe* (The Cloud Pump) (Hanover: Stegeman, 1920); Francis Picabia, *Poèmes et dessins de la fille née sans mère* (Poems and Drawings of the Girl Born without a Mother) (Lausanne: Imprimeries Réunies, 1918); Blaise Cendrars, *La Fin du monde filmée par l'Ange Notre-Dame* (The End of the World Filmed by the Angel of Notre-Dame), pochoir compositions by Fernand Léger (Paris: Editions de la Sirène, 1919).

olution which freed art from the task of representation and allowed the *livre d'artiste* to move beyond illustration, led to our dilemma. Illustration traditionally was successful when it convinced the reader that this was indeed the hero's face, the countryside through which he moved, the house in which he lived."[8]

Before surrealism came into existence as a movement, the cubists, for purely esthetic reasons, and the dadaists, for the sake of impish subversion, had revolutionized book illustration and even typography. The surrealists, who eschewed the formalistic preoccupation of the cubists and who replaced the programmed destructiveness of the dadaists with their own constructive approach to the dream world, dealt with the book in a less revolutionary and more practical manner than their immediate predecessors. Surrealist book illustration, while adopting many of the new techniques, did not at first break completely with nineteenth-century practices, as a brief comparison between the great Curmer edition of Bernardin de Saint-Pierre's *Paul et Virginie* (1838) and two surrealist books, René Char's *Placard pour un chemin des écoliers* (1937) with drawings by Valentine Hugo, and Tristan Tzara's *Parler seul*, with lithographs by Miró (1951), will show.[9]

The Curmer edition of *Paul et Virginie*, described by Jules Brivois as "la perle des livres romantiques,"[10] contains full-page steel engravings and woodcuts in addition to hundreds of illustrations within the text. Tony Johannot and Meissonier (among others) multiplied genre scenes, portraits, and representations of exotic fauna and flora, in an attempt to provide an all-inclusive visual commentary on the text, which tells of the idyllic but ephemeral adventures of the protagonists (Fig. 1). The visual commentary combines documentation (significantly, introduced by a map of Ile de France) with a full esthetic appreciation of the narrative. Not only do the artists make the sites in which the action takes place attractive, but they underscore Bernardin de Saint-Pierre's richly descriptive style with ornate initials appropriately framed with floral and animal patterns (Fig. 2). Documentation and esthetic appreciation enhance and corroborate each other; for the Romantics,

---

[8]Breon Mitchell, *Beyond Illustration: The Livre d'Artiste in the Twentieth Century* (Bloomington: The Lilly Library, Indiana University, 1976), p. 6.

[9]J.-H. Bernardin de St. Pierre, *Paul et Virginie*, illustrated by Tony Johannot, Charles François Daubigny, et al. (Paris: Curmer, 1838); René Char, *Placard pour un chemin des écoliers* (Poster for a Wayward Walk to School), with five drypoint engravings by Valentine Hugo (Paris: G.L.M., 1937); Tristan Tzara, *Parler seul* (Talking to Oneself), with color lithographs by Joan Miró (Paris: Maeght, 1951).

[10]Jules Brivois, *Bibliographie des ouvrages illustrés du XIXᵉ siècle* (Paris, 1883), p. 390.

FIG. 1. Woodcut after Tony Johannot, from Jacques-Henri Bernardin de Saint-Pierre, *Paul et Virginie*. Paris: Curmer, 1838.

ur le côté oriental de la montagne qui s'élève derrière le Port-Louis de l'Ile-de-France, on voit, dans un terrain jadis cultivé, les ruines de deux petites cabanes. Elles sont situées presque au milieu d'un bassin formé par de grands rochers, qui

1

FIG. 2. Woodcuts after François Louis Français and Charles Marville, opening page of *Paul et Virginie*.

truth should remain indistinguishable from beauty. This total visual account is of course given diachronically by, as it were, freezing episodes as they occur in the text. Each plate, whether it emphasizes fauna, flora, or human figures, is a self-contained dramatic scene that gives interest and intensity to the page, paragraph, or initial it embellishes (Fig. 3). All 318 plates are mimetic; none appears to arise from the free play of the imagination. In spite of the many artists involved and the many kinds of representation deriving from the various types of painting—portrait, landscape, genre, and even still life—continuity is maintained throughout, a continuity that coincides with the progression of the novel.

The harmony of text and graphic representation arises mainly through metaphor. Even the vignettes whose essentially decorative function make them seem extraneous still point to the dominant metaphor of an enclosed or hidden object, such as a nest, an egg, or a bird, to show the sheltered but precarious idyll of Paul and Virginie, continuously threatened by the world outside. Menacing storms, although not dominant until the end, all along threaten to arise from the unframed contours of the ocean and society (Fig. 4). Johannot, Meissonier, and their collaborators not only illustrated stages in a narrative progression but also gave visual representation to figures of speech.

Placard pour un chemin des écoliers is composed of a surrealist text by René Char illustrated by Valentine Hugo. Visual paraphrase has not been eliminated. In fact, the illustrator's interpretations sometimes seem quite literal. In the poems, dedicated to children victimized by Franco's legions, allusions to roads are numerous: unexpected misadventures distance mankind from roads, whose linear progression has become incompatible with an existence in dire need of transformation. Rupture and discontinuity predominate in a world where children cannot follow the paths their fathers took. Speed, direction, and even identity undergo reversals. As lines dissolve throughout the poetic text, alienation and estrangement increase. Safe routines and shelter give way to precarious activity; fragmentation replaces cohesion. Buffeted by all this dynamism, the reader envisages for the future either annihilation or a precarious regeneration. Love and desire cry out in a world where mineral, vegetable, and animal elements have lost almost all distinguishing features.

In most of Valentine Hugo's illustrations a head or heads are detached from the body and usually relegated to a corner of the landscape (Fig. 5). These realistically represented heads are juxtaposed with a dreamy landscape with which they seem to have little in common. Valentine Hugo succeeds here in simultaneously revealing the dreamer and his alienating dream. Her

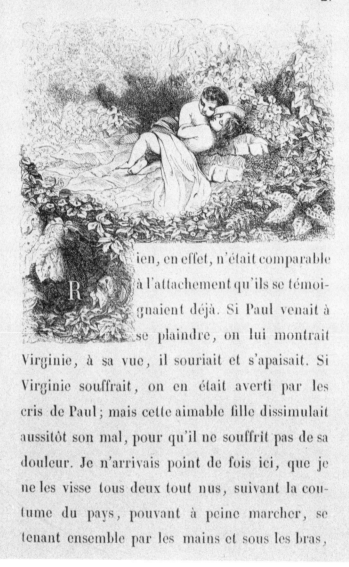

ien, en effet, n'était comparable à l'attachement qu'ils se témoignaient déjà. Si Paul venait à se plaindre, on lui montrait Virginie, à sa vue, il souriait et s'apaisait. Si Virginie souffrait, on en était averti par les cris de Paul; mais cette aimable fille dissimulait aussitôt son mal, pour qu'il ne souffrit pas de sa douleur. Je n'arrivais point de fois ici, que je ne les visse tous deux tout nus, suivant la coutume du pays, pouvant à peine marcher, se tenant ensemble par les mains et sous les bras,

FIG. 3. Woodcut after Charles Marville from *Paul et Virginie.*

FIG. 4. Woodcut after Tony Johannot from *Paul et Virginie.*

juxtapositions presuppose a lost unity or direction, whereas the poet retains a pervasive ambiguity. Several plates translate a passage in the text into a visual scene, an approach which other surrealists would have avoided as far too mimetic. Desire, present in the worlds of both the poet and the painter, provides a bond between text and image. Only the initial plate, which transgresses the conventional order of mimetic figuration, fully belongs to the order of surrealist representation (Fig. 6). The many heads of the schoolchildren are not inscribed in a delineable space; Valentine Hugo has here rejected perspective in favor of a mysteriously constellated space that corresponds to the ambiguity of the poem. In spite of her surrealist themes and imagery, Valentine Hugo can be considered in many ways a throwback to Romantic illustration, for her images tend to paraphrase, and only occasionally to mediate, the text, and they never engage in the full-fledged two-directional interplay of image and text expected of avant-garde illustration.

Joan Miró's interpretation of a poetic sequence by Tristan Tzara entitled *Parler seul* goes to extremes in breaking with the past. Small printed portions of text are surrounded or surmounted by vividly colored figures in the litho-

FIG. 5. Drypoint by Valentine
Hugo from René Char's *Placard
pour un chemin des écoliers*
(Poster for a Wayward Walk to
School). Paris: G.L.M., 1937.
© SPADEM, Paris; VAGA, New
York, 1985.

graphs (Fig. 7). It is not possible to detect correspondences between the objects named in the texts and the figures drawn by the painter or to decipher either one in the context of the other. The multiple ciphers drawn by Miró do not add up, as in *Paul et Virginie* or, for that matter, in *Placard*, to recreate on the visual level the major facets of a literary work. Tzara's poems can be called a verbal unleashing, where words generate or liberate words. They abolish shade and darkness, transforming writing into illumination. They no longer fall into set categories but acquire new attributes: "Le bras cassé de l'eau" (The broken arm of water) and "La langue de sucre dissout la lampe du sommeil" (The tongue of sugar dissolves slumber's lamp).[11] Every verbal cluster suggests either an unaccountable encounter or a dynamic escape. The terms of narrative or description cease to apply when autonomous elements expressing both spatial entity and rhythmic unity celebrate their triumphant liberation. These verbal clusters unleash in Miró's lithographs a number of spontaneous and mobile colored patterns which never interfere with or repeat

[11]Tzara, *Parler seul*, pp. 11, 15.

FIG. 6. Drypoint by Valentine Hugo, frontispiece for René Char, *Placard*. © SPADEM, Paris; VAGA, New York, 1985.

one another (Fig. 8). Each figure, whether black stroke or vividly colored blot, belongs to the world of painting, while functioning as an apparently meaningful sign. Thus the transformation of text into image is reversed: the image, instead of remaining a fixed representation, reaches out in its turn for signs in the text.

As this inclusion of *Parler seul*, a book written, illustrated, and published between 1948 and 1950, shows, we refuse to limit surrealist production to the narrow period roughly from 1924 to World War Two. In this respect among others, our study differs from Lothar Lang's thorough *Expressionist Book Illustration*, whose coverage hardly extends beyond 1927.[12] We have, however, followed Lang's example by including only interpretive graphics as opposed to documentary reproductions. We have excluded periodicals such as *La Révolution surréaliste*, *Le Surréalisme au service de la révolution*, and especially the abundantly illustrated *Le Minotaure*, even though the so-called informative material they contain, far from providing ordinary documenta-

[12]Lothar Lang, *Expressionist Book Illustration in Germany*, 1907–27 (Boston: New York Graphic Society, 1976).

FIG. 7. Lithograph by Joan Miró from Tristan Tzara, *Parler seul* (Talking to Oneself). Paris: Maeght, 1951. © ADAGP, Paris; VAGA, New York, 1985. Photograph courtesy of the Museum of Modern Art, New York, the Louis E. Stern collection.

tion, functions in the provocative manner of the "real scorpions" in Luis Buñuel's *L'Age d'or*, totally displaced from their habitual context. Moreover, such essays as *Le Surréalisme et la peinture* and *La Peinture au défi* differ markedly in their aims from the illustrated books we shall examine.[13] In the latter, artistic production, rather than designation, counts, while documentation, subversive or not, has no place except, incidentally, in Desnos' and Miró's *Les Pénalités de l'enfer*.[14] Indeed, in literary works such as *Les Chants de Maldoror*, the illustrator, instead of providing a relevant, if heightened, criticism of the text, asserts throughout his creative rights and liberties.[15] His own artistic preoccupations do not prevent him, however, from responding,

[13] Louis Aragon, *La Peinture au défi* (Painting Challenged), catalogue of the Galerie Goemans (Paris, 1930); reprinted in *Les Collages* (Paris: Hermann, 1965).

[14] Robert Desnos and Joan Miró, *Les Pénalités de l'enfer ou les Nouvelles Hébrides* (The Penalties of Hell or the New Hebrides) (Paris: Maeght, 1974).

[15] The obvious example is Dalí's illustration of *Les Chants de Maldoror* (The Songs of Maldoror) (Paris: Skira, 1934).

FIG. 8. Lithograph by Joan Miró from Tristan Tzara, *Parler seul.* © ADAGP, Paris; VAGA, New York, 1985. Photograph courtesy of the Museum of Modern Art, New York, the Louis E. Stern collection.

often with considerable intensity, to the text. It is this very duality that justifies our own interpretive approach.

Besides restricting our study of surrealist illustration mainly, if not exclusively, to books, we have regrettably had to exclude, merely by focusing on certain key texts, such prominent and gifted artists as Jacques Hérold, Victor Brauner, Oscar Dominguez, Toyen, Paul Delvaux, and Dorothea Tanning, most of whom are featured in *Le Surréalisme et la peinture.* We will concentrate mainly on the works of Joan Miró, Max Ernst, André Masson, Jean (Hans) Arp, Hans Bellmer, Sebastian Matta, Yves Tanguy, Wifredo Lam, Salvador Dalí, René Magritte, Joseph Cornell, and Rufino Tamayo. We have chosen texts either by fellow surrealists or by authors of the past, such as Lautréamont and Rimbaud, with whom surrealists could identify.

We aim not only to set up dialectical relationships between graphics and the written or printed word but also to situate and define the surrealist book in its various manifestations. But how is this to be done? A simplistic solution would be to insist on the artist's or writer's often precarious associations with the surrealist movement. This historical approach would hardly do justice to artists whose official connection to the movement may have lasted only a few years. Indeed, we may wonder whether the term *surrealism* adequately designates the work of an artist throughout his life. Is Ernst the illustrator of Eluard in the twenties the same surrealist who thirty years later illustrated Lewis Carroll? Critical works on surrealism usually include as authentic members of the group those who regularly contributed to *La Révolution surréaliste* or *Le Surréalisme au service de la révolution*. Except in our chapter on commitment, all texts and graphics included are by recognized if sometimes dissident surrealists or their fully "adopted" precursors. The allegiance of Aimé Césaire and Tamayo may appear peripheral or even questionable. Not only do they come from another continent and belong to a somewhat later generation, but they have their closest ties with Black awareness or a pre-Columbian heritage. Both, however, were affected by surrealism at a crucial stage in their careers. Césaire in *Cahier d'un retour au pays natal*, like Tamayo in *Air mexicain* (discussed in Chapter Seven), associates with a major surrealist and thus becomes, as it were, a fellow traveller.[16]

Terms such as *surrealist book, surrealist illustration*, even *surrealist painting* provide no more than convenient handles quite devoid of ontological significance. We have followed in the title of this study the example of André Breton, who entitled his meditations on painting *Le Surréalisme et la peinture*, perhaps less for reasons of philosophical prudence than to give precedence to his movement rather than to plastic art. We need not, however, emulate Breton's forbearance in regard to labels or accept his dogmas. We might even reinstate the ostracized but nevertheless useful term of *genre* in analyzing both texts and graphics. Luckily, no authority has ever taken the trouble to provide a binding definition of the term *surrealist book*.

Ideally, a surrealist book should unite the texts and images of two artists who were closely associated with the movement and, preferably, should have been acknowledged by André Breton, its tough-minded leader, at the time of its creation. The two artists should have worked in close collaboration, consciously manufacturing an artifact by merging their creative efforts. As might be expected, however, the actual works do not conform to this ideal. In Chapter One and especially in Chapter Two, we discuss books that closely approximate this ideal model. Collaboration between the two main creators is usually incomplete because of the time interval separating their contributions. Eluard and Man Ray in *Facile* and Eluard and Ernst in *Les Malheurs*

---

[16]Aimé Césaire, *Retorno al país natal*, preface by Benjamin Péret, illustrations by Wifredo Lam (Havana: Colección de Textos Poéticos, n.d.); Benjamin Péret, *Air mexicain* (Mexican Air), colored lithographs by Rufino Tamayo (Paris: Librairie Arcanes, 1952).

des immortels carefully planned, and worked closely together in the production of, their books. More often than not it was friendship that induced the painter to illustrate a poet's opus, as Masson did for Michel Leiris's *Simulacre*, Tanguy for Péret's *Dormir, dormir dans les pierres*, Ernst for Eluard in *Répétitions*.[17] Collaboration, as in the genesis of the illustrated book, was an essential surrealist practice. Periodicals were collaborative efforts, engendering, among others, a collection of oneiric accounts. *Un Chien andalou*, *L'Immaculée conception*, and *Ralentir travaux*, although produced in a single medium, were the work of several artists.[18] The pioneering *Les Champs magnétiques* allegedly resulted from the fusion of two minds producing an automatic text.[19] The high point may have been reached with *Ralentir travaux*, but unfortunately the collaborators, Char, Breton, and Eluard, failed to supply information concerning their method of collaboration or to specify the individual contributions of each poet.

The majority of our chapters, however, consider deviation from, rather than conformity with, the ideal pattern outlined above. Discrepancy between theoretical assumptions and practice pervades all fields of surrealist enquiry and endeavor. Chapters Five and Six are devoted to illustrations of nineteenth-century predecessors of surrealism, in connection with whom the very notion of collaboration becomes irrelevant. Surrealist painters, as we have mentioned, virtually appropriated these writers as contemporaries. They illustrated their texts less for esthetic reasons than because they saw them as proponents of revolutionary values. In other chapters, collaboration may seem even less applicable and decoding the rapport between text and image more problematic.

In Chapter Three, we discuss books illustrated by the author. As we have

[17] Paul Eluard, *Facile*, photographs by Man Ray (Paris: G.L.M., 1925); Paul Eluard and Max Ernst, *Les Malheurs des immortels* (The Misfortunes of the Immortals) (Paris: Librairie Six, 1922, reprinted by Librairie Fontaine, 1947); Michel Leiris, *Simulacre*, lithographs by André Masson (Paris: Kahnweiler, 1925); Benjamin Péret, *Dormir, dormir dans les pierres* (Sleeping, Sleeping in the Stones), drawings by Tanguy (Paris: Editions Surréalistes, 1927); Paul Eluard and Max Ernst, *Répétitions* (Paris: Au Sans Pareil, 1922).

[18] André Breton and Paul Eluard, *L'Immaculée Conception* (Immaculate Conception) (Paris: Editions Surréalistes, 1930); André Breton, René Char, and Paul Eluard, *Ralentir travaux* (Slow Down: Men at Work) (Paris: Corti, 1930). We do not include any book illustrated by several painters, such as *Oeuvres complètes*, by Isidore Ducasse, comte de Lautréamont, with illustrations by Victor Brauner, Oscar Dominguez, Max Ernst, Espinoza, René Magritte, André Masson, Matta Echaurren, Joan Miró, Paalen, Man Ray, Seligmann, and Tanguy (Paris: G.L.M., 1938).

[19] André Breton and Philippe Soupault, *Les Champs magnétiques* (Magnetic Fields) (Paris: Au Sans Pareil, 1921).

already stated, a reading of the illustrated book tends to take into account its genesis and to proceed, at least tentatively, from the earlier to the later of the two contributions. For books produced by double talents, we tend to have fewer clues as to which came first, the text or the image: in other words, we have difficulty in identifying which is the illustration, and which the illustrated. Among the artists included in that chapter only Arp can be considered a full-fledged double talent. His writings and plastic works arguably have attained equal status, whereas Miró's and even Ernst's writings are but occasional extensions or transpositions of preoccupations usually expressed in a plastic language. In these works, the verbal and the visual steadfastly remain in their respective places and the production of the book generally proceeds by conventional juxtapositions of the text on one side and the image on the other. Nevertheless, the awareness of a double talent at work complicates not only our reading but the very notion of illustration.

The threat to the relation between text and image becomes much more serious in Chapter Eight. In his collage novel Ernst takes over the literary form and almost completely dispenses with the text—but not with intertexts. For this reason Ernst must be examined as a graphic artist who creates novels by collages as well as by missing, because subtracted, texts. Breton, by including photographs in *Nadja*, by making himself responsible not only for verbal but visual elements—images that he merely borrows—undermines and complicates our role as a confident reader able to deal with illustrated books. [20]

In Chapter Nine we consider postwar achievements, major works resulting in large part from the initiative and participation of creative publishers. In Chapter Ten we see the process of illustration continuing to function in the absence of the book. Confronted with Cornell's boxes and Magritte's canvases, the reader again has to supply the texts.

The actual production of the book renders the autonomy of the illustrations problematic, insofar as the illustrator may have been diverted in the very act of reading the text. The most prestigious and influential among publishers of such books were Daniel-Henri Kahnweiler, Albert Skira, Georges Visat, Jean Hugues, Gérald Cramer, Guy Lévis-Mano, Louis Broder, Aimé Maeght, and that genius of many endeavors, Ilia Zdanevitch, known as Iliazd. [21] Several of these well-known publishers are artists and craftsmen in

[20] André Breton, *Nadja* (Paris: Gallimard, 1958).
[21] Cf. François Chapon, "Sur des livres publiés par Aimé Maeght entre 1946 et 1972," *Bulletin du Bibliophile* 1 (1982): 34–81; François Chapon, "Bibliographie descriptive des livres édités par Iliazd de 1940–74," *Bulletin du Bibliophile* 2 (1974): 207–16; *Iliazd* (Paris: Centre Georges Pompidou, 1978); Jean Hugues, *50 ans d'édition de D.-H. Kahnweiler* (Paris: Galerie Louise

their own right. They all edited a certain number of surrealist texts, but none was exclusively or even mainly committed to surrealism. Jean Hugues has shown a particular interest in René Char and Henri Michaux and has chosen artists such as Wifredo Lam and Joseph Sima to illustrate the former.[22] Aimé Maeght stands as the single most important publisher for Joan Miró. In his choice of texts he went beyond the confines of surrealism by favoring such poets as Yves Bonnefoy, André du Bouchet, and André Frénaud.[23] Many a *livre de peintre* would never have seen the light of day had it not been for these enterprising publishers bringing nascent affinities to light and presenting their educated guesses to a discriminating and wealthy public. We shall attempt to reveal their impact on the surrealist book, which on a few occasions they signed jointly with the artist and, whenever possible, with the author of the text. In several instances, our reading would be insufficient if we merely examined the relationship between text and image. The writer's possible participation in a typographical adventure and the painter's concern with format and packaging were now and again stimulated by the publisher's inventiveness. François Chapon aptly stresses in his article on Aimé Maeght the freedom that this publisher allowed the illustrator both in the implementation of his iconography and in the translation of the text.[24] However greatly the publisher may have experimented with the production of the book, his success ultimately depended on his ability to respond artistically to his fellow creators.

Little more than half of the works treated in our study come under the heading of *livres de peintre*. This raises the issue of the relation between these conspicuous artifacts, in which the signatures of the creators usually occupy a prominent but expected place, and ordinary illustrated books. Actually, the surrealists followed standard practice in this respect, for they rarely deigned to sign economically produced illustrated books. Anne Greet makes a useful distinction: "It is essential to distinguish between the *livre de peintre*, where the picture creates an atmosphere, and the illustrated book, where the picture

---

Leiris, 1959); *Daniel-Henry Kahnweiler* (Paris: Centre Georges Pompidou, 1984); *G.L.M.*, 1923–74 (Paris: Bibliothèque Nationale, 1981).

[22] René Char, *Contre une maison sèche* (Against a Dry House), with nine colored etchings by Wifredo Lam (Paris: Jean Hugues, 1975); René Char, *L'Effroi, la joie* (Fright, joy), with fourteen drypoint engravings by Joseph Sima (Paris: Jean Hugues, 1971).

[23] André du Bouchet, *La Lumière de la lame* (The Light of the Blade), with etchings by Joan Miró (Paris: Maeght, 1962); Yves Bonnefoy, *Anti-Platon* (Against Plato), with etchings by Joan Miró (Paris: Maeght, 1962); André Frénaud, *Le Miroir de l'homme par les bêtes* (The Mirror of Man through Beasts), with etchings by Joan Miró (Paris: Maeght, 1972).

[24] Chapon, "Sur des livres publiés par Aimé Maeght."

is content to accompany the text."[25] Esthetic considerations weigh heavily in the distinction she makes. The *livre de peintre* can only be assessed as an original work of art, whereas the illustrated book, a more modest volume with, generally, a wider circulation, depends on mechanical means of reproduction. Anne Greet assigns to the production of the latter type of book a far simpler task. As we include in our study both *livres de peintre* (for example, Bellmer's individually signed etchings with suite for Heinrich von Kleist's *Les Marionnettes*) and *livres illustrés* (for instance, Péret's *Dormir, dormir dans les pierres*, embellished with reproductions of drawings by Tanguy), we need hardly insist on such a distinction.[26] A number of the books we discuss were produced by somewhat ephemeral publishing houses or even sponsored by art galleries that were intimately associated with surrealism, in particular that of Jeanne Bucher. They did not as a rule enlist the services of renowned printers; we may even claim that some of these modest volumes unconsciously remain faithful to the tenets of surrealism by such no-name collaborations. It is likely that if an artist were to illustrate the same work, first with reproductions and then as a limited folio edition with lithographs or etchings, he would provide a different kind of reading and give a different status to the text. This may actually have occurred in Dalí's double set of illustrations for *Don Quixote*.[27]

The problems that confront the illustrator resemble and indeed compound those of the translator. The illustrator freely and assertively translates from one medium to another. The two more or less opaque languages, so he knows, will at best overlap, for any compatibility between them would depend on semantic transparency. Within the surrealist context, translation and transposition become acts of liberation rather than of allegiance and submission. The image-maker, instead of groping for equivalents, will most likely seek within the text encouragement to provoke and transgress rather than imitate and repeat. By neglecting the letter of the text he remains faith-

[25] Anne Hyde Greet, *Apollinaire et le livre de peintre* (Paris: Minard, 1977), p. 7. Anne Greet's definition supplements W. J. Strachan's: "The *livre d'artiste*, as the term implies, is a book containing illustrations carried out by the artist himself—a painter, sculptor or original engraver (*peintre-graveur*)—who will have himself employed some autographic process for the execution of his designs, be it lithography, engraving on wood, linoleum, copper or other material, some process of etching or indeed a mixture of media": W. J. Strachan, *The Artist and the Book in France* (New York: Wittenborn, 1969), p. 19.

[26] Heinrich von Kleist, *Les Marionnettes*, with engravings by or after Hans Bellmer (Paris: Visat, 1969).

[27] Miguel de Cervantes, *Don Quixote* (New York: Random House, 1946); Miguel de Cervantes, *Don Quichotte: Pages choisies* (Don Quixote: A Selection) (Paris: Joseph Foret, 1957).

ful to its spirit, especially when he can conjure up in relation to a revolutionary work the imp of the perverse lurking within him. Like the collage, the calligramme, the poem-object, the *tableau-poème*, and concrete poetry, the illustrated book manifests tensions as verbal and visual elements interact. Textuality can assume visual characteristics capable of transforming the channels by which it usually promotes communication, or it can even emerge within painterly outlines if the artist so wishes. The barriers that separate text from graphics can, at the whim of the illustrator, be abolished as though to proclaim the simultaneous merging and emergence of lettering and image. Such reflections of standard codification and the usual devices of closure suggest that most of these hybrid works are provocatively open-ended, in keeping with the free play generally advocated by surrealism. The text provides graphic interrogation and exploration without requiring solution or judgment. The resulting volume, with its contributions from various hands, becomes a communicating vessel whose shape and consistency remain amorphous.

In many instances the text, printed on one page, conventionally confronts a splendidly isolated image on the facing page. This traditional spatial arrangement may mislead the reader by suggesting a clear, prescribed progression of the literary and the visual. On the surface, parallelism dominates the relation of text to image. This parallelism, however, merely reflects the persistence of earlier models or practices; it does not indicate the presence of any fixed relationship between text and image throughout the book. In *Les Malheurs des immortels*, verbal collage confronts visual collage page by page, but without providing clues to their interaction. The reader will naturally be tempted to start his exploration by identifying the "original," which enjoys an autonomous existence apart from the illustration. The illustrator's contribution has to be deciphered in terms of the simultaneous involvement of a critical and a creative approach. For the surrealists, the work to be illustrated does not constitute a model or even an antecedent. Text, drawing, or photograph plays for the surrealist illustrator the role of an inner model that stimulates but never constrains his imagination. The reader faces two oddly dissimilar entities which simply refuse to move along parallel tracks.[28] In many books, particularly those adorned by Miró such as *Parler seul* and *A toute épreuve*, graphic outlines and typography swerve from their usually assigned

[28]Cf. in this context Anne-Marie Christin's valuable article, "Images d'un texte: Dufy illustrateur de Mallarmé," *Revue de l'Art* 44 (1979): 70: "The role of the illustration is comparable; however, instead of the visual effect being inscribed within the text, it is now put at a distance, as its principle is no longer the equivalence of terms but their duality."

order; their double invasion of the same space spells ultimate artistic appropriation.[29] Eluard and Man Ray's *Facile* amorously share their frame: the text of the poem in its spatial dimension and the accompanying photograph constantly seem to shape one another.

Methodological studies dealing with illustrated books and, in particular, their interpretation are not numerous. Ségolène Le Men suggests that most approaches do not retain their validity beyond the specific problem they investigate. She concludes: "The diversity of possible methods of approach, though beneficial to critical thought, had the adverse effect of preventing the assertion of a synthesizing conception that would have integrated traditional and new formulas in a generic definition."[30] The one exception she finds is A.-M. Bassy, whose semiotics of the book is too linguistically oriented for our purposes, for we seek to grant equal status to text and image.[31] Critics such as Louis Marin or, for that matter, Le Men apply the same terminology to a visual work that they use for a verbal one: "The painting is a representational text and a system of reading: it would be desirable, so as to understand the scope of this initial assertion, not to take the terms *text* and *reading* metaphorically, but to grasp them from the initial perspective of the frequently utilized metaphor of reading. What is reading? It is the perusal of a graphic ensemble and the deciphering of a text." And Marin reads paintings in precisely this manner.[32] Le Men considers both the verbal and the visual as text. The critical concern not completely to separate reader and viewer, or even image and text, directly addresses the problematics of reading illustrated books, ultimately generated by sequences of imbricated readings.

We have already mentioned the open-endedness of surrealist books, in particular where the relation between text and image defies closure, which in itself, according to Umberto Eco's theories expressed in *Opera aperta*, leads the reader to expand and develop the work.[33] But long before the public can make such optimal readings, the illustrator must have staged his own interpretive reading of the text, an activity which generates, if we adopt the terminology of Le Men, additional textuality.[34] It seems that as long as we ad-

[29]Paul Eluard, *A toute épreuve* (Proof against Anything), with eighty woodcuts by Joan Miró (Geneva: Gérald Cramer, 1958).

[30]Ségolène Le Men, "Quant au livre illustré," *La Revue de l'art* 44 (1979): 100.

[31]Alain-Marie Bassy, "Du texte à l'illustration: Pour une sémiologie des étapes," *Semiotica* II, 4 (1974): 294–334.

[32]Louis Marin, "Eléments pour une sémiologie picturale," *Les Sciences humaines et l'oeuvre d'art* (Brussels: Connaissance, 1969), p. 112.

[33]Umberto Eco, *Opera aperta* (Milan: Bompiani, 1962).

[34]It is only if we take the following statement out of context that Le Men expresses a different

here to the same terminology for the verbal as for the visual, we can legitimately regard an illustration as a metatext—a means of "writing" upon another text that makes it legible in different ways and increases its visibility. Illustration imposes a grid on the initial text by translating it into another language as well as by supplementing it with commentary.

Coming after, if not going beyond, the illustrator's complex commentary, our act of reading can hardly proceed in a linear and continuous fashion or on a single level, whether we begin with the alleged parallelism of the two texts or attempt to reconstruct the genesis of the book. We had better remember that the visual and the verbal never completely lose their autonomy in surrealist books; indeed, their complete fusion would subvert surrealist aims. Thus, if we do not acknowledge and take into account this cleavage, we may fail as readers not only of the surrealist book as a whole but of individual illustrations. An interpretation that refuses to admit that the illustrator continually rereads and rewrites fails to recognize the problematics of the avant-garde illustrated book. This complex reciprocity of production and viewing, entailing a prolongation of the reading process, serves to confirm the notion that such books are inevitably open-ended and thrive on the continuous modification of conflicting kinds of textuality. The endless interplay between verbal and visual in the surrealist book depends on the deliberate rejection of structures and harmonies.

Although Marin and Le Men have opened for us essential problematics, we have not adopted their terminology, for we still clearly distinguish text from image. Chapter Four deals with books in which the writer interprets or "reads" the painter, but in only a few of them do we find that the illustrator aims at restoring the visual within the verbal. A certain amount of self-serving manipulation on the part of the illustrator, verbal or visual, enters into the production of these works. As we shall see, several illustrators (Dalí more than others) consciously becloud their readings by repeating the iconography of their own earlier works. Since information concerning the genesis of the book can on occasion direct our interpretation, we examine certain texts obviously composed without any expectation that anyone would ever illustrate them. Although we have not attempted to reinterpret frequently discussed

---

point of view: "The illustrated poem thus forms an autonomous and closed circuit where each of the two expressions interprets the other." Later she states: "For the illustrated book does not limit itself to associating the readable and the visible in a unique space, but consists besides of two levels, where the initial 'text,' visual or verbal, is once again taken up and interpreted by a second text, also visual and verbal; the possible combinations are thereby multiplied." "Quant au livre illustré," p. 86.

masterpieces such as *Les Chants de Maldoror,* we have, in commenting on less famous texts, tried in our transitional or transpositional readings to highlight networks of images capable of provoking the attention of illustrators. In each instance, the text presents itself as an assault on the artist, who thus appears to respond to an aggression rather than to an invitation to embellish an "innocent" literary work. As these observations show, the reader cannot expect simple correspondences between text and image.

Simultaneous readings of text and image, however desirable, raise more problems when applied to avant-garde writings than to traditional literary works. In most cases, for instance, graphics, although distributed throughout the volume, lack captions and do not connect with specific passages. *Vers le blanc infini* and *Une Saison en enfer* are exceptions in this respect and thus lend themselves to attempts at simultaneous reading.[35] Usually, however, in decoding illustrations we shall merely strive to rediscover salient features of the text as we hope to find them "translated" in the illustration. As our reading constitutes both a critical search and a re-creation, which combine in surrealist practice, it should include not only consecutive but simultaneous decoding. Surrealist illustrations manifest differences that can be evaluated only by keeping in mind the notions of repetition and sameness. Finally, we cannot overlook in our reading other writings such as manifestos, essays, or dream accounts of which the illustrator had cognizance. We cannot read textuality, either verbal or plastic, in isolation—we cannot read without intertexts.

. . .

The surrealist book takes advantage of the reevaluation of certain arts, through the experimentation of artists daring in their collaboration and in venturing to go beyond established genres.[36] It also appropriates new techniques capable of transforming the book itself. As Rosalind Krauss shows, the illustrations in *Nadja* undermine both its esthetic and its documentary projects.[37] Man Ray in *Facile* introduces the process of solarization to make contours more fluid and surfaces more transparent. Hans Bellmer's *Les Jeux de la*

---

[35] Jean Arp, *Vers le blanc infini* (Toward Infinite White), eight original etchings (Lausanne: La Rose des Vents, 1960); Arthur Rimbaud, *Une Saison en enfer* (A Season in Hell) (Paris: Les Cent-Une, Société de Femmes Bibliophiles, 1961).

[36] Cf. Antoine Coron's comments in *Le Livre et l'artiste* (Paris: Bibliothèque Nationale, 1977), p. viii.

[37] Rosalind Krauss, "When Words Fail," *October* 22 (Fall 1982): 91.

poupée makes use of photographs to reveal unbelievable distortions.[38] Surrealist books are experimental not only in their use of medium but in the presentation of the book itself. In *Maximiliana* Ernst and Iliazd combined various verbal and visual possibilities: woodcuts and etchings, together with various types of lettering, invented writing most appropriate for a book focusing on the art of seeing.[39] Aimé Maeght's inventive typographer, Otthoffer, experimented with highly stylized and at times archaic characters that graphically undercut Miró's plates as well as Desnos's modified proverbs and maxims. The most consistent territory of experimentation was that of collage, through which the surrealists were able to throw off their dependence on and allegiance to painting as an established art form. The introduction of the collage as a borrowed or modified visual image, as a juxtaposition of icons, led to Ernst's famous collage novels in which the function of words, as we have stated, is greatly reduced. In *Les Malheurs des immortels*, verbal and visual collages accompany one another without revealing their interrelations. Thus, the rapport between text and image always remains problematic, even mysterious. In the surrealist book, the relation between text and image presupposes the same kind of threshold that is posited between the everyday and the surreal world. And this may explain why referentiality and mimesis are so often excluded.

According to most surrealist critics, surrealism, with its Hegelian underpinnings, is rooted in a dialectics of paradox rather than in mimesis, and its opposition to logic stems from the rejection of one-track argumentation or clear-cut resolutions. What stands out as mutually exclusive when reason governs becomes simultaneous presence through surrealist transformation. Any surrealist work of art, whether verbal or visual, openly designates its enterprises as paradoxical, consisting as it does of surprising juxtapositions, often as spectacularly displayed as those in Lautréamont's metaphor. From the beginning, surrealists have been resolutely iconoclastic. Breton's manifestos in particular attack, among other institutions, the conventional novel, while stressing the need of inventing undefined and preferably undefinable genres, of elaborating new languages and techniques capable of fulfilling the revolutionary aims of the movement.

The collage, the archetype of these innovations, undoubtedly played a key role as an agent both of subversion and of experimentation. Its presence can

[38] Hans Bellmer, *Les Jeux de la poupée* (The Doll's Games), illustrated with texts by Paul Eluard (Paris: Les Editions Premières, 1949).
[39] Max Ernst and Iliazd, *Maximiliana ou l'exercice illégal de l'astronomie* (Maximiliana or the Illegal Practice of Astronomy) (Paris: Le Degré Quarante et Un, 1941).

be detected in works that do not bear the name or label of collage. It includes paradox in its structure and is composed of elements that refuse to relinquish their identity as they intermingle. Collage affirms the differences among the parts that simultaneously compose the image and interfere with one another. Such relationships guarantee that equilibrium will never be restored. It can be argued that in surrealist illustrated books the interaction of text and image to a large extent assumes the functions of collage. It is partly for this reason that these books remain open-ended. Dissimilarities between the verbal and the visual, for example, the "transgression" of writing into image, cannot be overcome even if exchanges of their functions were allowed to take place. Rather, text and image must assert their differences and even their *différances*. In most instances the book not only includes an acknowledged surrealist text, which supplies its own tensions and paradoxes, its own imagery, its own system of collages, but it reinforces all these characteristics by interrelations of the verbal and the visual capable of abolishing parallelism.

The book can in a way be considered the most representative surrealist art form, and the manner in which it evolved adds one more paradox. Volumes that we consider masterpieces of this Janus-faced genre, such as Péret and Ernst's *La Brebis galante* or Eluard and Miró's *A toute épreuve*, appeared after World War Two—long after the heyday of surrealism.[40] The careful craftsmanship that went into their production bears little resemblance to the automatism so strongly advocated in Breton's first manifesto and practiced in the initial stages of creativity by such artists as Masson and Matta.[41]

[40] Benjamin Péret and Max Ernst, *La Brebis galante* (The Sexy Ewe—a pun on *brebis galeuse*, "black sheep") (Paris: Les Editions Premières, 1949).

[41] Cf. Matta's illuminating comments made at the Moderna Museet of Stockholm in 1959 in *Matta* (Paris: Centre Georges Pompidou, 1985), p. 287.

CHAPTER ONE
BEGINNINGS

According to many authorities, including some of the surrealists themselves, surrealism proper arose from dadaism in 1924 or thereabouts and lasted only approximately a dozen years. Surprisingly, the illustrated texts of this so-called "classical" period appear rather tame, particularly if we compare them to their dadaist predecessors, notably the special number of 291 designed by Picabia and the entire run of 391 or the dadaist-inspired *La Fin du monde filmée par l'ange Notre-Dame,* in which Fernand Léger collaborated with Blaise Cendrars.[1]

We may recognize the apparent frame of a narrative in Cendrars's text and detect cubist techniques in Léger's *pochoirs,* but the subversion of the words and images overpowers recollections of other works or genres with which we may wish to compare them. As the title indicates, Cendrars simultaneously ushers in a new world and ends the old one. The figure of the angel becomes the key reporter of radical transformations. Hierarchies and distinctions disappear as god, demoted to the status of bureaucrat, has lost his grip. This is not simply satire—written satire—for language itself has lost its conventional prestige. Modern techniques, more than obliquely involved, have disrupted all verbal conventions and displaced expected spatial representations. Montage and "telescopage" have freed language and undermined the apocalyptic narrative. The images engage in audacious bouts with a text whose guidelines are no longer respected. In fact, the illustrations rival and invade the text. They take possession of letters and words reduced to formal residues in a dynamic and liberated space. An occasional understated sign within the image may refer to the text, but only as an assertion of discontinuity and distortion at the expense of relevance. In a multiplicity of ways Cendrars and Léger transgress frames.

[1]The review 291 appeared in 1915 in New York; its successor, 391, in 1917 in Barcelona and then at irregular intervals from 1919 to 1924 in Paris.

Simulacre, Dormir, dormir dans les pierres, and *Au défaut du silence* show greater subservience to traditional methods and tastes in book illustration. [2] They reflect the professionalism of their publishers or designers far more than the revolutionary preoccupations of their authors and illustrators.

SIMULACRE

The appearance in 1925 of *Simulacre*, the first collection of Michel Leiris's poetry, marks the debut of his collaboration with André Masson, of which *Glossaire, j'y serre mes gloses* (1939) and *Toro* (1951) constitute the most important landmarks. [3] To these ornate volumes of lithographs we must add *André Masson et son univers* (1947) and *Massacres et autres dessins* (1971), volumes which include the prefaces or the poems Leiris dedicated to his artist friend. [4] The "discursive" series and the "figurative" series that make up *Simulacre* exist independently of each other, according to Leiris. [5] Nonetheless, it is difficult to believe in a simple juxtaposition of poems and lithographs. The poet who wrote several texts in the studio at rue Blomet certainly found inspiration in certain canvases. Even if the lithographs do not directly illustrate the poems, they set up a dialogue with them. Certain among them, as rough sketches, may have preceded the poems in such a way that text and image intertwine and complete each other.

The poems of *Simulacre* evince an extraordinary density. The majority of the phrases are models of brevity, at times recalling Latin constructions. The causality of relations is revealed only rarely, for this syntactic density is the corollary to a total absence of legend, anecdote, or dramatic unfolding, whether emotional or philosophical. The poem consists of constructions of solidly massed elements, excluding even the slightest trace of the presence and thrust of the creator. Leiris, author of *Glossaire, j'y serre mes gloses*, stresses the verbal intricacies of poetry while reducing to the minimum preoccupations with referentiality and message. [6] In his own textual comments, defined as glosses, Leiris abolishes traditional distinctions without

---

[2] Paul Eluard and Max Ernst, *Au défaut du silence* (By Default of Silence) (Paris; n.p., 1925).
[3] Michel Leiris, *Glossaire j'y serre mes gloses* (Glossary, There I File My Glosses) (Paris: Galerie Simon, 1939); *Toro* (Paris: Galerie Louise Leiris, 1951).
[4] Michel Leiris, *André Masson et son univers* (André Masson and His Universe) (Geneva: Trois Collines, 1947); André Masson, *Massacres et autres dessins* (Massacres and Other Drawings) (Paris: Hermann, 1971).
[5] Personal communication, 1974.
[6] Cf. Philippe Lejeune, "Glossaire," *Sub-Stance* 11/12 (1975): 117–18.

substituting new connections. He gives a body to that which seems destitute of any substance, while undermining the substantial givens of accepted reality. By this verbal gesture he creates a double simulacrum wherein language, armed with a metamorphosing force, is characterized also by its mobility, thus making manifest its proper being:

> *Le passage des gloses ondule*
> > [Orbe intangible]
>
> The passage of the glosses undulates
> > [Intangible Orb]
>
> *hors des perspectives du langage*
> *le règne des ossatures s'abreuve*
> *au nid muet de l'énigme.*
> > [Intervalle exilé]
>
> Outside the perspective of language
> the reign of skeletons quenches its thirst
> at the mute nest of the enigma
> > [Exiled Interval]

Even if Leiris abolishes categories, he tends to conceive of the universe in contrasting terms, and this multiplies paradoxes. Time, stripped of continuity and even of flux, appears in scattered allusions, sometimes as a solid block linked to eternity, sometimes as an ephemeral passage. Leiris recovers the characteristics of an indescribable, unrepresentable if implacable landscape which although impossible, nonetheless exists.

The stars do not figure as indices of the seasons or of moments but are bound into constellations, establishing a circuit, a series of signs. Temporary, they carry no names but are woven into ideograms. And the light, which certainly fails as a guide, becomes a manifestation of the storm, the bolt of lightning. It is difficult, indeed false, to separate the elements of a landscape whose essence springs from movement and where turmoil is conceived only in relation to the episodic affirmation of repose, just as light is conceived only in relation to shadows. While evoking the force of the wind or the tide, the poet speaks essentially of traces—of their passage, their trajectory, their perspective. He inscribes the line and the vector that sum up the displacement of present or past. His universe, equivalent to a radical stylization, nearly reduces itself to a typographical sign or incipient writing. Poetry delivers the translation of reality and its metamorphosis:

Eveil des mains secrètes
aux replis du courage rapide
cabrée la trajectoire corporelle des urnes
sens incurvés sur des abîmes.
[Souveraine fuite]

Awakening of secret hands
at the retreat of swift courage
while the bodily trajectory of urns rears
senses incurved upon abysses.
[Sovereign Escape]

Leiris displays in these lines a fundamental mobility of the cosmos, its cul-minating points, its abysses. The poet unites what sets in motion and what is moved, thereby transforming trace and passage into line and writing.

We have already indicated that Leiris tends simultaneously to efface sepa-rating barriers and to set up paradoxes. Thus the pronounced tendency to in-scribe curves, arrows, coils with their ascending and descending displace-ments combines with the effacement of boundaries and the striving toward transgression. Movement seen as the essence of life is manifested, however, without continuity or regularity. The alternation of discontinuity and pro-gression, indirectly perceived, deprived of categorical beginning or end, is triggered by jumps, by sudden emergences. The landscape of Leiris under-goes not only displacement but also chemical changes, metamorphoses. The poet reveals the process of transformation instead of defining the object undergoing displacement. Petrification and finally dissolution or pulveriza-tion testify to metamorphoses which, by operating on a geographical and geo-logical scale, push the past back to the surface. These terrestrial transforma-tions join with those of the celestial orbs. And the same confrontations, the same bursts, rise up and disappear at the level of man and vegetation. Despite the analogies and other unifying tendencies, the Leirisian universe in no way evolves toward harmony. On the contrary, rekindled tensions lead to a dra-matic confrontation in which the actor becomes inseparable from the act.

In this world where the spectrum is limited to grayness, subterranean cav-ities and prisons produce, by multiplying, more imprints and shadows. The allusions to death and sickness reveal the obsession, the drive toward transgression, where life and death become interchangeable. Man, deprived of a definite or definable being, is characterized by anonymity, reduced to a silhouette where a glacial eroticism is inscribed. Present mainly as skeletal portions of his anatomy, he once more witnesses this reduction to a trace, a sign inseparable from localization.

Phalanges d'aube hissant l'obstacle des chevelures,
incrustations de la lumière vierge d'ossements,
les nuages contournent le creuset
au ras des gisements pétrifiés par le déluge.
Gravite lentement le rite complice des paroles,
ressuscite la bavure primitive submergée par le futur,
cendres pour enchaîner les racines ensevelies.
Les cartilages dissous s'insinuent en fusées criminelles
avec le cortège rauque des désastres,
délicatement montent au sillage aboli du néant propice,
facettes floconneuses des semences
           dépouillées par les morsures révolues,
tendre présage illimité des flammes :
lèpre limpide.

FIG. 9. Lithograph by André Masson from Michel Leiris, *Simulacre*. Paris: Kahnweiler, 1925. © SPADEM, Paris; VAGA, New York, 1985. Photograph courtesy of the Bibliothèque Nationale, Paris.

By poetic *écriture* Leiris not only sustains tension, even in the reductive state of simulacra, but also sets it against multiple fragmentation, against the flight toward invisibility. While negations multiply and disasters appear ever more threatening, poetry, conversely, reinforces its ritualistic and incantatory functions.

The lithographs of André Masson are characterized by an alternation between architectural and organic elements (Fig. 9). The contours of battlements, arenas, and Greek temples reveal the sometimes mythological and ritual direction of this universe. An architectural order is manifested by straight lines and, less frequently, by curves. The cornices, friezes, galleries, and arenas, far from providing the illusion of tangible substance, are reduced to diagrams. The particulars of the landscape—clouds or suns—far from asserting their autonomy in relation to these architectural diagrams, are modified by them. The most fluid contours, alluding to vegetable, animal, or human organisms, by their juxtaposition with architectural shapes create a tension between rigidity and fluidity, between the conceptual and the existential, being and becoming. In addition to fixing, constraining, and structuring, the lines are implicitly situated within time. Gradually geometry tends less to incarnate a recognizable architecture than to establish a net-

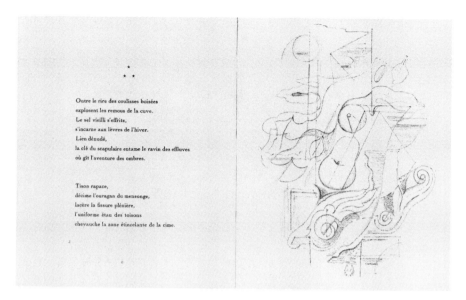

FIG. 10. Lithograph by André Masson from Michel Leiris, *Simulacre*. © SPADEM, Paris; VAGA, New York, 1985. Photograph courtesy of the Bibliothèque Nationale, Paris.

work. Within incipient structures preliminary oppositions tend to harmonize: the organic forms sometimes compose the container of geometrical lines which, by being forced to bend in their upward thrust, assume an air of fluidity.

The book cover plainly exposes this reconciliation of contrary ideas, this transition of the pedestal and the geometric frieze into round forms. The skull and the eye, repeated with many variations, propose that man cannot escape a force lying beyond him: the dream. The three heads constitute the generating points of a network. Throughout the series, the missing center of gravity is replaced by a diagram that reconciles the diverse shapes in all their variations. By analogy, the vegetative contours are integrated into a much vaster system of organic forms. Masson, like Leiris, stresses the analogies among different realms, among different creatures. By attenuating the differences, Masson, no less than Leiris, allows ambiguities to subsist, ambiguities that in one way or another result in a diagrammatic focus. This schematization would be abolished if movement did not prevail in the painter's universe, where all contours and all organic forms directly express metamorphosis—a continual becoming that tends to abolish classification (Fig. 10). Moreover, schematization not only operates among different creatures but embraces all elements—fire, air, water, earth—without representing them directly, without resulting in a landscape. It is useless to distinguish between an isolatable element and the impetus that it produces within the diagram, because being and making merge in the painter's work as well as the poet's. Masson, like Leiris, unites planetary regions, terrestrial or submarine, not in the same space but by the same sign, the same anagram. The multiplication of organic forms occasionally prevails over the geometry, as we have said, without, for all that, weaving tighter networks.[7] This conjunction of several categories within the plastic realm is manifested by the rarification, even the abolition, of superfluous contours.

For Leiris, certain terms allude to a void, to a clearing away of space. In the lithographs, the faults and discontinuities are integrated into a diagram, thereby transforming the drive toward profusion into deprivation. In the lithographs as in the poems, these diagrams resemble charts, with anatomical, geographical, or astronomical outlines. The contour of a sole inscribes movement as a trace and the organic as a manufactured object. In his aspiration toward simplicity of form, the artist refrains from any assertion of mastery of the universe. Indeed the "I" of the poet appears only once and rather as a target than as a projectile.

> Au-delà des ébauches du fléau
> s'insurgent
> les ronces phosphorescentes de mes membres
> [Crêtes des siècles]

> Beyond the adumbrations of the plague
> rise in revolt
> the phosphorescent thorns of my limbs
> [Crests of centuries]

The epigraph to *Simulacre*, taken from Raymond Lully, pertains no less to the painter than to the poet: "From one place to the other, without a break." To the magic invocations of the poet corresponds in Masson a denial of the everyday, as the allusions to mythological places seem to indicate. Without transition, without anecdote, the collaborators juxtapose dreams and memories with the more visible signs of life. They grapple with the faults and voids that it is incumbent upon creators to fill or at least to cover up. On the lithograph-frontispiece appears the twice-broken word *sim-ula-cre*. This fragmentation is linked to others: incomplete buildings, busts separated from

---

[7]In this context it is interesting to quote Masson's commentary on *grande peinture* in *Le Plaisir de peindre* (Paris: La Diane Française, 1950), p. 73: "The creation of a canvas is based on the weaving together, the fusion of various elements. Bound together, integrated, forming a unity. The intervals matter as much as the bodies that determine them."

pedestals, as well as syntactical ruptures. Text and image are conjoined so as to aspire to a unity without breaks by transforming the wreckage that encumbers the beginning. But poet and painter maintain throughout an awareness that their creation will never be more than a simulacrum.[8]

DORMIR, DORMIR DANS LES PIERRES

Dormir, dormir dans les pierres was one of the early surrealist books, kindled by the enthusiasm of a new friendship.[9] It is divided into five sections, each preceded and followed by a vignette. This first poetic text by Benjamin Péret followed his important short story *La Brebis galante*.[10] Benjamin Péret and Yves Tanguy were particularly well suited to publishing a book together. Enthusiastic, spontaneous creators, they seem less concerned than most others with the theoretical aspects of surrealism, provided we disregard Péret's political polemics. In 1926 and 1927 Tanguy was freeing himself from a representational, narrative style of painting. We do not wish to imply that when he discovered his way of painting dreamscapes peopled by haunting *machines célibataires* he ceased to be representational, but it then became impossible for the viewer to identify the scene or to construct a referential event. Tanguy's 1926 canvases *La Peur* and *La Dormeuse* exemplify this important turning point. In *La Peur*, where a horse is abandoned by his hardly visible rider in the very act of escaping, the landscape is composed of an aggressive, erotic vegetation. In *La Dormeuse* the sleeper is visible under the surface of the water; the dream landscape suggests the decomposition or dispersion of the

[8]Pierre Chappuis defines the title of Leiris's volume: "With uncanny precision, this first title designates the ridge on which Michel Leiris, divided between his taste for spectacle and his mistrust of embellishment (his fear of giving himself the star role) uncomfortably stands, this ridge separating the true from the false, the authentic from the inauthentic or, just as fittingly, poetry from the denial of poetry": Pierre Chappuis, *Michel Leiris* (Paris: Seghers, 1973), p. 6.

[9]In *Yves Tanguy* (Brussels: André Dérache, 1977), p. 15, Patrick Waldberg states: "To this intimacy we owe one of the most compelling volumes of surrealist poetry, *Sleeping, Sleeping in the Stones*, in which Tanguy's spellbinding illustrations combine with the text. . . . It is clear that for the illustration of his first book Tanguy could not have dreamed of a text better suited to his deepest inspiration." Péret dedicated to Tanguy a poem, "Les Lycées de jeunes filles sont petits" (Girls' schools are little) in *De derrière les fagots* (From Beneath the Woodpile—a place where the best bottles of wine are hidden). See *Oeuvres complètes* (Paris: Losfeld, 1971), vol. II, p. 107. "Yves Tanguy ou l'anatife torpille les Jivaros" appeared in *Cahiers d'Art* X, 5 & 6 and is reprinted in the Tanguy catalogue of the Centre Georges Pompidou retrospective, 17 June to 27 September 1982.

[10]According to Jean-Louis Bédouin, *La Brebis galante* was written as early as 1922 or 1923: *Benjamin Péret* (Paris: Seghers, 1961), p. 73. *La Brebis galante*, illustrated with etchings as well as *pochoir* colored drawings by Max Ernst and published in a limited edition by Editions Premières (Paris, 1949), is considered a major surrealist illustrated book.

dreamer's identity; the various elements become autonomous and assert their dynamism. We feel that by 1927 Tanguy would have omitted the dreamer, the horse, and the rider. Toward the same period there seems to be a considerable change in Tanguy's use of titles: the 1926 *La Peur* and *La Dormeuse*, for instance, remain conventionally descriptive. Later titles such as *L'Humeur des temps* (1928) and *Essai sur les erreurs populaires* (1927) mystify rather than explain and possess obviously literary qualities which show the impact of surrealist contacts.

In *Dormir, dormir* Tanguy's drawing and vignettes represent landscapes—more specifically, dream landscapes, which, however, do not fully represent the imaginary world. Their chief characteristics are their mobility and changeability. The viewer does not confront a moment which will immediately be outdated, but a panorama where every element asserts the process of change and mobility. As we suggested, these drawings show some but by no means all aspects of the paintings of the same period: within a relatively uncluttered page various components manifest organic characteristics and functions. In the canvas's spatial depth the absence of lines of demarcation and the strangeness of the luminosity contribute to that otherworldliness for which Tanguy is noted but which lies outside the scope of the drawings. There are no clearly defined organic structures; almost no recognizable living creatures emerge (the end of the third poem provides the only exception). The mountain or group of mountains in the early plates recurs as a mere outline that can hardly be ascribed to a specific location. And this vague outline could in some instances refer to the sea and the tides no less than to mountains. Moreover, it combines upward and downward directions at the expense of substantial referentiality.

The changeability of the contours is suggested by the presence of several differently shaped elevations which function as variations on one another. All elevations and declivities give birth to some germination or growth. Here again Tanguy avoids single, unambiguous appearance; germination and growth are represented by a group of wavy lines, a patch of small tufts, a series of more or less curved stems. Undoubtedly all these constellated lines, whether shorter or longer, higher or more widely spaced, more curled or straighter, refer to the vegetable world, particularly to its most visible forms—stems and blades. Tanguy thus outlines a fundamental, undifferentiated mountain-seascape in which we seek in vain for a unilateral relation between the organic and the mineral world. As the elevations can be interpreted equally well as motions of the sea or upheavals of the land, so the tufts and the blades or stemlike lines can denote or summarize not only flora but fauna—including humanity. Growth, extension, expansion bind together the many lines, because they always seem to lead to an uncharted, mysterious domain, predictable because they occur in structured clusters interrelating all the contours that the viewer gradually uncovers and which discourage him from construing Tanguy's world in terms of regression or curtailment. Although spatial invasion, so characteristic of Tanguy's late paintings, has little relevance here, forms do tend ever so slightly to encroach on one another, but without depth or substantiality such encroachment merely increases the sense of transformation and kinship.

Tanguy's drawings are erotic, even though the only direct human reference is three hands assembled in the foreground of the first drawing and colored in flesh tones. As often occurs in surrealist art, they suggest at once gloves and hands with their mobile fingers, obviously sexual motifs, echoed by other figures in the drawing. Hands become merely a more stylized or less explosive version of tentacles, detectable in several of the drawings. Most groups of lines indirectly refer to hair. Eroticism becomes universalized; the landscape and the organism mirror each other in their subjection to forces that excite motion, give rise to invisible waves, propagate storms in every direction. All elements remain present, each one echoing, completing, and fertilizing the others. Elevations twist into enticing spirals; the mountain's silhouette, with its almost geometrical pyramid or cone, suggests the female pubis. Spitting, sprouting flamelike bushes of hair bring to mind a volcano. Sea and sky, underground and above become almost indistinguishable. As the container is always transgressed by the contained, as the delineating contours germinate leaves or petals, so the landscape of the first drawing can be replaced by the strange, at once mutilated and all-inclusive, creature in the second. Headless but not handless, this unrecognizable cloud shape or endlessly transformed sequence of elevations is both erect and seated.

It seems that Tanguy has added only a few modulations to his iconography in order to adapt to Péret's poetry. If we view the hors-texte and the vignettes as a sequence with both recurring elements and a development, we encounter toward the end an element of stabilization. In fact, if we do not take into account the title page (which is, in our opinion, Tanguy's best drawing), there seems to be a movement of intensification that becomes especially strong at the end of the first section. The somewhat repetitive emergence of lines toward the end paradoxically results in greater autonomy for each line and an increased emergence of interlaced patterns exemplified by a greater prominence of chains and extended ribbons. The shapes are not only subject to simultaneous upward, downward, and diagonal thrusts but also to circular motion, which diminishes distances and increases cohesion. Later emerges a movement of relative ebbing, where horizontality dominates in the landscape and tensions subside.

On the title page the painter scatters the letters in a meandering downward motion (Fig. 11).[11] Numbers and letters recur in other drawings, though to a lesser degree; they are not exclusively used as signs of another system of representation, but function as "actions" in the scene. Introduced in a linear fashion, they do not follow a recognizable numerical, alphabetical, or semantic order. Moreover, these letters and numbers actively participate in the system of spatial dislocation while providing pictorial meaning. For Tanguy they do not remain separate; they are scattered over the page in a manner similar to parts of the landscape. Germination and dissemination, appearing as multiple grains and dots (belonging to the floral while serving as linguistic signs) surround both the numbers and the various shapes as though to establish the interchangeability of the quantitative and the qualitative realm. The landscape is generated by the letters in which they become objects. From other lines in the drawing may germinate the contours of words to come, which in their turn may embody mysterious stones. These promises of the title page are repeatedly broken throughout. They announce in a twofold and hence equivocal manner the adventures of dreams, the vertiginous itinerary of possible tribulations, from which the recognizable image of the stone remains conspicuously absent. In Tanguy's drawings substance and matter have no place, for the forces of gravity do not govern the universe of dreams.

How does this order created by the painter correspond to Péret's text? We know little, perhaps nothing, of how Tanguy may have read the poems. And we might even claim with some plausibility that Tanguy was primarily struck by individual poetic lines or images and that his illustrations responded to certain verses or metaphors, which served as catalysts to the ebb and flow of his own pictorialization. The following lines taken from different poems could conceivably have played such a role:

> *Tous ses tentacules n'arriveront jamais à transformer le ciel en mains*
> [p. 55]

> All its tentacles will never succeed in transforming the sky into hands

> *et le sommeil de l'air est propice à la naissance des montagnes*
> [p. 55]

> and the slumber of the air fosters the birth of mountains

[11] In 1947 Tanguy contributed still another illustration, a frontispiece, to *Dormir, dormir dans les pierres*. Cf. Benjamin Péret, *Feu central* (Paris: K Editeur, 1947), p. 16. Tanguy created a single erect figure manifesting erotic aggression.

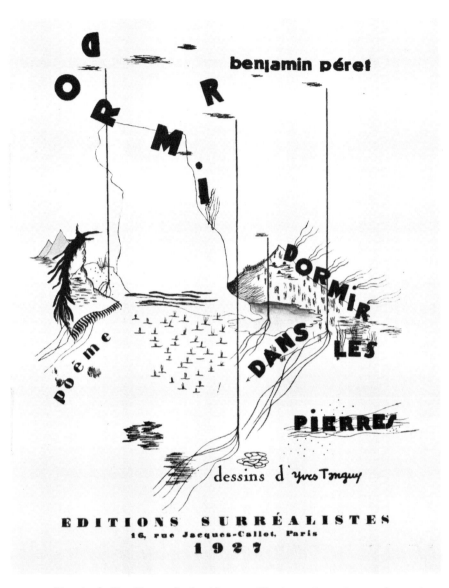

FIG. 11. Drawing by Yves Tanguy for the title page of Benjamin Péret, *Dormir, dormir dans les pierres* (Sleeping, Sleeping in the Stones). Paris: Editions Surréalistes, 1927. © SPADEM, Paris; VAGA, New York, 1985. Photograph courtesy of the Museum of Modern Art, New York, the Louis E. Stern collection.

Tanguy's illustration suggests the disregard of proportions, the analogy and interrelation of tentacles and hands, the active principle of metamorphosis which can be generated from a single element or from the persuasiveness of the landscape, the passage from movement to immobility, from flowing to ebbing, characteristic of the dream that is the unifying creation of all. Moreover, the key function given to physically suggestive words such as *mountain, hands, tentacles* may have struck the painter seeking reductive equivalents (Fig. 12). At that time (1926) Tanguy painted his well-known *Genèse*, which explicitly reveals his preoccupation with the creative process. Even if we were to select individual images as starting points for the illustrations, it would not be for their inherent descriptiveness. Although vision and visual elements play a significant role in Péret's poetry, they could hardly possess sufficient power to instill in the painter an urge to imitate. As the hand or the mountain could represent, as we have suggested, a strong link in a network of contours and lines, Tanguy might conceivably have put the emphasis on such words, all the more because they corresponded to the iconography of his own paintings at the time.

Tanguy did not misrepresent or distort Péret, the only poet for whom he illustrated two volumes. All the characteristics we have discovered in the Tanguy drawings are finally grounded in the poems, for Péret's landscapes or dreamscapes are based on the complete interchangeability between the natural world and the body.

> *Entourez de vos mains le corps fragile des vents*
>
> [p. 47]
>
> Encompass in your hands the frail body of the winds
>
> *d'une corde à noeuds et d'un pendu*
> *tous deux se regardent avec des yeux d'horizon*
>
> [p. 56]
>
> with a knotted rope and a hanged man
> both of them peer at one another with the eyes of horizon
>
> *le sternum de verre que polit le soleil des caves*
>
> [p. 55]
>
> The glass sternum polished by cellar suns

Elsewhere in the poem other parts of the body are mentioned: *oeil, chevelure, tête, veines, sang, lèvres, mains*—eye, hair, head, veins, blood, lips, hands. However, they never display their anatomical function or enter into relationship with other parts of the world. Indeed, these physical qualities and parts

FIG. 12. Drawing by Yves Tanguy from Benjamin Péret, *Dormir, dormir dans les pierres.*
© SPADEM, Paris; VAGA, New York, 1985. Photograph courtesy of the Museum of Modern
Art, New York, the Louis E. Stern collection.

belong to a system of false or displaced attributions, a system where the barrier between animate and inanimate is broken down, where exchanges between the active and passive elements make interchangeability compulsory. Moreover, since physical outlines characterize the unlimited or invisible (winds or horizon), the mysterious kinship between single elements and complex organisms is revealed. It would be erroneous to claim that Péret renders the body visible or gives to natural elements a physical stability or presence. On the contrary, his metaphors affirm the principles of metamorphosis and affinity that mark Tanguy's illustrations as well as his paintings.

We have already insisted on Tanguy's repeated use of revealing shapes and movements to insure the compelling presence of eroticism. Péret shows far greater complexity in his poetry, introducing subtle erotic elements: the relentlessly devious provocation of winds and storms, capable of displacing in multifarious directions the surface as well as the depth of the water. In addition, Péret's poetry relies on synesthesia:

> *De la corne du sommeil aux yeux révulsés des soupirs*
> *il y a place pour une cornemuse bleue*
> *d'où jaillit le son fatal du réséda fleuri*
>
> [p. 45]

> From slumber's horn to the turned-up eyes of sighs
> there's room for a blue bagpipe
> whence springs the fatal sound of blooming mignonette

or

> *qui salissent les regards bleus des squales*
> *voyageurs parfumés*
> *voyageurs sans secousses*
> *qui contournent éternellement les sifflements avertisseurs des saules*
>
> [p. 51]

> who sully the blue glances of sharks
> perfumed travellers
> unjolted travellers
> ever circumscribing the warning whistles of willows

In the first quotation, vision and sound are doubly linked as *soupirs* endowed with sight, and flowers become sonorous. *Corne* and *cornemuse* are akin in both sound and form, as both become generators of words and images. Péret's dream manifestations are not solely a ritual for the eye; vision is not separated, but accompanied or generated by sounds, songs, expressions. In addition, growth, regeneration, and eclipse do not merely, as in the drawings, result in the undulations and fertilization produced by a concatenation of forces. Touch manifests its presence and even asserts itself as an active force; caresses, tactile encounters, alternations of freezing and thawing, odd sensations passing through strange stages in which the sun becomes frostlike and consists of germinating moss (*soleil mousseux*, "frothy sun") play a significant part and display erotic dominance.

Péret's universe appears strongly, if not overtly, sensuous compared to Tanguy's. This stems not only from the collusion of all senses in his universe but from the pervasive presence of matter and substance. Tanguy, in his use of the drawings, created landscapes consisting of forms and lines, deliberately bypassing both depth and matter, which play such a significant role in the text. In other words, the manner and the style of drawings Tanguy chose (note that the use of color is very restricted) enabled him to insist on the dynamic process, on its cosmic and organic constituents, on time almost as much as on space. He proceeded in a stylized manner without providing allusions to textures, distances, transparency, or opacity. Péret's universe multiplies the very stones which, as we intimated, Tanguy omitted. Not that the word *pierre* is a key term. Chemical bodies, elements, and metals abound in the poetry: *charbon, agate, silex, quartz, mercure, cristal, aluminium*. The word *pierre* occurs coupled with signs of life and transformation: *pierres fleurs, pierres frémissantes*. The title itself strikes by the contradictory nature of the wish, for it destroys the identity of stone as hard, cold, inflexible matter. *Dormir, dormir dans les pierres* suggests a death wish combined with the continuity of dream work. Hence the attainment of a depth incompatible with a state of awakening. The many recurrences of hard elements constitute merely metonymic transformations of the stone, dark or light, adamant or dusty, liquid or solid. The stone, with its many transformations, cannot be isolated; its alchemical powers are unlimited, so that even were it absent, its force would still make itself felt, as that of the sun and the stars, in a nonhierarchical system, in a discourse that disrupts accepted proportions and classifications, constituting one link among many. The earthly substances acquire the power of reflection, of reverberation, of dispersion and germination, intensifying both tactile and visual manifestations and asserting above all their affinities.

In Péret's poetry the reader discovers a constant transition from the hidden, the mysterious, the miraculous to the overt in order to return to another depth or secret, such as the pattern of the complex bloodstream with its multiple veins or arteries. The dark substances which can be dispersed into dust or transformed into sources of light often allude to tunnels or labyrinths or radically shift to angry cataracts.[12] In other words, "it has at its disposal in each link of the syntagmatic chain a far more extensive paradigm than that of any other poetry."[13] Péret does not localize the pursuits, escapes, and encounters, which take place in the sea as well as in the sky. The sensations of depth and of spiral motion alternately emerge and disappear. The poet's world is, in the fullest sense of the word, that of the surrealist adventure from which Tanguy has abstracted his drawings. While schematizing the poems, Tanguy's multiple lines add innovative shapes on which we may arbitrarily bestow more or less suitable names without destroying their anonymity.

Péret's world is one of presence, where every word has the power to name or assumes an identity. Beyond the tangibility of his universe, the reader senses the intensities of passion, of happy and desperate love or irretrievable anguish. He addresses a flower as a woman caressed or attached by forces and objects set free by losing their proper function. From the light touch to the steady forces of rivers as well as to the violence of waterfalls, the equilibrium shifts from hope and prophecy to boredom and emptiness. Often the poet gives a semblance of logic and a superficial continuity to manifestations that function merely by unleashing their dubious vitality. "Car . . . car," "parce que . . . parce que": such words are multiplied only to mask the lack of validity of an outer order and to replace it:

> La poudre s'ennuyait dans le désert des mains
> dont le superflu s'épanche sur des gorges pâles
> issues du miroir que nul ne découvrit
> car il part et revient comme une feuille
> car il est bleu
> car il est rouge
>
> [p. 46]

> Powder wearied in the desert of hands
> whose superfluity spreads on pale throats
> issuing from the mirror nobody discovered
> for it leaves and returns like a leaf
> for it is blue
> for it is red

---

[12] Since many *livres de peintre* are unpaginated, we have, whenever possible, quoted from more easily available reprint editions. Benjamin Péret, *Oeuvres complètes* (Paris: Losfeld, 1969), vol. I, p. 51. All quotations are from this edition.

[13] Jean-Christophe Bailly, *Au-delà du langage* (Paris: Losfeld, 1971), p. 31.

We have mentioned Tanguy's implied acknowledgment on the title page that he was interpreting or transforming a literary work. Péret's poem includes allusions to the act of writing poetry:

> *Et telle plume qui disparaît comme un ABCD*
> *se retrouve au printemps sur la tête des cieux*
> *car les cieux sont faits de vos plumes*
>
> [p. 46]
>
> And such a feather that disappears like an ABCD
> reappears in the spring on the head of the heavens
> for heavens are made of your feathers

The acts of writing, lettering, numbering, creating, destroying, as well as the pervasiveness of a network, the mirroring of manifestations together with their unlimited variations and their reconstellations comment each in its own way on poetic activity, on a productive process never defined, never arrested, never isolated. This process does not originate in a persona, but corresponds to the manifestations of the dream, which contains tangible as well as intangible worlds. Tanguy could not have included this aspect of Péret's poetry once he had abstracted "le fer et le sang." Although his title page clearly suggests that literature is not "above" but "within," although he refused to distinguish between literary signs and representations of visual objects, although he undermined verbal stasis, he did not really respond in his illustrations to the fundamental nature of poetic creation. It seems that Tanguy's title page can be construed as an acknowledgment of his role as illustrator and an assertion of the aims of the illustrated book. As he strove for the fusion of his own contribution with that of Péret, he did not have to absorb into his drawings the specifically linguistic aspects of the enterprise or worry about verbal referentiality. It also seems that Tanguy's title page can serve as a program, as a sort of blueprint of which he carried out only a part.

Critics have repeatedly stressed the revolutionary, subversive qualities of Péret's writings.[14] Humor and parody abound in his verse, including *Dormir, dormir dans les pierres*. First of all, Péret uses and dismantles popular expressions such as *tirer à la courte paille* ("draw straws") or *jeter le froc aux orties* (leave a [religious] order, literally, "throw the cowl to the nettles"). The reader recognizes the expression even though it is taken out of context, fragmented, reversed, and perverted.

---

[14]Especially Guy Prévan in "Trajectoire politique d'un révolutionnaire poète," in *Benjamin Péret*, edited by Jean-Michel Goutier (Paris: Henri Veydrier, 1982), pp. 80–106.

et crier Orties Orties
Jetez les orties dans le gosier du nègre
borgne comme seuls savent l'être les nègres
et le nègre deviendra ortie
et soutane son oeil perdu

[p. 52]

and shout Nettles Nettles
throw the nettles in the Black man's throat
one-eyed as only Blacks know how to be
and the Black will become a nettle
and cassock his lost eye

Froc is replaced by *soutane* as well as by *orties*; its dark color, by *nègre*. Objects become persons, persons objects; liberation assumes the appearance of cruelty; what is discarded takes on a new personality. Péret restricts the apparent arbitrariness of his verbal games. Since the nettles grammatically take the place of the frock, so the Black man must take the place of the nettles. Therefore the nettles regain their propensity to sting. Tanguy's art is undoubtedly free of the need to subvert and in this respect he differs from Péret, who turns an expression into a sequence of verbal explosions and equates words that are semantically at odds with one another.

Péret subverts not only modern expressions but biblical and mythological allusions such as that of the heron who drops a stone, in order to wake the other birds, when danger approaches. *Lentilles*, lenses rather than lentils, seems to evoke the biblical Esau, who fits perfectly into this modern text where mirrors and echoes actively participate in the always unexpected emergence of simultaneous or juxtaposed images. Péret's poems are full of odd literary recollections of shockingly distorted and disconnected interests. Here he displaces an echo from Gérard de Nerval's sonnet inspired by Goethe, "Do You Know the Land"; elsewhere lines from Baudelaire's "Le Voyage" change a life itinerary into a surprise party, "Ah que le charbon est beau sur les routes tournesol" (Oh how beautiful is coal on sunflower roads) to which he soon adds parodies of Rimbaud and Mallarmé. Péret apes Lautréamont overtly:

belle comme un trou dans une vitre
belle comme la rencontre imprévue d'une cataracte et d'une bouteille

[p. 60]

beautiful as a hole in a pane
beautiful as the unexpected encounter of a cataract and a bottle

celui qui provoque la rencontre dans l'escalier des bouteilles
d'une orange et d'un portemonnaie

[p. 56]

The one who provokes the encounter in a staircase of bottles
of an orange and a purse

Undoubtedly Péret does not so much stress Lautréamont's revolutionary esthetics, his substitution of the ordinary and casual for the eternal and necessary, as he parodies the celebrated metaphor concerning the encounter of a sewing machine and an umbrella until it disintegrates into a stubborn refrain. He also shows that this metaphor can be indefinitely multiplied and still maintain its vigor. The intertextuality of Péret's poems participates in its characteristic process of ebb and flow as the poet alternates threadbare and newly invented imagery. Jean-Christophe Bailly's commentary seems pertinent here: "Poetry and surrealist poetry in particular abound in these grammatical phrases that 'have no meaning,' but the meaning they do not have is common sense, trusted by Chomsky. They have another, emancipated meaning."[15]

By this metaphorical game, any term can participate in magic transformation and in the dream. Tanguy's illustrations are, we have suggested, a schematization of Péret's dynamic dream images in which he stresses affinities rather than equivocation. That he sought or found no equivalent for the complex verbal rejuvenation of the verse, if indeed he grasped it, is not surprising. His drawings point to typically surrealist adventures and themes. However, his approach, free of misunderstanding as it may be, cannot, insofar as it faithfully paraphrases Péret's basic narrative, be termed surrealistic. He tends more to mimesis than inventiveness. He uses Péret's text as a restraining guideline in his drawings rather than as an encouragement to multiply explosions or prolong the bewildering concatenations by which grammar turns autonomous imagery against itself. Thus though Tanguy implies by his vignettes that the structure of *Dormir, dormir* corresponds to the alternations of flux, such a structure does not do justice to Péret's verbal pulsations.

AU DÉFAUT DU SILENCE

Au défaut du silence (1925) is a mysterious book, for it retains in a published work the intimacy of a private universe. Its edition, limited to fifty-one cop-

[15] *Au-delà du langage*, p. 32.

46

ies, provided no name of publisher, printer, or date. Preceding the title, several preliminary pages enclose the text. Twice the words "Au défaut du silence" appear alone on a page without even an intimation of the name of the poet or painter. Philippe Soupault wrote:

When a poet like Paul Eluard publishes without signature a book even a few pages long, I cannot help but cry, miracle! and voice my astonishment that in a lugubrious, dreary, and, as it were, coarse atmosphere, the fieriness of poetry should flower.[16]

The book withholds the basic information readers expect. Such secrecy normally belongs to political pamphlets the author of which must remain anonymous to avoid prosecution. Pornographic books, which transgress institutional codes, also tend to keep the identity of the author concealed. Do Ernst and Eluard, in collaboration with their unknown editor, imply that for one reason or another this work should never have appeared? Such an answer would account for the paradox; and the refusal of the book's creators to make it a full-fledged venture in the open provides a meaningful sign. Mystery surrounds what is said, for it should perhaps have been left unsaid.

We may ask what qualities of the text or the drawings invite censorship. Eluard has written poems far more sensuous and erotic than those contained in *Au défaut*. The poet here strives more toward purity than scandal. Ernst's portraits have nothing subversive or even challenging about them. Still, the poet and the painter, by remaining unnamed, imply that in the domain of intimacy, love, and dream they cannot or may not make their revelation without embarrassment, without a feeling of intrusion. The semi-secrecy of the book becomes synonymous with self-censorship. Ernst and Eluard do not wish to violate their usual standards and positions, an attitude which can be termed Freudian, for *Au défaut du silence* is far less daring than their earlier *Les Malheurs des immortels*. The title confirms these ambiguities: the words and the drawings replace silence, which would have been preferable. Consequently, the series of sketches and pen-and-ink drawings become so many approximations replacing the violated blank page, and the words inadequately express what should have been left unsaid. In this sense, both the text and the illustrations are doomed to failure. Conversely, words and lines assault the purity of silence left without defenders. By means of the verb, the voice, the line, silence is made vulnerable. A fissure, an interval in space has been created; into this "défaut du silence" Ernst and Eluard reluctantly allow their reader/spectator to penetrate.

[16]Paul Eluard, *Oeuvres complètes* (Paris: Bibliothèque de la Pléiade, 1969), vol. I, p. 1369.

Eluard's poems are love lyrics: two verse poems, two prose poems, and many single-lined texts. *Au défaut du silence* can be considered a single poem composed of sections, several of which later, in *Capitale de la douleur*, acquired the status of autonomy. Since many directly address the woman, immediacy prevails, but in some, and especially in the last poem, the woman is referred to in the third person and the reader's presence is implicitly acknowledged. The voice of the poet repeatedly returns to the present tense, modulating distances created by various time spans and recollections. The primarily thematic unity of these poems, inspired by and addressed to the same woman, is acknowledged by the illustrator. Ernst draws for each poem another variation on a portrait of Gala Eluard that precedes the first text. *Au défaut du silence* verbally proposes constantly changing attitudes and approaches, moments never to be duplicated and rarely reversible. Dream and reality, constituting opposing poles both in flux, set up tensions. When the poet declares at the beginning that he belongs to the world of dream, he has not definitively relinquished the outer world, for he will seek to restore it by vision or by memory: "Ta chevelure d'oranges dans le vide du monde" (Your hair of oranges in the emptiness of the world)[17] and "Ta bouche aux lèvres d'or n'est pas en moi pour rire" (p. 167) (Your mouth with golden lips is not in me for fun). Space, in which only dream images appear, has no truly recognizable characteristics. The woman, at first evanescent, becomes a starlike luminosity in a world of shadows where the poet stretches out his hands so that he may get a grip on something more tangible. When a clearly ordered reality emerges, even encompassing a degree of intimacy, the poet denies its solidity.

Terms that denote circularity, suggesting either embrace or imprisonment, recur; they express fulfilled or unfulfilled desire, the intermittent hope for plenitude. Such hopes take into account the cyclic course of nature: birth, rejuvenation, fruition, fertility. The changes in distance or closeness of the woman undermine the completion of the circle, and this the poet interprets as a threat of failure.

> —*Je t'ai saisie et depuis, ivre de larmes, je*
> *baise partout pour toi, l'espace abandonné*
>
> [p. 166]
>
> —I grasped you and since then, drunk with tears, I
> make love everywhere, for you, to the abandoned space

[17] Ibid., p. 165. All quotations from Eluard are from this edition.

Et si je suis à d'autres, souviens-toi
[p. 167]
And if I belong to others, remember

Moments that suggest fusion, simultaneity are outnumbered by those that denote the loss of precise forms, the loss of response. The poet or, rather, his persona experiences the urge to recapture by words and gestures his own presence, his strength. He seeks to evoke his beloved, then to assess the role of the woman who in her triumph might become the container of the world, close the cycle, provide access to communion, to the visibility of contours. But the persona is constantly reminded that woman also reinstates fiction, illusion, and error. These paradoxes are not irrelevant to the title and the presentation of the book.

The drawings represent the woman made textually present and, when absence verbally replaces presence, her still persistent power. No eclipse seems possible; the drawings strengthen both desire and enigma but do not fulfill or answer. On one page Ernst provides a single portrait; in all others he presents the same face in multiple versions (Fig. 13). He responds by prolonging what the poet has inaugurated or invoked. But has he not intruded into the poet's intimate life by making a recognizable portrait of Gala, whom the poet dares not address by name? Whereas the poet often relegates her to the world of dream, where he vaguely identifies her as "bouche aux lèvres d'or," the painter indiscreetly multiplies fairly tangible and assertive portraits. Ernst's faithfulness to Eluard's text appears questionable: his drawings are portraits and thus "replicas," imitations of reality. They differ in essence from his other illustrations, such as those in *Les Malheurs des immortels* and *La Brebis galante*, composed of surprising juxtapositions, creatures that nature would never bring forth, "machines célibataires." Moreover, portraiture as a genre seems somewhat incompatible with modern poetry.

In some of the well-known surrealist paintings such as Ernst's *Au rendez-vous des amis* (1922) or Valentine Hugo's *Aube* (1932), the painters stressed paradox: they bestowed "photographic" resemblance on the figures they depicted, yet moved them into a spatial context at variance with any recognizable world. However, Ernst's drawings eschew space of any sort. Once he had decided—undoubtedly with Eluard's consent—to represent Gala, he had to solve the difficult problem of rendering the fluid, changing characteristics of Eluard's verse. Ernst chose, as we have stated, to repeat with relatively little variation the same face and indeed the same expression. Gala's portrait serves

Je me suis enfermé dans mon amour, je rêve.

FIG. 13. Drawing by Max Ernst from Paul Eluard and Max Ernst, *Au défaut du silence* (By Default of Silence). Paris: no publisher, 1925. © SPADEM, Paris; VAGA, New York, 1985. Photograph courtesy of the Bibliothèque Nationale, Paris.

as a suitable surrealistic illustration only by subverting mimesis. In spite of this extraordinary reduction of the illustrative material and this accumulation of the same instead of the other, Ernst, strange as it may seem, has drastically and immediately cut off the outer world (see Fig. 13). The face in its multiple and multiplied presence exists outside any background, surrounding or interfering. It invariably appears and reappears on the left preceding the lines of poetry, over which it seems to preside by assuming the dominant role of mediator. Reality as such is completely undermined. What distinguishes one illustration from the next are the number of portraits represented, their relative darkness and luminosity, the sizes of the heads. A single representation cannot be isolated after the first drawing and no permanent image is allowed to impinge itself on the viewer.

In the second drawing Ernst presents about twenty heads; the exact number is difficult to determine, for the multiplication process seems never to end. Since images continually emerge, the viewer relates them to the dream and the entire sequence to an inner vision. Ernst has repeatedly, for instance in *Une Semaine de bonté*, suggested dream productivity by a similar multiplication of analogous images. In *Au défaut du silence* repetition cannot be reduced to an endless process of duplication. The faces cannot be counted, because the viewer never finds a system or method to account for them, and they overlap not only spatially but in time. Indeed, some of the heads are coming into being while others are about to vanish. Thus the viewer, being among a majority that remain pointedly present and continuously straddling the barrier between absence and presence, could easily conclude that the contours, incipient, evanescent, or fully defined, elude tangible reality and attain to a vision quite compatible with Eluard's.

This second plate arouses the viewer's expectations for, and seems to generate, an entire sequence. The viewer usually faces only one side of the contour, and upper or lower parts may also be missing. Although basically the eyes repeat the same contours and maintain the same relations with the rest of the face, vacant pupils alternate with a complete blackening of the eye zones. This alternation of sight with eclipse depicts fluxion, the crossing of the secret threshold between sleep and awakening. It is not an outer pose that transforms the portrait, but the inner forces of the dream which flow among the multiple portraits.

In most of the drawings, curled, spiral, and curved lines circumscribe or expand the woman's hair, and they stress the act of drawing or writing to the point of transforming them by an autonomous and self-generating sign of creativity. Ernst represents these constellated clusters on a screen together with their withdrawing or projecting forces, their tensions and abatements.

In spite of the apparent uniformity of the illustrations as well as the endless repetition of the same portrait, the distance between text and drawing varies far more than one might expect. Some very precise encounters can be established provided we focus on specific sections of the poem together with the portraits appearing on the opposite page: for instance, when the poet alludes to the hair of the woman, the corresponding portrait is composed of innumerable curly lines which, instead of circumscribing, closing, or confining the face possess a liberating force ultimately transmitted to the features, which become less recognizable than usual.

> *Ta chevelure orange dans le vide du monde*
> *Dans le vide des vitres lourdes de silence*
> *Et d'ombre où mes mains nues cherchent tous tes reflets*
>
> [p. 165]
>
> Your orange hair in the void of the world
> In the void of windowpanes heavy with silence
> And shadow where my naked hands seek your every reflection

As outer reality is obliterated, the reader is pulled further into the domain of the imaginary and the dream, the inner landscape where the glow generated by the woman's hair abolishes recognizable contours. In Ernst, this dream emerges by means of dissolving, receding, and expanding contours, which inevitably omit emotional and lyric intensity as well as the direct interplay between the self and the other. Nonetheless, Ernst's drawing immediately and freely responds to the first line of the poem, "Visage perceur de murailles" (wall-piercing face), remaining faithful to its dominant principle. The poet refers to the woman's magic power to transgress matter, to appear through opaque surfaces. She enters a nocturnal realm which she metamorphoses by planting luminous seeds. The accompanying drawing consists of an intensely darkened surface.

Whereas in many drawings ink lines circumscribe faces, eyes, mouth, and hair, here black diagonal lines cover the space between the faces. The blackening that invades the drawing suggests the strokes of the artist's pen. The creative effort coincides with the emergence of the wall to be pierced, evoked in the poem by the manifold emergences of the face. The drawing provides an amplification; it develops the poem's full potential. Ernst represents Eluard's verse not as a state of being but as a becoming, a constant transformation while we as viewers continue to straddle the borderline between dream and reality. Although Ernst chose Gala's portrait as the sole basis of his illustration, he has not provided a visual equivalent to Eluard's mysterious beloved. He reacts to fluctuations of the poetic text and in addition creates variations generated by his own initial portrait. Ernst even modulates the degree of realism in his drawings, however limited it may seem: drawings with a high degree of stylization alternate with others richer in detail. Representations seemingly capable of breathing and seeing follow others on the verge of obliteration and dispersion. In opposition to the text, Ernst has introduced moments of distanciation.

"La forme de tes yeux ne m'apprend pas à vivre" (p. 167) (The shape of your eyes does not teach me how to live): Ernst adds to the irony of Eluard's nostalgic pun—the expression *apprendre à vivre* can also mean "to teach better manners"—by showing a multiplicity of divergent eyes, protruding or masked, in heads clustered more closely than elsewhere. But whether in deference to his friend, to his model, to a poet, or to art, Ernst refrained from isolating the specific features of a woman. Rather, he evokes her for a selected public, while refusing to retain her as a prized possession.

Compared to the blatant innovations of Dada, this group of early surrealist books seems a timid and somewhat confidential venture. The "privacy" of these books corresponds to the intimate bond linking painter and poet. Taken separately, text and image propose nonrepresentational elements while adumbrating a foreground for surprising imagery. Nevertheless, in the relation of text to image mimesis holds its own, for the painter seeks to remain faithful to the writer even if it introduces paradoxes in his own artistic project.

CHAPTER TWO
SURREALIST COLLABORATION

INDIVIDUALISTIC THOUGH THEY APPEAR TO BE, surrealists deeply valued collaboration—for example, in their famous game the *cadavre exquis* (exquisite corpse), practiced both verbally and graphically, as well as in their most celebrated team activity, automatic writing. The *cadavres exquis*, preserved in museums and reproduced in critical studies, cannot be considered a mere pastime. Like surrealist art, it was signed by all its contributors. From its collaborators it prompted responses to a hidden verbal or visual fragment. Its practice stressed a desire for unanimity in creation; it depended on spontaneous activity and minimized all forms of conscious elaboration. The interference of critical intelligence was supposedly completely eliminated.[1]

It is therefore not surprising that the authors of collaborative works such as *Les Champs magnétiques* and *Ralentir travaux* gave barely any hints about their modes of collaboration and the respective shares of individual participants. In illustrated books such as *Facile* or *Les Malheurs des immortels*, contributors revealed themselves, at least to a certain degree, through their medium, so their collaboration is not to the same degree shrouded in mystery.[2]

Chronologically *Les Malheurs des immortels* and *Répétitions* belong to

---

[1]Jean-Clarence Lambert states in his article on *cadavre exquis* in *Dictionnaire général du surréalisme*, edited by Adam Biro and René Passeron (Fribourg: Office du Livre, 1982), p. 74: In his presentation, Breton emphasizes the aspects that should really matter in this activity: collective creation (in Lautréamont's sense), disclosure of the instinct of play, suspension of critical judgment, surmounting the antinomy serious/nonserious, liberating the metaphorical activity of the mind, satisfying the pleasure principle, tacit communication among the participants (not to say thought transmission). *Cadavre exquis* assures, by means of repeated juxtapositions, the distanciation indispensable to Lautréamont's metaphor. Indeed, distance takes causal precedence in generating an illusion of continuity. For further comments on Lautréamont's metaphor, see Chapter Six below, "Illustrating the Precursors."

[2]The propensity to collaborate did not cease when the revolutionary zeal of the movement abated; see, for example, Breton's and Masson's joint *Martinique charmeuse de serpents* (Martinique the Snake Charmer) (Paris: Sagittaire, 1948).

dadaism. Although the uncompromising satire contained in their pages fits with the aggressive practices of that movement, however, the highly constructive and even systematic nature of these joint ventures departs from the improvisational, even slapdash dadaism and points to the mainstream of surrealism.

RÉPÉTITIONS *and* LES MALHEURS DES IMMORTELS

In 1922 Max Ernst and Paul Eluard jointly published *Répétitions*, a series of poems, some of which are accompanied by collages.[3] In the unusual nature of their collaboration they hoped to unite not only their conscious but their subconscious minds. Surrealist art often uses repetitive devices referring to the unending chain of events that characterizes both the dream and the creative process.[4] In the eleven collages and thirty-five poems such recurring elements stand out, both within the framework of a single page and from one page to the next. In the plate that serves as frontispiece to the volume, four schoolchildren, turning their backs on the master and the spectator, identical in their postures and gestures, provide the first instance of "répétition" (Fig. 14). In this example, repetition, far from being produced mechanically, involves variation, a disquieting, frequently used factor that actually insures the repetitive movement of the entire series. Partitions open unexpectedly, windows hide or disclose a mystery; above all, arms and heads pop out anywhere, while the rest of the body remains invisible. Ernst lures the spectators by means of the apparently familiar quality of repetition in order to disrupt their complacency more thoroughly.

In Eluard's poetry, words and lines are repeated within a poem and from one poem to another. Repetition has little to do with a refrain, a return to the familiar. It synthesizes paradoxical qualities:

> *Signal vide et signal*
> *A l'éventail d'horloge*
> [A Côté][5]

> Empty signal and signal
> At the clock-shaped fan
> [On the Side]

[3]Max Ernst and Paul Eluard, *Répétitions* (Paris: Au Sans Pareil, 1922).
[4]Cf. "Troisième poème visible" ("Third Visible Poem") in Max Ernst, *Une Semaine de bonté* (Goodness Week) (Paris: Pauvert, 1963). Cf. also René Passeron, "Poétique et répétition," pp. 9–21 in *Création et répétition*, edited by René Passeron (Paris: Clancier-Guénand, 1982).
[5]Paul Eluard, *Oeuvres complètes* (Paris: Bibliothèque de la Pléiade, 1969), vol. I, p. 112. All quotations from Eluard are from this edition.

FIG. 14. Collage by Max Ernst from Paul Eluard and Max Ernst, *Répétitions*. Cologne: Galerie der Spiegel, 1962. © SPADEM, Paris; VAGA, New York, 1985.

The words as they recur assume different functions and bring about a change in tempo. Repetition thus includes a shift from the knowable to the mysterious in both the poems and the collages.

"Répétition" also implies the idea of lesson, a notion that Ernst, before Ionesco but long after Lewis Carroll, deliberately subverts. In the introductory plates, the pupils, by not facing the teacher but positioned so as to write answers on a missing blackboard, have in a way turned their back on his knowledge to seek new adventures and new contacts. Eluard gives the impression of initiating his reader in words of wisdom, but in reality he leads the innocent away from boredom toward the night and the dream:

> *Ferme les yeux visage noir*
> *Ferme les jardins de la rue*
> [Les Moutons, p. 109]
>
> Close your eyes black face
> Close the street gardens
> [The Sheep]

Répétition in its meaning of "rehearsal" is demonstrated in the drama evident in the work. Climactic but puzzling situations accentuate the mystery: a well-dressed, upper-middle-class gentleman is hoisted into the air by a strange pump while another is forced by the same machine to stand on his head, showing no sign of discomfort (Fig. 15). Ernst and Eluard, in driving home the idea of rehearsal, remind the public that they are carrying out exercises leading to a performance that will never take place. Rehearsal approaches synonymity with the surrealist refusal to create finished works of art or to seek perfection.

Repetition also raises, at least implicitly, the problem of originality versus imitation. Ernst and Eluard, in their joint creation, aim at a fusion capable of minimizing the differences in their media. Ernst states and prolongs in his

FIG. 15. Collage by Max Ernst from Paul Eluard and Max Ernst, *Répétitions*. © SPADEM, Paris; VAGA, New York, 1985.

collages what Eluard depicts in his poems, or, conversely, Eluard develops what Ernst has assembled. Thus neither artist gains, so to speak, an edge on the other. Originality and imitation, inspiration and interpretation belong equally to both. Imitation, a form of repetition, is unavoidable even when both the poet and the painter proclaim their revolutionary intentions and seek a complete break with the past—which they will put only partly into effect. Eluard cannot help repeating the words of the French poets from whose tradition he wished to dissociate himself. Amid typically lyrical verses worthy of Apollinaire, such as "le coeur sur l'arbre vous n'aviez qu'à le cueillir" (That heart on the tree, you had only to gather it) ("Poèmes"), we encounter purposely banal expressions that disrupt any possibility of continuity and subvert the functioning not only of poetic but of ordinary language, such as "Je ne vous entends pas" (I do not hear you) ("Oeil de sourd," p. 119) and "Pouviez-vous prendre plus de libertés" (Could you have taken more liberties) ("Rubans," p. 116). Nor could Ernst elude imitation. Collages by their very nature employ borrowed elements in a new context. Ernst cuts out figures or fragments from old journals and assembles them in surprising ways. These collages, refusing to hide their origins, blatantly proclaiming themselves as copies, invest the imaginary with a striking degree of absurdity. In Eluard's poems contours are dissolved, obstacles eliminated, and a breakthrough into more mysterious zones becomes inevitable; familiarity breeds unfamiliarity. Through such metamorphoses the poet effects a fusion of objects that usually remain separate. He singles out part of the human body at the expense of the whole and grants autonomy to each part by depriving it of its function and turning it into a disquieting, potentially magic object. Ernst's collages make this transformation even more pronounced (Fig. 16). A similar interplay can be seen between association and dissociation in text and image, but Eluard's approach may be termed *positive receptivity*, Ernst's *corrosive denunciation*. So far at least, our analysis seems to confirm Michel Sanouillet's comment: "We can hardly speak either of 'illustrations' or of 'legends,' and even less of repetitions, but, rather, of miraculous correspondences."[6]

Although the same artists collaborated in *Les Malheurs des immortels*, notable differences prevent us from treating one merely as the extension of the other. *Les Malheurs des immortels* consists of twenty poems accompanying twenty collages, and Ernst participated with Eluard in the creation of the texts. Thus the two books differ in the method of assembling text and image, as well as in the nature of the collaboration. Jean-Charles Gateau has exam-

---

[6]Michel Sanouillet, *Dada à Paris* (Paris: Pauvert, 1965), p. 362.

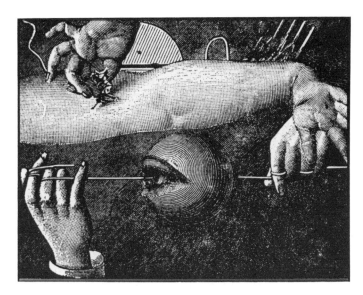

FIG. 16. Collage by Max Ernst from Paul Eluard and Max Ernst, *Répétitions.* © SPADEM, Paris; VAGA, New York, 1985.

ined the problem of the respective contribution of Ernst and Eluard to the poetic text. In an analysis of "Les Ciseaux et leur père," he shows that from the beginning to the end of the poem, fragments of sentences by Ernst alternate with verbal contributions by Eluard. The collaborators did not concoct their text by sitting around a table, but through a correspondence. Since the collages were completed before the poems, each time Eluard added to the unfinished text he had to respond to an image as well as to words; we cannot consider this a spontaneous creation, but, as Gateau calls it, "a faked image aiming at poetic surprise."[7] It becomes clear, then, that the poems are themselves collages of small groups of words composed by each of the two authors who hardly bothered to correct, let alone censure, one another. These "fabricated poems" also include paraphrases or intertexts, for example, from Alphonse Daudet's *Le Petit Chose.*[8]

The collages are composed of fragmented representations, usually taken from scientific or technological treatises. It appears that the artists emphasized the arbitrary quality of their juxtapositions. For instance, the diminutive pine tree, though not rooted in the ground, asserts its upright posture (Fig. 17); a man with a bird's head proclaims his bourgeois identity (Fig. 18). By such juxtapositions the artists challenge the spectator's naive insistence on

[7]Jean-Charles Gateau, "Découper, se couper, se recouper," pp. 217–27 in *Le Livre surréaliste: Mélusine IV* (Paris: 1982). Cf. by the same author, *Paul Eluard et la peinture surréaliste* (Geneva: Droz, 1982), pp. 53–63, 74.
[8]Ibid., p. 219.

FIG. 17. Collage by Max Ernst, "Les Ciseaux et leur père" (The Scissors and Their Father), from Paul Eluard and Max Ernst, *Les Malheurs des immortels* (The Misfortunes of the Immortals). Paris: Editions de la Revue Fontaine, 1945. © SPADEM, Paris; VAGA, New York, 1985.

established relations. By giving the same spatial importance to a thimble, a bucket, and a constellation, the artists suppress all hierarchy and thereby eliminate normal relationships. Ernst and Eluard reveal the falsity of such relationships even more clearly by introducing diagrams, maps, anatomical charts. These networks of lines appear far more lively than the human, who is often represented by a mannequin wearing stiff, ceremonial attire. The spectator dutifully struggles to decipher the curves and with even less success endeavors to set into motion the magic but functionless machines that Ernst and Eluard have set up.

The prose poems make their point in a matter-of-fact journalistic style. By pretending to narrate, to explain, the two poets leave no room for lyricism or at least for the clichés that identify a text as poetic. Moreover, the writers often provide a rapid inventory of fragmentary incidents that have little or no bearing on issues they were supposed to settle. This play at substitutions forms a verbal process that closely resembles the collage. The reader is subjected to word-games consisting mainly of expressions that take on unexpected literal meanings:

> *L'application des serins à l'étude n'a pas de mesures.*
> ["Réveil officiel du serin," p. 124]

> The way canaries apply themselves to study cannot be measured
> ["The Canary's Official Awakening"]

> *Mais on ne peut pas être ivre toute sa vie*
> ["Le Fagot harmonieux," p. 124]

> But you cannot be drunk all your life
> ["The Harmonious Bundle of Sticks"]

The poets constantly introduce paradox and deliberately misdirect our attention. In the collages parts are cut out, making us aware of what is fragmented or absent. In the poems similar processes occur through repeated references to what has disappeared or been forgotten. In the collages as in the poems, the natural and the mechanical, the organic and inorganic enter into many surprising relations; all barriers seem to disappear. And in both collages and poems, normal proportions and distances are abandoned: a hand manipulates the sky with ease. Such curtailments and liberation, far from unleashing boundless energy, result in a perpetual but meaningless agitation.

Unlike *Répétitions*, whose title implies serialization, lack of novelty, lack of originality—processes belied by both the text and the collages—*Les Malheurs des immortels* promises paradoxical adventures involving divinities, normally protected against such ups and downs: in other words, anything but repetitions. The first difficulty the reader-viewer encounters is that of recognizing these immortals, for their day-to-day misfortunes have often quite obscured their identities. Venus and Saturn, though diminished by circumstances, are still unmistakable. In the collage entitled "A la Recherche de l'innocence" (In search of innocence) Venus emerges, legs first, from a glass bowl, a minimal artificial sea serving as a womb (Fig. 19). In the collage entitled "Mon Petit Mont Blanc," Saturn, recognizable by its rings, is no more

FIG. 18. Collage by Max Ernst, "La Rencontre de deux sourires" (The Meeting of Two Smiles), from Paul Eluard and Max Ernst, *Les Malheurs des immortels*. © SPADEM, Paris; VAGA, New York, 1985.

than the buttocks of a woman, of whom we can also see the breasts and thighs. The Twins, a sign of the zodiac, look like prostitutes putting on their war paint, next to Capricorn reduced to an object floating in a bucket. By reducing the immortals' stature and transforming their spirituality and symbolic prestige into physical needs or mere exhibitionism, the poets replace, subvert, and invert the exemplary values usually associated with classical mythology. The statue, so often the embodiment of the superhuman and the universal, becomes a mannequin or an empty piece of clothing in "Le Fugitif," "Les Ciseaux et leur père" (see Fig. 17), "Conseils d'ami." Strange esthetic or ethical concepts are represented by the immortals: halo-shaped illuminations radiate from a rudimentary wooden mannequin; a caged canary officiates at a ceremony in an open landscape.

In the poems "the divinities" experience similar devaluations, often expressed by change or substitutions:

voyez les femmes, à quarante ans, elles laissent leur coeur dans le tronc des pauvres et remplacent les légumes par des attitudes classiques. ["Conseils d'ami," p. 128]

Consider women, at forty they leave their heart in the poor box and for vegetables substitute classic attitudes. ["A Friend's Advice"]

In a single sentence Ernst parodies both classical tradition and romantic love. In the following examples, as they replace higher by more ordinary but not less unexpected values, the poets indirectly suggest the subjection of the immortals to daily misfortunes:

Personne ne connaît l'origine dramatique des dents
["Les Agréments et l'utilité," p. 131]

Nobody knows the dramatic origin of teeth
["The Pleasures of Usefulness"]

Les crocodiles d'à présent ne sont plus des crocodiles
["Des éventails brisés," p. 132]

The crocodiles of today are no longer crocodiles
["Broken Fans"]

The immortal is either placed in an unsuitable situation or is replaced, within recognizable circumstances, by a less exemplary protagonist such as an object. Such paradoxes are sustained by both text and image.

As in *Répétitions*, again and again the one replaces the many, sameness substitutes for difference. In the poetic texts a certain type of repetition surfaces immediately: the first and last sentences of certain poems are identical ("Des éventails brisés"), or several paragraphs begin with the same sentence pattern ("Les Ciseaux et leur père"). This minimal concession to standard versification and refrains in the context of the prosaic use of language, in several instances imitating the style of short news items, actually undermines traditional poetic practice and calls into question the act of repetition. "Des éventails brisés" includes two types of repetition, "Les crocodiles d'à présent *ne sont plus*" and "*il n'y a plus.*" Suggesting the void of the present compared to better times, these poems function as parodies of Romantic poems of regret as well as of clichés expressing dissatisfaction. Taken literally, they depreciate the past together with the present taken as rhetorical mode of presentation. Such repetitions, by making the reader aware of clichés grafted on other clichés, suggest a kind of stereotyped impotence. Words and tropes suggest mechanical reiteration far removed from the musical repetitions characteristic of poetic language: "Il n'y a plus de vraies hydrocyclettes, ni microscopie, ni bactériologie" (p. 132) (There are no longer any true hydrocycles, or microscopy, or bacteriology). This statement suggests a semantic levelling. The poet may include words poetic or scientific, imaginary or banal, without producing different meanings and effects. In certain instances at least, this method differs from the procedures followed in *Répétitions*, for variety degenerates into sameness.

Eliane Formentelli has discussed in great detail the relation of text and collages of "La Rencontre de deux sourires" and "Les Ciseaux et leur père." The following two quotations summarize her findings and have, to a certain degree, guided us in our study of "L'Heure de se taire" and "Des éventails brisés":

Between the "representation of objects" and the "representation of words" functions a system of exchange that is neither translation nor transposition but, rather, work, inscription, game, which, in both sectors, involves the trace.

The technique of the collage silences a garrulous rationalism by means of a bruise, a scratch, or the violence of mute appearances; the accomplishment wrought by collage provides the proving ground for the playful verbalizations of poetry. [9]

In the collage "Des éventails brisés" (Fig. 20) we can detect a certain amount of repetition, but not on the obvious mechanical, functionless level that prevails in the poem. Repetition binds, to a certain extent, text and collage. The following words are represented plastically by their respective images: *crocodiles, bicyclette, coureurs, équilibristes, cordes tendues, les quatre points cardinaux*. We see "les crocodiles d'à présent ne sont plus des crocodiles" as a

[9]Eliane Formentelli, "Max Ernst, Paul Eluard ou l'impatience du désir," *Revue des Sciences Humaines* 164 (Oct.–Dec. 1976): 503.

FIG. 19. Collage by Max Ernst, "A la recherche de l'innocence" (In Search of Innocence), from Paul Eluard and Max Ernst, *Les Malheurs des immortels*. © SPADEM, Paris; VAGA, New York, 1985.

parody of nostalgia. In this context of the collages another set of meanings surfaces, at least partially. The crocodile in its stretched-out position, far away from water, upside down, with a bicycle-like contraption in lieu of its stomach, is no longer an animal. Text and collage jointly contribute to the destruction of identity. The crocodile here merely repeats the shape and texture of a crocodile; it is nothing but a reproduction. Even if the curved line dividing the space into a lighter and a darker zone were to be seen as outlining a wave of water, the "crocodile" is out of its element. A being renowned for its murderous power, here, separated from any meaningful existence and reduced to inaction, it joins the immortals. Text and collage repeat each other,

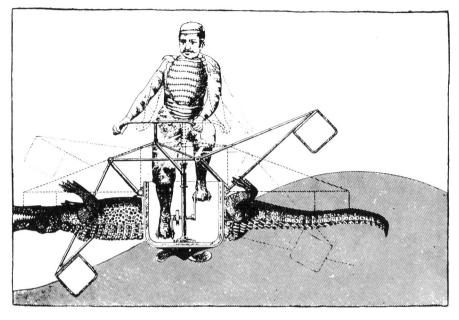

FIG. 20. Collage by Max Ernst, "Les Eventails brisés" (The Broken Fans), from Paul Eluard and Max Ernst, *Les Malheurs des immortels*. © SPADEM, Paris; VAGA, New York, 1985.

extend each other. In a sense, each becomes the impossible replica of the other.

Contrasting with the immobilized, "etherized" crocodile demoted to the rank of a defunctionalized object, the upright cyclist pedals away. Contrast or difference soon merges into sameness: the front of the cyclist treacherously resembles a crocodile's scales. However strenuously he pedals, he is no more mobile than the crocodile, and he is just as powerless in displaying energy as the crocodile is in displaying none. Cyclist and crocodile, represented in a quasi-photographic realism, are reproductions or repetitions of a nonexistent reality. In addition to the cyclist and the crocodile, the collage includes geometrical, abstract or schematized components. The geometrical contraption conveys the image of a machine endowed with a mobility that the cyclist, glued to his seat, and the stretched-out crocodile do not possess. Not a single but several positions are conveyed, outlining the direction to and from which the "flying" machine will swing. The painter maps out different positions of the cyclist's hand, both present and absent, establishing relations between the mobile bars and the cyclist's hands without indicating whether the hands generate movement or follow it, in what appears to be a vicious circle. The viewer may have to accept the interference of the arbitrary and irrational, even if their status and nature remain undefined.

The title provides additional clues to the interrelations between the parts of the collage. The term *éventail* refers to an object depending on the unfolding of its parts according to a given pattern: it is made up of repetitions. The cyclist's movable hand, the crocodile's stretched-out legs, the geometrical contraption are all fan-shaped. Consequently one could consider that the collage presents a visual translation (by more than one method) of the image of the fan. *Eventail*, however, suggests not only a shape but a range. Ernst includes a range of divergent elements that end up not being as fully divergent as they appear at first. The fan used for cooling, constantly swung back and forth, is subjected to the very movements we have detected in the collage, the pedalling within spatial confinement. The title "Des éventails brisés" surprises us, for everything represented within the collage seems intact. The mutilation, the paralyzation comes from the way the parts of this *machine célibataire* are joined, how they affect each other.

In the text, as in the collage, dissimilar elements tend to become similar; we enter into the structure of a gadget-like contraption the function of which ultimately escapes us: "Autrefois, les bons vieux poissons portaient aux nageoires de beaux souliers rouges" (p. 132) (In the past, the good old fish wore pretty red shoes on their fins). Fish and men, like the crocodile and the cyclist, become interchangeable. They possess no natural affinity, and the expression quoted does not suggest its revelation; the surprising juxtaposition merely precludes their separation. Several clauses in the imperfect tense refer to the past as a lasting state of affairs. They imply a positive set of gestures introduced by "les bons vieux aventuriers" or "les bons vieux poissons," so essentially different from the now living, unnatural crocodile. Can we conclude that in the poem, unlike the collage, we chance upon a system or past network of immortals? Each statement calls upon the reader to grasp a precarious operation vulnerable to its own lack of reality, to follow a path soon to become traceless, to recognize almost totally disguised protagonists. It seems that Ernst and Eluard have deliberately transformed their readers into cyclists (or aviators) pedalling frantically in order to get nowhere, for the most familiar objects elude them in spite of all attempts to circumscribe them.

Just as the collage represents a series of fans and their thwarted movements, so the text reveals a constant attempt at unfolding that will inevitably result in collapse, as lines or words always fall short of providing the expected results. As both crocodile and birds can be considered fan-shaped, collage and text, so our chosen example would indicate, held together only by the title, far from lending themselves to metaphorical parallels, form a single contraption. In any event, text and image cannot be decoded separately but, as was suggested, only in terms of their mutual interference. The final sentence, except for the introductory "ma parole" (my word), merely repeats the first. The whole poem therefore serves to prove the veracity of the initial statement, which belies our perceptions and defies all scientific categories. In the context of the collage, it stresses both lack of change and lack of reality. We have to fall back on the same old reproductions or simulacra.

Certain words in these poems, denoting movement, directly refer to visual elements in the collage and thus temporarily create the illusion of a close correspondence. Verbs such as *accrocher* and *appuyer* (to hook, to support) pertain both to objects that appear in the collage and to our tentative efforts to decipher the text. As we juxtapose words with certain figures, we contrive collages even more haphazard than those of Max Ernst and Paul Eluard. Our readings confirm the fan-like structure—we take off, reach midair, only to fall back again, almost literally to square one: "Suivant la vitesse du doigt, les coureurs aux quatre points cardinaux se faisaient des compliments" (p. 132) (According to the speed of the finger, the runners at the four cardinal points paid compliments to one another). The rotating movements of the arms and the rectangular structure of the contraption, perhaps no more than a superstructure of the fan-rooted bicycle or flying machine, suggest that at least here text and collage coincide.

The correspondence between the single cyclist of the collage and the multiple *coureurs* provide just one example of the many confrontations between the visual singular and the verbal plural. Eliane Formentelli mentioned examples in "Rencontre de deux sourires" where the single hairdresser, woman and serpent, of the collage corresponds to the multiplicity in the poem ("dans le royaume des coiffeurs," "ces femmes coiffées en papillon," "ces petits serpents") (in the kingdom of hairdressers, those women with the butterfly hairstyle, those little snakes). In "Des éventails brisés" the single cyclist appears as a reduction of a plurality, which itself is generated by the singular, in both senses of the term. In the sentence quoted that ends with the compliments of the runners, disruption suggests the arrest of movement, which transforms itself into repetitions and clichés, another "éventail brisé."

The text contains multiple references to what may be considered feminine attributes—daintiness, graciousness, smiles, politeness, and, last but not least, red shoes. The text alludes to seduction, though hardly in a continuously overt manner; the voice that speaks is presumably male. If seductiveness seems to be missing in the collage, overt sexuality emerges in the relationship of the cyclist's effort and his position in regard to the crocodile. Nonetheless, the poem ends on a regretful note: "les crocodiles ne sont plus des crocodiles," which, because of the interference of the collage, has more important functions than the simple parody of Romantic nostalgia.

Interference also plays an important part in "L'Heure de se taire" (Time to Shut Up), where in the text the female protagonist, characterized by her desire to attract the opposite sex, displays her image with all its calculated reflections. By her anatomy and her gestures she becomes the creator of a landscape. Displays and expansions alternate with curtailments and contractions. The woman by means of her reflections, associated with fluidity, appears to have the power of imposing order or creating chaos. In the collage outlining a vegetation of extreme density no trace of the woman is visible (Fig. 21). The foliage grows not in a vertical but a horizontal direction. The viewer soon detects that he is looking at a cross-section that lies below the surface: "Près de la lèvre vue dans l'eau" (Close to the lip seen in the water). The vegetation constitutes an inner growth which, if compared to other Ernst collages, seems to represent the human muscular system.

In the text, the watery surface provides an entry into the hidden domain. Water is not altogether absent in the collage: the plumbing fixtures and the watering can provide obvious references. They belong to the fabricated world, as opposed to the natural or organic universe to which we have referred so far. They suggest virility and male aggression—the apparently indispensable partner to female coquetry—or perhaps the man's desire for female acquiescence. We once more encounter intensely female elements in the text and predominantly male elements in the collage. The relation of text and collage necessitates a lateral reading in order to generate their mutual interrelation. The underground organic system becomes definitely the territory that the "erect" elevated watering can and the plumbing outlets irrigate. When we become aware of this vigor, the rapport with the concluding poetic statement becomes more intimate: "Elle étend la mâture de ses seins au pied des ruines et s'endort au crépuscule de ses ongles rongés par des plantes grimpantes" (p. 128) (She spreads the masts of her breasts at the foot of ruins and falls asleep at the dusk of her nails bitten by climbing plants). Male and female elements are, at this stage, interwoven, as sexual intercourse has almost run its course. The final words of the text, "plantes grimpantes," have their visual equivalent, which ultimately becomes indistinguishable from the pilar system. Outer and inner dusk intermingle, the coquette succumbs to sleep, everything confirms that it is "l'heure de se taire."

Ernst engaged in simultaneous creation with Eluard, but he was interpret-

FIG. 21. Collage by Max Ernst, "L'Heure de se taire" (Time to Shut Up), from Paul Eluard and Max Ernst, *Les Malheurs des immortels.* © SPADEM, Paris; VAGA, New York, 1985.

ing an already written tale when he provided both a preface and collages to Leonora Carrington's *La Maison de la peur.*[10] In this, her first tale, the authoress relates the extraordinary in matter-of-fact prose, by the frequent misuse of language alerting the reader to the presence of the unusual. Phonetic spelling leads to confusion concerning verb endings, to the substitution of one gender for another, and to the generation of strange contexts. The main character, at the same time a horse and a human being, belongs by rights to the realm of the fantastic. The horse lures the female narrator to a party where she penetrates into a world unknown to her. The narrator enters a dream-like domain where the one is transformed into the many, where estrangement entraps like a chill. Fear corresponds not only to an atmosphere; it also represents the owner of the haunted house while coinciding with the horse's seductive power. The owner imposes rigorous games in which musi-

[10]Leonora Carrington, *La Maison de la peur* (The House of Fear) (Paris: Collection Un Divertissement, 1938).

cal and mathematical prowess combine and ultimately silence the narrator; the tale ends in the middle of a sentence.

Max Ernst illustrated this text with three collages in which the horse appears in various shapes and disguises. As we glean from the captions, he does not follow the order of the tale. Ernst first introduces the *patronne* (boss, mistress) without conforming to the postures and disguises described by Carrington. His horse-headed, long-maned, acrobatic, gracefully clad creature holds a phallus-shaped club adorned with a feminine bow. In the second collage Ernst again takes liberties with the narrative as he represents two horses, one going up and one going down, in a setting reduced to a geometric structure (Fig. 22). Moreover, the horses are badly assembled, as if the transformation from human to animal remained incomplete. Letters, lines, and numbers "build up" the structure made of parallel and diagonal lines, suspending the characters outside reality. The viewer, seeing the soles of two sleepers, associates Ernst's reference to the dream with the hypnotizing effects described by Carrington. Both allude to the multiplication of the protagonists as well as to their shifting nature. In the final plate Ernst interprets the denouement of the tale. The horse stands propped up like a monument on a pedestal, whereas the woman—invisible heretofore—plunges dizzily into the air. Upon a soft-contoured setting where sea and land fuse into one another, Ernst glues two cut-out figures representing Carrington's paradoxes as she imposes her eyewitness account upon the irrational, dream-like events. Taken as a group, Ernst's three collages display discontinuity in style as well as in their relation to the text.

In his preface Ernst introduces his own characters, who entice us to read *La Maison de la peur*. These creatures belonging to his own iconography establish links between his painting and Carrington's fiction. Ernst mentions several of his "protagonists": sun, nightingale, cloud, a horse called Mariée du Vent (The Wind's Bride), and, most important, Loplop, Superior of the birds, who in various canvases has assumed many shapes and made many introductions. Here Loplop is called upon to introduce La Mariée du Vent— an encounter between Ernst's most frequently recurring character or alter ego and Carrington's favorite personification. In addition, the title of the preface indicates that Leonora's horse and La Mariée du Vent will merge. In the painting bearing that title, horses interlaced, propelled by winds, suggest endless cloud shapes. By denying the separation between these protagonists Ernst provides an "introduction" to the tale; *La Maison de la peur* becomes not only a collaboration between Ernst and Carrington but also between their creatures.

je remarque avec ettonnement que le cheval...

FIG. 22. Collage by Max Ernst from Leonora Carrington, *La Maison de la peur* (The House of Fear). Paris: Collection "Un Divertissement," 1938. © SPADEM, Paris; VAGA, New York, 1985.

As Ernst adds more double creatures to his repertoire and combines his creations with those of Carrington, he creates, as in *Répétitions* and *Les Malheurs des immortels*, both verbal and visual collages. Therefore, because it faces the preface, the first collage cannot be construed as being merely the portrait of La Patronne de la Peur. Her feathered skirt and hat link her both to La Mariée du Vent and to Loplop, who changes according to the person he is called upon to introduce. In spite of the captions, Ernst's interpretation of *La Maison de la peur* constitutes, not a mere reading of a text where the narrative is disrupted, but a conscious revamping of his own amphibious impersonations, inspired by a tale where language and identity assume the characteristics of a collage.

FACILE

The slim volume entitled *Facile* (1935) appeared shortly after Eluard's marriage to Nusch, which followed his meeting with Man Ray. Nusch, Man Ray's professional model, participated in the creation of the book. It includes five of the poet's major love poems, hymns to joy, beauty, and communion, and eleven photographs, surprising views of a woman's body. On the title page we read "Poems by Eluard, Photographs by Man Ray." No definite information is provided as to whether one preceded the other. The book is the fruit of intimate and continuous collaboration among Man Ray, Paul Eluard, and Guy Lévis Mano. Nicole Boulestreau refers to an initial planning between photographer and poet at the initiative of the latter.[11] According to Boulestreau, Man Ray and Mano adopted a somewhat different design from the one originally conceived by Eluard and Man Ray. Arturo Schwarz claims that the conventional order of illustration is reversed, that Eluard illustrates Man Ray.[12] Roland Penrose, in his study of Man Ray, rich in biographical data, views *Facile* as a document testifying to the intensity of the Eluard–Man Ray friendship: "They are going to collaborate on a volume entitled *Facile*, containing poems where Eluard expresses his love for Nusch and illustrated with nude photographs of the young woman."[13] *Facile* marks the beginning of the Eluard–Man Ray collaboration; *Les Mains libres*, the second and more voluminous book in which Eluard illustrated Man Ray's

[11] Nicole Boulestreau, "Le Photopoème *Facile*: Un Nouveau Livre dans les années 30," *Le Livre surréaliste: Mélusine IV* (Paris, 1982), pp. 165–68.

[12] Arturo Schwarz, *Man Ray: The Rigor of Imagination* (London: Thames and Hudson, 1977), p. 240.

[13] Roland Penrose, *Man Ray* (Paris: Chêne, 1975), p. 125.

drawings, was to follow two years later.[14] The cohesion between text and photography, as well as between various poems and various photographs, suggests analogies with musical orchestration of theme and variation. *Facile*, with its photographs of a model and actress, provides an example of the status gained by photographs from Man Ray's creative powers and discoveries. Photography plays an esthetic role equivalent to the drawings in *Les Mains libres* or to Max Ernst's frottages illustrating Benjamin Péret's *Je sublime*, two titles that appeared in the same period.[15] In his illustrations Man Ray employed the then-experimental process of solarization, effects regarding texture, exchange between mellow and sharp outlines. Critics refer to the fine dark contours that accompany photographs exposed to solarization, which painters hoped to rival; such outlines appear on several pages of *Facile*.

In the eleven photographs of Nusch, Man Ray avoids repetition. Each provides a new perspective, a new focus or angle. Each represents a different posture, a different gesture. Man Ray makes visible various parts of the body; he explores the woman's anatomy in order to discover new landscapes, to unveil a heretofore invisible beauty. He avoids being the copyist of nature who strives to represent the full-size portrait. Never capturing the entire body, he selects parts: the torso, the arms, the legs. The head appears only once, reversed. The eyes remain invisible. Man Ray refuses the limitations that outer reality might have imposed and that would have undercut his emphasis on flux, surprise, variation. Although he photographed the woman who inspired Eluard's love lyrics, Man Ray aspired no more than the poet to make her immediately recognizable or to distinguish her from others. Painter and photographer masterfully bypassed everything that could be construed as characterization. Rather, the model becomes the mediator of beauty, thus acquiring universality. The artist's vision changes from one page to the next, moving from daytime to night, from front or back to profile, from modesty to blatancy. Viewed as a suite, the photographs exemplify the paradox of surrealism, the contradictions it aspired to reconcile.

The contrasts between dark and light have been ingeniously exploited by Man Ray in the frontispiece, occurring both as simultaneity and alternation. Here dark zones appear as shadows; elsewhere they rival light zones, ceasing

---

[14]Paul Eluard and Man Ray, *Les Mains libres* (Free Hands), drawings by Man Ray illustrated by Paul Eluard's poems (Paris: Editions Jeanne Bucher, 1937). Anne-Marie Christin has devoted a lengthy study to this work: "Le Poète-illustrateur: A propos du recueil *Les Mains libres* de Man Ray et Paul Eluard," pp. 323–45 in *Ecritures II*, under her editorship (Paris: Le Sycomore, 1985).

[15]Benjamin Péret, *Je sublime* (I Sublime), with four frottages by Max Ernst (Paris: Editions Surréalistes, 1936).

FIG. 23. Photograph by Man Ray from Paul Eluard, *Facile*. Paris: G.L.M., 1925. © ADAGP, Paris; VAGA, New York, 1985.

to reflect another reality. On the cover (Fig. 23), letters constitute luminous zones projecting imposing shadows. The words become an active force, as does photography. The shadows stemming from the geometrical letters have no curving contours. They are brush-strokes, once more the denial of the shadow as a replica. The printed letter on the cover, by casting shadows, expands space. A slight displacement, once more disturbing the geometrical patterns and immobility, creates the impression of light, forming windows or suggesting the outlines of a castle. The spectator confronts a universe that invites penetration, yet prevents it because of the two-dimensional reduction of the cover. The contrast between oversized "industrially produced letters" on small pieces of paper and "handmade" brush-strokes on large zones of canvas suggests transgressions. We confront ambiguities between sign and image, reflection and creation, reading and perceiving, all multiplied as geometry generates the organic. The two arts, poetry and photography, have established themselves as communicating vessels, where communication through love leads without effort to universal harmony. Hence the title, *Facile*. From cover to cover the book points to a single universe expressed by two different

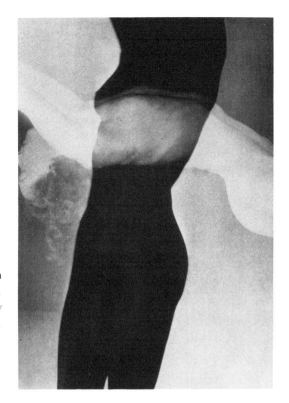

FIG. 24. Photograph by Man Ray from Paul Eluard, *Facile*. © ADAGP, Paris; VAGA, New York, 1985.

languages. The poem is made up of images, and the images coalesce into a poem. Nicole Boulestreau in her article on *Facile* has coined the term *photopoème*, which she defines as follows: "In the photopoem, meaning progresses in accordance with the reciprocity of writing and figures: reading becomes interwoven through alternating restitchings of the signifier into text and image."[16]

When Man Ray simultaneously represents two images of the woman, for instance one vertical and one horizontal, the shadow-like figure is in the upright position; the luminous one, head tilted down (Fig. 24). Both become dream figures and dreamers: one by her absence of dimension, the other because of her closed eyes. The latter is endowed with creative power as the downward-floating hair mirrors a seascape, the undulation of water. An analogy comes to view between the waving motion of the woman's body and the sea, an analogy which Eluard's verses may parallel:

[16]"Le Photopoème *Facile*," p. 164.

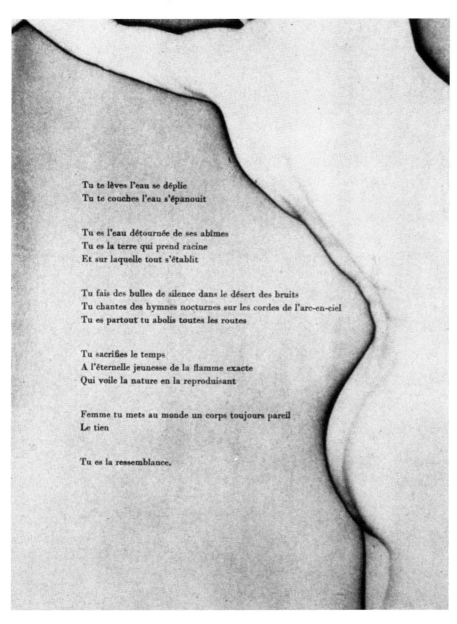

Tu te lèves l'eau se déplie
Tu te couches l'eau s'épanouit

Tu es l'eau détournée de ses abîmes
Tu es la terre qui prend racine
Et sur laquelle tout s'établit

Tu fais des bulles de silence dans le désert des bruits
Tu chantes des hymnes nocturnes sur les cordes de l'arc-en-ciel
Tu es partout tu abolis toutes les routes

Tu sacrifies le temps
A l'éternelle jeunesse de la flamme exacte
Qui voile la nature en la reproduisant

Femme tu mets au monde un corps toujours pareil
Le tien

Tu es la ressemblance.

FIG. 25. Photograph by Man Ray from Paul Eluard, *Facile*. © ADAGP, Paris; VAGA, New York, 1985.

Tu te lèves l'eau se déplie
Tu te couches l'eau s'épanouit

[p. 460]

You arise, the water unfolds
You lie down, the water blossoms forth.

In addition, Eluard suggests a more subtle parallelism between the woman, or perhaps Man Ray's representation of her, and a page in the book (*déplie*), as well as an exchange of characteristics between her and the water, *s'épanouit*. As the two lines indicate, Eluard, just like Man Ray, creates contrasts which he then disperses or dissolves. In the photographs, overlapping dark zones may create transparency instead of opaqueness, so that the shadow loses its identity (Fig. 25). The joining of two contrasting areas can bring about an illumination violating natural laws or rationality. A third dimension emerges, a relief dream and reality produce surreality, at once the work of imagination and of photographic manipulation.

The integration of poetic and visual elements comes partly from the placement of photographs and text in the same space. Man Ray departed from the usual forms of separation, which consist of putting the illustration on a separate plate or of dividing the page horizontally between the two. In several cases the photographs supply a frame without duplicating the outlines of the page (see Fig. 25). The undulations of the woman's body give shape to the poem; the arabesque of the human figure harmonizes with the typography. By means of the fluctuations of the dividing lines, one zone may expand or retract at the expense of another and thus increase ambiguity. When the curve delineated by the photograph coincides with that traced by the poem, the text and the image belong to the same configurations. Boulestreau claims that Eluard's poems, at least implicitly, refer to solarized photographs where the effects of light and shadow have been subtly manipulated. Fluctuations are revealed not only by varying degrees of contrast between opaqueness and transparency but by their relation to the typography of the text (Fig. 26): "Henceforth, it carries throughout the book its vibrating halo and, in the by-play of its declensions, the form of the poem whose very contours it has embraced. . . . The axial contrariness of woman and poem somehow situates the impossible union of body and discourse, even though the engraver digs into the night so as to penetrate to the immaculate stratum."[17] Such apparently paradoxical statements are resolved by the distinction Boulestreau makes between typographical and fantastic space.

[17] Ibid., pp. 173–74.

78

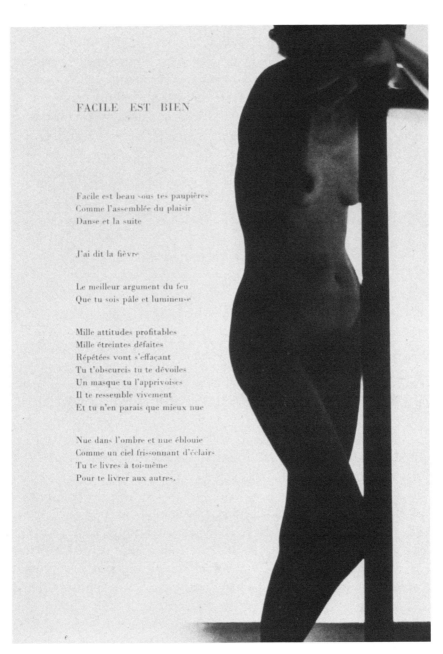

FACILE EST BIEN

Facile est beau sous tes paupières
Comme l'assemblée du plaisir
Danse et la suite

J'ai dit la fièvre

Le meilleur argument du feu
Que tu sois pâle et lumineuse

Mille attitudes profitables
Mille étreintes défaites
Répétées vont s'effaçant
Tu t'obscurcis tu te dévoiles
Un masque tu l'apprivoises
Il te ressemble vivement
Et tu n'en parais que mieux nue

Nue dans l'ombre et nue éblouie
Comme un ciel frissonnant d'éclairs
Tu te livres à toi-même
Pour te livrer aux autres.

FIG. 26. Photograph by Man Ray from Paul Eluard, *Facile*. © ADAGP, Paris; VAGA, New York, 1985.

Eluard's poems, by stressing creativity and proximity as well as focusing and mirroring, are closely related thematically to the modalities of representation. In *Facile*, as in other love lyrics, Eluard evokes the creative power of woman. This power emerges from constant association with and comparison to flowers, objects conveying the idea of growth, unfolding, germination. Eluard's point of departure is always the woman. In the course of the poem, a number of substitutions take place: one gesture replaces another, one perception displaces another. Eclipses, obliterations, and dispersions are outweighed by multiplication and enrichment. The universe expands. It will suffice to quote some terminal lines:

> *Tout le temps d'une rue qui n'en finit pas*
>
> [p. 462]
>
> Through the entire duration of a road that never ends
>
> *Couché aux pieds de son reflet*
> *Un couple illimité*
>
> [p. 464]
>
> Lying at the feet of its reflection
> A limitless couple

This enrichment, this unfolding resulting from the woman's power—at once moral, esthetic, and erotic—means that ultimately Eluard includes the entire universe. Reality with its restrictive boundaries is transcended; universal analogy dominates. Woman not only asserts but endows everything with her identity, by making hidden affinities tangible through her gestures. In several of Eluard's poems, woman, initially at the center, appears to expand toward the circumference.

The mirror associated with the germinating force of the flower suggests, in Eluard's poetry, the possibility of increasing and abridging distance; it therefore has a central function in his pursuit of immediacy; indeed, the first poems about Nusch were entitled *La Vie immédiate*. In addition to its function of bringing closer, of eliminating intermediaries, the mirror becomes the seminal image in a universe whose referent is the dream, a universe in which confusion reigns between the reality and the image, the sound and the echo. Such interchanges, coupled with Eluard's metaphors of growth and fertility, provide for spatial expansion. Likewise, the photographer produces fusion by means of his art. Man Ray's figures are by no means circumscribed by the page, but stretch far beyond (Fig. 27). In most of the photographs the woman moves beyond the frame of the page. The viewer is urged to use his imagination to transgress the limits of the paper. In both the poems and the

FIG. 27. Photograph by Man Ray from Paul Eluard, *Facile*. © ADAGP, Paris; VAGA, New York, 1985.

photographs, a movement stemming from the woman as focal point is propelled to larger spaces. The fluid contours of the woman suggest (as was mentioned) a seascape. Man Ray's figure adopts surprising postures; she dances; she is bereft of weight. The viewer moves between opaqueness and transparency, between consolidation and dematerialization. Similarly, Eluard aspires to the luminous qualities associated with the dreamer. Analogies with clouds, movement of winds, gestures of dance, eliminate all obstacles:

> *Mains qui s'étreignent ne pèsent rien*
> [p. 461]

> Hands that embrace weigh nothing

> *Ou bien rire ensemble dans les rues*
> *Chaque pas plus léger plus rapide*
> [p. 460]

> . . . or laughing together in the streets
> Each step lighter and faster

Both Eluard and Man Ray create the image of a woman, present yet forever changing, and pertaining both to being and to doing. They refer not only to a present moment, a spatial presence, but to "passages," some earlier and others yet to come. The physical presence of the body in the poems is undeniable. Eroticism pervades the text no less than it does Man Ray's photographs. Eluard, to say the least, does not aspire unilaterally to purity, to spiritualization, to the dissolving of contours. The word *corps* (body) recurs:

> *Le creux de ton corps cueille des avalanches*
> [p. 460]

> The hollow of your body gathers avalanches

> *Tu es toujours en train de rire*
> *Mon petit feu charnel*
> [p. 461]

> You are always laughing
> My little carnal fire

It is the physical nature of the woman that makes her, as in Man Ray's photographs, the creator of landscapes. These rapidly evolving scenes with their ever-new vistas embrace all elements, but fire perhaps more strongly than the others. Eluard refers to the nude body:

> *Tranquille sève nue*
> [p. 461]

> Tranquil naked vitality

> *Il te ressemble vivement*
> *Et tu n'en parais que mieux nue*
> [p. 465]

> It vividly resembles you
> And you look all the better in the nude

> *Nue dans l'ombre et nue éblouie*
> [p. 465]

> Nude in the shade and dazzled nude

These terms establish an obvious analogy with Man Ray. The term *nue* is in keeping with the search for purity, with the aspiration to communion and harmony. It refers to a course that is obstacle-free, that by establishing fundamentals eliminates intermediaries. Eluard's woman, always associated with creative powers and dissociated from the past, remains unknown, performing an original gesture.

Simultaneity of paradoxical elements characterizes both Man Ray and Eluard. Only the latter leads the reader to the heart of a continuous process. He alludes to traces, imprints suggesting the self-reflexive process of creation. Man Ray, a viewer once removed, does not attain the same intimacy. Dream and metamorphosis in his photographs depend on distance and make no reference to the identification of the "You" and the "I," of the creator and the created, emerging from the poems. The directness of the poet's voice makes the woman present, a presence intensified by but hardly originating in the photographs. This immediacy in no way weakens the dream quality so pronounced in this collaborative work.

The books discussed in this chapter are contemporaneous with or even earlier than the works analyzed in Chapter One. Indeed, collaboration implies more than a mere personal link, for it leads to experimentation with new techniques such as collage and solarization and implies a concomitant rejection of established methods such as lithography, etching, and wood engraving that are inappropriate for collaborative adventures where difference may matter even more than unity.

CHAPTER THREE

THE FOCUSING OF
A DOUBLE TALENT

ALTHOUGH THEY MAY NOT HAVE gone as far as the dadaists, the surrealists did reject the traditional categories and neat distinctions that had prevailed in the creative arts since the time of Pericles and of which Gottfried Ephraim Lessing was considered the most respected theoretician. They ironically entitled one of the chief journals of the movement *Littérature* (1919–21)—a journal no less uncompromising than *La Révolution surréaliste* or *Le Surréalisme au service de la révolution* in reducing to absurdity the generic distinctions that gave a feeling of security to the bourgeoisie. For this reason, we should in a sense have refrained from referring to surrealist *poems*, *essays*, or *novels*. The general and, since post-structuralism, more loaded term *text* suits their writings better. André Breton, for instance, considered the classification of *Nadja* as a novel offensive. He, as well as other members of his group, favored aggressive and undifferentiated creativity, as *cadavre exquis* and automatic writing or drawing demonstrate.

It is therefore hardly surprising that they tried to break down the barriers between writing and the plastic arts or that many of them should have tried their hand, sometimes simultaneously, at both: Breton himself, Georges Hugnet, and Paul Eluard practiced collage; conversely, Jean (Hans) Arp, Max Ernst, and Joan Miró, as well as Salvador Dalí, André Masson, Hans Bellmer, and Jacques Hérold, produced innumerable texts that it would be foolhardy to classify as creative or theoretical.

Some of these artists were less successful in their writings than others, and it might be rash to claim that all of them truly had a double talent. In our opinion, Arp, Ernst, and Miró show remarkable verbal dexterity. Jean Arp, whose poetry might have sufficed to bring him fame, published a considerable number of volumes both in French and in German, whereas Ernst's and Miró's efforts at texts were no more than sporadic. In illustrating their own books, the three painters vary considerably. *Vers le blanc infini* (1960) and *Le*

Soleil recerclé (1966) show Arp's mastery both in the texts and the designs.[1] In his *Le Lézard aux plumes d'or* (1971) Miró stages a confrontation between textual and graphic representation, and in *Paramythes* Ernst produces a remarkably integrated illustrated book, though not a *livre de peintre* in the strictest sense of the term.[2]

VERS LE BLANC INFINI *and* LE SOLEIL RECERCLÉ

Ever since his dadaist period, Jean Arp has illustrated many of his books. Small volumes both of French and of German poetry, as well as the collected editions *Jours effeuillés* and *Gesammelte Gedichte*, are accompanied by drawings.[3] We would expect that Arp, a bilingual poet famous for his sculptures, wood-reliefs, tapestries, collages, and graphic works, would create illustrated books showing a deep and natural cohesion between word and image. Yet Arp, in his sparse theoretical writings, never explicitly denied, whatever the context might be, the autonomy of the verbal and plastic arts and he never mentioned their possible fusion. We may safely speculate that Arp would not consider his poetic texts as mirror images or echoes of the plates, or vice versa, or that their simultaneous publication constituted an indivisible unity. Since the concept of metamorphosis is central to both Arp's literary and his plastic works, it is possible that in his illustrated books, text and image relate by different manifestations to a similar change, or one art may suggest the prolongation or the arrest of a movement initiated by the other. Arp did not, then, diminish the role or impact of the poems when he added drawings. Toward the end of his life Arp published two *livres d'artiste*, *Vers le blanc infini* and *Le Soleil recerclé*; the great care that was taken in the publication of the two books, including in their typography and engraving, seems to invalidate Arp's claim that his creations were highly spontaneous and that he disregarded esthetics.

The eight poems and eight plates composing *Vers le blanc infini* had previously been unpublished. The book begins with an etching, followed by a

---

[1]Jean Arp, *Vers le blanc infini* (Toward Infinite White), with eight original etchings (Lausanne: La Rose des Vents, 1960); *Le Soleil recerclé* (The Re-Ringed Sun) (Paris: Louis Broder, 1966).

[2]Joan Miró, *Le Lézard aux plumes d'or* (The Lizard with Golden Feathers) (Paris: Louis Broder, 1971). *Paramyths*, in the Copley Gallery's *Max Ernst: Ten Years of His Work* (New York, 1949); *Paramythes* (Paris: Le Point Cardinal, 1967). A trilingual edition is available: *Paramythen-myths-mythes* (Cologne: Spiegelschrift, 1970).

[3]Jean Arp, *Jours effeuillés* (Defoliated Days) (Paris: Gallimard, 1966); Hans Arp, *Gesammelte Gedichte* (Collected Poems), 2 vols. (Zurich: Arche, 1963).

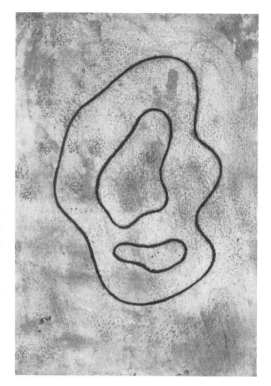

FIG. 28. Etching by Jean Arp from
Vers le blanc infini (Toward Infinite
White). Lausanne: La Rose des
Vents, 1960. © ADAGP, Paris; VAGA,
New York, 1985. Photograph
courtesy of the Bibliothèque d'Art et
d'Archéologie, Paris.

poem—an order repeated seven times. The poems bear titles, which in most
cases do not seem relevant to the plates. No one-to-one correspondence can
be established between each poem and the etching that precedes it. The
reader-viewer deals with two sequences, constantly interfering with each
other, neither progressing in a linear fashion, each undergoing modulations
and coming to a closure at the end. The oft-repeated terms *constellations* and
configurations used by Arp for some of his sculptures and wood-reliefs, may
provide an explanation, for we are dealing simultaneously with individual
stars and with sets of overlapping figures. The rapport of text and image will
be more fruitfully established by viewing the entire sequence than by attempting to find a parallelism between pairs of entities.

Arp has used titles descriptively, as an inventory; he has also used them
in the surrealist manner, as word-games. Such titles bring out chance associations—for example, navels and forks; they stress the irrelevance of associations with an everyday world and the affinities acquired through creative gesture. With the possible exception of the title poem, however, the headings of
Vers le blanc infini provide neither inventories nor verbal creations. The title
itself proposes the poet's aspiration towards purity, his effort to escape past all

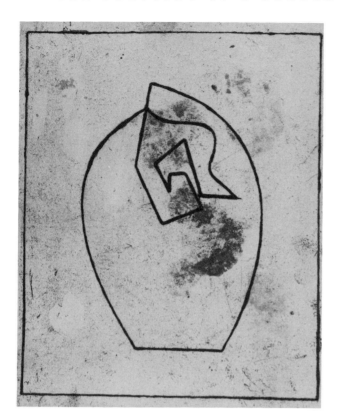

FIG. 29. Etching by Jean Arp, "La Cathédrale est un coeur" (The Cathedral Is a Heart), from *Vers le blanc infini.* Photograph courtesy of the Bibliothèque d'Art et d'Archéologie, Paris.

the barriers of the everyday world. No impeccable whiteness appears in the graphic suite. Its black contours recall wood-reliefs and sculptures that Arp created during the same period. In the etching, a limited number of forms and black lines emerge from a gray surface (Fig. 28). Its streaks and pigmentation suggest vibrancy and substance, testifying to the concreteness of art, proclaimed by Arp in a text of *Les Jours effeuillés*.

The outline of the first etching consists of an arch surmounting a straight line (Fig. 29). This shell has affinities with the accompanying poem, "La Cathédrale est un coeur" (The Cathedral Is a Heart); the truncated heart delineates the aisle of a cathedral. The three interconnected shapes of the etching are inseparable, enclosing a mystery not unfolded. In the plates preceding "Vers le blanc infini" (see Fig. 28), "A travers les myrtes du rêve" (Through the Myrtles of Dream) (Fig. 30), and "Poupée" (Doll), the black contours suggest organic shapes; straight and geometric lines, which would give the impression of having been drawn with angular precision, are excluded. Whereas the first illustration conveys the impression of complete rest, these three etchings—by their undulating lines, by the relative positions of the

FIG. 30. Etching by Jean
Arp, "A travers les myrtes du
rêve" (Through the Myrtles of
Dream), from Vers *le blanc
infini*. Photograph courtesy of
the Bibliothèque d'Art et
d'Archéologie, Paris.

contours and shapes—impress the viewer by their motion as well as by the
projected change of forms they reveal. These etchings inscribe constellations
corresponding to the ambiguity between woman, flower, and star, constellations which recur in many of Arp's plastic works as well as in his poems. One
constellation proposes the ultimate reduction of a woman's torso. Two others
are multi-shaped: three similarly shaped contours embrace, reflect, give birth
to, or displace one another. These constellations, molded like waves and
leaves, are tokens of a continuous creation that defies mimesis. The last
plate, preceding "Une Onde blanche" (A White Wave), maps out a design or
chart: an oval shape floats in the upper section and in it a complex road is
inscribed; below it lies a structure composed of loops and straight lines (Fig.
31). Geometric forms are more numerous here than organic ones. In relation to the initial plate, an expansion, an unfolding has taken place. If we
compare two or three plates, we notice a constant relocation of the elements,
a switch in roles between the container and the contained, an avoidance of
symmetry and repetition. Yet in none of the eight plates does Arp disrupt harmony as he constantly remaps the designs and their allusions. He proposes

FIG. 31. Etching by Jean Arp, "Une Onde blanche" (A White Wave), from *Vers le blanc infini*. Photograph courtesy of the Bibliothèque d'Art et d'Archéologie, Paris.

forms that waver between fluidity and concreteness; he strives toward transparency as he approaches a dream that lies on the road leading from dematerialization to spiritualization.

"La Cathédrale est un coeur," "Tu fus une onde blanche" (You Were a White Wave), "Je suis une poupée" (I Am a Doll). Taken by themselves, such definitions might indicate that the poems do not move in the direction of the graphic suite, at once so schematic and ambiguous. Arp often pursues a definition when he raises a question. What initially appears to be a definition turns out to be a hypothesis which the poet questions, belabors, and metamorphoses until the statement becomes part and parcel of a process of change, of becoming. Thus "La Cathédrale est un coeur" sets into motion the transformation of an architectural structure into an organism. Arp proceeds by a cohesive molding of shapes; he testifies to their bond, which constitutes the focal point of a universe where a swallow, the heart, and the church interweave. The poem may be termed a celebration belonging to a realm freed from the forces of gravity, where upward and downward motions become interchangeable. A complete reading of the poem will show the merging of forms, the interpenetration of their affinities, thereby offering strong ties with the plastic suite: the heart, the core, the center will never be relinquished.

Such affinities do not imply that the etchings have lyric qualities or that the poems abound in pictorial or descriptive dimensions. In his poetry Arp makes abundant use of verbal games based on homonyms, onomatopoeia, rhythms; apparently conventional repetitions and refrains recur. Spatial forms and interrelations on which "La Cathédrale est un coeur" depends cannot be isolated from the role played by sound effects: the progression *ciel, ailé, air, anges* produces a gradual opening. Synesthesia and word-games are effectively introduced in "Le Maître-Cloueur" (Master-Nailer), "La Poupée," and, especially, in "Qu'est-ce que c'est que ça?" (What Is That?) In this poem a gradual spatial expansion emerges. The initial impetus comes from the sequence *corbeau, corbillard* (raven, hearse), semantically and etymologically unconnected words which, by means of repetition, begin to interrelate. Later in the poem, *toujours* is followed by Arp's verbal creation *tounuits* (all-nights), producing a continuity in time and space intensified by the recurrent "il s'endort, il se réveille" (he goes to sleep, he awakens) until dream and awakening, day and night become reversible. Finally, Arp metamorphoses "Lazare lève-toi" (Lazarus, stand up) into "Lazul, lazul que me veux-tu" (What do you want from me). This verbal device of substitution seals the sequence by a touch of magic and ethereal blueness. When sleep and awakening alternate with such ease, all obstacles belonging to the everyday are removed. By poetic means, by hidden fluctuations of language, Arp, without passing through tensions, reaches a dream world compatible with the domain outlined in the plates. He reveals the uninterrupted testimony of metamorphosis, where no single identity is relinquished for the sake of another.

As Arp suggests the passing of thresholds, the elimination of barriers between dream and reality, he also encompasses the domain of death. In the title poem and in "A travers les myrtes du rêve," speaking to Sophie, his dead wife, he negates distance and separation. The impact of the images is enhanced by the brevity and simplicity of the syntax. The two poems, written in the imperfect tense, suggest the uninterrupted catalyzing action of the woman in a domain where distance in space and time are of no significance. She radiates light, absorbs differences, conjures affinities. A process of liberation and expansion is generated; terms such as *déployer* (to unfold), *envahir* (to invade), *se glisser entre* (to slide between), *étaler* (to display) abound, accompanied throughout by rhythmic activity. As sounds or colors glide into one another, the intimate comes to assume cosmic dimensions. In "Vers le blanc infini" the woman shares her existence, or merges, with flowers and stars. She provokes upward motions, even under the impact of downward forces, rendering sky and earth interpenetrable; she endows the unreal with substance. In "Poupée," too, Arp generates a poetic process that obliterates limitations and classifications. The doll deplores the reduction and separation which originate in her identity. She longs for a soul and the expansion of an inner landscape.

The final poem, "Une Onde blanche" (see Fig. 31), closes a cycle that has not evolved according to any regular progression but which, by recurrent metaphors and structures, coheres. "The White Wave" takes on a centripetal force due to its fluid power, its color, its applicability to both woman and landscape. Contrary to most of the preceding poems, wherein hope and aspiration manifested themselves by motions and configurations, "Une Onde blanche" suggests distancing of the pure white image which clings to memory as a past vision but which no longer provides promise of a return. Grayness, barring any possibility of transparency, any opening to other dreams or horizons, invades the domain so intimately linked to silence. It prevents the appearance of new constellations and effaces the traces of creativity to which Arp has been alluding: *peindre* (paint), *clouer* (nail), *tisser* (weave), *pinceaux* (brushes), *crayons de couleurs* (crayons). "Poupée" had already revealed signs of separation, discrepancy, or reduction, thus at least partially reversing the tendencies toward growth and fertility suggested in the earlier poems of the collection. Compared to "La Cathédrale est un coeur" (see Fig. 29), where all elements move toward or appear close to a hypothetical center, where a fall becomes a move toward a womb—"Elle se laisse tomber dans le ciel ailé, dans l'air des anges" (she lets herself fall in the winged sky, in the air of angels)—"Une Onde blanche" points toward disintegration and dispersal. This is reflected in the two corresponding plates. All the shapes shelter each other in the first plate, whereas divergence characterizes the final one. We are tempted to say that the sky and its constellation have been separated from the rest.

Time is not recorded in a uniform manner throughout the eight poems. "Qu'est-ce que c'est que ça," written in the present tense, is composed of narrated sequences or anecdotes that move at varying speeds. "Vers le blanc infini," written primarily in the imperfect tense, suggests time as a continuum generated by a central force, a woman. In several plates ("Vers le blanc infini" [see Fig. 28], "Poupée") undulating contours reflect the passage of time or situate a moment within a continuum. In the first plate, the shape with closed walls, anchored like a statue on a straight base, escapes time's dichotomy. This two-dimensional enclosure without open-ended vectors character-izes a tensionless stability, which to a certain degree recurs in the final plate. In both the poems and the etchings time is necessarily linked to the process of metamorphosis, of becoming, always intense even though the third di-mension, of time and space, memory and perspective, is never made explicit. Within a single poem or a single plate constant rhythmic fluctuations create coherence for the reader or viewer progressing through the *livre de peintre.*

It would be erroneous to say that Arp's plates extend the domain of poetry or that poetry extends that of the etchings or that they form simultaneous expressions in different media. In many cases the poems were conceived be-fore the plates and, in all probability, separately. Arp is not truly an illustrator, although we are indebted to him for many illustrated books. Generally their genesis remains mysterious. Rather than commenting on one another, the etchings and the poems manifest the creative gesture in different ways. Prompted by a common dream and aspiration, they result in a unity that dwells below surface divergences. The arrangement of eight plates each fol-lowed by a poem by the same artist necessarily changes our reading of both texts and images. The former tend to fall within the context of schematiza-tion provided by the plates; the latter assume some of the continuity provided by poetic language.

It would be even more difficult to construe *Soleil recerclé*, Arp's last illus-trated book, as a simultaneous creation than to do so with *Vers le blanc infini.* The plates and the poems were composed independently of one another. The texts do not constitute a cycle in the strict sense of the word, and the colored woodcuts appear to be variations on a limited number of motifs. Compared to those of *Vers le blanc infini,* which recall Arp's rather streamlined sculp-tures and wood-reliefs, the 1966 colored woodcuts possess the characteristics of his paintings. In most cases several pages of poetry correspond to the space of a single almost abstract woodcut. In addition to the nine brightly colored plates, Arp has included several monochrome vignettes, most of which sug-gest organic forms in motion, recalling the illustrative principle of some of Arp's earlier books. In the plates, geometrical forms—squares, circles, and ellipses—which do not attain the regularity of abstraction, in addition to sim-ple, complex, or composite amoebic forms, compose Arp's imagery. Most of them present the basic components of natural sites, but, due to their sche-matization, they can be read as maps. They are characterized by an interplay between container and contained: all the plates have a rectangular frame that contains a circle in addition to smaller round or organic forms either within the circle or outside it.

The frames and the circle appear to imply immobility. Movement, which governs most of Arp's art, stems from the fluctuation of shape of the organic forms, the wide variety of protrusions and retractions, the invading and withdrawing action of two differently colored surfaces. The viewer cannot discern the source of energy. The movements refer simultaneously to life in a simple cell and to the complexity of an entire organism's birth, growth, and reproduction (see Plates 1, 2). The autonomy of each organism, each container and contained, is evident; this autonomy encompasses the larger forms we labelled geometrical. Because one never occupies the hypothetical center of the other and inclinations or tiltings are the norm, the viewer has the impression that a shift has taken place or is taking place. One woodcut suggests a two-dimensional night created by a large bluish square containing an irregular golden shape, either star or sun, with a black circular heart. This image still has relevance to our outer reality, yet, while asserting the principles of artistic creation, it defies the concept of imitation. As in *Vers le blanc infini*, Arp alludes to life as a constant and mysterious becoming. *Soleil recerclé*, the title of the volume as well as of this plate (and corresponding to a line in "Nuit recachetée"), reveals the encounter of enormous power, size, and distance made intimate by the creative act. As the poet or painter recircles the sun, he transforms its relation to the sky. The sun simultaneously contains and is contained; the sky and sun shape and limit each other. Art, freedom, and chance are linked, as they bypass the inessential, the unnecessary, and drive toward reduction. *Recerclé* refers to repetition, whereby the outlines of the sun are rewritten. No constellation reveals a completely new world or scale in relation to the preceding one, nor does it provoke contradiction or tension. Every plate presents an equilibrium between what could be paradoxical forces, between distance and closeness, abstraction and concreteness, light and darkness. By a constant effort of refinement and stylization, the painter has created images of relative simplicity. Arp's constellations, so eminently plastic, bear little overt relation to poetry.

Most poems of *Soleil recerclé* abound in humor, word-games, and surprise effects. Word-games restore to verbal expression a literal, somewhat forgotten sense. More often than in *Vers le blanc infini*, Arp here manufactures new words that mystify or that emphasize rhythmic and vocal patterns. The lightness of tone, the anecdotal manner of presentation, the childlike fantasy and game-playing situate the poems in a different context than the plates. "Ne cueille plus bougie" (No Longer Gather Candle), characterized by relative simplicity, narrates the story of a man drowning, his efforts to master the situation, his gradual loss of control, his eventual sinking. The poet gives, in a matter-of-fact account, the detailed record of an observer who refrains from interpretation. Ironically, the drowning swimmer, who will soon have no need for his shadow, discovers himself. As he falls into the water, by setting a calm surface into motion the swimmer inscribes a line in the greenish plane, a line which rapidly becomes obsolete or irrelevant. The poet repeatedly alludes to disappearing contours:

> *Mais l'eau n'a plus de bords bateaux*
> *radeaux rochers concours conforts*[4]

> But the water no longer has any banks boats
> rafts rocks contests comforts

Both the movement of the water and the swimmer's gestures amount to an obliteration of contours and, implicitly, of the outer world. Upon turning the page, the reader loses sight of "la plage"—the events are "literary" rather than real. After the eclipse, the swimmer's convolutions, whether flower or star, survive in the growing darkness or flickering light. The poem alludes to the stages of reduction and elimination pertaining to the production of an engraving. Simplicity comes not from lack of elaboration, but from renunciation. The artist intimates that shapes, contours, outlines entered into the making of the plate without leaving visible traces. By writing the poem, Arp recreated in another medium the steps of his graphic procedure, and thus returned to origins. The action of reduction, the groping for an image pervades the text, whereas the engraving presents the results, a relative stabilization.

If "Ne cueille plus bougie" obliquely refers to the quest for identity, "Qu'est-ce que c'est que cela" drives at definition, as the dream through its fluctuations manifests its presence. The title poses a question. Others follow, enhancing the childlike tone, giving rhythmic continuity, exhibiting the similarity of patterns and motives. Such questions are not raised by a defined grammatical subject. Their often impersonal nature increases the discontinuity that arises from the very continuity of questioning, and this discontinuity shows the impossibility of classifying, recognizing, and defining.

Every element the poet names is prone to disappear, because of either its mysterious nature or the ephemeral quality of its being. Snow, ephemeral in itself, disintegrates more rapidly when "chauffé à blanc" (white-hot), even though, from a poetic point of view, it may appear that it has then found its essence. Frailty becomes even more pronounced: new associations, as they

---

[4]Jean Arp. *Jours effeuillés*, p. 492. All quotations refer to this edition.

emerge, create paradox. The chain of queries and accumulation of mysteries as well as shadowy contours of identity result in an oblique affirmation of poetic freedom. This is not proclaimed by ideological or thematic means, but emerges from the power of words that are not circumscribed by their semantic and logical connotation and that do not lead to distinctions between visible and invisible, abstract and concrete—least of all, between logical and illogical. As the poet repeats, changes, negates, he disengages many words from their narrow everyday context. By use of commonplace expressions such as *chauffé à blanc* or *cartes blanches* (white cards), he turns whiteness into a protean protagonist, present even on the book's cover. Whiteness, however, hardly carries an allegorical meaning such as innocence or purity. On the contrary, whiteness assures a constant elimination of reality in the general reductive movement. Moreover, Arp bypasses or rejects the relationship between word and referent, between word and idea, just as in the woodcuts he prevents trite associations from entering into the act of interpretation or even recognition (Plate 3). His colors actually preclude the assignment of symbolic or psychological value. As forms must not coincide with each other, as words have to be separated from their accepted meanings, negation or subtraction plays a predominant role.

The link we have established so far between text and image in Arp's work has very little to do with surrealistic theory and practice, such as a common creative principle operative for all genres or a mode of perception leading to similar inventions in visual and verbal expression. Rather, we have stressed the purely verbal quality of the text and the assertive plasticity of the plates. Nevertheless, Arp's poems in *Soleil recerclé*, much more than in *Vers le blanc infini*, do have surrealistic characteristics insofar as the words act as liberating forces, overcoming restrictions and abandoning established associations.

In "Nuit recachetée" (Night Sealed Once More), Arp does more than set the word at odds with its accepted referent. By a *mise-en-abîme* of creative activity, he recasts the role of language and standard poetic devices. The poem evokes a succession of day and night, of black confinement, repeatedly overcome by new rosy shades until these contrasting moments become simultaneous. Several images correspond to the act of writing, to its full-fledged creative, nonreferential assertiveness: snails leave suggestive traces; full stops and commas lose their mechanical functions and their subordination (Fig. 32). The title itself is suggestive: *recachetée* refers to a letter, a message repeatedly hidden, contained in the night. The initial traces of this seal bearing the image of a sun or star were prophetically introduced by the snails,

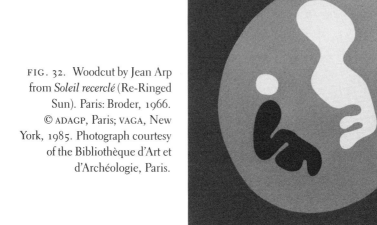

FIG. 32. Woodcut by Jean Arp from *Soleil recerclé* (Re-Ringed Sun). Paris: Broder, 1966. © ADAGP, Paris; VAGA, New York, 1985. Photograph courtesy of the Bibliothèque d'Art et d'Archéologie, Paris.

then perpetuated by clouds of confetti and the recircling of the sun. The title bears the promise of a vast container enclosing mysterious signs where being created and creation become interchangeable, repetitive and thus equivalent. In the plates the simultaneous presence and interplay of organic and geometrical components indicate the principle of metamorphosis, of growth and motion in its most general sense. In the poems, by a process of defunctionalization, Arp also suggests the transformation of objects:

> un long, long boudin immangeable
> derrière soi
> suivie de l'unique chasseur de chez nous
> qui est sans fusil.
>
> [pp. 584–85]

> A long, long, black, inedible sausage
> behind itself
> followed by the only hunter from our side
> who goes without a gun.

In "La Maison" Arp speaks of a street that, by losing its bearings and running in all directions simultaneously, ends any possibility of a spatial order and a referential system. However, another short poem, by aligning the container and its contents, seems to run counter to the dispersals detected in other texts:

Un mur dans une lettre
un voilier dans une forêt
une flamme dans une cage
une clef dans une bouche
un mât d'ivoire aux fruits de neige

[p. 510]

A wall in a letter
a sailboat in a forest
a flame in a cage
a key in a mouth
an ivory mast with fruits of snow

Arp springs a series of surprises, of unexpected relations, of secret associations, for the frame or the container always houses an object that it could not encompass in ordinary existence. He abolishes all proportion. He dislocates rather than locates. The four disjunctions lead to a landscape where the natural and the fabricated, the durable and the ephemeral become indistinguishable and attain a unity defying fragmentation. Containment becomes a form of liberation, a process of emptying out the ordinary. The poem continuously writes itself and erases itself so that the graphic sign can emerge. The juxtaposition of two sequences presents a complex commentary on the artist's labors, but no more than in *Vers le blanc infini* does Arp illustrate poems by woodcuts or woodcuts by poems. The texts situate themselves in relation to a prior creation to which the reader as spectator has to return and which can manifest itself only through the revolt of the signifiers against the signified.

LE LÉZARD AUX PLUMES D'OR

Joan Miró has made fewer theoretical statements than Dalí, Magritte, Ernst, Bellmer, or even Arp. The most important texts by Miró about his art are interviews with Georges Charbonnier, Georges Duthuit, and Georges Raillard.[5] Although he was always willing, if not eager, to answer questions, he apparently never felt the urge to reveal the theoretical or methodological foundations of his art. The word *dream*, recurring in such texts as "Je rêve d'un grand atelier" (I Dream of a Large Studio) or *Ceci est la couleur de mes rêves* (This Is the Color of My Dreams), suggests that Miró speaks about his

---

[5]Georges Charbonnier, *Le Monologue du peintre* (Paris: Juillard, 1959); Georges Duthuit, "Enquête," *Cahiers d'Art* 1–4 (1939): 65–75; Joan Miró, *Ceci est la couleur de mes rêves* (This Is the Color of My Dreams), "entretien avec Georges Raillard" (Paris: Seuil, 1977).

aspirations rather than his technique or method, about his pursuits rather than his relationship to his medium.[6] He showed little concern for his role in the surrealist movement and viewed Breton and other surrealists as personal friends rather than as members of a movement.

Miró is essentially a painter who explores by means of colors and lines, who seeks adventures that will lead to creation of his own space. Although his art shows considerable variety, no radical change took place during his career. Paintings, gouaches, woodcuts, etchings, lithographs, watercolors, sculptures, and ceramics constitute almost but not quite the sum of his lively, luminous artistic creations, for Miró now and again tried his hand at poetry: "Jeux poétiques" appeared in the 1946 issue of *Cahiers d'art*.[7] As far as we know, Miró always—sooner or later—illustrated his texts.[8]

"Jeux poétiques," only slightly revised, provided the text of *Le Lézard aux plumes d'or*, published by Broder in 1971 as "poème de Joan Miró enluminé par l'auteur." If we are to judge by the title page, Miró puts the stress on his poetic creation, to which he seems to subordinate his lithographs; in other words, he assigns the lithographs a purely functional role. The publication of the text within the frame of an illustrated book must have been of great importance to Miró. In volume III of his complete lithographs, eighteen lithographs dated 1967, intended to accompany the poem, are reproduced.[9] However, this first edition of the book was never circulated. Because of a defect in the paper, the color was so distorted that Miró withdrew the entire edition. In fact, the eighteen lithographs never really accompanied the text, for they were published as "Des suites des lithographies en simple page . . . tirées sur vélin des Rives" (suites of single-page lithographs . . . printed on Rives vellum paper). Thus we do not know how the text in the suppressed edition may have been related to the illustrations.

The reader of the "Jeux poétiques" confronts a typical surrealist poem: a rich sequence of images, evoking gesture and movement, a colorful display which avoids stasis or an eclipse. The syntax and the arrangement on the page encourage continuity, as does the absence of punctuation. The sections are sometimes arranged horizontally, using the full length of the line, in a manner reminiscent of the prose poem, sometimes vertically, by reducing a line

---

[6]"Je rêve d'un grand atelier," *XXème Siècle* 1.2 (1958): 25–28.
[7]"Jeux poétiques" (Poetic Games), *Cahiers d'Art* 20–21 (1946): 269–72.
[8]See Patrick Cramer, *Joan Miró, 60 livres illustrés* (Geneva: Galerie Patrick Cramer, 1979), for a description of *Ubu aux Baléares* (Ubu in the Balearic Islands) (Paris: Tériade, 1971), as well as *L'Enfance d'Ubu* (Ubu's Childhood) (Paris: Tériade, 1975), with texts, colored lithographs and calligraphy by Miró.
[9]*Miró lithographe*, vol. III (Paris: Maeght, 1976).

to very few words. Spatial arrangements on the page play a definite role. The vertical and horizontal forms together further the sense of continuity. Their conjunction shows that Miró seeks to overcome any unidirectional arrangement. Because subordinate clauses are singularly absent from these configurations, all elements voiced in the poem receive equal stress. Like several of André Breton's early prose poems included in *Le Révolver à cheveux blancs*, Miró's text gives the impression of narrative continuity. However, the ceaseless shifting of protagonists and scenes of action undercuts the technique on which continuity usually relies.

The change from the initial "Jeux poétiques" to the final version, *Le Lézard aux plumes d'or*, consists of the replacement of two stanzas containing the games most difficult to imagine, to follow, to represent, to transform into a visual sequence—in a strict surrealist context, the closest to automatic writing. The term *jeu* does not necessarily or exclusively indicate lack of seriousness or playfulness or the mischievous quality often attributed to Miró's art. The surrealists labelled many of their activities, especially those of a collaborative nature, *jeu*, as a way of expressing their allegiance to chance, their refusal to be dominated by fixed rules and reason. Miró's title suggests a claim to freedom, a desire to move at random wherever words may lead him, rather than a predetermined or predefined goal or message. By changing the title, Miró does not point in the second version to a single or specific protagonist. *Le Lézard aux plumes d'or* is neither the subject nor the key image of his poem. At best, the title suggests the enigmatic quality of his text. It may appear that Miró's titles are more descriptive than those of other surrealist painters. The sun and the woman so often named in his titles are present in the painting, etching, lithograph, or woodcut; the mystery arises, however, not from their absence or presence but from their unexpected disguises and their stylizations. Mystery depends on the interrelation of the images mentioned in the title, whether one object reflects or attracts the other, and on how their rapport produces ambiguity. *Le Lézard* is not mentioned in the poem itself. The word, it is stated in *Ceci est la couleur de mes rêves*, was frequently used by Miró. It may even be considered, like Ernst's famous Loplop, as denoting the painter's alter ego. Miró suggests that it is a slightly diabolic figure, probably endowed with powers of transformation and exorcism. The lizard participates in the creation and re-creation of a landscape where the real borders on the fantastic. The mobility of its long tail, its mysterious eyes, and the relationship of its multi-patterned skin with its surroundings may well have contributed to Miró's fascination with the reptile. By calling it a golden-feathered lizard, he transforms it into an amphibious creation, half bird, half reptile, and gives it alchemical, mythical, and fantastic dimensions.

A lizard suggests a constant shifting, a succession of movements. Moreover, the adjective *lézardée* describes the crannied sequence of the text, as the title alludes to the lizard's jerky movements, indirectly announcing the erotic elements abounding in the poem:

—*Un oeillet rouge sur le bout du parapluie*
a red carnation at the end of the umbrella

—*Les points rouges de ma cravate piquaient le ciel*
the red dots on my tie pricked the sky

—*une danseuse nue à la chevelure rousse*
a naked dancer with red hair

—*Amour pur qui chatouille la gorge des hirondelles*
pure love that tickles the throat of swallows

—*Un papillon écarlate fait son nid dans le décolleté de mon amie*[10]
a scarlet butterfly makes its nest in my girl friend's décolleté

The relation established between one object and the next, one creature and the next, often has erotic overtones: a series of provocations implying a chain reaction. By this eroticism Miró introduces a form of transgression into forbidden territory. Trespassing, which subverts the expected order of the landscape, inevitably leads to upheavals where no established division of space can prevail.

The text in *Les Cahiers d'art* is accompanied, though by no means illustrated, by a sequence of reproductions, most of them entitled "Femme devant le soleil." The outline of the woman's body always implies proximity to the sun as well as the possibility of every creature or object entering into the others' fields of attraction. It suggests flexibility of motion and infinite ways of reconstellating multiple figures, of surrounding sun and woman, such as astronomical changes determined by the very agents we have detected in the poem. Whether Miró intended it or not, the accompanying reproductions reveal the affinity of the poem to his paintings, as they both bypass order and divisions characteristic of everyday reality.

Within the text itself, the emphasis on words, particularly adjectives denoting color, is striking: *oeillet rouge* (red carnation), *neige rose* (pink snow), *dames habillées en noir* (ladies dressed in black), *les points rouges de ma cra-*

---

[10]"Jeux poétiques," pp. 269–71.

vate (the red dots on my tie), *dessous bleus* (blue undies), *des poissons violets* (purple fish), *bébé rose* (pink baby), *maman brune* (brunette mommy), *le lait blanc* (white milk), *la cerise rouge* (red cherry). In the definitive illustrated version Miró eliminated such pleonasms as *lait blanc*. The abundance of basic colors coincides with the surface of the object named. The poem becomes equivalent to a painting, where colors shift into each other's orbit, often as a means of provocation. Tactile gestures together with the alternation of groups of two or three words (object plus color) characterize the poem. They lead to the rainbow, suggesting the presence and union of all primary colors as well as the shape of the arch, and thus they build bridges, which combine distance with proximity. The counterpart or complement of the rainbow in the text is the shooting star, scintillating, explosive, ephemeral. Rainbow and shooting star become synonymous in Miró's poem. Poetically they are related to the lizard, particularly in their connotations of alchemy and enigma. Miró's paintings do not merely precede his poems; his basic iconography is reflected in his verbal experimentation. Syntactically the poem avoids subordination. Thus grammar reflects imagery where all parts "stretch out" and move into greater proximity, producing the effect of autonomy, of instant dazzling visions. As we "chase" the protagonists or seek to circumscribe outlines, we reassess the place and time of action, retrace their flux, their reflection, their projection. The poem does not move toward clarification but proceeds toward the strangely luminous trace of the dream image, which transcends the landscape contours encountered in the course of the itinerary.

Miró modified his text in *Le Lézard aux plumes d'or*. He omitted the most intricate verbal chains, with which the deliberate simplicity of his iconography could never cope. The typography he adopted also made the poem more fluid and accessible. The poem printed by Féquet and Baudier reproduces Miró's handwritten text. At the time of the publication of the volume, the use of handwriting instead of printed characters was practiced by several painters in their *livres de peintre*—for instance, Reverdy's *La Liberté des mers* illustrated by Braque.[11] As early as 1928 Miró had published an illustrated book with handwritten rather than printed text: *Il était une petite pie*, text by Lise Hirtz.[12] However, handwriting is not used for the same reasons in all illustrated books. In *Il était une petite pie* the handwriting gives a naive quality to the book, as though it had been produced by a little girl. At the same time, it is undeniably ornamental. Above all, it clearly shows the intent of the *livre*

---

[11] Pierre Reverdy, *La Liberté des mers* (Freedom of the Seas), with seven original lithographs by Georges Braque (Paris: Maeght, 1959).

[12] Lise Hirtz, *Il était une petite pie* (There Was a Little Magpie) (Paris: Jeanne Bucher, 1928).

de peintre to avoid at any cost the industrial aspects of book production. In *Il était une petite pie* these same homemade, natural, spontaneous features characterize the *pochoirs en couleurs.*

Handwriting in *Le Lézard* has a different function. The letters are not formed with regularity; the relative thickness of the lines varies considerably. Moreover, the sizes of the letters expand and shrink within the frame of the same page. The letters slant in different directions on the page and in relation to one another. Critics have said that Miró's paintings reflect a child's world, a statement that readily applies to the handwriting in *Le Lézard.* Its childish scribe, unlike the little girl in *Il était une petite pie,* has not mastered the art of perfect penmanship for which elementary school teachers used to provide inimitable models. The awkwardly formed letters of each word are undeniably "tied" together to reconstitute the unity of the word. Expressions such as "les points rouges de ma cravate" remain clearly delineated simple entities or clusters. The handwriting discourages both standardization and mechanization. Each page, each cluster, each word, each letter asserts its uniqueness and thus pushes in the direction of art as irresistibly as its graphic accompaniment does.

Miró gives to each word a distinctive trait, which he further increases by the distribution of the words on the page. Regular straight lines and geometric parallelism are avoided. The quantity of writing appearing on each page also varies, and a sentence or line can begin anywhere on the rectangular space of the paper. Not only are the lines crooked, but they may form loops, going upward or downward or wherever the "jeu poétique" may lead. The end of the page does not coincide with a normal break in the syntax. Lines that do not form a regular pattern of distribution of letters or words on the page defy the conventions of printing and typography. By the fact that he confronts a somewhat unpredictable design, the reader is disturbed in his habits.

The poem as it is set on the page for *Le Lézard aux plumes d'or* no longer follows the patterns of verse and prose of "Jeux poétiques." In fact, any reference to prosody now seems irrelevant. The poem written on the page assumes stronger visual dimensions at the expense of verbal and literary qualities. The very first letter of the title is attached to a line sloping downward from a star figure or upward toward it. Does this not mean that Miró lifts his words out of the conventional space of the sheet of paper into a pictorial space where time and again the star emerges—not golden in order to represent what we see, but black in order to coalesce with the handwriting? Alain Jouffroy has summarized Miró's innovations:

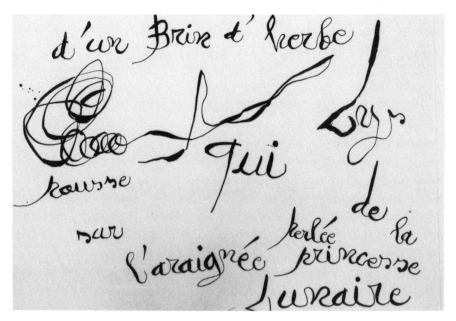

FIG. 33. Lithograph by Joan Miró from *Le Lézard aux plumes d'or* (The Lizard with Golden Feathers). Paris: Broder, 1971. © ADAGP, Paris; VAGA, New York, 1985. Photograph courtesy of the Bibliothèque d'Art et d'Archéologie, Paris.

The Lizard with Golden Feathers is above all an example, a message of freedom. It is most surprising to see this poem dance on the page according to pictorial laws, destroy the system of verticality and horizontality to which writing always conforms. Miró thus goes from sign language to verbal language by means of the language of graphic displacements: the swelling of the thick strokes, the shrinking of the thin strokes, the stressing of nonlogical connections between sentences, the visual space between words.[13]

Indeed the reader's eye is prevented from moving repeatedly and systematically from left to right. His hand seems to turn the pages at random, to multiply surprises. As it follows the words on the page, the eye has to meander back and forth (Fig. 33). Often it returns to the beginning of the page to find the final word at the upper left corner floating in isolation instead of tacked onto a sentence. Elsewhere the reader is caught in a new set of ambiguities, for he can fit the same word, by reason of the place it occupies on the page, into two different syntactical patterns. Moreover, he becomes involved not

[13] Alain Jouffroy, "Le Lézard aux plumes d'or," *XXème Siècle,* "Hommage à Miró" (1972): 129.

only in deciphering but in retracing footsteps mysteriously emerging and abruptly ending. He thus participates in the movement of the never visible lizard. The clumsy-looking letters, with scratches and blots, suggest the traces left by the passage of the trailing tail or the sliding paw (Fig. 34). Loops, tails, and doodles expand the verbal text. As the reader wanders on the page, he becomes an accomplice in unprecedented adventures. Miró subtly subverts our reading habits by this use of writing, as, by the poetic quality of his text, he lures the reader into his voyeurist transgression. Repeatedly the letter does not begin or end but merely fits into the patterns of designs. Circles, spirals, scribbles, perhaps not fully belonging to our world, extend the words, as if the scribe responsible for the scribbles may move back and forth between "here" and "elsewhere." In addition, those ornaments link the plastic to the poetic world and thus form transitions between lines in drawings and lines in writing.

We do not know the relation of the original lithographs to specific passages of the text, but we do know that they differ considerably from the final set. In fact, at best two lithographs possess a certain similarity, for both suggest a labyrinth with a double opening: a heavy black line circumscribes two colored circles (Plate 4). The viewer may relate the figure to the front view of a mys-

FIG. 34. Lithograph by Joan Miró from *Le Lézard aux plumes d'or*. Photograph courtesy of the Bibliothèque d'Art et d'Archéologie, Paris.

terious animal. The complex black line simultaneously hides and circumscribes the outline of the creature's body through stylization. Rather than delineate its contours, the line suggests their flux, their ever-changing motion, their mysterious itineraries. The figure emerges on both lithographs from a lighter background, speckled and spotted, flecked and vibrating, perhaps a transformation simultaneously reflecting a reptile's skin and the pigmentations rapidly moving through the atmosphere. The final published version of the lithograph includes several zones, especially in the lower section, uniformly covered with opaque but luminous colors, clearly delineated. Each zone shines in a primary color. Black dominates the episodic recurrence of red, blue, green, and yellow.

The original lithographs seldom, if ever, display such luminosity and opaqueness. They do not rely on monochrome color areas; they rarely use color zones circumscribed by lines. The space appears open, as great transparency and fluid shapes predominate. Barely any continuity or obvious area of affinity holds from one lithograph to the next. The plates could almost be independent pieces of work reflecting the artist's style of a given period, rather than belonging to a single set. Curved vectors and vigorous color splashes convey an immediate vitality. Thick, colored lines avoiding geometric precision display the irregularities always characteristic of Miró's craft. The vibrating gestures of the hand as well as the uneven thickness of the color-paste often lie side by side with thinly drawn black lines, arrows, curves, and starlike figures, varying manifestations of the artist's intervention. Color splashes add explosive movement and luminosity, analogous in function to the verbal cluster. The perplexed viewer is confronted by a constant meshing of creation and deconstruction, attraction and dispersion, by the perpetual stretching and condensing of happenings in spatial contexts. We watch the transformation of weblike constellations without ever seeing permanent images that crystallize the painter's vision of either dream or reality. Movement emerges anywhere: lines, vectors, splashes are never integrated or anchored and seem to move away from, rather than toward, a state of equilibrium.

The black lines, meeting one another, crossing one another, forming loops or arrows, obviously present analogies with writing in their common search for a language, for a code, for a state where the pictorial and the textual can merge. The painter avoids circumscribing contours that might tempt us to a recognition of familiar shapes. He avoids identification as he combines in eighteen different ways color zones, color splashes, curved lines, yet he always maintains their freedom and even suggests further expansions, further multiplications of the signs that refer to the artistic process. Lines not overtly linked to a color display, eventually curving into shapes, echo or simulate certain letters and thus establish further bonds with the poetic text. Both text and image create chains and clusters.

Stylistically, as we have suggested, there is a significant change as we confront the final plates. They reflect more directly what Miró claims on the title page: that he has *enluminé* the text. The poem is accompanied by very bright, luminous ornamentation. The color scheme differs from the subtle nuances of the first set of plates. Its reds, yellows, blues, greens, and blacks boldly assert their identity. The primary colors are displayed throughout, combining in lines, squares, and triangles. Far from undergoing dispersion or coagulation, they form a luminous stained-glass window (Plate 5). The painter shows the windows in which he captured the poetic movement of the text. As we turn the pages, the colors, set in their frames, assemble and reassemble, telling the "story" of their variations, a story that is continuous but nevertheless without theme, without the traditional distinction between characters and scenes, a story that defies analysis and divisions.

The three-legged hunched figure that illuminates the title page appears to be more recognizable here than elsewhere (see Plate 4). It belongs to an undefined mythology and seems endowed with the extraordinary ability to move in either direction. Arrows pointing to both the right and the left further increase the confusion. Several lithographs give the impression of wider spaces, more directly reflecting the liberating gestures of the text. Can we view the title, perhaps added as an afterthought upon the publication of the book, as an enticement to look for an ever-evanescent discourse? The title would indicate that representation has become desirable just because of its impossibility. The lizard is at once a bird and a star, an elusive amphibious creature.

We may endeavor to look at text and lithograph in conjunction with one another, while assuming all along that both constantly return to unknowable genetic and generating origins. Here and there the painter establishes precise points of contact between the text and the image; for example, the circles that occur again and again in the illustrations have a polyvalence similar to verbal play in the text—they suggest the eye as well as the woman's breast. The spotted ties can also be traced in the plastic work. Such overlaps serve merely to multiply discrete points of contact. Moreover, we cannot discount the fact that the painter has avoided parallel arrangements between text and image. Some lithographs occupy two adjoining pages; conversely, the text, on occasion, occupies the page on the right, thus taking the place regularly assigned to the lithographs, as though to imply that one can substitute for the other. Considered independently, the textual arrangements cause disruption and

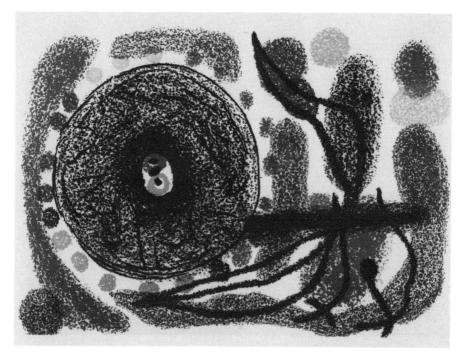

FIG. 35. Lithograph by Joan Miró from *Le Lézard aux plumes d'or*. Photograph courtesy of the Bibliothèque d'Art et d'Archéologie, Paris.

discontinuity. The lithographs confirm and intensify this tendency toward interference: luminous constellations, faint echoes of the transposed rainbow, far from imposing any regular recurrence, compound the challenge for the adventurous reader who, as we have shown, can never allow himself to remain merely a reader but must always function as a viewer (Fig. 35).

Miró, the painterly poet who verbalizes colorful images, the visual poet who lets his text create and enforce its own spatial rules on the page, adds a series of illuminations. Thus it appears that he goes full circle, for he finally fixes the vision. The landscapes, hidden paths, transgressions inherent in his poem crystallize into colorful stained-glass windows. Even though Miró began with the poem, the reader does not move unidirectionally from text to image, for their arrangement in the book asserts their reciprocity. When we try to isolate the text, its imagistic arrangement creates a demand for plastic representation. Conversely, the lithographs, however painterly they may appear, have many of the linear qualities of writing and thus seem to demand confrontation with a text. We cannot fail to notice that the text asserts its fragmentation, for letters cease to be recognizable as letters. The lines are assembled, juxtaposed, and meshed, but never link up into a chain. The last two pages form a disarray of arches, dots, and lines. Letters and words throughout tell a story of dispersion and discontinuity. The sequence of luminous maps, more and more enshrining and reconciling, embraces both the eye and the field of vision. It ultimately makes repetitious the further flow of the text, whether created by the movement of a hand or retracing the passage of a claw.

After it has vibrantly inscribed its code, the poetic language disintegrates, whereas plastic language then reaches its highest point. The fact that Miró has capitalized words denoting color, as though to stress their objectivity and their autonomy, should have warned us from the beginning that in spite of all appearances he intended to subordinate the poet to the plastic artist. The poetic text, like the lizard, symbolizes the trajectory that leads to creation, the domain where "les cordes de cette guitare déchirent le ciel" (the strings of that guitar tear up the sky). The strings and the lines, together with their recorded and unrecorded vibrancy, thus lead to a vision where poetry and painting finally unite in the subordination of the verbal to the plastic.

PARAMYTHS

In 1949 the Copley Gallery in Beverly Hills included, in its publication *Max Ernst: Ten Years of His Work*, *Paramyths*, a suite of eight collages and eight poems. This illustrated work for which the painter composed both the poems and the collages undoubtedly serves as the single best example of Ernst's combined talent as verbal and graphic artist. In *Les Malheurs des immortels* Eluard collaborated in the writing of the text; in *La Femme 100 têtes* (1929) and *Une Semaine de bonté* (1934) Ernst attempted to reduce, if not suppress, the textuality of his fiction.[14] Prior to 1949 Ernst had published some writings in French and German. In 1955 he translated the only text he wrote in English into his native German, and in 1967 he assisted Robert Valençay with the French translations that he later revised for inclusion in *Ecritures*, a collected edition of his writings published in 1970 by Gallimard. The painter's repeated efforts to translate and revise his own text indicate a commitment to writing unusual for a painter. Whereas he made no changes in the collages, he displayed complete freedom in transforming his text from English into other languages; in fact, he provided practically new poems in German.

The title *Paramyths* itself, the conjunction of two verbal entities, a prefix

[14]Max Ernst, *La Femme 100 têtes* (The Woman 100 Heads); phonetically, it could be *sans tête*, "headless," or *s'entête*, "shows stubbornness" (Paris: Carrefour, 1929); *Une Semaine de bonté* (Paris: Jeanne Bucher, 1934).

and a noun, constitutes a verbal collage coining a new word. In Ernst's book dealing with myths, he refers to Venus, Pallas Athene, Castor and Pollux, Hercules, and others who eventually, in more or less disguised form, become recognizable in the collages. As the prefix *para* is, in most cases, derived from the Greek, Ernst's new verbal unit maintains plausibility. *Paramyths* is not in the dictionary, but various word combinations with the same prefix can provide analogies, if not models. Some such terms denote objects, such as *paravent, parachute, parasol, paratroupes*; others are linguistic or literary, such as *parable, paradigm, paragraph, paragon, paraphrase*. If we review the collages, we discover the presence of a parasol used by Hercules (sixth collage), a screen (*paravent*) shielding a divinity (fifth collage), a parachute barely sustaining a recognizable creature in midair (the term *parachute* also denotes the membranes between the wings of the flying squirrel). Linguistic and literary terms also have relevance: the English poems in their concision can be defined as parables with a somewhat hidden moral. Ernst, who, as we shall see, borrowed freely from various books to create his collages and who introduced various ready-made expressions into his texts in several languages, indeed mastered the art of paraphrase. Paradox governs Max Ernst's collages, in which juxtaposition brings out the incongruous: in the first plate of *Paramyths*, a youthful divinity and a decayed birdskull together form a statue. If we consider the prefix *para* by itself it can mean either "near" or "alongside" (spatial location), "similar to" (comparison), "beyond," or "wrongly." We shall discover that Ernst's verbal and visual juxtapositions exemplify all these possibilities. The painter, whether he practices "closeness," "similarity," "trespassing," or "opposition," never fits his combinations together so as to form an organic unit. *Paramyth*, a word, as we have shown, in itself relevant to both the verbal and the visual, comes close to meaning *new myths*, while, at the same time, the reader/viewer feels warned against making such an assumption. He soon realizes that for Ernst the game of substitution itself matters more than whatever may result.

In the first collage, images seemingly fitted into each other turn out to be a series of misfits and disproportions (Fig. 36). Three layers, one behind another or, more appropriately, on top of one another, compose the plate. The front or top layer shows the graceful statue of a sun god, holding a sunwheel in one hand, a zigzagging whip in the other. Due to the muscles visible in both his knees and abdomen, the statue also seems to be a live body. The god's nudity is displayed: his meandering tunic is barely wider than the whip, and the figleaf merely outlines and frames his penis. Out of the background, or from the bottom layer, safely hidden from the god's nudity, emerge the eyes,

FIG. 36. Collage by Max Ernst, "puis-je en croire mon tympan" (Can I Believe My Tympanum), from *Paramythes*. Paris: Le Point Cardinal, 1967. © SPADEM, Paris; VAGA, New York, 1985.

toes, and outstretched hands of a woman. Enough of her clothing protrudes to reveal that she is fully clad. Between the female figure and the god, pieces of clothing are stacked, extending one another without forming a unit. The scarcely visible female figure is overwhelmed by the clothes, and she in turn dwarfs the sun god who, paradoxically, is strong enough to step on her feet. By their style, the clothes—a petticoat, a piece of belting, a night jacket, laces, pleats, frill and collars, suitable to the Victorian age—do not fit the Greek "paradigm," but if they are scrutinized carefully, classical decorative patterns can be discerned. This night attire, stacked up layer by layer, offers a protective wall (*paravent*); rich in décolletés and drawn curtains, it suggests indiscretion.

A bird skull crowns and partially replaces the barely visible woman's head. An ostentatious yet incomplete substitution provides an ironic example of *para* as "nearby": a burning candle, modestly echoing the sun, holds the skull in position, a contraption which also serves as lightning rod (*paratonnerre*).[15] A heavily twisted ram's horn, echoing the meanders of whip and male tunic, replaces the roots or pedestal of the tree-like statue. Ernst, as he juxtaposes incongruous images of Greek divinities and Victorian lace, creates ironic distinctions between female straight-"laced" outline and complex "ram"-i-fications.

In the second collage, the painter replaces juxtaposition by narration, displays by spectacles with spatial expansion. The moth is ordinarily incompatible with the light to which it is attracted. Here the painter contracts into a single image these two visually discrepant entities. Paradoxically, his moth has absorbed large quantities of light, which it radiates. The main protagonist, a daring girl on a ladder—still encumbered by frills, though they are somewhat less prominent than those of her predecessor—is fascinated by this ex-"parasite" turned into a heretofore unknown mythical creature perched on an erect pole. In the foreground two serpentine shapes, vestiges of the sun god's passage and traces of his temptations, are drawn to the girl. In the background, startled, half-obliterated men wearing bowlers or top hats catch glimpses of the frills and pleats of the girl. Her sun-shaped hat, crowning her hair, may come within their reach. As Ernst changes the moth from victim to source of attraction, he engages in a series of reversals, substitutions, and disguises. Disproportion, change of scale, characterizes the collage, into which Ernst deliberately introduces an optic equivocation.

The statue of an identifiable Venus continues the paraphrases of the divinities. As Werner Spies says: "The Venus of Milo, that most famous art motif emerging from the work, remains most easily recognizable."[16] The celestial body has shrunk to a candle and her hair assumes the shape of a butterfly. Obliterating her facial features, a diagrammatic "parabola" shows the lines of a magnetic field. Margot Norris says of this Venus:

The lines crudely trace a pattern resembling the orbital shape of eyes and an intersecting nose or proboscis—a pattern suggesting the exaggerated and grotesque features of an insect. Ernst might also be using the magnetic field as scientific analogy of Venus' esthetic and emotional power to attract and to control.[17]

---

[15] Several verbal cognates such as "paratonnerre" and "paravent" are present in the French text only, as this language is particularly rich in terms of Greek and Latin origin.

[16] Werner Spies, *Max Ernst—Collagen* (Cologne: DuMont-Schauberg, 1974), pp. 202–16.

[17] Margot Norris, "Deconstruction in the Works of Max Ernst," *Structuralist Review* 1 (Spring 1978): 10.

This "paragraph," with its oppositions between the scientific and the sensuous, between light and blindness, which provide different codes, replaces the myth and the love, harmony, and beauty which made Venus immortal.

The representation of two hovering, winged mammals departs from the previous iconography (Fig. 37). The nocturnal creature who has reached a higher zone and whose wings are further outspread claims the freedom denied to the hidden creature, with imprisoned arms, on the first collage. What distinguishes the two mammals is not a matter of degree but of species. Ernst suggests a paradoxical encounter between bat and beaver. Whereas Venus is

FIG. 38. Collage by Max Ernst, "le protège-mythe" (The Myth-Protector), from *Paramythes*. © SPADEM, Paris; VAGA, New York, 1985.

reduced to a candle, bat and beaver occupy regions of the sky, now synonymous with the poles of a magnetic field and exerting their power in the same instead of opposite directions. Throughout the series, the paramyths subtly invert similarity and opposition.

Werner Spies in his *Max Ernst—Collagen* includes book illustrations borrowed by the painter. His Venus (third collage), his Hercules (sixth collage), and his Three Graces (eighth collage) gloss plastically and verbally titles and representations included in *Stories of Gods and Heroes*.[18] By additions and

---

[18]Mark K. Jensen maintains that the three graces derive from Canova's sculpture of 1815–17. He refers to Fred Licht, *Canova* (New York: Abbeville Press, 1983), pp. 203–11.

modifications, Ernst twists the chronological references and cultural information provided by the textbook. He creates new verbal and visual adventures at the expense of the divinities' timeless past. In "le protège-mythe" (Fig. 38), Hercules' majestic body and frightful club are overshadowed by a huge umbrella burdened with pleats and decorations that in the first two plates had belonged to the feminine protagonists. The "parasol" affords an ironic protection to an invisible hero whose face is hidden by the back view of a woman's hair. Ernst, who has raised the underground beaver to the sky, here mixes male and female allusions.[19] The muscular and fleshy hero grows in unexpected places not only hair but frieze-like decorations unfit to serve as shield. Is he still capable of accomplishing his mythical promises now that the distinction between hero and statue has become as shaky as that between body and garment?

In addition to the book on gods and heroes, Ernst used a natural history treatise, borrowing bats with wings spread and closed, as well as miscellaneous snails. These "designs in nature," reproduced in *Paramyths* in various perspectives and contexts, provide a thread that mysteriously winds and unwinds "beside" and "beyond" the images of gods and heroes. Recurrent motifs, having lost their relationship to nature, belong to a world of dreams and hallucinations. Ernst, in his liberal borrowing, appears to tinker rather than invent, but the transformative process that these borrowings have to undergo reduces them to mere ingredients.

In the original English version Ernst did not title poems and collages. He refused to provide overt links—at least at that level. In the first English poem, however, by his juxtaposition with "phallas athene," goddess, Sade "the divine marquis" reinforces his phallic divinity. Moreover, *marquis*, pronounced "marquee," suggests that the collage functions both as canopy and as spectacle. In creating paradoxes without warning, in relating incompatible codes, Ernst refrains from using parallel misfits in text and image. The Greek goddess, chaste according to the age-old myths, is made to exchange characteristics with the most famous author of erotic texts. Her sexuality, which contradicts the principle of the ancient goddess's divinity, serves as a basis for "modern" immortality. These exchanges, without requiring confrontation, stem from a lopsided affinity between a warlike goddess and the sadistic aggressor. In the world of *Paramyths*, Pallas Athene, rather than imposing wisdom, becomes a willing or knowing victim, while the cold calculations of the marquis assume an air of innocence. Ernst's associations through verbal dis-

[19]In the sixth text, both in French and in English, Ernst refers to Prince Elizabeth; in the first poem, English version, to Phallas Athene.

placements such as "divine marquis" result in the destruction of the traditional attitudes toward these protagonists. The marquis's or "marquee's" contradictory attributes, which add up to an accumulation as defunctionalized as the stack of clothes in the plate, deny identity and, because they imply transgression, they can never attain fusion. The principle of the collage has been transferred to the text.

In assembling the verbal and the visual, Ernst does not assume the burden of matching the protagonists of the two series. By including multiple invocations and exclamations he manipulates the reader, for whose benefit he seems to record the reactions of a puzzled or misguided observer rather than giving literal translations or paraphrases. The introductory words of the first English text, "strange hallucinations," promise distorted realities matching those of the collage and justify the discontinuity and fragmentation of the literary discourse. The poetic text, which neither explains nor imitates, reflects on and magnifies the enigmas of the collages.

The contact between text and image is usually strongest at the beginning and gradually tends toward dispersion. Ernst adds and suppresses as he transposes from one medium to another; as he "cuts out" and "glues on," his verbal transposition and deconstruction simultaneously decode and cipher visual images.

In the second text the streetlight, functioning as protagonist, watches "high-heeled oranges." By this poetic statement the writer proposes a contraction, a new perspective as well as the metamorphosis of a girl into a tree. Alluding to Goethe's *Hermann und Dorothea* (cf. "tag und nachtgleich") he provides one more erotic association between the equivocal gods and the respectable bourgeois, by coupling through verbal substitutions the versatile, cunning messenger of the gods with the virtuous German heroine.

The first two texts come closer to narration, as they raise the expectancy of events, while the third begins like a fairy tale, proposing as hero a mouse, a creature usually found in fables. In replacing by a purely verbal expression Venus and her best-known statue, which is present in the collage, as well as the prince or princess of fairy lore, Ernst deconstructs two acceptable forms of Western culture. His short text leaves the telling of the tale, which might describe how the rodent forced the goddess to take refuge on a pedestal, up to the reader, cast as a perplexed accomplice in the creation of *Paramyths*.

If words about the mouse of Milo widen the rift between text and image, the poem facing the fourth collage, which represents a winged bat and a beaver in the sky, provides additional clues to their abrasive associations. The two night-creatures Castor and Pollux are demigods known for their similarity and inseparability and are also called the Gemini, a constellation. Ernst paid special attention to the ambiguity of their names. The French word *castor* means beaver. Ernst ironically links Pollux to pollution, for language, especially poetic language, encourages substitutions in accordance with sound and morphology. But while the collage humorously represents this constellation of unoffending stars, the text dissolves the bond between them by insisting on their eclipse and invisibility. Chaste Castor merely leaves footprints; Pollux, a by-product of pollution, fortunately leaves no trace at all. The initial rapport between text and image also disintegrates as the syntax undergoes the same process of dissolution as the two protagonists. After all, a collage cannot be recast in the words of a closed poem without denying its paradoxical nature. In the English version Ernst, by avoiding integration of word and image, proclaimed above all the integrity of the collage.

Since only minor differences appear in Robert Valençay's French translations from the German, these two versions may be examined together. The revisions made for inclusion in *Ecritures* further reduced the slight differences in meaning.[20] In 1955 the painter-poet seemed less concerned with enticing his audience than with writing poems that would establish more dramatic encounters with the collages. In the French and German texts, based, like the English, on contraction, amplification, and substitution, contact with the collage tends to intensify toward the denouement. The absence of capital letters and punctuation emphasizes the spatial appearance of the texts. Several poems are divided into stanzas; others include refrains. Words generate each other by sounds parodying conventional patterns of versification:

ihr bodenloser los, "bottomless fate" ["die obskuren"]

viehzucht noch unzucht, "animal breeding or unbreeding" [ibid.]

singulièrement le cor de la vie corne, "singularly the horn of life trumpets forth"
    ["une vie de héros"][21]

Ernst attracts the reader's attention to the auditory quality of his poetry, not only phonetically but semantically:

prête l'oreille à la cueillette, "lends an ear to fruit picking" ["equinoxe"]

horch aufs apfelsinen-pflücken, "listens to the picking of oranges"
    ["tag und nachtgleich"]

---

[20] For instance, *il inspecte son cheval de bataille*, "he inspects his war horse," is replaced by *il inspecte son dada*, "he inspects his hobby-horse," a more literal translation of *steckenpferd*.
[21] For reasons of expediency we use titles rather than page numbers in citing this trilingual book.

puis-je en croire mon tympan, "can I believe my eardrum" *täuscht mich das trommelfell,* "does my eardrum deceive me"

Synesthesia results not in the creation of metaphors but in the transformation of clichés or standard expressions. In the second example, the French suggests even more associations than the German. *Tympan* refers also to the frieze of a Greek temple, transformed in the collage into a stack of clothes. Is Pallas Athene, the goddess of sewing and embroidery, hiding behind these patterns and parodies for fear of becoming involved in Ernst's verbal expansions? The poet, by his texts, asserts difference, yet invites us to pursue with him the process of juxtapositions so typical of the collages.

Other rhetorical devices such as personification and animation are introduced into Ernst's poetry:

> *unermüdlich plätschert der lebensweg*
> *durch festland und murmelt quatsch*
> ["ein heldenleben"]

> indefatigably the path of life splatters through
> solid ground and murmurs nonsense
> ["a hero's life"]

> *sans relâche le chemin de la vie murmure*
> *à travers la terre ferme*
> *chemin bafouilleur*
> ["une vie de héros"]

> ceaselessly the path of life murmurs
> through solid ground
> stammering path
> ["a hero's life"]

This poem does not allude to a recognizable celebrity either by name or in action. The hero is a passive model amid change that springs from the course of life itself. In repeatedly introducing comparisons or hypotheses by terms such as *comme, comme si, als wären,* Ernst uses a poetic device to imply falsity or disguise and to arouse the reader's or viewer's mistrust.

> *le peintre peint le jour par moitié*
> *il peint la nuit tout entière*
> *il peint le prince elizabeth*
> *et sonne de la hache avec force*
> ["combien de couleurs dans la main"]

> the painter paints the day by half
> he paints the night in its entirety

he paints Prince Elizabeth
and strongly rings out the ax
["how many colors in the hand"]

der maler malt den halben tag
er malt die ganze nacht
er malt den prinz elisabeth
und bläst das beil mit macht
["wieviel farben hat die hand"]

the painter paints half a day
he paints all night
he paints Prince Elizabeth
he blows into the ax with force
["how many colors does the hand have"]

Because of the carefully synchronized substitutions of bat and beaver, the reader of "les obscurs" ultimately suspects that this coupling must also mysteriously interact with a group of words referring either auditorily or semantically to *souris* (this is pertinent only to the French texts).

un sourire dans l'arbre à feu, "a smile in the fire tree" [puis-je en croire mon tympan"]
la fable de la souris de milo, "the fable of the mouse of milo"
toutes deux se tiennent coites souriceaux pollux en chauve-souris, "both of them
    remain quiet, little mice pollux as a bat" [les obscurs"]
l'homme-chauve-souris chevauche, "the batman rides on a horse (*or*, overlaps)"
    ["la nuit du jugement dernier"]

The recurrence of terms has a function quite similar to that of the snails in the collages and provides mysterious signals. Like the title *Paramythes*, "la souris de milo" can be considered a verbal collage, for the mouse and Milo have no true connection. Cultural associations can create bonds that language may not foresee. Milo is known for the statue of Venus, with which we associate the smile of its near neighbor the *Mona Lisa*. Ernst's verbal collage, which depends on the displacement of a single word, assaults our threadbare cultural heritage. In the German text, significantly entitled *märchen* and not *fable* as in the French, Ernst sets up a clash between the child's world, expressed through diminutives, and the adult one, thereby compounding dissonance at the expense of the harmony expected of a Greek goddess and pertinent to the escapism of the fairy tale.

Lines from "wieviel farben hat die hand" or "combien de couleurs dans la main" combine two expressions:

et sonne du poignard (dagger) *avec force*
et sonne de la hache avec force

und bläst den dolch (sword) *mit macht*
und bläst das beil mit macht

As readers, we sort out the two actions that the poet has welded together, *sonner le cor* and *frapper de la hache* (*in das horn blasen* and *mit dem beil schlagen*). Both expressions evoke the type of heroic action by which myth and art have prospered. *Sonner du poignard* creates a disorienting but concrete effect quite appropriate to the collage.

Ernst repeatedly informs his reader, especially his French reader, that he constructs his poems strictly according to logic and seemingly in keeping with adherence to classical models:

ainsi donc la raison de l'homme frôle son aride tunique, "thus does man's reason brush its arid tunic" ["puis-je en croire mon tympan"]

ce qui explique leur insondable destin, "this explains their unfathomable destiny" ["les obscurs"]

man kann mit sicherheit daraus schliessen, "we can conclude from this with certainty" ["die obskuren"]

These claims to logic clash with the incongruous associations we have discussed and clearly invert poetic practices, which involve readers in a participation quite different from their approach to the abrupt English "para"-graphs.

If we are to judge by the examples provided, the French text contains ramifications specific to that language (for instance, the polyvalence of *tympan* or the homonyms of *souris*, smile, mouse). The French poems permit expansion of the text-image relation by means of verbal ambiguity, but the German text more directly reflects the nature of the collage. Logic, reason, or, more appropriately, the surrealist para-reason manifests itself on the surface in *ainsi donc*, echoing the terminology of Descartes, Boileau, and mathematical reasoning. In the German text, compound nouns with recurring parts seem to point to an inescapable order: in "*die jüngste nacht*" (the youngest night), *oberdrachentöter* (superior of the dragon-killers) and *oberkörper* (torso) are present in the same line. Although *ober* is by no means synonymous in the two expressions, the movement of the dragon-killers, a vertical movement already present in the collage, depends on the false assumption of their synonymy. In the German text, Ernst untiringly juxtaposes or couples words without prior connections, using and misusing linguistic models.

pestfahnen, "pest flags" ["täuscht mich das trommelfeld"]

mythenschirm, "mythical umbrella"

fledermensch, "batman" ["die jüngste nacht"]

oberdrachentöter ["die jüngste nacht"]

urgrosswald, *urgrossmutterschaft*, "great/grand forest, great/grand motherhood"
  [ein heldenleben]

"Fledermensch," for instance, is composed of two parts, instead of three as in the French *l'homme chauve-souris*. The German just as clearly conveys the meaning and the surprise elements, but it also creates in the reader the awareness that scissors have been active, that something has been taken out as a new object was created.

Repetitious elements, as was mentioned earlier, parody the versifications, refrains, assonances that result from the overwhelmingly synthetic nature of the German language. "ein heldenleben" includes recurring units: the prefix "un" at the beginning of several lines, nouns composed with "leben" toward the end, as well as nouns composed with "ur." The repetition of *un—unerbittlich* (inflexible), *ungewöhnlich* (unusual), *unermüdlich* (indefatigable)— is semantically relevant to heroic life and is reinforced by *lebensweg* (way of life), *lebenshorn* (horn of life), *lebensbild* (life's picture); this terminology seems to frame, although somewhat irregularly, the poem and confirm its title. However, disturbances occur as terms, casual in tone and meaning, emerge between the outline of the frame: "unermüdlich *plätschert* der lebensweg," "durchs festland und *murmelt quatsch*." Heroism becomes devalued as it loses its appropriate context. It no longer stands as a way of life, as a series of meaningful exemplary deeds. By means of juxtapositions whereby the expected noble words and deeds give way to *quatsch*, the prefix *un* may appear to be placed or displaced so as to avoid too dangerous a proximity with *unmensche*, *unvögel*, and *unzucht*, which Ernst coined in "täuscht mich das trommelfell," when Pallas Athene denatured various sounds and visions of our customary world. It appears that the recurrent prefix *un* proclaims once again the impossibility and unsuitability of "our gods and heroes." Nonetheless, the collage shows an apparently reassuring family portrait of the hero, his wife, and his child in a determined posture capable of restoring our confidence (Fig. 39). The examination of "les obscurs" suggests that resemblance and difference are not really opposing categories. In this collage the male hero originates in anatomical plates; he even wears a medieval helmet, while his spouse descends once more from Olympus. In the text we find direct references to the "model" child. This is ironically reinforced by the statement

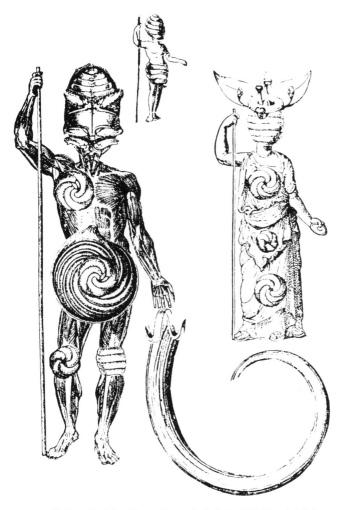

FIG. 39. Collage by Max Ernst, "une vie de héros" (A Hero's Life),
from *Paramythes*. © SPADEM, Paris; VAGA, New York, 1985.

that the hero "turned out well himself," through heroism, ancestry, or good
luck, even though such distinctions are never stated. When Ernst refers to
urgrossmutterschaft and *urgrosswald*, two words he coined in order to extend
human heredity to the vegetable world and child-bearing to old age, by
merely adding prefixes and shuffling them around he subverts all possibility
of a heroic career. By his deft lexical as well as syntactical manipulations,
Ernst shows that in his native tongue, more compatible with collage than
either French or English, he has achieved a mastery comparable to his
achievement in graphic assemblage.

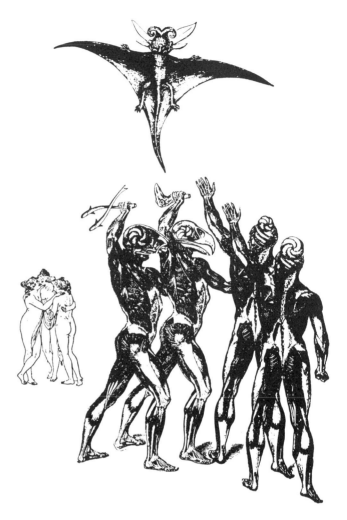

FIG. 40. Collage by Max Ernst, "la nuit du jugement dernier"
(The Night of the Last Judgment), from *Paramythes.*
© SPADEM, Paris; VAGA, New York, 1985.

A comparison between the final collage and the French and German texts shows even more clearly than its predecessors just how Ernst makes literary and graphic assemblage both complement one another and collide (Fig. 40). Beside three nude women, forming a tight and tender group by their embrace, four naked heroes (or are they anatomical models?) join in battle. In preparation for their strenuous activity, they display bulging, skinless muscles contrasting with the smooth skin of the three Graces. Above them hovers a hybrid creature combining human, animal, and vegetable traits, but whose wings resemble clothing, for they are barely stuck to the arms.

The warriors present another stage and a multiplication of the preceding warrior ("une vie de héros": see Fig. 39), recognizable by the same muscular representation and snail shapes. The hybrid creature presents in its pattern and shape a modification of the bat and the beaver as well as of the Venus head and the streetlight moth. Its spatial location suggests that it also stands for a heavenly body: god, angel, moon, sun, or star.

Max Ernst has concocted a collage of incongruous juxtapositions that simultaneously construct and deconstruct a make-believe world in search of a storyteller. The warriors display their musculature. The viewer sees beyond their skin and even into the snail-like convolutions of their brain. Ernst has not relied on a single anatomical chart but has borrowed from a variety of plates muscles, bones, and perhaps nerves, all the while cutting, deforming, castrating, until all that is left intact is the outline of the human figure. The numerous "fibers and threads" of the human anatomy are interwoven, braided, or wound as though to expose and parody myths of structure, cohesion, and organicism.

The poems are based on repetitive patterns of ready-made expressions such as *de-ci de-là*, *hin und her*, *de temps en temps*, *dann und wann*, suggesting a shaky regularity in the stanza where spatial expressions alternate with temporal ones. Ernst also refers to *mädchen*, *jeunes filles*; *oberdrachentöter*, *tueurs de dragons*; *fledermensch*, *homme chauve-souris*. Allusions to male and female, time and space, never carry the same associations when repeated or, rather, rotated. Such poetic uses or misuses therefore tend to protrude rather than blend. Just as the muscle and the bone do not originate in the same chart, just as the anatomical representation leads to the downfall of heroes, so verbal expressions juxtaposed in the poems seem to work against each other (especially in the French text):

> *les jeunes filles déchaînées se dandinent*
> *clopin-clopant*
>
> *hin und her am langsamen ort*
> *schaukeln die ausgelassenen mädchen*

Ernst suggests movements, rhythms, intentions that logically annul one another but which, as in the collage, increase their strength by grinding against each other.

Text and collage are held together by a title borrowed from the New Testament, "la nuit du jugement dernier," "die jüngste nacht." But what about the three Graces, who derive from a Greek model? And if the origins of the protagonists hardly call for a Christian interpretation, perhaps the location will prove to be more helpful. The hovering hybrid creature substitutes for Christ as represented in paintings of the Last Judgment and the Ascension. This dragon-shaped miniature may even turn out to be the devil, thus adding one more inversion to a long list. The world of muscles and bones introduces a nocturnal landscape. These "écorchés" (flayed ones) belong to Christian mythology, even if they do not perform like martyrs. "bergauf bergab" (up and down hill), "clopin-clopant" (limping along), "nach rechts nach links" or "à droite à gauche" (to the right, to the left) suggest a casual routine hardly appropriate to the Last Judgment but helping to explain the protagonist's lack of concern.

They create, although by different verbal usages, the same discrepancies we found in "ein heldenleben." Ernst has repeatedly provoked confusion about human time in the context of his chosen so-called immortals, beginning with the first poem, where Pallas Athene throws her watch into the ocean. In his last poem, residues or chips from the last collage function as objectified memories capable of fitting into the world of the collage. They show that poetic time is propelled according to different rhythms. The poem ends in silence and eternity without direct mention of the Last Judgment. Yet repeated allusions to horses' steps suggest that Ernst scatters "chips" from the Apocalypse. Now the hybrid creature in the collage takes on an additional identity: if we fully assume the double role that Ernst has foisted upon us, we too contribute to the paramythical representation of the Beast of the Apocalypse.

Arp, who showed equal talent in and equal familiarity with the visual and the verbal arts, tended to remain faithful to his prior or habitual practice and thus appears more conservative and less daring in his illustrated volumes than the two artists who wrote only occasionally. In presenting both art and literature in the same *livre de peintre* he obviously did not run the risk of experimentation. Ernst and Miró, on the contrary, by their use of language in the context of the illustrated book trespassed from one medium into another by means of a single experimental act whereby they broadened the basis of their creativity while destroying the barriers between the two languages.

CHAPTER FOUR

THE TEXT AS ILLUSTRATION

THE SURREALISTS WERE FAR FROM THE FIRST to produce books in which the order between text and image was reversed. William Combe, a minor British poet who produced a considerable amount of doggerel, wrote his most successful verse late in life, in the *English Dance of Death* as illustrations for Thomas Rowlandson's blackly humorous hand-colored etchings.[1] Alfred de Musset and P. J. Stahl in *Voyage où il vous plaira* embellished with their imaginative texts a series of fantastic woodcuts by Tony Johannot, probably the most prolific and successful book illustrator of the Romantic period.[2] Reversed or not, nineteenth-century book illustration remains stubbornly mimetic; writers as well as graphic artists provide close readings of the text or image they intend to translate into a different medium.

Obviously, mimetism is lost when the surrealists reverse the usual relationship between writer and graphic artists. René Char in *Dent prompte*, Breton in *Constellations*, and Eluard in *Les Jeux de la poupée* treat the text as a suggestive and challenging invitation to reinvent their own worlds.[3]

DENT PROMPTE

Dent prompte provides a striking instance of the poet cast in the role of illustrator. Ernst had completed a series of ten large panel collages which Pierre-André Weill wanted him to transform into lithographs and for which René

[1] *The English Dance of Death*, "from the designs of Thomas Rowlandson, with metrical illustrations by the author of *Doctor Syntax*" (London: Ackermann, 1815–16).
[2] Tony Johannot, Alfred de Musset, and P. J. Stahl, *Voyage où il vous plaira* (A Trip to Suit Your Fancy) (Paris: Hetzel, 1843).
[3] René Char, *Dent prompte* (Ready to Bite), with color photolithographs by Max Ernst (Paris: Lucie Weill, Galerie au Pont des Arts, 1969); Joan Miró, *Constellations*, with introduction and twenty-two parallel proses by André Breton (New York: Pierre Matisse, 1959); Hans Bell-

Char was to provide a poetic sequence—Weill had appropriately selected a major poet long associated with surrealism. Another editor, Gérald Cramer, also brought painter and poet together for the creation of A *toute épreuve*, where, as we shall see, the visual contribution outweighs the verbal in a different manner. In A *toute épreuve*, as in other books illuminated by Miró, the illustration provides an expansion. In Char's case, the literary illustration represents a considerable reduction when compared to the lithographs. Moreover, in *Dent prompte* the painter's contribution is in itself a transformation rather than an original creation.

According to Lucie Weill, Ernst's lithographs stimulated Char not to comment on or to describe, but to transpose the visual into the verbal. The lithographs, originating in collages, remain assemblages even if they are no longer three-dimensional and multi-textured. They are composed of assembled sections that require the viewer to overcome vacant spaces and to restore plenitude. Char saw his role as that of a reconciler who searches for unity. Since in his poetry he avoids syntactical subordination, this aspiration was for him all the more challenging. The brevity and ellipsis that dominate in his texts result from a struggle to seek balance without insisting on a prior statement of differences or on experiences of rifts.

The first lithograph consists of three parts. One is a somewhat unevenly cut piece of wallpaper representing a field full of promise of rich autumn harvest (Plate 6). Painterly luxuriance suggests vitality in this "canvas" where we can recognize scarcely any individual plants. The second component is a picture of a palette covered with patches of paint which also suggest fabrication, for they too are just clumsily cut out, like the wallpaper. We may wonder whether we have before us a painting or a ready-made object. The third part is a collage of a yellow basket and two bird legs glued to a green strip of paper. If the viewer of the palette does not quite know whether the colors have come haphazardly out of a tube or whether the fabricated patches compose an abstract painting, he is even more puzzled by the third section, where representation creates an ambiguity between raw materials and their transformations.

<hr />

mer, *Les Jeux de la poupée* (The Doll's Games), illustrated with texts by Paul Eluard (Paris: Editions Premières, 1949). The earliest surrealist book where the poet functions as illustrator is probably *Les Mains libres* (Free Hands) (Paris: Editions Jeanne Bucher, 1937), with drawings by Man Ray illustrated with poems by Paul Eluard. This book has recently been discussed by several critics: J. C. Gateau, *Paul Eluard et la peinture surréaliste* (Paris: Droz, 1982); Nicole Boulestreau, "L'Emblématique des *Mains libres*," *Bulletin du Bibliophile* 2 (1984): 194–221; Anne-Marie Christin, "Le Poète-illustrateur: A propos du recueil *Les Mains libres* de Man Ray et Paul Eluard," in *Ecritures II*, under her editorship (Paris: Le Sycomore, 1985), pp. 323–45.

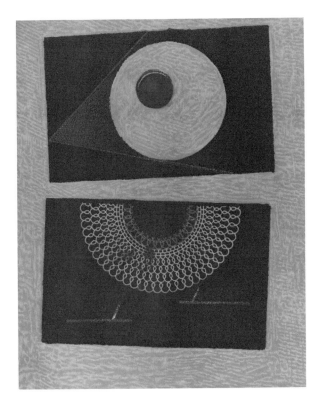

FIG. 41. Color photolithograph from René Char, *Dent prompte* (Ready to Bite). Paris: Lucie Weill, Galerie au Pont des Arts, 1969. © SPADEM, Paris; VAGA, New York, 1985. Photograph courtesy of the Bibliothèque Nationale, Paris.

The elements employed are not simply reducible to brush strokes or color but also function as objects from the ordinary world, defunctionalized by inclusion as well as juxtaposition. The golden basket loses its fabricated essence to become a sun; the green strip does double duty as a lawn. Strangely enough, the false sun, which owes its solarity far less to the play of illusions such as trompe-l'oeil than to the willing collaboration of our imagination with the painter's substitutions, even casts shadows. By spatially separating the three parts of his lithograph, Ernst stresses artificial fragmentation, which eludes all unifying illusion, while referring to the conflicts between art and nature.

Char's brief poem singles out the most incongruous element in Ernst's lithograph, the unreal sun casting shadows. He begins with the interplay of light and shade in the higher zones and, after a downward movement, ends with a harvest. At the speed of light he crosses a space that corresponds to Ernst's two-dimensional reduction, for it encompasses a movement across the various segments. Char alludes to the anvil and, implicitly, to the hammer by the lightning gesture which throughout his poetry represents creativity. Thus it constitutes a suitable metamorphosis of the palette. He views the world as a scene of dissonance and harmony acting simultaneously ("concordance ennemie"). He seeks to overcome the dichotomy present in Ernst's collages, assembled as stimuli for his efforts.

In the sixth lithograph two rectangles are attached unevenly to a marbled frame (Fig. 41). The upper rectangle contains a circular shape, an eye trapped in a triangle; the lower one, a semicircular lace collar strutting on two stylized split-level legs. The relation between the upper and the lower section tends to be more strongly conceptual than thematic. Both parts approach being abstractions based on circular forms; both exhibit striking luminosity; both suggest movement by use of slant angles; both are truncated representations serving as reductions of the human figure or its parts. The eye represents the head; the collar, the neck or belly. Each part remains autonomous but belongs to a clearly divided whole. The two joined parts suggest motion and vision: again they point to artistic creation as a process while providing a completed, self-sufficient artifact in which the collar and the lacework seem to link the visible to the invisible, continuity to fragmentation. The very nature of the collage traps the viewer in a complex game where concreteness and abstraction multiply similarities and opposition.

> *Veilleuse au seuil de nos terrassements*
> *Découple la beauté*
>
> *De moins en moins de charge*
> *Obstruant la glissière*
>
> *Disparus sur les humeurs du soleil*[4]
> Night-light on the edge of our earthworks
> Uncouples beauty
>
> Less and less of a load
> Obstructing the groove
>
> Vanished on the humors of the sun

With extreme concision Char sketches a landscape both cosmic and anthropomorphic. Once again the first line provides the strongest tensions and contrast. *Veilleuse* introduces light with night; *terrassement* alludes to earth, defeat, opaqueness; hence darkness predominates at first. The poet "conjures" an overcoming of obstacles, a filtering of matter, a reduction to essentials. By evoking an upward direction of increasing luminosity that is nowhere out-

---

[4]René Char, *Oeuvres complètes* (Paris: Gallimard, Pléiade, 1983), p. 119. All quotations are from this edition.

lined in the lithographs, Char nevertheless responds to the painter's dominant signs: the eye and its watchfulness in the upper part; the "mini"-sun with
its lace loop in the lower. *Humeurs*, invoking fluids and the eye, provides another link in the poem between seer and seen, between microcosm and macrocosm, between the two parts of the lithograph. Char's upward thrust abolishes our sense of perspective, while Ernst both respects and reverses the
usual spatial structures: the eyeball and the globe, the collar and the sun become synonymous and interchangeable. Char proposes a continuity pertaining to the poem as autonomous and a conciliation between aspects that in
Ernst at first seem separate.

The fourth lithograph repeats the spatial separations into parts; on the upper section a red circle, on the lower a grayish, rectangular wall. These cut-
out pieces on a dark background remind us again that the original version was
a collage. By surrounding the gray board with a frame, Ernst introduces the
paradox between fragmentation and completion. As in the first lithograph,
the viewer hesitates between reality and representation, art and artifice. The
red circle, reminiscent of the sun, creates the illusion of a cut red rose and
pieces of lace. The artificiality of flower and lace is made to coalesce with
"natural" light. A wall represented with photographic realism, stressing the
third dimension, dominates in the lower half. The two parts form a landscape
reduced to sky and earth, solidity and transparency. Both are represented, as
in the previous lithograph, by signs simultaneously suggesting intimacy and
distanciation.

In the accompanying poem Char establishes a series of contrasts, not between different levels of reality but between the timeless and the timebound,
between death and life. The initial word *liège* can, to a certain extent, illustrate the cycle of disappearance and rebirth: cork deriving from a tree, turned
into lifeless matter, is reborn from the sea by flotation. By evoking its color as
"l'étourdissement du linge" Char obliquely calls up the lace as well as the
wall in Ernst's lithograph:

> *Au liège rendu par la mer*
> *Couleur de l'étourdissement du linge*
> *J'ai adossé l'étape de sa source*
> *Le phénix du sel s'est deployé sur elle*
> *Elle a joui*
>
> [p. 118]

> Against the cork returned by the sea
> Color of the linen's giddiness
> I leaned the stage of its source

Salt's phoenix unfurled on her
To her enjoyment

Char endows the mythological phoenix with sexual proclivities, but also, by linking him to both fire and water, combines what in Ernst's collage seems divided. The painter separates a fiery red circle and an ash-colored wall, sky and earth, the everyday and the cosmic. He evokes return and rebirth as well as evanescence and frailty, which express a need for stability and mutual reliance. The phoenix belongs to Char's Heraclitean universe. In the poem inspired by the fourth lithograph, the poet attributes to the painter the metamorphoses of bird, fire, and ashes. Ernst's ash-gray wall, red sun, flower, and lace have transgressed the confines of identity.

Char excludes any description, narration, and comment that derives directly from Ernst. He does not read or decipher the lithographs. Between the poet and the painter there is no immediately recognizable affinity, even though they both proceed by reduction, concision, economy. Char recognized that Ernst's simplified figures are complex but not isolated signs. Ernst's division aroused in him aspirations that were habitual to him but that he undoubtedly and mysteriously also attributed to the painter.

For both Ernst and Char, the search for immediacy takes the form of a dual retreat from mimesis.

CONSTELLATIONS

Unlike other works we have examined, Joan Miró and André Breton's *Constellations* has given rise to several studies.[5] Moreover, separate studies have been devoted to Miró's series of gouaches and to Breton's sequence of prose poems. Jacques Dupin, poet and art critic, situates the series in the develop-

---

[5] Jacques Dupin, *Joan Miró* (Paris: Flammarion, 1961); Anna Balakian, "From *Poisson soluble* to *Constellations*," *Twentieth Century Literature* 21 (Feb. 1975): 48–59; Georges Raillard, "Comment Breton s'approprie les *Constellations* de Miró," *Cahiers de Varsovie* (Nov. 1973): 171–81, and "Breton en regard de Miró: *Constellations*," *Littérature* 17 (1974): 3–13; J. H. Matthews, *The Imagery of Surrealism* (Syracuse: Syracuse University Press, 1977) (the most comprehensive study interrelating surrealist art and literature); Matthews, "André Breton and Joan Miró: *Constellations*," *Symposium* (Winter 1980–81): 353–76; Renée Riese Hubert, "Miró and Breton," *Yale French Studies* 31 (1964): 52–61; Laurie Edson, "Confronting the Signs: Words, Images, and the Reader-Spectator," *Dada-Surrealism* 13 (1984): 83–94; Willard Bohn, "Semiosis and Intertextuality in Breton's 'Femme et oiseau,'" *Romanic Review* LXXI, 4 (1986): 415–29. Edward B. Henning, *The Spirit of Surrealism* (Cleveland: Cleveland Museum of Art, 1979), and Rosalind Krauss, "The Structure in Joan Miró's *Magnetic Fields*," in *Magnetic Fields* (New York: Guggenheim Museum, 1972), provided many insights.

ment of Miró's art. Anna Balakian, on the other hand, defines the role Breton's twenty-two prose poems play in his evolution. Such studies, in considering either text or images as autonomous, are, according to J. H. Matthews, somewhat debatable. Although *Constellations* was planned jointly, it is not strictly speaking a collaborative work. Miró composed his gouaches in 1941, away from the scene of military action and with full faith in the generative power of artistic creation. Breton, who was soon to reside in the United States, had at that time no contact with the painter. He did not compose the prose poems until 1959, shortly before Pierre Matisse published his deluxe volume in which the gouaches were reproduced side by side with the prose poems, sharing the same title.

The volume might better be classified as a portfolio or album rather than as a *livre de peintre*, since visuals unimpeded by text retain their space as in the original gouaches. The 1959 album, limited to 350 copies, includes colored photoprint reproductions of the gouaches in their original format. Printed by Daniel Jacomet, it bears the signatures of both Breton and Miró. Lithographs printed by Mourlot and engravings printed by Lacourière accompanied a limited number of copies, presented in a box illustrated by Miró. Only these few copies come close to fulfilling the conditions of a *livre de peintre*.

In at least two editions, André Breton's *Constellations* appeared with black-and-white reproductions of Miró's series.[6] This indicates that Breton continued to consider his texts as illustrations of the gouaches. Both Georges Raillard and J. H. Matthews have discussed *Constellations* as an illustrated book; they have attempted to assess the relation of the painter's to the poet's contribution, the transformation of the visual into the verbal. Raillard rejects an approach based primarily on parallelism: as each plate generates further images without disrupting the chain, it cannot be deciphered out of sequence. The gouaches provide a pre-text, but not pretexts. Matthews questions parallelism not so much on intertextual grounds as by reason of the density of prose and poetry: "And so André Breton's parallels are most prosaic, we notice, when on the surface their author reveals most directly the nature of his indebtedness to Miró. Hence, as they move further from prose, increasing therefore in poetic intensity, the less easy it is to say how they relate to the pictures they accompany."[7] Matthews cautiously refrains from seeing either competition or imitation in the poetic texts, and he carefully examines what

[6]André Breton, *Poésie et autre* (Paris: Le Club du Meilleur Livre, 1960), and ibid., *Signe ascendant* (Paris: Gallimard, 1968).
[7]Matthews, "André Breton and Joan Miró," p. 374.

FIG. 42. Gouache by Joan Miró, "Femmes au bord d'un lac à la surface irisée par le passage d'un cygne" (Women on the Shore of a Lake, Its Surface Made Iridescent by the Passage of a Swan), from his *Constellations*. New York: Pierre Matisse, 1959. © ADAGP, Paris; VAGA, New York, 1985. Photograph courtesy of the Pierre Matisse Gallery, New York.

he calls Breton's motivation, a fundamental desire for inquiry or investigation the poet detected in the painter and that led him to self-inquiry.

The title of the volume provides the first link between poems and gouaches. It produces a sign or "figure" that enables reader and viewer to penetrate the dual series and eventually to form it into one. The title, *Constellations*, applicable to much of Miró's art, designates a group of luminous stars as well as mediators between the human and the celestial. Pertaining both to the realm of perception and to that of representation, constellations were, so to speak, the first work of art or the first hieroglyphic cypher. Miró proposed programmatic titles for the individual gouaches rather than names of constellations. In general, the painter's titles tend toward description or inventory ("Portrait de femme" [Portrait of a Woman], "Escargot, femme, fleur, étoile" [Snail, Woman, Flower, Star]); some refer to the protagonist of a scene ("Personnage blessé" [Wounded Character], "Femme sur la plage" [Woman on the Beach]), still others such as "Femmes au bord d'un lac à la surface irisée par le passage d'un cygne" (Women on the Shore of a Lake Whose Surface Is Made Iridescent by the Passage of a Swan) (Fig. 42) by lyrical language suggest mysterious interactions. If Breton's prose poems are indeed responses to the titles as well as to the gouaches themselves, complex shifts between verbal and visual must have determined the creation of the poems. We cannot decode poems and gouaches merely by reading them in relation to a title. The title prompts the reader/viewer to extend his vision, to search for signs, to follow or foresee their metamorphosis. "L'Echelle de l'évasion" (Ladder for the Escape) (Fig. 43) embodies some of the chief characteristics of the series. The lines are inscribed on a surface to which patches of color are applied; the pigmentation fluctuates, moving between darkness and luminosity, transparency and opaqueness. This two-dimensional sky, which changes according to mysterious laws of attraction or fluidity, transcends the separation between the cosmic and terrestrial. The five dominant colors deny shadings. The blue does not simulate the sky. Colors declare their visibility, convey the presence of mobile contours, and when they glide into each other they do not mix according to natural laws but change radically as upon entering into new magnetic fields. In his preface Breton tells us that the gouaches are both *champs magnétiques* (magnetic fields) and *chants magnétiques* (spell-binding songs), for the line of demarcation between the organic and the geometrical cannot be clearly drawn.[8] Circles, triangles, rectangles, and curves blend or expand, as though to suggest the continuing process of reshaping, of rewriting, of re-

[8]*Constellations*, p. 9.

FIG. 43. Gouache by Joan Miró, "L'Echelle de l'évasion" (Ladder for the Escape), from *Constellations*. Photograph courtesy of the Pierre Matisse Gallery, New York.

juvenating signs. Each form assumes an identity by analogy with others, an identity immediately invalidated by the very nature of the process wherein becoming overshadows being. A discovery, for example, an analogy between the sun and a spider, undermines their phenomenal reality.

According to the title, the ladder plays a central role. An upward motion surfaces in a paradoxically concrete world. As the bars of the ladder lean toward each other, groping for a meeting point, they do not encounter the obstacle of matter or volume. Snail tracks and sickle moon aspire to create further ladders, so that eventually one element may substitute for another. Dupin states: "Thus by this other sort of ladder, whose rungs are equivalent and interchangeable, all exchanges are permissible, no hierarchy among beings and things has a profoundly rational foundation."[9] The ladder with its multiple connotations—upward lift, passage into the open, progression—

[9]Dupin, *Joan Miró*, p. 308.

FIG. 44. Gouache by Joan Miró, "La Poétesse," from *Constellations*. Photograph courtesy of the Pierre Matisse Gallery, New York.

can become a constellation, multiple but single; just as Miró's gouaches simultaneously form twenty-two separate constellations and at the same time a single constellation governed by repetition and transformation, Breton's poem departs from Miró's gouache as it unfolds in time. The first sentence implies a birth, a forthcoming awakening; the second sentence, more intertwined and meandering, suggests a projection outward, a rapid growing up; the third evokes a leap into freedom. The time sequence, compressing all activity into a single moment, relinquishes continuity, functioning as a third dimension. The poet's syncopation presents affinities with the painter's schematization. Breton names many objects without inserting them into a fixed space or defining their identity. He forces the reader to seek the lines, the forces that bind his swift-moving constellations. He overdetermines verbs that denote expansion or retraction across space—*annelé* (ringed), *froncer* (wrinkle), *hérisser* (bristle), *épandre* (spill), *bâiller* (yawn)—as does the interjection *Ooooh*; nouns such as *tuyau* (pipe), *boîte* (box), *bouton* (button), *chausse-trape* (trap) refer to open or closed containers. The sequence of concrete terms used by Breton shows affinities with Miró's patterns of squares, spirals, and circles, which open up and stretch; it repeats the multiple possibilities, present in the gouaches, of proportions rapidly changing, of evolutions dictated by mysterious rhythmic laws.

Breton's *Constellations* not only inscribe wavy, upward, expanding movements corresponding to those of Miró, but also suggest the painter's dominant reds (from the hidden poppy petals to the fiery beard) and blacks (the chimney sweepers). Breton does not apply color by "strokes," but lets them explode and retrospectively illuminate his whole poem, thereby echoing the painter's secret network. The terms we have stressed before—*annelé* (ringed), *hérissé* (bristled), *froncé* (wrinkled)—suggest potential ladders and thus potential leaps into the open. The ladder becomes the image of language itself, a ladder of verbal action; the "Oooh" makes a network of form and sound that carries the message of art, reiterating the ambiguity between *champs magnétiques* and *chants magnétiques*. "La Poétesse" (Fig. 44), the thirteenth gouache in the series, is far less mimetic. Even if objects emerging in a stylized, disembodied fashion are recognizable, they do not belong to the outer world as full-fledged beings. Later, when they become reduced to shapes and silhouettes, their autonomy recedes further. Graphic patterns emerge from which specific figures cannot be extracted. Networks, evoking a map of the sky with its rhythmic ebb and flow, move toward greater density and intricacy in the course of the sequence. However, figures such as the ladder or the snail, which emerged earlier in the series, will be neither abandoned nor submerged.

"La Poétesse," compared to "L'Echelle de l'évasion" (see Fig. 43), reduces the autonomous representational elements and increases the spatial forms tending toward greater abstraction, enhanced by density and overlapping contours. The color range broadens to seven, a number that, even though the colors themselves do not correspond to the spectrum, indicates the completeness of scales as well as the transformation of the ladder into an all-pervasive pattern of signals. On a background considerably lighter and more transparent than that of "L'Echelle de l'évasion" abound luminous circles, often divided into different color zones. Their interference produces chemical or magnetic effects. Motion is implied as strongly as in "L'Echelle de l'évasion." When colors move into one another's zones, they spark flames. Circular forms resulting from distortion and fragmentation tend toward more organic shapes. Triangles and rectangles intersect round areas, composing new constellations. "La Poétesse" tells more clearly than "L'Echelle de l'évasion" that constellations are not primarily fixed forms, established images, but are "constellating acts." According to Breton's preface to *Constellations*, Miró proposes less the folding and unfolding of scenes than the unfreezing of space, "la décongélation de l'espace." Interpenetration of live elements tends toward their lowest common denominator, while vision and visibility become inseparable in his spectacle. The presumed protagonist remains invisible; her intangible mediation enriches the spectator's horizon, which is lit by new solar systems. Although repeated all over the surface, no two stars or spiral forms appear identical. Creation is primarily related to the infinite variation of the same basic patterns relying on centrifugal or centripetal expansion and retraction. A network of lines where continuity and discontinuity alternate presents a complement to the color zones. By inscribing meandering lines that simultaneously bind and separate, the artist avoids trapping the viewer into an itinerary. These lineaments, not the poetess's dwelling but her powers of seduction, are also hinted at by evanescent contours of breasts and mischievous eyes.

According to Raillard, the gouaches constitute the initial spark, the germinating object of the prose poem.[10] Breton wishes to prolong the gouaches by an equally intense projection. His multi-layered text has to be read like a cryptogram, reducing Miró to one presence among many. Breton's intertextuality is of course undeniable, as Anna Balakian shows.[11]

The poem "La Poétesse" introduces the poetess Louise Labé, known as La Belle Cordière. In addition to reincarnating Renaissance woman, she becomes, with her braided cords and musical strings, the embodiment of surrealist fate. By her activities, *grésiller* (crackle), *joncher* (strew), *amorcer* (entice), *couver* (hatch), *onduler* (undulate), she mediates the power of Miró's barely visible poetess. As we read a phrase such as "le soleil qui doit devenir noir comme un sac de poil" (the sun which must become black as a bag of hair), we look back on Miró's fragmented, undulating lines, absorbing themselves by solar transformation into a black network without relinquishing their power. As these examples indicate, magnetic and chemical changes do not shape a narrative but reveal the structure of the poem and the gouache. The text of "La Poétesse," with its multiple allusions to fire, lightning, and explosions, displays both a mobile, luminous firmament and the persistent destruction of outer reality: "Lamiel, le tison aux doigts, s'apprête à incendier le Palais de Justice" (Lamiel, a fire-brand in her fingers, gets ready to set fire to the Palace of Justice).

[10] Raillard, "Comment Breton s'approprie les *Constellations*," p. 179.
[11] Balakian, "From *Poisson soluble* to *Constellations*," p. 53.

The poet's references to the erotic, alluring, yet poisonous effects of poetry (*Belladone*), a term denoting poison and a red-belled flower while suggesting by its etymology a beautiful lady, urge the reader to form his own constellations in passing from Miró to Breton. The poet's transposition of the plastic into the verbal, necessarily at once poetic and metapoetic, does not effect a merger, for such a merger would require that poet or painter relinquish the language that is his own.

LA POUPÉE

Bellmer's doll, a key surrealist innovation, had a fairly complex development. In its first incarnation it appeared to be little more than a provocative sculpture, a three-dimensional representation of human anatomy. It differed from other surrealist sculptures by the strange effect it produced, for it enticed the viewer to follow the artist in his game of assembling, reassembling, and disassembling, thus repeatedly and almost mechanically enhancing deformations, tensions, and distortions. Hence, from the very beginning, the doll was, literally and figuratively, both single and multiple. Subsequently the artist provided, in addition to the model, its endless variations. He presented a doll that can have one head and four legs; it turns simultaneously a back and a front view, apparently both toward and away from the spectator who, with a single glance, catches one pair of heels, one pair of toes, the buttocks, and the vagina. Bellmer holds in store an even more disconcerting spectacle: a doll suspended over a set of mirrors, in addition to creating the expected triple image or reflection, engenders three new dolls, three new views, three discoveries.

Bellmer relentlessly multiplies his dolls, revealing the unlimited number of "parts" that make up the anatomy, unveiling unsuspected features or eliminating seemingly essential aspects of their habitual context, while surreptitiously making believe that he has added imaginary dimensions. In his various representations of the doll Bellmer juxtaposes the pieces so as to bring forth abstract and mechanical potentials side by side with the most sensuous and enigmatic evocations. Between a faceless mannequin made up of straight rods that a switch could conceivably set in motion, and a pair of thighs adorned with lace draperies folded in flower shapes or calices entangling the viewer in a labyrinth of silken pleats and stitches, a multiplicity of variations must emerge. The doll, while remaining a sculpture, evolves into a surrealist object, the solidified token of our desire; this necessarily distorted form corresponds to our dreams.

We introduce Bellmer's doll into our study because of the 1949 *Les Jeux de la poupée* by Hans Bellmer, "illustré de textes par Paul Eluard." *Les Jeux de la poupée* had a long developmental history. In 1934 the *Minotaure* reprinted a set of eleven black-and-white photographs entitled "Variations sur le montage d'une mineure articulée" that had been published anonymously the same year in Karlsruhe under the title *Die Puppe*.[12] In 1936 G.L.M. brought out the first French edition of *La Poupée* which included a text by Bellmer translated by Robert Valençay. In 1939 *Jeux vagues la poupée* was published, consisting of fourteen poems by Eluard and two photographs by Hans Bellmer.[13] *Les Jeux de la poupée* includes Bellmer's "Notes au sujet de la jointure à boule" (Notes concerning Knobbed Joints) written in collaboration with Georges Hugnet.

Les Jeux de la poupée played an important part in Bellmer's subsequent drawings and paintings: "These drawings and the paintings derived from them are airy constructs, where the gossamer quality of the line belies the opacity of the doll."[14] In the issue of *Obliques* devoted to Bellmer the editors included a tale by Eluard, entitled "Appliquée," that had originally appeared in the *Minotaure* in 1935, illustrated by Man Ray and Bellmer.[15] Although Eluard does not refer to the dolls, "Appliquée," in certain of its sections, anticipates *Les Jeux de la poupée*: "Sur le tapis, en lentes processions rectangulaires, Appliquée multiplie ses pieds nus et les chemins qui ne mènent nulle part" (On the rug, in a slow rectangular procession, Appliquée multiplies her bare feet and the paths that lead nowhere).[16] Eluard emphasizes the endless interplay of self and other, the inner and the outer world, capable of generating the kind of imagery featured in the poems illustrating Bellmer's doll. In *Les Jeux de la poupée* we have not merely a remarkable illustrated book but by all odds the prime surrealist example of a collaboration where the quite separate ventures and development of the two partners mysteriously come together. The artist included fifteen specially colored photographs, a technical innovation which he supervised. Although he lacked the professional expertise of Man Ray, he did understand some of the creative potential of photography. He succeeded in changing proportions by a novel use of blow-up, a technique eminently suited to making concrete and exterior his peculiar vision of the unconscious workings of the mind.

[12] Hans Bellmer, *Die Puppe* (Karlsruhe: n.p., 1934).
[13] Quoted in Eluard, *Jeux vagues la poupée* (Playful Vagaries the Doll) (Paris: Editions de la Revue Messages, 1939).
[14] Paul Eluard, *Oeuvres complètes* (Paris: Gallimard, Pléiade, 1969), vol. II, p. 1568.
[15] Paul Eluard, "Appliquée," in *Bellmer*, a special issue of *Obliques* (Nyons) (1975): 93–94.
[16] Ibid., p. 94.

The title immediately invites us to clarify the notion of game, to see the doll of *Les Jeux* not only as a nonspecific surrealist object but as a mannequin. The long series of surrealist mannequins began with de Chirico's faceless assemblages, which were multiplied and metamorphosed by Ernst, Magritte, and Dalí. It exemplified some of the surrealists' basic paradoxes concerning animate and inanimate, object and subject, the real and the imaginary, for it abolished barriers and made contradictions irrelevant. Between a mannequin in a show window and a doll, the size and the relative adaptation to the child's world consitute the major differences. Bellmer's *poupée* combines the characteristics of a doll and a mannequin, not so much by deliberate distortion as by the ambiguous nature of its body, which juxtaposes adult with immature features. Not unlike Breton with Nadja, Bellmer projects the simultaneous but hardly angelic presence of child and grown-up for the purpose of overt sexual aggression. The *jeux* in the title refers to the doll's secret maneuvering as well as to the game the author plays with his audience.

Surrealist artists and writers played, as we have repeatedly mentioned, many games of their own invention, particularly that of *cadavre exquis*, a minor variation on a childhood game we all remember (its final product, usually colored drawings, often displayed with other surrealist art, looks like a distorted doll). The grown-up who plays at *cadavre exquis* substitutes for everyday behavior the liberating but disquieting force of chance. Bellmer, with his erotically provocative but still recognizable childhood toy, relies on similar substitutions. His doll, instead of submitting in predictable fashion, defiantly reveals inner tensions and stress. Her strangely distorted anatomy matters less as a fantastic or playful representation than as an invitation to subconscious sport. By her posture she lures the viewer into a ludic world where transgression and constraint are reconciled, thus turning him into not only a partner but an accomplice. There the difference between self and other disappears and the principle of identity becomes meaningless, for only reversibility can prevail. Bellmer himself, in his introductory statement, insists on the continuity of the game:

The best game feeds its exaltation less on the predetermined images of an outcome than on the idea of the perpetuity of its unknown sequels. Thus the best toy will be the one that gives no inkling concerning the implementation of its prearranged operations.[17]

[17]*Les Jeux de la poupée*, p. 13. Subsequent quotations are from this edition.

By means of the game the doll is thrust into a timeless flux; it becomes an enigma constantly rejuvenating its seductive powers. [18]

Bellmer photographs artifacts or objects that he has assembled or disassembled so as to suggest the possibility of an indefinite number of variations. In this respect his fifteen pictures only begin an endless progression or series and thus serve as initiation into a game where the doll performs, as we have already stated, as object and accomplice. The painter in his preface refers to the built-in "poetic" dimension of his work, which, of course, preceded Eluard's illustrations and the very notion of a book. By the term *poésie expérimentale* Bellmer refers to the process of creation, to the rejection of an originating order. He also undoubtedly considers poetry the common denominator of all artistic endeavors. Intertextually he prepares the ground for the poet. He alludes to multiple meanings, most of them unexpected, and disclaims any single, definable message. In his numerous critical texts Bellmer repeatedly uses the term *anagramme*, which he defines as establishing a relationship between the physical and the spiritual, between language and the body:

Anagrams are words and sentences obtained by permuting the letters of which a given sentence or word is composed. It is astonishing that—since the renewal of interest in the verbal creations of the insane, of mediums, and of children—no attention has been paid to the anagrammatic, coffee-cup divination of the letters of our alphabet.—We did not know much about the birth and anatomy of the "image." As a matter of fact, human beings know less about their language than about their bodies: the sentence is comparable to a body urging us to disarticulate it, so that its true contents can be recomposed through an endless series of anagrams. [19]

Bellmer dismisses any theory of language that would separate it from the image. The games of disassembling and reassembling serve to diminish the space of the unknown, to discard some of the false notions we have always accepted about both words and physical reality.

The doll thus becomes an anagrammatic puzzle, where organs and limbs seem out of place: here arms replace the head, elsewhere the buttocks replace the bust. In the "organic" language proposed by Bellmer, substitutions run apace and old parts are eliminated or assume new meanings and thus transform the whole. According to Monique Broc-Lapeyre, "Bellmer is crazy

---

[18]The doll conforms in this respect to standard surrealist practice. Max Ernst in his collages and Jean Arp in his ambiguous forms also force the viewer to pursue the creative process, to extend it indefinitely into the realm of the unknown.

[19]Hans Bellmer, "Post-scriptum à oracles et spectacles d'Unica Zürn," *Bellmer*, p. 109.

about these anagrammatic games, but in what way? The practice of verbal inversion is tantamount to disorienting the corpus of words so that other meanings therein contained as unsuspected potentialities may blossom forth."[20] The anagrammatic game results on the one hand in mutilations and amputations, absence of limbs and permutations; on the other, in distortions and amplifications: a blown-up navel looks like an apple, both signifying origin (Plate 7). But the game of substitution, as it curtails the unknown, also produces, by the new order it proposes, an abyss of mystery and an unsuspected enigma.

The viewer-reader who takes in a frontal view of the doll simultaneously with a glimpse of its back may indeed sense that he is involved with dream syntax. As the navel blown up into an apple proposes a strong forward motion, the vagina seems to withdraw, while the head is pushed between shoulders rounded like breasts and thrust upward. Bellmer grants freedom to the body. As J. B. Pontalis states in his introduction to Xavière Gauthier's *Surréalisme et sexualité*: "she insists on the destructive dimensions [of these sexual perversions], on their defiance."[21] The body in *Les Jeux de la poupée* has, so to speak, acquired an autonomy that discounts mimetism and adopts the language of desire (Plate 8). The outer and the inner world become reversible; in other words, concentricity and eccentricity become interchangeable. Therefore, exaggerated buttocks ultimately point to interiorization. These fuller, rounded sections are the counterparts of hollowness or the void. The anagram of the body creates a new context even though nothing has actually been added to what constitutes the body. Invention is not a new departure but is the revelation of the anatomy, of its potential seen with the inner eye. This vision corresponds to a language where words cease to follow preordained patterns, where they are set free.

Bellmer does not fabricate illusions so that his viewer may take the doll for some form of reality, for an accidental misshaping of nature or creation. Missing legs are not omissions but commissions. Bellmer uses both artificiality and exaggeration to tell his public that he has not duplicated a child's toy or the image of an adolescent girl. His doll wears make-up. As light falls upon her, it produces bewildering chiaroscuro stage effects. She is obviously made not of flesh but of papier-mâché. The anagrammatically repeated constellations constitute an assault on identity. The squinted eye informs the viewer that the protruding navel may serve, for the time being, as the center of the

---

[20] Monique Broc-Lapeyre, "Hans Bellmer ou l'artisan criminel," *Erotiques*, special issue of *Revue d'Esthétique* 1–2 (1978): 242.
[21] Xavière Gauthier, *Surréalisme et sexualité* (Paris: Gallimard, 1971), p. 14.

world. But can we henceforth recognize her when only one eye remains visible, though colorless? How can the doll, hairless from top to bottom, emerge crowned by black hair tied with a stained ribbon? A yellow strawlike coiffure may be a wig, removable at will. Her stockings or gaiters dramatize the nudity of the rest of the body. All these changes somehow relate to obsession.

"La Jointure à boule," added only in the final version, constitutes, according to Bellmer, the most important feature of his doll:

However close or far it may be positioned and swing in the confusion between animate and inanimate, it will always be a question of the personified, mobile, passive, adaptable, and incomplete object; it will, finally, . . . be a question of the mechanical factor of its mobility, of the Joint. [p. 13]

Jointure is both a contraption and a metaphor in the strictest sense, a bridge between two fragments or, rather, two words. Bellmer displays fragmentation by disassembling the doll through strong color contrasts or by its hollowness. Often the joint or its function remains invisible. It also can replace limbs or other parts of the body, as in the second photograph, where it substitutes for the breasts; and it can even assert its kinship with eyes, mysteriously glaring. In the text from which we have quoted, Bellmer again establishes analogies with language: "They probably function according to all the equations, even now slightly obscure, of interanatomical images, and according to each 'method' that, like the interlocking of sentences, grammatical dismantling, permutation . . . does not belong only to the specialist or to nature" (p. 25).

Bellmer's doll displays the repeated loss and recovery of an equilibrium, an alternating tension and relaxation. The multiplication of the "jointure à boule" dislocates the center of gravity, replacing a real and perhaps painful limb with its plastic or verbal representation. Substitutions deriving from prohibition lead to the restitution, by desire, of a forbidden territory. The representational or virtual body is conceived by Bellmer, in the case of the doll, as a language, precisely because it permits a deconstruction of bodily functions. The "jointure à boule" also emphasizes that the doll, always in motion, executes nonrepeatable gestures and postures (Plate 9). They resemble acrobatics: she stretches out unbelievably or curls up in knots, floats in a state bordering on weightlessness or sinks into a cushion. Even when she is reduced to carefully disassembled fragments or parts, she can still make menacing gestures. She is simultaneously the self and the other.

In spite of the absence of a partner, of an outer source of stimulation and seduction, we cannot consider the doll independently of her surroundings. Voyeurism is not confined to her squint or her vacant eye; it also comes from the setting or context in which she operates, a context that has to be read ana-grammatically in conjunction with her movements. The doll coiled against the wall, hiding as much of her anatomy as possible, is nevertheless ready to spring forward as though to belie her defensive gestures. Significantly, the wall against which she squeezes reveals a chasm rather than a crack; else-where a door enticingly remains ever so slightly ajar.

The cane chair that she confronts in more than one photograph creates, by undergoing changes similar to her own, an intimate interrelation between object and subject. The chair appears at first glance to show a predictable pat-tern, capable of offsetting the transgressions of the doll's anatomy. In one photograph both doll and chair, broken into fragments, are scattered on striped pieces of cloth (Plate 10). In this disquieting still life, discreet shadows interact among the parts. The chair plays the role of intermediary between the doll and her surroundings; the cane underlines the suggestive game of hide-and-seek. Throughout the series the cane serves as a filter of light and shadow falling randomly on limited surfaces, accentuating the virtuality born from the repeated paradoxes of transparency and opaqueness, fullness and void, organic and mechanic. If the doll's limbs and clothes, scattered around the broken chair on the green runner, suggest a still life, the next three images could qualify as landscapes where the doll participates in the changing pat-terns of branches. A dead tree crowns her head with abundant foliage. Death and life, artificiality and natural growth interweave to produce this astound-ing landscape. The accumulation of ecstatic elements—the overblown hip, the misplaced vagina, the triple breast, the "jointure à boule"—enhance and to a certain degree generate the eroticism of these landscapes.

In spite of the subversive transformation of objects, everyday rituals are by no means eliminated from these photographs; here the doll lounges in a featherbed, there she "recuperates" next to dishes partially filled with food, activities which seem at once successive and simultaneous. These everyday references are, however, ultimately subsumed under the various forms of transgression and contribute signs in the anagrammatic puzzle. In one pho-tograph an invisible carpet-beater slides its menacing shadow across her body, apparently without affecting her. This shadow of sadistic impulses carries more power than the actual act of beating. The amalgamation of the dead trunk with an instantaneously halted posture—four legs, two down, two raised, forming an anagram of the cross—provides an intense representation of Georges Bataille's conjunction of eroticism and death.[22] In another pho-

[22]Georges Bataille, *L'Erotisme* (Paris: Les Editions de Minuit, 1957).

tograph, the doll's limbs and a dead tree combine to suggest both an erotic trance and a crucifixion.

In composing his prose poems in response to Bellmer's photographic series Eluard inevitably became a partner or perhaps an opponent in the game. By this intrusion of a new player, the presumed rules had to be altered. The image of the doll provoked the poet and plunged him into a state conducive to surrealist activity. Its erotic mediation enabled him to reenter an abiding world of dream and desire where the figure of the doll ceased to be indispensable.

Eluard's poems do not establish close or manifest ties with individual photographs or even with the series taken as a whole. Descriptive statements concerning the doll as an objective presence in space are almost completely absent. Some scattered poetic images do, however, allude directly to the photographs. "L'Homme aux aguets" (The Watchful Man) (Plate 11) refers to the dark, decapitated figure watching from behind a tree the headless, four-legged, flaming-red dancer, which Eluard translates as "Flammes rondes et dures" (Round and Hard Flames), thus suppressing the dancer in the dance, the object in the passion. Elsewhere he looks for the breasts of a bald-headed girl and obliquely alludes to her nudity by mentioning dressing and undressing. The effect produced by visual images reverberates in shifting responses formulated by the poet. Thus word and image rarely coincide, for the poet avoids establishing parallelisms. Nor does he invent a narrative texture, for in all but two instances he provides no transition from one poem to the next. Eluard merely adds a richly filtered textuality to the game initiated by Bellmer's configurations.

In Eluard's own game he circumvents the object so as to gain access to a common inner world: "Gonflant ses joues, gourmande, avalant une fleur, odorante peau intérieure. Bouche forcément rose, même au fronton de la forêt toute noire" (Bulging her cheeks, greedy, swallowing a flower, fragrant interior skin. Mouth perforce pink, even at the facade of the pitch-black forest) (p. 46). Although Eluard in this text refers to physical attributes, even to greed, the poem manifests a strong drive toward interiorization and expansion. From Bellmer's outer wall, blown-up cheeks, the text by subtle transformations leads to poetry and perfume, to a mysterious language, clear manifestations of a hidden world. Under the impact of such an undefined landscape, an integration of contours takes place. Desire, even when stated in terms of hunger, overdetermines the inner world. And the poet abolishes perceptual distinctions between the visible and the invisible, implying at the same time the absorption of the physical. Several words refer to parts of the face, and the mouth suggests erotic transgressions as well as more spiritual exchanges. The rest of the body remains unmentioned. Bellmer's photographic image may well have provoked the quoted text, in which the very nature of desire undergoes metamorphosis, if not purification. Nonetheless, Eluard's transformation provides no more than a departure, since it does not lead to ecstasy but to a distillation, to purity. Bellmer's dream presupposes repressions requiring the compensation of transgression, whereas from the beginning Eluard's dream expresses and coincides with aspiration.

Elsewhere Eluard alludes to other parts of the body: eyes, heads, breasts, and the "ambiguous" heart, which have always played an important part in his terminology and mythology. They maintain their usual emotional intensity when they serve to illustrate or at least accompany Bellmer's images. Eyes, breasts, and the heart quickly lose their status as physiology by becoming involved in the polarities to which Eluard's poetry always seems to gravitate. He does not offer a mediation for Bellmer's universe or seek an equivalent in another medium, but searches for the parts of Bellmer's territory, limited though they may be, that he can reconcile with his own.

While some poems, as we have shown, derive from details in a photograph, others appear to arise from the sequence itself as verbalized by the poet rather than represented by the photographs. Whereas the immediate generative impulse could lead to endless problematics, we can fruitfully investigate the varying distances between image and text. In some poems, as we have already noted, Eluard dispenses with the doll. Elsewhere he urgently addresses her so as to present her as an object of desire who is capable of asking and even answering all the essential questions. Like the sphinx, she brings forth enigmas and sets traps. The voice of this often invisible incarnation cannot be heard. The poet, as in "Appliquée," tells about this being a story that he barely situates in space. This spatial void, without reverting to virtuality and protrusion, evokes a nostalgia echoing the distance between desire unfulfilled and satisfaction. Fear appears as the counterpart of desire. Eluard believes in a utopia, a realm outside the present context, but his cracked walls and desolate corners seem to belong to a world threatened with collapse. Are the echoes of Bellmer's enclosures accomplices of his doll's grotesque postures? The poet's polarized universe also contains shifting centers.

Bellmer's photographs preceded Eluard's prose poems. In 1945 Eluard had become concerned with brotherhood, communism, and social justice. As a result, his unformulated image of the doll belongs no more to the dream than to the fear of solitude and isolation. The absence of a voice becomes to a certain extent synonymous with a compulsion to be heard, and the need of the self for the other leads to the denial of identity, to the implicit affirmation of the anonymous. Eluard aspires to identity by fusion and by communion in his drive toward interiorization.

The doll circumscribes for Eluard a realm where poetic tradition has ceased to operate. It obliquely alludes to creatures reminiscent of some of Rimbaud's *Illuminations,* especially "Enfance." As in Rimbaud, the prose poems are composed of cryptic statements, words "assembled," leaving to the reader the responsibility of formulating transitions. Eluard establishes a system whereby he can compensate for the ruptures that occur both on the verbal and on the kinetic level. Unison motivates the poet, who has rejected fixation and stagnation, for stone, marble, and the statue must be thrust aside so that he can discover a mysterious road lacking visible traces. Metamorphosis or transformation plays an important part both in the poet's and in the painter's world. Eluard functions primarily as mediator for the realm of imagination at the expense of Bellmer's restless provocations. Imagination lies at the other end of absence, poverty, physical need. Its survival is linked to liberation. The emergence of nostalgia suggests the possibility of beholding once again a golden age.

Ultimately Eluard's prose poems establish a system of *vases communicants,* and the variations within the text are tantamount to a swinging back and forth between fear and longing. Childhood, to which Eluard's doll belongs more nearly than Bellmer's, may generate confidence and trust, even if its domain cannot be recaptured without distortions, restrictions, and obstacles. As absolute fiction, it is not fully attained by verbal means: "Dans le plus petit espace de la vue la plus étroite, on cherche en calculant, en ergotant la place de son coeur, on evalue la foi en l'enfance" (In the tiniest space of the narrowest view, we seek through calculation, through quibbling, the location of our heart, and we evaluate our faith in childhood) (p. 11). Eluard's pendulum swings back and forth; fear and hope, intimacy and expansion cannot forever exclude one another. Bellmer never deals with such fusions.

The poem accompanying the photograph of the doll squeezing itself into a dilapidated corner gives rise on Eluard's part to an inventory of secret dream objects contained in a child's closet, unrelated treasures simultaneously illuminating, alluring, and threatening. The pseudo-treasures have nothing to do with Bellmer's bold distortions of desire, for they replace obsession with the marvellous and gravity with childlike grace.

When the verbal, in keeping with surrealist practices and principles, serves to illustrate visual texts, it avoids the invitation to describe or the temptation to deviate into metacritical discourse. Nonetheless, Char, Eluard, and

Breton, in taking as their point of departure photographs, lithographs, or gouaches, fail to break out into a new kind of verbal expressiveness. On the contrary, their reaction to the provocative suites provided by the painters consists simply of adding earnest ideological and ethical considerations, as though they wished to endow the artists' purely plastic endeavors with moral value.

CHAPTER FIVE

SURREALISM AND THE
NINETEENTH CENTURY

THE SURREALISTS ESSENTIALLY treated Lautréamont and Rimbaud not only as charter members of their association but as exemplary figures who stood out against the lurid background of the age of Napoléon le Petit. They also respected, admired, and even followed several other nineteenth-century writers—Nerval, Baudelaire, Mallarmé, Poe, Lewis Carroll, and, as a group, the German Romantics, notably Kleist and Achim von Arnim— though they could not readily identify them with their own preoccupations and practices. They no doubt felt that they had to come to terms with these major figures because of their creative accomplishments, their continuing influence and, especially, their challenging theories. They paid less attention to the more pompous French Romantics such as Victor Hugo or that genius of all trades, Goethe, whose politics they abhorred.

A key aspect of nineteenth-century literature was the complex, even ago-nizing conflict, so characteristic of German Romanticism, between intense emotional commitment and incisive intellectual inquiry.[1] This conflict par-ticularly preoccupied Ernst and Bellmer, not so much because they had been steeped since early youth in German Romantic literature as by reason of their unceasing efforts to explore and structure intellectually the irrational world of dreams and eroticism. Both chose to illustrate seminal texts that ventured beyond the borderlines of literature by addressing theoretical problems of art, philosophy, and even logic. For instance, Ernst favored Lewis Carroll's play-ful paradoxes connected with language and reasoning over *Alice in Wonder-land*, from which he selected only one chapter, the Tea Party. Carroll ob-viously has little in common with Kleist, Arnim, or the Jena group; nonetheless, his humor and his love of paradox stimulated many of the sur-

---

[1]Cf. Jean-Luc Nancy's comments on *Witz* in this context: "Literary Dissolution," *Sub-Stance* 21 (1978): 23–25.

realists, including Breton himself.[2] The other major surrealist artists, unlike Ernst and Bellmer, never strayed far from the mainstream of nineteenth-century literature. André Masson chose Nerval's *Aurélia*, Mallarmé's *Un coup de dés*. Both Joan Miró and Sébastian Matta lavishly illustrated Alfred Jarry's popular *Ubu roi*, while Dalí, as we shall see, commented graphically on every aspect of *Alice in Wonderland*.

SUR LE THÉÂTRE DES MARIONNETTES

Critics concur in interpreting Kleist's frequently discussed *Über das Marionettentheater* in terms of Romantic aspirations toward harmony and unity.[3] Man, who occupies an intermediate position between animal and God, is unable to rely on reflexes, for his propensity to reflect slows down his gestures and makes him painfully aware of his limitations and his duality. The mirror in which he pursues his reflection, revealing his inability to repeat his gestures, becomes a metaphor for his duality and the limits of his control.[4] Man ineffectually longs for a lost paradise, a return to a golden age. Thus Kleist is clearly an exponent of Romantic idealism. His dancer belongs to the illusory world of dream, where spiritual forces overcome the material world and its rigorous scientific laws. In the course of the dialogue, the dancer formulates theories that challenge classical esthetics. Since many of man's beliefs have been shattered, he faces, in the absence of a reliable tradition, a world that has suddenly become uncertain and opaque. Kleist, in opposing the puppet to man, puts weakness and inferiority on the latter's side. This problem has been addressed by Bernhild Boie:

Just like an animal or like a man "without a reflection," it [the puppet] exists in a prelapsial state of innocence. Thus it is opposed to the adolescent contemplating his image, to the fencer observing himself, and, in the ultimate chapter of universal history, it finds an equivalent in the infinite consciousness of God.[5]

Moreover, man needs firm ground for support and rest, whereas the puppet touches the ground ever so lightly, exemplifying an obstacle-free course.

[2] In his *Anthologie de l'humour noir* (Paris: Sagittaire, 1940), Breton does not include any texts by German Romantics.

[3] Cf. Hanna Hellman, "Über das Marionettentheater," pp. 17–31 in *Kleists Aufsatz über das Marionettentheater, Jahresausgabe der Heinrich von Kleist Gesellschaft* (Berlin: Erich Schmidt, 1956–57); Hal Rennert, "Affinities in Romanticism: Kleist's Essay *Über das Marionettentheater* and Keats's Concept of Negative Capability," pp. 177–85 in Alexei Ugrinsky and Frederick Churchill, *Hofstra Cultural and Intercultural Studies* 3 (New York: AMS, 1980).

[4] Cf. Jean Starobinski, *L'Oeil vivant* (Paris: Gallimard, 1968), p. 186.

[5] Bernhild Boie, *L'Homme et ses simulacres* (Paris: Corti, 1979), p. 166.

The dialogue between dancer and narrator provides provocative and opposing points of view. Both interlocutors reopen old questions even when they abandon or modify previous positions. "Allerdings, antwortete er, das ist das letzte Kapitel von der Geschichte der Welt" (It is true, he replied, that this is the last chapter of the history of the world).[6] This closing statement is ironically substituted for the formulation of a theory enabling man to find once again a solid basis for his existence.

Although Kleist proceeds dialectically and addresses philosophical questions, his essay cannot, strictly speaking, be considered a philosophical discourse, for, like Denis Diderot's writings, it lacks sequential reasoning, a system of abstraction, and a general conclusion.[7] Kleist presents to his reader examples, anecdotes, and speculations rather than consistently developed reflections. Erich Heller goes a step further in suggesting that Kleist's text in itself transcends the purely literary and in a way calls for illustrations: "There are few literary works in which intellectual discovery transforms itself without resistance into the visual as in the *Puppet Theater*."[8]

Hans Bellmer has provided the major surrealist illustration of Kleist's essay.[9] A few years later, the British painter S. W. Hayter, who had strong ties with the surrealists, gave seven drawings to Guy Lévis Mano for his edition of *Les Marionnettes*.[10] Two vignettes signal the opening and closure of the text and provide a frame. Here horizontality dominates. The five others, where the vertical direction takes over, include two illustrations based on the juxtaposition of heavy and thin lines and three that are executed with lines of equal thickness. The representational element plays a subdued part compared to that of the movement or mobility of the lines. The formal element counts heavily in the work of a painter who, like Masson, has occasionally been associated with abstract art.

The initial and final vignettes include, in addition to heavy and light lines, dotted or broken lines, suggesting two levels of activity and introducing virtuality and hypothesis. The initial design includes a marked degree of geo-

---

[6]Heinrich von Kleist, *Sämtliche Werke und Briefe* (Munich: Karl Hauser, 1952), vol. II, p. 342.

[7]Hilda Brown, "Diderot and Kleist," pp. 139–45 in *Hofstra Cultural and Intercultural Studies* 3; Paul de Man, "Aesthetic Formalization in Kleist," p. 269 in his *The Rhetoric of Romanticism* (New York: Columbia University Press, 1984), introduces an analogy with Diderot so as to stress the importance of the dramatic as opposed to the persuasive.

[8]Erich Heller, "Die Demolierung des Marionettentheaters,"*Merkur* 354 (1977): 1074.

[9]Heinrich von Kleist, *Les Marionnettes*, translated by Robert Valençay, with ten colored etchings by Hans Bellmer (Paris: Georges Visat, 1969).

[10]Heinrich von Kleist, *Les Marionnettes*, translated by Flora Klee Palyi and Fernard Marc, illustrated by S. W. Hayter (Paris: G.L.M., 1972).

FIG. 45. Drawing by S. W.
Hayter from Heinrich von Kleist,
Les Marionnettes. Paris:
G.L.M., 1972. © Courtesy of
the artist.

metricality: triangular and rectangular shapes compete with an elliptical form sketched in heavier lines (Fig. 45).[11] Kleist's text alludes to the swerving from a straight to a curved line as he refers to the puppet's motions and the mechanism manipulating them and as he argues for the dichotomy between the organic and the quantitative, as well as their eventual fusion. Thus Hayter's illustration fits into an intellectual and esthetic context. The dynamism or kineticism of the first and last plates seems restrictive in comparison to that of the intervening ones. The more heavily interwoven lines and the horizontal equilibrium give the impression of a network not yet fully in action and extended. The final vignette, where bold shapes counterbalance rather than confront one another, provides a response to an open-ended text where implications remain merely latent. Hayter does not directly or indirectly ac-

[11] Georges Limbour, *Hayter* (Paris: Le Musée de Poche, 1960), pp. 30–32, stresses the creative aspect of Hayter's lines: "The engraved line is thus a pure creation of the hand and the mind; it has its own meaning, determined by the nature of the incision, and does not need, by means of imitation, to borrow from nature any of its aspects."

count for Romantic aspirations but reduces his illustrations to traces, including the hypothetical or potential movements of the dancer, which show man's effort toward liberation and his urge to create art.

The other illustrations emphasize movement, trace the continuity of the gestures, and provide their graphic synopses. It is tempting to see here analogies with Masson's automatic drawings. In certain illustrations the dancer appears recognizable; in one case he remotely resembles a bear. The struggle for liberation, the disengagement from material things, from weight or gravity, has its graphic parallel in the constantly curving lines, in their spatial meander. In spite of the remnants of representation, of a certain verisimilitude, Hayter does not introduce mimetism or take Kleist's text as a model for visualization.

He seeks the unifying element of various episodes by proposing a constant process of transformation. The dancer cannot be separated from the dance; the viewer remains unrelated to any form of reality, since he can grasp no more than threads of thoughts. Hayter presents a meta-illustration of artistic performance and creation, for which dance serves as a metaphor. The painter's surrealism in these illustrations comes from the drive of the Romantic heritage to overcome duality. He relates to the text by an intellectual strategy, not by theme, narrative, or ideological pursuit. Like Bellmer, Hayter reads the *Marionettentheater* as comment and reflection on art, but unlike the author of *Les Jeux de la poupée*, he proposes only minor deviations from or inversions of Kleist's esthetics.

Bellmer's interest in Kleist's essay is in keeping with the surrealists' affinity with German Romanticism. Among the most important works that testify to this kinship are Breton's preface to *Les Contes bizarres*,[12] Julien Gracq's preface to *Penthésilée*,[13] and Ernst's graphic comment on Caspar David Friedrich's *Paysage marin avec un capucin* and the accompanying texts by Arnim and Kleist (which we shall discuss later). Bellmer's affinity with German Romantic art and literature is strengthened by his belief in a basic analogy among all forms of artistic expression: "I think that the various modes of expression, pose, gesture, act, sound, word, handwriting, creation of an object, all result from the same assemblage of psychophysiological mechanisms, that they all obey the same generative law."[14]

Kleist's literary piece, by concentrating on performance in order to estab-

---

[12] Achim d'Arnim, *Contes bizarres* (Strange Tales) (Paris: Arcanes, 1933).
[13] Heinrich von Kleist, *Penthésilée* (Paris: Corti, 1954).
[14] Hans Bellmer, *La Petite Anatomie de l'image* (Small Anatomy of the Image) (Paris: Losfeld, n.d.), p. 11. Subsequent page numbers refer to this text.

lish analogies with painting and sculpture, could hardly fail to fascinate Bellmer. In the course of the dialogue, Kleist attributes the more challenging
point of view not to the "I" of the dialogue but to the dancer, who strives to
penetrate into the mystery of artistic creation by observing as spectator the
puppet theater. Bellmer, as generator of his doll, might originally have aspired to substitute plastic equivalents for the theatrical allusions in Kleist's
text on puppets. Its various connotations—robot, homunculus, mannequin,
toy—lead the viewer or reader to speculate about the relationship between
creator and creature, a reversible relationship capable of obliterating the very
distinctions which had given rise to the dialogue. Indeed, in the course of the
discussion, animate and inanimate, subject and object are gradually and paradoxically reconciled. The doll or puppet, in mirroring man without ever becoming his replica, expresses his limitations as well as his dynamic potential.
As Boie put it:

The puppet follows the curved lines described by the movement of its center of gravity; the strings that people had considered a mark of servitude will, in Kleist's view,
enable the doll to free itself from the inertia of matter, to gain access to the domain of
perfect movement, which is also the domain of absolute freedom.[15]

For Bellmer, on the contrary, the doll or its equivalents become by its gestures, by its distortion, the representative of dream and desire rather than a
referent for a clearly defined concept (Figs. 46, 47). Bellmer's doll has much
in common with the surrealist mannequin *objet désirant* or *machine célibataire*.[16] Nonetheless, even before undertaking his illustrations of Kleist he
had probably skirted the ambiguous territory of the *Marionettentheater*,
where freedom of movement and autonomy of gesture merge in the course of
a theoretical discussion on the inevitable interference in man between physical and spiritual forces. Kleist focused his arguments on such issues as the
relative power in man of the limbs and the location of the center of gravity,
which generates mobility. The puppet's dynamism, on the contrary, emanates from a single cross-shaped center. Bellmer, in his *Jeux de la poupée*, had
also questioned the limits and potentials of human movement by means of a
system of displacement that puts the emphasis on articulation. In viewing the
puppets Kleist's dancer gains awareness of his own being and art. In a sense
he becomes an apprentice all over again. According to Paul de Man: "*Über*

---

[15] *L'Homme et ses simulacres*, p. 170.
[16] The *objet désirant* is a surrealist erotic personification of an object, and *machine célibataire*
is an imaginary fabricated machine with obvious erotic suggestiveness; cf. Duchamp's celebrated *La Mariée mise à nu par ses célibataires, même* (The Bride Laid Bare by Her Bachelors,
Even).

FIG. 46. Colored etching by Hans Bellmer from Heinrich von Kleist, *Les Marionnettes*. Paris: Georges Visat, 1969. © ADAGP, Paris; VAGA, New York, 1985. Photograph courtesy of the Bibliothèque Nationale, Paris.

das Marionettentheater is also a text about teaching, stages all the familiar devices of pedagogy."[17] Bellmer represents his doll from the point of view of an ideal partner who experiences transformation from within.

One of the chief characteristics of Bellmer's art is the distortion of human anatomy. Other surrealists, too, introduced deformations, disproportions in representation. Masson in his 1939 *Gravida* reduces the body to a sexual labyrinth with open bloody walls; Magritte's 1939 *Viol* substitutes the female sexual parts for the face. Ernst's *Une Semaine de bonté* shows a male watching a woman whose intestines are escaping from her womb. Like Bellmer, these painters, each in his own manner, make visible the hidden dimensions of desire; by provocative displays, by departures from traditional representation, they aim at releasing the viewer from his repressions. The body ceases to be circumscribed by barriers that artificially separate the self from the other or from the outer world (Plate 12). By these distortions of the anatomy the surrealist artist thrusts the viewer into the world of dream and desire, where physical laws, including gravity, no longer apply. Bellmer states that our normal patterns unconsciously make us deny or efface zones of conflict. As we have suggested, by substitution and repression he suppresses parts of human anatomy; he juxtaposes and even joins together unrelated areas, thereby creating ambiguous images.

Bellmer practices further transformations and distortions by multiplying as well as sectioning organs and limbs (Fig. 48). In *La Petite Anatomie de l'image* he refers to "sexe-épaule" as a girl in her daydream touches her shoulder with her chin: "As soon as, by means of the intuitive gesture of the chin, the analogy between sex and shoulder ["sexe-épaule"] has been established, the two images merge their contents through superposition, placing the sexual parts on the armpit, the leg naturally on the arm, the foot on the hand, the toes on the fingers" (p. 13). By making noncontiguous parts coincide, the artist overdetermines analogies in shape, for example, breasts and buttocks: "From the dictionary of images—from that monstrous dictionary of analogies/antagonisms—we should learn especially that a particular detail, such as a leg, can be perceived, in short is real, only if desire irresistibly takes it for a leg. An object identical to itself has no reality" (p. 38). Here Bellmer clearly justifies and explains his method of representation, a system of transformation, a system which incorporates tension and analogy, a system alternating between opposition and fusion. He relies on shockingly distorted relationships with reality.

---

[17] "Aesthetic Formalization in Kleist," p. 269.

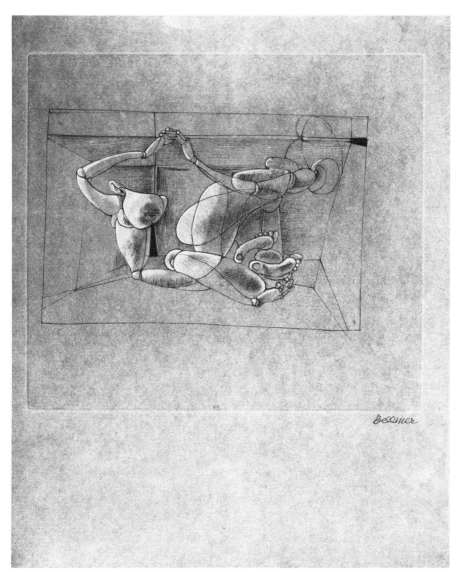

FIG. 47. Colored etching by Hans Bellmer from Heinrich von Kleist, *Les Marionnettes*.
Photograph courtesy of the Bibliothèque Nationale, Paris.

Kleist considers the physical or material aspects of existence a weakness, which man may overcome, at rare privileged moments, while seeking deliverance from duality or from his second fall, characterized by an alienation from nature and a paralyzing self-consciousness. As we have suggested, this purely physical domain assumes in Bellmer's universe a different meaning. For the German writer's aspiration toward a paradisiac state he substitutes the immediacy of dream and desire. The body serves as junction between the self and the other. In the act of penetration where freedom, pleasure, and magic combine with cruelty, the body, far from behaving as a soulless extension of man, functions as the primary intensifier or transgressor.[18]

Bellmer's illustrations of Bataille's *Madame Edwarda*, where he provides the human figure with the gesture of a puppet so as subtly to underline the interplay between revelation and innocence, might suitably have accompanied Kleist's text.[19] Indeed, to a certain extent they resemble the copper engravings of the *Marionettentheater*. Many of Bellmer's figures display perspectives, gestures, or postures that transgress the restrictions imposed by conventions.

The placement of the illustrations in the 1970 *livre de peintre* seems to indicate that the artist studiously avoided drawing any close parallel between specific images and the text, thus leaving to the reader all responsibility for interpretation. The painter multiplies, however, discernible links among various plates. As can be noted in other surrealist books, interpretation has to rely even more on the interrelation of the images than on the rapport that may exist between illustration and text. The fourth plate (see Fig. 47) can be construed as an echo of the second (see Fig. 48), for both introduce strong theatrical elements; the locale of the theater appears in schematic form; slanted lines create the perspective of a decor and curtain. The acrobatic alertness that emerges in the fourth engraving seems transformed in the eighth by an emphasis on articulations which form a skeletal chain no longer separable into limbs. These plates presenting circular gestures differ considerably from the third and the fifth, which feature constellated vertical movement surrounded and crowned by elliptical red shapes, functioning simultaneously as female genitalia and lips.

---

[18]Jérome Peignot, in *Bellmer*, p. 232, gives a different interpretation which leads him to affirm a greater affinity between the writer and the painter: "You have to read Kleist's text not only with the eyes but with all the senses. In other words, Kleist invites us not so much to a reading as to a fusion, an adherence of our entire being to what he says. It is to this very different kind of reading that Bellmer devoted himself."

[19]Georges Bataille, *Madame Edwarda* (Paris: Georges Visat, 1965).

FIG. 48. Colored etching by Hans Bellmer from Heinrich von Kleist, *Les Marionnettes*. Photograph courtesy of the Bibliothèque Nationale, Paris.

In general, when two or three plates echo one another in the Bellmer series, one of them is characterized by reduction of complexity and greater
structural integration. Bellmer's plates do not provide a "recognizable" reading for Kleist's characters, and episodes cannot be identified. In addition to
gestures, decors, curtains, and clothing pertaining to the theater, the presence of the actor or the dancer provides a unifying element among many
plates as well as between text and image. The painter obviously addresses the
problems and techniques of the Kleistian text. In plate 9 (Fig. 49), for instance, Bellmer, by distinguishing two levels of reality, alludes to the tale
within the tale—a container which, paradoxically, has broader implications
than the contained—the episodes of the mirror and the bear. Bellmer does
not introduce Kleist's protagonists into his illustration: the confrontation between bear and man is not represented, but the essence of the writer's paradox
is intimated by the painter.

In the eighth plate (Plate 13) Bellmer brings movement to a point of idealization that goes hand in hand with the reduction of matter. The puppet
dancer no longer touches the floor, but floats in the air. In two engravings the
soles of the feet constitute the summit, the crown of the figure. Through
these substitutions the anatomy is reconstellated, most probably in response
to Kleist's inquiry into art and imagination and his somewhat provocative
reversals.

In an early passage Kleist states the paradoxical situation of coherent motions stimulated by minimal gestures executed by the hand that activates
the many threads of the puppet. His paradox rests on the doll's superiority
over man, who because of his division is reduced to an impotent shadow.
Bellmer is concerned with the autonomy of movement as an esthetic problem. He establishes affinities and resemblances between the hand that
holds the thread and the arm that performs the dance: they create a single
figure. The first etching presents a "puppet," composed of five limbs, simultaneously arms, legs, male organs, extending in various directions the central
region of partially overlapping hips from which movement originates (see
Fig. 46). Upright and hanging "penduli," to use Kleist's metaphor, participate without distinction in rhythmic performances. In spite of the marked
transformation and perhaps the increased complexity, Bellmer encourages
an interpretation that fuses the hand that pulls the thread and the arms that
move the dancer and the puppet; the puppet and the puppeteer merge in this
and subsequent plates, so that Boie can claim: "Bellmer's doll is at the same
time a point of departure and a principle of art. The two aspects merge in the

FIG. 49. Colored etching by Hans Bellmer from Heinrich von Kleist, *Les Marionnettes*.
Photograph courtesy of the Bibliothèque Nationale, Paris.

desire experienced by the self for representations of the 'thou.'"[20] Whereas Boie insists here and elsewhere on the fundamental differences between the Romantic writer and the modern artist, we believe that the merger between creator and creation is alluded to in Kleist's text:

Er setzte hinzu, dass diese Bewegung sehr einfach wäre; dass jedesmal, wenn der Schwerpunkt in einer graden Linie bewegt wird, die Glieder schon Kurven beschrieben; und dass oft, auf eine bloss zufällige Weise erschüttert, das Ganze schon in eine Art von rhythmische Bewegung käme, die dem Tanz ähnlich wäre.

He added that this movement is a simple one; that each time the center of gravity follows a straight line, the limbs describe a curve and that often the entire body, accidentally set in motion, performs a rhythmic gesture resembling a dance.[21]

As we have shown in our discussion of *Les Jeux de la poupée*, gestures and movement are intimately linked to language. In the sixth engraving of *Les Marionnettes*, a mouth doubling as genitals is surrounded by multiple leg-shaped lines, by constantly sliding surfaces. The opening, enhanced by ovoid shapes or ellipses in the background and necessarily associated with language, provides another meeting point between writer and painter. The simultaneity of tension and depth evokes the generative act which, in Bellmer's art, links pleasure and pain. The final plate may be construed as a crescendo of the sixth. Tension and depth, life and death confront each other directly by means of the representation of the skeleton with its erotic blandishments. The dance of death, in which the fragmentary and multiple are integrated and which contrasts with the statuesque immobility of the previous plate, also points to a zestful new beginning. Kleist's denouement appears equally paradoxical, as though to imply the possibility of continuing the debate indefinitely.

Bellmer does not keep his viewer at a steady distance as he shows the sprouting of new limbs, autonomous fragments, spastic tensions, and powerful embraces. The viewer moves to and from invisible zones, regions that cannot be identified as skin, bone, or muscle but from which gestures emanate. Kleist's essay does not present a stylistic uniformity, whether we view it as an anecdotal narrative or from a philosophical point of view. Bellmer's plates oscillate between animate and inanimate, the image and its reflection,

---

[20] *L'Homme et ses simulacres*, p. 173.
[21] Heinrich von Kleist, *Sämtliche Werke und Briefe* (Munich: Karl Hauser, 1952), vol. II, p. 336.

the more or less marked intrusion of painterly qualities into dominant linearity. In the second plate mere outlines interact with precise and detailed forms of representation. Flat, transparent poles attached to one another contrast with the firm grip of phalanges, showing the gesture of the puppet by the dichotomy of stress and relaxation.

In his illustrations the painter combines geometrical forms—squares or circles—with contours that refer to human anatomy. Geometrical allusions in Kleist tend to suggest a drive toward conceptualization, whereas Bellmer searches for a new order, new forms of compatibility. Moreover, in plates 3 and 5 the painter, referring to the sky, transgresses Kleist's idealism by his ambiguities, which always include eroticism and desire. Artistic creation, for Bellmer, does not mean overcoming the inertia of matter, for the body becomes the instrument of transgression. It is unrelated to good and evil, since the puppet has never been exiled from paradise. The circle, symbol of geometric perfection, is bound to take another meaning in Bellmer's art, since paradise is bypassed or invalidated. René de Solier states: "The points of juncture, the sphere or half-sphere, this completed, nonmechanical rotation haunts man, who discovers the limit of his gestures."[22] In Kleist's work the circle assumes its full meaning; he does not question the existence of a center, a focal point, whereas Bellmer suggests a multiplicity of focal points substituting for one another: "What do you want me to call you when the inside of your mouth ceases to resemble an utterance, when your breasts kneel down behind your fingers and when your feet open or hide your armpit, your beautiful face afire?"[23]

This lyric sentence by Bellmer could be a comment on one of his works of art, revealing his inversions of conventional and religious attitudes, but never, as in Kleist, a nostalgia caused by their absence. Bellmer's drive toward esthetic criteria is relocated, metamorphosed, and liberated, so that Kleist's aspirations could only survive in a state of dissonance. Bellmer, rather than bring out the hidden characteristics of the inner world, makes the surface equivalent to penetration. He responds to Kleist's text as to a series of philosophical questions and specific literary devices. His engravings translate the dialectic of the Romantic text and its inquiry into art and creation. His modernization suppresses the irremediable distance implied in the Romantic longing that still separated man from image and stasis from movement.

[22] René de Solier, "Les Dessins de Hans Bellmer," *Bellmer*, p. 168.
[23] *La Petite Anatomie de l'image*, p. 47.

FIG. 50. Painting by Caspar David Friedrich, *Mönch und Meer* (Seascape with Monk). Berlin: Staatliche Museen Preussischer Kulturbesitz, Nationalgalerie Berlin (West). Photograph courtesy of Jörg P. Anders, Berlin.

PAYSAGE MARIN AVEC CAPUCIN

Ernst's overt relation to Romanticism can be traced to two works, a painting, *Quasi feu le romantisme* (Almost Late Romanticism, 1960) (Plate 14), and a book, *Paysage marin avec capucin* (Seascape with Monk, 1972).[24] The latter includes a translation of texts by Kleist, Arnim, and Clemens Brentano commenting on a painting by Caspar David Friedrich, and six collages which can be considered illustrations of segments of the text, as well as a lithograph which can be construed as still another gloss, though from a different period and in a different medium.

Friedrich's *Mönch am Meer* (Seascape with Monk, 1809) (Fig. 50) is important because it remains Romantic by virtue of its atmosphere and philosophy while anticipating more modern art forms by its technique. Kleist differed from Arnim and Brentano as he tried to assess the merits of the work and confront its controversial nature. He expressed his exaltation, communicating his feelings rather than explaining the painting. Brentano and Ar-

[24]Heinrich von Kleist, Clemens Brentano, and Achim von Arnim, *Paysage marin avec capucin* (Zurich: Bolliger, 1972).

FIG. 51. Lithograph by Max Ernst from Heinrich von Kleist, Clemens Brentano, and Achim von Arnim, *Paysage marin avec capucin* (Seascape with Monk). Zurich: Bolliger, 1972. © SPADEM, Paris; VAGA, New York, 1985.

nim, on the contrary, adopt an attitude of irony by juxtaposing the artist's attitudes toward nature and society with the shallow opinions of some hypothetical middle-class Philistines.

Ernst's lithograph represents a seascape without a monk (Fig. 51).[25] The absence of a human element eliminates the overwhelming feeling of disproportion between man and nature that dominates the Friedrich painting. While the lithograph reacts to the painting, the collages serve the dual purpose of commenting on the dialogue and representing the points of view of various spectators, including ourselves.

Friedrich is above all a landscape painter interested in depicting the mood of a particular time of day as well as the effect of the light, which transforms the wide spaces of the sea, forest, sand, and sky. His subdued and secondary

---

[25]Philip Miller, in "Anxiety and Abstraction: Kleist and Brentano on Caspar David Friedrich," *Art Journal* XXX, 13 (Spring 1974): 205–11, explains the paradox emanating from the spatial expansion suggested by the painting and the exclusion of the spectator: "Penetrability has been called the essence of the landscape painting, but Friedrich has indeed created the paradox of a vast, inviting distance against geometric horizontality which suggests flatness and opposes penetration."

colors suggest the mysteriousness of nature. A few of his paintings have general titles such as *Die Lebensstufen* (The Stages of Life), while most of them refer to specific geographic location and reveal unusual aspects of familiar areas. Friedrich's landscapes offer a multitude of realistic touches: the trees in *Felsenschlucht* (Rocky Gorge) and *Kreidefels am Rügen* (Chalk Rock), for instance, are depicted with careful attention to detail. However, such precision is usually offset by fluid outlines on the verge of blending into each other, metamorphosing; for example, trees receding into the background assume the characteristics of the sea or sky. Luminosity does not necessarily derive directly from the sky, sun, or moon. In the painting of the monk by the sea, the opaque sky gives an impression of heaviness, of closing in rather than opening up, and contributes to the mysterious and somewhat ambiguous ambience of the painting.

The presence of human beings in many of Friedrich's paintings usually expresses some form of isolation. Buildings are abandoned or in ruins. When the painter shows an altar perched on a rock, exposed to the elements, Christ seems barely accessible to humanity. Human figures usually turn their back to the viewer and from this perspective appear to contemplate the landscape with awe. What matters more than the suggested identification between the figures and the viewer is the separation between the figures and the landscape. As contemplators they do not belong to the landscape; they are in need of the spectacle without participating in it. This becomes manifest in paintings such as *Mann und Frau den Mond betrachtend* (Man and Woman Contemplating the Moon) or *Kreidefels am Rügen*. In some instances the characters appear physically separated from the landscape, as if there were a foreground to which they belonged and a background coinciding with nature. These entrapped but privileged spectators peer through a window framing and enhancing an unusual natural spectacle. In some paintings, Friedrich evokes imminent danger but the canvas-bound spectators remain quite safe while witnessing metamorphoses; for example, a mist invading the mountains assumes monstrous shapes.

The great emotional effect of *Mönch am Meer* comes from the extraordinary amount of space occupied by the sky. Earth and sea combined become almost insignificant in comparison. The sky with its threatening opaqueness and its somber and mobile clouds constitutes an evocative, protean landscape in constant flux while the sea and the land, reduced to narrow strips, have few secrets to reveal. With the sole exception of the monk, everything in the painting follows a horizontal direction. This incongruity creates a feeling of isolation, for exiguous man stands in nature where he cannot find security or

shelter. Robert Rosenblum describes Friedrich's human figures as "so reduced in scale that they seem on the verge of that kind of spiritual absorption
described by transcendental poets and writers of the romantic era."[26] The
monk wears the costume of a Capucin or Franciscan preaching friar, as is
pointed out by Ernst in the French title, *Paysage marin avec un capucin*. The
monk can define his mission and find his message in the presence of the sea
and thus become an artist as well as a religious figure; he is alienated, isolated, and overwhelmed by grandeur, but is nonetheless capable of transforming disproportion into vision. The Romantic poets point out in their dialogue a relation between the infinite expansion of nature and the infinity of
feelings aroused by nature, while fully recognizing that artistic interpretation
must to a certain extent fail because of a loss of immediacy and the reduction
imposed by a specific medium.

Ernst's lithograph, as we mentioned, does not explore the relation between
man and nature or between the artist and life. The horizontal line divides the
surface not into three parts as in Friedrich's painting but into two (see Fig.
51). This reduction makes both the lower and the upper part ambiguous; and
the spectator, who cannot know whether all three elements remain present,
presumes that he witnesses framed or cut-out surfaces which may extend indefinitely. In spite of the lack of a third dimension, in spite of the lack of major variations, both sections of the lithograph suggest motion, organic and
geological if not cosmological. The surface is rich in ambiguous depths. The
serpentine or undular motions on the upper half could equally well reflect
stormy action among the clouds, dislocation on the ground, or swells in the
sea. In the lower section straight lines deviate from parallelism because of
constant disturbance. Ebb and flow seem to have come to a stand-off. In both
sections, forces and counterforces, visible primarily by their effect, govern
the process of construction and deconstruction. The Ernst landscape obviously requires deciphering in addition to scrutiny, suggesting as it does expansion in space and continuity in time as well as constancy of variation independent of precipitation, acceleration, or centralization. The viewer, in
spite of the constancy of the upper and lower patterns which bar major disruptions, cannot find a central organizing principle; he cannot dominate the
mystery in spite of the relative simplicity of the pattern, for its vitality, its vibration exist everywhere.

The Romantic text emphasizes the absence of the sea, only a relative absence in Friedrich's seascape, where sky covers most but not all of the canvas.

[26] Robert Rosenblum, *Romantic Art and the Northern Tradition* (New York: Harper and Row,
1975), p. 23.

FIG. 52. Frottage by Max Ernst from his *Histoire naturelle* (Natural History). Cologne: Galerie der Spiegel, 1964. © SPADEM, Paris; VAGA, New York, 1985.

In spite of the horizontal divisions, interrelation is produced by reflection. Dark and light movements in the sky, among the clouds, reverberate in the blue sea and the golden sand. Ernst has taken cognizance not only of his horizontal division and of disproportion but also of the interaction or interplay between the zones. The dark traces caught between parallel lines may well be echoes of the turbulence above. More than echoing or reflecting, this interaction, consisting of echoes and reflections, comes close to a kind of synthesis or conjunction: the lower section in particular may well represent a plurality of elements.

The surrealist painter, like the Romantic artists, aimed at the discovery of a unity beyond the obvious divisions. By eliminating the figure of the monk, by letting the presence of the elements subsist while increasing their ambiguity, by suggesting inner texture rather than mere surface representation, Ernst has maintained the visionary quality of the landscape but has suppressed the subjective note, the meditation on loneliness, the salutary perception of death within life. Whether or not Ernst was fascinated by the true Romantic expressiveness of Friedrich, he did not want to emulate his search

FIG. 53. Painting by Max Ernst, *Cloud, Sun and Sea*, 1952. © SPADEM, Paris; VAGA, New York, 1985.

for beauty and sublimity. In translating the text that epitomizes Romantic art criticism Ernst decreased its intensity, its sentimental expansiveness. By the very act of penetration into the text, as well as into the painting, he found his way back to his own uncharted course. In its strokes and technique his lithograph is reminiscent of the frottages that Ernst assembled in *L'Histoire naturelle* (Fig. 52).[27] In its structure and composition it is reminiscent of several paintings entitled *La Mer et le soleil*, all of them horizontally divided, with differently textured lower and upper parts (Fig. 53). In other words, the painting is a variation on a number of Ernst's own works, as well as both an homage to and a parody of the German Romantic painter.[28]

As Ernst reveals in *Au-delà de la peinture*, he did not eliminate subjectivity from his art. Self-portraits with a comic vein pervade surrealist art and literature. Collage and frottage led Ernst not only to technical innovations but to self-discovery. Romantic longing and contemplation, at the root of nineteenth-century self-discovery, provided a somewhat passive if effective

[27] Max Ernst, *L'Histoire naturelle* (Paris: Jeanne Bucher, 1926). Cf. reprint (Cologne: Galerie der Spiegel, 1964).
[28] An extensive list is given by Werner Spies in his *Catalogue raisonné* (Cologne: Dumont, 1969).

method to attain this end. Surrealist desire makes its requirements for the here-and-now felt in a far more active and obsessive way. The visionary quality of surrealist creation may be aroused by an insignificant object or event—for example, by the irregularity of wood. The Romantic artist departs from vaster perspectives which still may serve as a model. Surrealists claim to chance upon hidden qualities, arousing unconscious activities of the mind, making such notions as example and imitation irrelevant. In one of his many penetrating essays on Max Ernst, Werner Spies mentions that in the frottage, primarily two planes of reality coincide: a structure refers a priori to something unrelated to the pictorial object. Artist and creation become indistinguishable.[29]

We have pointed out earlier that it is difficult to label sky, earth, and sea in Ernst. We have noted both omission of one element and simultaneity of several through the technique of stratification. The outer landscape has become unimaginable or nonexistent. By the same token Ernst calls into question the rational and the explicable, as through his very gestures or strokes he renders nature inexplicable and indescribable. He brings forth an image in which the order of creation is all-embracing. He does not refer, as Friedrich does, to an absence related to a void or a fear of nothingness—or, as Kleist does, to death.

Kleist speaks of death, of instability, of lack of centralization when confronting the Friedrich painting; it may seem like a personal response from a writer who experienced more deeply than others the conflict of the artist. Romantic writers did not unilaterally define death as void or nothingness. Many, above all Novalis, found that life-giving elements, cyclic forces, were deeply linked to death. These theories too were profoundly transformed in Ernst's works, so often Romantic in their origin, but never in their realization. In Ernst's lithograph and even more in some of his key paintings such as *Totem et Taboo* (1941), everything contributes to the entwining and unravelling forces where life and death function simultaneously. In Romanticism polarity survives to some degree until the natural has reached its transformation into supernaturalism. As transgression is often the point of departure in surrealism, we can safely say that Ernst's lithograph belongs to an "elsewhere."

Brentano and Arnim in their introductory statement, despite their somewhat exalted language, do not give a very high place to art or, in particular, to the painting by Friedrich, which must rely on the mediation of the monk, who makes empathy possible. In addition, the poets state the impossibility of

---

[29]Werner Spies, *Max Ernst, Frottages* (New York: Abrams, 1969), p. vi.

expressing the total impact of this or any other painting in words. Because of these doubts they agree, in their search for a more worthy interpretation, to include allegedly overheard comments of museum-goers. In relation to the transcendental aspiration of the seascape, the critic, unlike the creator, operates from a limited perspective—that of fidelity, rather than inspiration. However, the two Romantic writers aim less at translating the visual universe into words than at assessing the impact made on the viewer as he grasps the basic disproportion between emotions and rational thought, a discrepancy reflecting the division of humanity itself.

The alleged commentaries undercut the subjectiveness of the first part, especially the poet's suggestion concerning the painter's identification with the monk. This dual approach appropriately reflects the controversy that arose in 1810 about the painting, purchased by the Crown Prince, which was little appreciated by the public. The Arnim/Brentano text is composed of two widely differing sections, the juxtaposition of which has some qualities of a literary collage. In addition, the dialogue composing the second section is part of a sequence of fragments, a number of mini-scenes, each a non sequitur because the two speakers are not attuned. This discontinuity pertains to the painting itself, which, as we mentioned earlier, is dominated by distance and alienation. Moreover, its literary quality, attributable to the mediation of the monk and compounded by a peculiar use of perspective, also implies distanciation. Brentano's indirect approach is appropriate not only to the painting but to his own use of dialogue. The reader finally realizes that the aspiration toward unity collapses socially, intellectually, emotionally, and esthetically. The remarks, sometimes highly perceptive and penetrating but more often a string of clichés set in an unusual context, show rifts, reveal a latent discrepancy and misunderstanding. The work of art accordingly remains out of reach much of the time. More importantly, the dialogue indicates the difficulties of assessing art and nature, of transcribing feelings beyond the scope of everyday existence. It also suggests that art does not necessarily transform man and that only a superior person can grasp the mediation of art.

The museum-goers are people of all ages, widely differing in their relations to one another and thus capable of looking at a work of art in many ways. They give examples in capsule form of various aberrant or suitable approaches to the world of painting. Kleist's rewritten statements absorb passages from the dialogues, but instead of seeming two-edged, ironical, and fluctuating, they become serious, mainly by stripping away the bourgeois, Philistine comments in which Brentano and Arnim had delighted. The poets

FIG. 54. Collage by Max Ernst from *Paysage marin avec capucin*. © SPADEM, Paris; VAGA, New York, 1985.

had castigated the middle-class desire to possess, to recognize, to identify, and had accused the bourgeois of a propensity to reduce knowledge to facts and to make art perfectly safe by explaining it away, so that the painting became a substitute for emotional involvement and a means of covering up the emptiness of a world based on possessiveness. The bourgeois needs mediation, but hardly on the level of the painter who had to create the monk. This restricted and impoverished level reduces the mediation between the artist and nature to a kind of irony.[30] The painting thereby loses its immediacy and its visionary presence.

It would therefore have been inappropriate for Ernst to include a reproduction of the painting itself. Moreover, to include a reproduction would restrict the audience by making them read the remarks only in the context of a single painting and by forcing them to operate on the level of relativity or comparison rather than on the level of imagination. Instead of showing the painting in the distorting context of irrelevant remarks, Ernst shows only the faces of the speakers (Fig. 54). That is his creation. He thus completes a literary repertory consisting of poetry, art criticism, and dialogue by transforming it into a full-fledged drama with visible actors. He adds gestures to words. The faces

[30]Je voudrais être le capucin qui, éternellement solitaire, enfonce son regard dans la sombre mer et dans ses promesses (I should like to be the Capuchin friar who, in his eternal solitude, sinks his gaze into the dark sea and its promises): *Paysage marin*, p. 16. These comments from a dialogue of Brentano's text, however ironic, are most revealing.

FIG. 55. Collage by Max Ernst from *Paysage marin avec capucin*. © SPADEM, Paris; VAGA, New York, 1985.

become even more tellingly present when we think of the doubly absent face of the monk, who now must not only turn his back on the public but contemplate a forever missing sea.

The figures in the collage match the speakers of the dialogue. Presumably they face us, the readers of the book, but they also face the absent painting. This gives the missing painting with its absent sea greater power, by increasing poetic ambiguity. Even though everyone contemplates it, it is nowhere. The museum-goers are represented by collage. Ernst did not create these figures, but cuttingly uncovered them in a discarded fashion catalogue (Figs. 55, 56). Their apparel matters far more to them than their expression. Anachronistic from a Romantic as well as a surrealist perspective, they exclude identification while perfectly achieving the status of a cliché. By their precision, meticulous clothing, calculated pose, rigor, and ostentatious lack of freedom, spontaneity, and suggestive moods they represent the opposite of the seascape with its almost invisible sea, its mysterious inner reality. Nor do the mannequins all peer at the painting; scattered on the page, two children, one góverness, and two gentlemen, quite unaware of one another's presence,

FIG. 56. Collage by Max Ernst
from *Paysage marin avec
capucin*. © SPADEM, Paris; VAGA,
New York, 1985.

look in various directions. Obviously, they could not all stand enthralled behind the empty space where the Friedrich masterpiece would be hanging.
They have nothing to do with it. Ernst has substituted one display for another: the Friedrich exhibit has been taken over by a fashion show, from a
catalog, it is true, but hardly one in which art patrons might find a reproduction of the seascape. Perhaps the collage characters seek information about
the monk condemned to wear the same outfit through the ages while they
display the wardrobe of a given season. The irony has gone full circle as the
guide becomes only an outline and Ossian's harp, a mere metaphor, emerges
as a visible medallion (Fig. 57). Absence and presence, illusion and reality,
mirroring technique as well as distortions create a never-ending labyrinth.

By heterogeneous juxtaposition, the essence of the collage, Ernst has clev-
erly displaced and replaced Romantic notions depending on continuity of
time and space. Including a reproduction of the painting might have introduced, in the guise of a third dimension, space and time, and, above all, personal reactions quite alien to Ernst's process. He leaves it to his readers to put
together the lithograph, the collages, and the textual juxtapositions of anonymous phrases, clichés, and parentheses in whatever order they wish. The
elements juxtaposed produce surprise, but to make the collage effective, they

FIG. 57. Collage by Max Ernst from *Paysage marin avec capucin.* © SPADEM, Paris; VAGA, New York, 1985.

must eventually fit together. Kleist distorted Arnim and Brentano, whose texts distance yet mediate the Friedrich painting. The six collages increase mediation while pushing distance out of sight. The lithograph boldly and definitely displaces the painting, but at the same time it merely adds itself to the numerous echoes and reflections, originating in the seascape, that stubbornly refuse to be eclipsed. A pictorial emanation sporadically hovers over the collage, like the grin of the Cheshire Cat.

Illustration, commentary, translation, and interpretation, heaped upon one another, give us not only a playful awareness of our limitations, but also an appreciation of our freedom in understanding and communicating by means of art. Romanticism preoccupied Ernst because it could provide him with the image, the original problematics. By using Romantic themes and images in his own creative process, Ernst was led to self-assertion and self-discovery. His title *Quasi feu le romantisme* clearly states that for him Romanticism never really died. Indeed, it kindled new creations throughout his career.

WUNDERHORN

In addition to devoting three paintings to Alice, Max Ernst illustrated several of Lewis Carroll's other works: *Symbolic Logic* (1966); *The Hunting of the Snark* (1968); and *Lewis Carroll's Wunderhorn* (1970), an anthology of texts that includes the Mad Hatter's Tea Party.[31] Since Max Ernst had used some of the illustrations of *Symbolic Logic* in the *Wunderhorn*, we can assume that he was not as interested in illustrating specific passages or scenes as he was in providing responses to the problematics raised by Carroll. The title of the chapter from *Alice in Wonderland* is not a German translation of "A Mad Tea Party," but "Aberwitz und Fünf-Uhr-Tee" (Wit and Five O'Clock Tea). This suggests that Ernst was preoccupied with the logical, linguistic aspects of the tea party, which for him was not an encounter among characters or a satire on Victorian mores. He gives visual expression to issues that surface as the dialogue touches on syllogism, time, meaning, and other problems of language. Ernst immediately breaks through the spectacle offered by the tea party as an odd scene and delves into the conceptual aspects underlying the bewildering non-sequitur discourse. Most of the lithographs are composed of geometrical patterns: triangles, circles, ellipses, and graphs, in various combinations, as well as freer, less predictable contours which cannot be readily labeled (Plate 15). These schematized elliptic, humorous patterns obliquely refer to human activities or gestures. Often Ernst opposes shifting, spontaneous lines referring to human movements with straight vectors probably suggesting aspiration, demonstrating their incompatibility.

The first lithograph, which appears below the title, consists of three designs beneath a stretched-out outline (Fig. 58). Were a similar design not also used in Ernst's *Symbolic Logic*, illustrating three different types of propositions and their interrelations, we would be tempted to construe the three designs as referring to the three protagonists drinking tea at the table. These figures may, however, suggest propositions characterizing the operations of the protagonists' minds. Such complex lines indicate that operations of the mind are crooked; no straight path can be drawn to separate right from wrong, spatially or verbally.

Another lithograph presents three anthropomorphic creatures, each with its upper limbs raised to one side of the triangle containing a circle, the action stressing their mobility as opposed to the immobility of the triangle and circle, their unpredictability versus the strict rigor of the geometrical figures. Again, Ernst is not commenting on three figures at a tea table. Indeed, in this lithograph, characterized by more diversification and fewer repetitious elements, identification appears even more remote than in the first one. The

---

[31]Lewis Carroll, *Logique sans peine*, illustrations by Max Ernst (Paris: Hermann, 1966); *La Chasse au snark* (Paris: L'Age d'Or, Aux Editions Premières, 1950); *The Hunting of the Snark*, lithographs by Max Ernst (Stuttgart: Manus Press, 1968); *Lewis Carroll's Wunderhorn*, lithographs by Max Ernst (Stuttgart: Manus Press, 1970).

Aberwitz und Fünf-Uhr-Tee

FIG. 58. Lithograph by Max Ernst from *Lewis Carroll's Wunderhorn*. Stuttgart: Manus Presse, 1970. © SPADEM, Paris; VAGA, New York, 1985.

effort of groping, of searching for something unattainable is suggested by the outlines, as opposed to the absence of hesitation conveyed by the triangle.

The Mad Hatter's Tea Party can be interpreted as a discourse that aims at logic but passes from contradiction to contradiction. It shows the discrepancy between our reality and its underlying principle, between our words and the sense we hope to convey. Can the Hatter claim that there is no room for Alice, while one side of the table is empty? Can the dormouse be fast asleep, yet assert that it heard every word of the conversation that went on? Cannot Alice have more tea, because she has not had any? Perhaps we can conclude that all is relative, as the characters clash with one another. Their unmodulated aggressive statements falter in the presence of facts.

The clash between theory and practice, between abstract and concrete reality, becomes evident in the arguments concerning time. It is always five o'clock, so the protagonists claim. Are there any facts to bear out their statement, which contradicts our ideas and experiences regarding time? They are always drinking tea—that proves it is five o'clock; the dormouse is asleep, so time does not march on; the watch is stopped up with bread crumbs, so time is arrested. To avoid seeing the passing of time, the characters change seats: a clean cup means it is five o'clock. Through words and gestures used by his protagonists, as well as through a series of games, Carroll shows that we cover up problems. His players make up rules that operate in their favor. They claim that time is like a person whom they have the power to kill, but they certainly do not master it on a higher level, as a concept. Ernst's lithograph displays the characteristics of games, especially of children's games.

In the final lithograph (Plate 16), Ernst once more suggests various inter-relations. This time he seems to go beyond the incompatibility of the two systems, the insufficient link established between the concept and the fact, the theory and the object. He implies that verbal activity is not directly linked to a speaker by a tight leash, but, rather, that it creates its own ambiguous ramifications. Such ambiguities frequently occur in the text. For instance, "talking over the dormouse's head" and "beating and killing time" become both literal and figurative, preventing a mere linear continuity of the text.

When the reader reaches the end of the chapter, he can safely say that Carroll's protagonists have played many games; telling or not telling time, parodying nursery rhymes, inventing variations on musical chairs and on sundry bedside stories. Above all, they play word-games; most of the time they use the written and unwritten rules of language at cross-purposes. The reader becomes aware that all these non sequiturs and absurdities are based on the mis-use of discourse. By verbal prowess the characters turn each other into winners and losers. They try to make every statement, however relative it may be, into part of an infallible syllogism. Finally they focus on a single letter and enumerate words beginning with the letter *m*. This game shows once more the arbitrary nature of signs and linguistic categories. Even the alphabet, basic to all verbal systems, begins to founder. Faith in language must ultimately result in chaos.

Ernst's designs, especially the final one (see Plate 16), suggest that as discourse continues, as one sentence follows another, linear progress comes to a standstill and single or simple evidence becomes irrelevant. The spiral suggests that the abyss of game within game, of derivation upon derivation within language, creates opaque patterns far removed from transparency of meaning. Words and a world full of people and objects remain far apart. In one of the lithographs we may perhaps recognize a chair. But as we try to label it as though it were an object, we begin to hesitate, remembering that the dormouse doubles as a cushion and has a place in the teapot. Identity is a real problem, so Carroll tells us all along. Ernst for his part undermines the world and questions the autonomy of its objects. He reveals the disturbance in our pursuits, the disorientation of our groping mental activities. His strange patterns simultaneously call to mind a child's attempts at figure drawing and the gestures of handwriting.

ALICE IN WONDERLAND

Alice in Wonderland is unusual in that the author himself provided drawings in the original version, entitled *Alice's Adventures Underground*.[32] Although they could have been intended as suggestions to John Tenniel, the artist who was to illustrate the final version, Tenniel may never have seen the sketches. Among the many later illustrations, those by Dalí, a prolific book illustrator, are the most provocative.[33] Lewis Carroll, who is included in *L'Anthologie de l'humour noir* and in *Le Dictionnaire du surréalisme*, was held in high esteem by the surrealists, who praised his polemical and his fantastic tendencies.[34] Dalí's and Ernst's interest in *Alice in Wonderland* cannot be construed as accidental; therefore the ways in which these surrealist painters distorted or enriched a text that acts at once as children's literature, adventure story, and satire against Victorian manners should be most revealing.

Carroll always conceived of *Alice* as an illustrated book; according to Harry Levin, this explains the scarcity of description.[35] Carroll's sketches show an ordinary girl who encounters extraordinary beings and undergoes incredible transformations. The girl's reactions are emphasized, not the setting; for example, a room conveys the idea of imprisonment. Carroll's drawings encourage his reader to identify with his character and her sudden physical changes and discomforts. Animals with eyes expressing self-awareness are put on a more or less equal footing with Alice. Her almost unchangeable countenance maintains the continuity of her identity, a continuity about which the literary character, especially in the final version, manifests doubt. With the appearance of the King, Queen, and Duchess, Carroll introduces caricature. Stiffness, extreme formality, and anachronistic attire and setting make the behavior of the "heartless" Queen appear absurd. Because *Alice's Adventures Underground* is about a girl to whom adventures happen, whereas *Alice in Wonderland* deals with a heroine who goes on a journey, Carroll's sketches and Tenniel's drawings do not really pertain to the same text.

---

[32] See the facsimile edition of the 1864 manuscript (New York: Dover Publications, 1965).
[33] Lewis Carroll, *Alice in Wonderland* (New York: Random House, 1969).
[34] E.g., Paul Eluard and André Breton, *Dictionnaire abrégé du surréalisme* (Paris: Galerie des Beaux Arts, 1938); reprinted in Eluard, *Oeuvres complètes* (Paris: Gallimard, 1968), p. 731.
[35] "Wonderland Revisited," *Antioch Review* (1965): 591–616.

In Tenniel's illustrations Alice again plays the central role, but this time she expresses awe, fear, or surprise at the transformations she constantly undergoes and the unexpected emergence and behavior of the other protagonists. The animals are endowed with more pronouncedly human expressions and greater individualization. Tenniel concentrates on quickly recognizable vignettes of Alice's adventures, often reducing the setting to bare outlines. The continuity of the plot is subordinated to the representation of key moments. Only the illustrations for "You Are Old, Father William" are closely modeled on the humorous ups and downs of its nonsense verse. Again, a different style characterizes the scenes involving the Queen of Hearts. Spontaneity, animation, and concision are replaced by stylization, heraldic design, and static pictorialization. In many scenes the attire of the characters stresses hierarchical functions to which neither their expression nor their gesture may conform. Tenniel has taken cognizance of a shift within the book that Gilles Deleuze explains: "As we progress in the narrative, movements of sinking and burying give way to lateral movements, to sliding from left to right and from right to left."[36] Tenniel's court ceremonies heighten the paradox that amphibious creatures have introduced from the beginning by their upright position and ambiguous dialogue with Alice.

Tenniel's interpretations, which have no symbolic dimension, obviously did not pave the way for the numerous psychoanalytical studies. Recently Hélène Cixous and Gilles Deleuze added their version of Carroll's works to those of John Skinner and Martin Grotjahn, which appeared about thirty years ago in the *American Imago*, all of them attempting to explain the puzzle of the mathematics tutor who wrote imaginative children's books, the confirmed bachelor who enjoyed the companionship of the daughters of his friends.[37] In his "Child as Swain" William Empson gives a penetrating reading, both Freudian and contextual: "A fall through a deep hole into the secrets of Mother Earth produces a new enclosed soul wondering who it is, what will be its position in the world, and how it can get out. It is in a long low hall, part of the palace of the Queen of Hearts (a neat touch), from which it can only get out to the fresh air and the fountains through a hole frighteningly too small."[38] Empson takes Carroll's sketches as partial proof of his Freudian

---

[36] *Logique du sens* (Paris: Editions de Minuit, 1969), p. 18.

[37] John Skinner, "Lewis Carroll's Adventures in Wonderland," *American Imago* (1947): 3–31; Martin Grotjahn, "About the Symbolization of Alice's Adventures in Wonderland," *American Imago* (1947): 32–41; Hélène Cixous, "Au sujet de Humpty Dumpty toujours déjà tombé," pp. 11–19 in *Lewis Carroll* (Paris: Cahier de l'Herne, 1971).

[38] "Alice in Wonderland: The Child as Swain," in *Some Versions of Pastoral* (New York: New Directions, 1960), p. 259.

FIG. 59. Drawing by Lewis Carroll from *Alice's Adventures Underground*. New York: Dover Publications, 1965.

interpretations; Carroll's Alice (Fig. 59), when imprisoned in the rabbit hole, looks like a foetus; Tenniel's does not (Fig. 60). As Alice suddenly grows bigger, then suddenly shrinks—for she is occasionally given the control of her growth or development—Carroll, so Empson explains, unfolds the complexities of the child-adult dichotomy.

Empson also discusses political, literary, and verbal parody, as well as Victorian beliefs and attitudes toward science, economics, and ethics; intellectual systems in general are devalued. Certain characters, such as the White Rabbit and the Duchess, satirize famous Victorians. Literary parody refers to Romantic and especially to Wordsworthian beliefs concerning a union of nature and child. Martin Gardner and Harry Levin allude to other forms of parody, such as the poems that are take-offs on popular songs of Carroll's time and to a "burlesque or pathetic fallacy echoed from Tennyson's *Maud*."[39] Literary parody becomes untranslatable when, as in Tenniel's illustrations, it entails change of medium in addition to change of genre.

Numerous studies have been devoted to the verbal and linguistic preoccupations of Lewis Carroll—among others, Elizabeth Sewell's book on nonsense verse and the seven articles in the section on the "Discours" included in the *Cahier de l'Herne* edited by Henri Parisot.[40] Critics were even tempted to

[39] Martin Gardner, *The Annotated Alice* (New York: Clarkson N. Potter, 1960), which includes Tenniel's illustrations; Harry Levin, "Wonderland Revisited," p. 599.
[40] Elizabeth Sewell, *The Field of Nonsense* (London: Chatto and Windus, 1952).

FIG. 60. Drawing by John Tenniel from Lewis Carroll, *Alice in Wonderland*, in *The Annotated Alice*. New York: Clarkson N. Potter, 1960. © 1960 by Martin Gardner. Used by permission of Bramhall House, a division of Clarkson N. Potter, Inc.

extend logical positivism and Wittgensteinian theories not only to *Symbolic Logic and the Game of Logic* but also to *Alice in Wonderland*.[41] During the early adventures, Alice's questions remain unanswered. Communication becomes so difficult that the polite, well-mannered heroine experiences a threat to her identity. During the later adventures, especially the tea party officially labeled as mad, discontinuity lies beneath the surface of the dialogue. Explanations given as logical or foolproof depend on homonyms or verbal plays that tend to invalidate or distort systems of semantics. Words become the accomplices of dreams that can thrust Alice into new domains or open up their "gardens." Linguistic as well as spatial explorations fascinate the level-headed Alice.

According to Sarane Alexandrian, Dalí did not wish to translate a literary text into another medium but to provide a complementary experience, thus rejecting, at least implicitly, Tenniel's mimetic representations.[42] Both illus-

[41] Cf. Jean-Jacques Lecercle, "Une Case en avant, deux cases en arrière," *Cahiers de l'Herne*, pp. 41–50.
[42] *Dalí illustré* (Paris: Grands Musées, 1974).

FIG. 61. Drawing by John Tenniel from Lewis Carroll, *Alice in Wonderland*. New York: Clarkson N. Potter, 1960. © 1960 by Martin Gardner. Used by permission of Bramhall House, a division of Clarkson N. Potter, Inc.

trators show Alice's "overgrown" arm emerging through a window frame. Tenniel remains faithful to the narration: the heroine blindly seeks to grab the rabbit (Fig. 61). Dalí's interpretation stresses eroticism: the shape and color of the arm, its relation to the caterpillar, the squashing of the butter-fly—all bring out and even add to the implications of the text (Plate 17). Each chapter includes an illustration, sometimes lacking any overt correspondence with the text. Their presence can, however, be explained by the continuous unfolding and recurrence of certain images. Moreover, in the loose-leaf *livre de peintre*, the illustrations tend to acquire a certain autonomy. The narration, the social dimensions, the role of most characters, the obviously recognizable elements have not been transposed; in fact, they have almost disappeared in Dalí's graphic interpretations.

Alice, an adolescent girl if not a grown-up, appears on all plates turning a jumprope, accompanied by her less feminine shadow (Plate 18). Her duality, for she is at once child and no longer child, agrees with Empson's interpretation.[43] She shows no sign of involvement in the scene or its sequels. The rope that encircles her creates the dream images through which she skips,

[43]Note the analogy with *Nadja*.

FIG. 62. Drawing by John Tenniel from Lewis Carroll, *Alice in Wonderland*. New York: Clarkson N. Potter, 1960. © 1960 by Martin Gardner. Used by permission of Bramhall House, a division of Clarkson N. Potter, Inc.

weightless and with floating hair. This figure was not invented in 1969; it had already appeared with its accompanying shadow and double in 1931 in Dalí's illustration for *Nuits partagées*, where it enhanced Eluard's love communion in the dream world. In the 1936 painting entitled *The Suburb of the Paranoiac-Critical Town*, the same illustration forms one of the panels. This recurring creature establishes not only a conscious link among Dalí's works and with the paranoiac-critical method but also an affinity with one of de Chirico's creations, the girl with the hoop who, in *Mélancolie et mystère d'une rue*, runs as unconcerned with her surroundings as Dalí's Alice.

The etched frontispiece accompanying the introductory poem shows Alice and her shadow outdoors, with hills and clouds in the background; a figure seated in the foreground probably alludes to the pilgrim mentioned in the poem. Careful scrutiny establishes a relationship between the floating hair and the fluid outlines of the landscape; the mysterious force that lengthens the skirt also extends the ground, which recedes dramatically and undermines its tangibility, thus setting the stage for the simulacrum or illusory representation. Henceforth Dalí bypasses the narrative and the human exchange between characters, while retaining the animals which, instead of appearing in successive chapters, are shown together, at the expense of plot development and narrative time (Plate 19). Dalí predicates that all creatures try to assert their visibility from the first.

Windows, doors, holes, frames abound, abolishing the distinction between seer and seen and creating a sense of depth. All creatures partake of visions, ready to exhibit their colorful webs, their immanent radiance. By their shapes, their mellow lines, Dalí proclaims the mysterious affinity of all elements rather than their individuality. The caterpillar barely differs from a reptile. Toadstools, tea table, and caterpillar become symbols that can substitute for one another in various episodes (Plate 20). The toadstool represents the initial reincarnation of the tea table. The rabbit, on several occasions, appears embedded in a gardenlike surface; through color scale and fluctuations he simultaneously suggests moving clouds (see Plate 19). Elsewhere, delineated by black outlines, he signals the passage from text to image as well as the fluctuations of the dreamscape, which is dominated by spirals and dotted lines. Each plate includes luminous zones, where colors melt into each other, and dark centers, from which explosions erupt. These sum up the dual trend toward concentration and dispersion, the flux that governs Alice's voyages and visions. [44] Both Carroll's and Tenniel's (Fig. 62) interpretations of the pool of tears are literal—a girl swimming vigorously in the rising waters. Dalí shows stages of a solidifying and liquefying process, of concretion and dissolution (Plate 21). The single drop with its alchemical lure belongs to the same phenomenon as the waves of the ocean, which reiterate the movement of the sky. Dalí insists not on simple being but on complex becoming, which the viewer, once alerted to it, may extend. The painter bypasses the adventure that literature has already fully told.

Having abolished outer time, Dalí retains the essence—sudden shifts and transformations. The repeated presence of butterflies in addition to caterpillars—in fact, the multiplication of butterflies in the later plates—can be construed as references to a parodoxical union of diachrony and synchrony. Dalí reduces space to surface, eliminating, as he did with time, mimetic representation. In his interpretation of the tea party, one of the immediately recognizable scenes (see Plate 20), the surrealist painter introduces one of his soft watches, thus reducing even further, by his own myth, the rigorous and unidirectional unfolding of time. However, the presence of soft watches must

[44] The terms *concentration* and *dispersion* may correspond to Lacan's use of *métaphore* and *métonymie* in his discussion of Freud's *Traumdeutung*. Cf. "L'Instance de la lettre dans l'inconscient," p. 511 in *Ecrits* (Paris: Seuil, 1966).

not be construed as arbitrary or governed by *hasard objectif*, or as a mere repetition of the artist's obsessive images. It relates to Carroll's text, where the Mad Hatter's persistent and prolonged tea-drinking ceremony constitutes a softening or elimination of the constraints imposed by ordinary time, a shifting toward the dream. Moreover, because the watch face doubles as tabletop, it subverts its normal function. The principle of transformation, which does not seem to affect Alice, is inherent in the wonderland that she creates in Dalí's illustrations but that in the text as well as in Tenniel's illustrations she merely viewed and experienced.

Animated playing cards in Carroll's world point to the precariousness and limitations of the world of grown-ups. Dalí depicts them with a seemingly sharp realism, so that, at first sight, their stereotyped, artificial qualities may appear convincing. Yet Dalí perverts the realistic aspect when he adds a third dimension to the heart, club, and diamond by transforming the pictures on the cards (Plate 22). The surrealists created playing cards to display their revolutionary purpose: Sigmund Freud and Novalis replaced decapitated kings and idols. Dalí extends the knave's nose so that, like those of many of his characters—for example, Violette Nozières's—it needs a prop.[45] He thus gives sexual dimensions to emblematic figures that for Tenniel represent the shallowness of the grown-up world. Dalí's Queen holds a flower close to her obliterated face, in a gesture reminiscent of medieval symbolism. The cards constitute the false fronts of two pairs of shadowy, equally flat figures, perhaps the final variation on François Millet's peasants, who, as the next chapter will show, had undergone many a metamorphosis both in Dalí's *Chants de Maldoror* illustrations and in his *Mythe tragique de l'Angélus*.[46] In one of their appearances, they acquire amphibious features; an underground and undersea adventure under the startling illumination provided by black sea-urchin constellations preceded this metamorphosis.

In the last illustration, corresponding to the chapter entitled "Alice's Evidence," the viewer faces the Queen of Hearts transformed into the Virgin holding another figure in her lap (Plate 23). The playing cards and Dalí's parodies of Leonardo and Raphael are fused into a single image. The distorted phantom of Renaissance painting may even correspond to one of the numerous pictorial transformations of Gala. However, Dalí has not altogether overlooked Carroll's text in thus updating these reminiscences of his former paintings, for he also evokes Alice awakening in the lap of her sister. All the elements coalesce into a single image: Alice, the card Queen, the figures bor-

[45]*Violette Nozières* (Brussels: Nicolas Flamel, 1933).
[46]*Le Mythe tragique de l'Angélus* (Paris: Pauvert, 1963).

rowed from earlier paintings, the sharply outlined and colored representation, the phantom. The simulacra stand in apparent contrast to the flower of the Queen of Hearts, now an autonomous untouchable symbol, which, however, is but a copy of a mystic symbol.

These interpretations come closer to Deleuze than to Empson: "Pure becoming, limitlessness, is the material of the simulacrum insofar as it eludes the action of the Idea, insofar as it challenges both model and copy."[47] By his denial of Alice's identity, as well as by the rejection of the model in favor of the simulacra, Deleuze is speaking not only of Carroll but also, in a sense, of Dalí. As Haim Finkelstein points out, the paranoiac delirium in itself constitutes a form of interpretation that can function both on the verbal and the visual level.[48] The image of Alice accompanied by her shadow, with whom her relationship is forever changing, by combining objective and subjective phenomena introduces from the beginning the notion of simulacrum. The double image of the playing cards, of a "photographic" copy pinned to the shadowy, faceless figures, further stresses the functioning of Dalí's own myth. The dissolving and solidifying forces of the teardrops indicate that Carroll's text acts as a stimulus for the painter's deliberately irrational mental activities. Reality is destroyed most dramatically in the sense suggested by Dalí's own words: "to systematize confusion and to contribute to the total discredit of the world of reality"[49] by the constant reconversion of elements from colorful to shadowy appearances, substituting for one another, alternately provoking corrosive and generating forces.

Although outer time, as we have stated, is abolished, allusions to twilight, which Dalí considered so significant in Millet's painting and which he explains at length in his *Mythe tragique*, are very pronounced in his *Alice* illustrations. Bright lines and dark zones alluding to constellations and their obliterations appear again and again with new variations. Twilight is not, as in Millet, associated with atmosphere, but with double images—so destructive, as in many other surrealist works, of reality, of the outer scene. The paranoiac-critical method makes visible involuntary thought, exemplified in the erotic shapes of caterpillars, nightbirds, ladders, and reptiles.

We have mentioned that Dalí complements the text instead of submitting to it. To a certain extent his everchanging signature, sometimes overshadowed by a big crown, sometimes framed in an emblematic sign, sometimes

---

[47] Gilles Deleuze, *Logique du sens* (Paris: Editions de Minuit, 1969), p. 9.
[48] "Dalí's Paranoia-Criticism or the Exercise of Freedom," *Twentieth Century Literature* (February 1975): 59–71.
[49] "L'Ane pourri," *Le Surréalisme au service de la révolution* 1 (1929): 9.

on the verge of total dispersion, indicates the degree of visibility of his creative ego asserting itself in the presence of the text he illustrates and that he is bound partially to destroy. Thus, the surrealist artist attempts primarily to integrate the text into his work, written and plastic.

Even if Dalí subordinates the literary text to his own theory—*theory* in the etymological sense of spectacle—even if he dismisses "objective" readings, he nevertheless takes cognizance of important aspects of Carroll's book. With her jumprope Alice generates autonomous images that obliterate every simplistic order of the everyday world. Subtly the painter conveys that the Victorian author questions the rational, the apparently evident, as well as the standard linguistic patterns that erase all levels of reality but the most superficial.

Romantic art and literature, with its wealth of innovative practices and theories extending over half a century, underwent major reductions under the hands of admiring surrealists. They retained and even amplified the Romantic use of irony, which could continue to serve as a redoutable weapon against the bourgeois, while underplaying Romantic ideology, including its insistence on individualism and subjectivity. Thus they could appropriate in the same self-serving fashion the Victorian Carroll and such thorough Romantics as Arnim, Brentano, and Kleist. Indeed, in surrealist eyes Romantics could never stand as true revolutionaries in the manner of Lautréamont and Rimbaud, in whose texts they found scandals and challenges akin to their own.

PLATE 1. Woodcut by Jean Arp from *Soleil recerclé* (Re-Ringed Sun). Paris: Broder, 1966. © ADAGP, Paris; VAGA, New York, 1985. Photograph courtesy of the Bibliothèque d'Art et d'Archéologie, Paris.

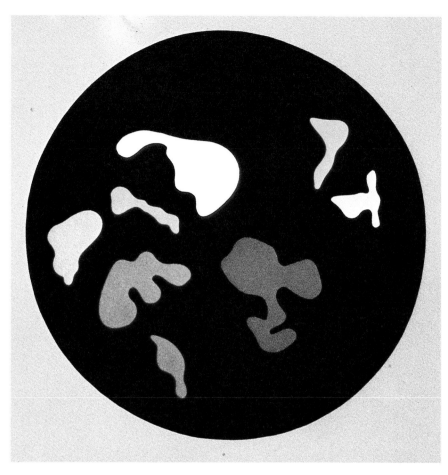

PLATE 2. Woodcut by Jean Arp from *Soleil recerclé*. Photograph courtesy of the Bibliothèque d'Art et d'Archéologie, Paris.

PLATE 3. Woodcut by Jean Arp from *Soleil recerclé*. Photograph courtesy of the Bibliothèque d'Art et d'Archéologie, Paris.

PLATE 4. Lithograph by Joan Miró from *Le Lézard aux plumes d'or*. © ADAGP, Paris; VAGA, New York, 1985. Photograph courtesy of the Bibliothèque d'Art et d'Archéologie, Paris.

PLATE 5. Lithograph by Joan Miró from *Le Lézard aux plumes d'or*. Photograph courtesy of the Bibliothèque d'Art et d'Archéologie, Paris.

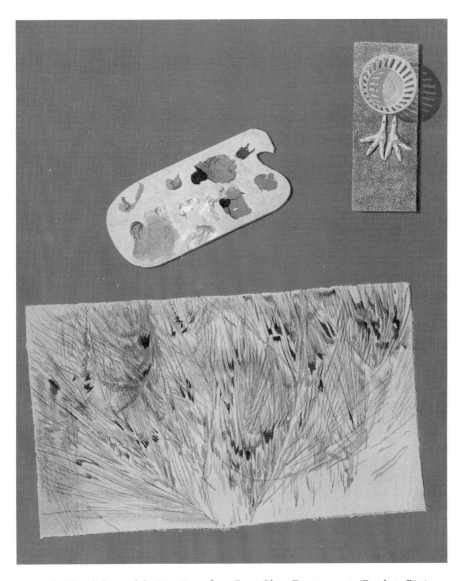

PLATE 6. Photolithograph by Max Ernst from René Char, *Dent prompte* (Ready to Bite). Paris: Lucie Weill, Galerie au Pont des Arts, 1969. © SPADEM, Paris; VAGA, New York, 1985.

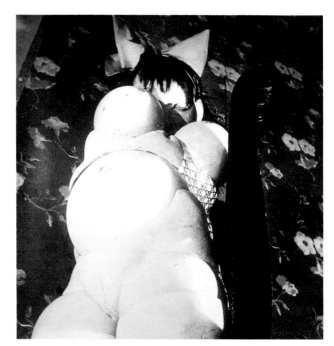

PLATE 7. Photograph by Hans Bellmer from *Les Jeux de la poupée* (The Doll's Games), illustrated with texts by Paul Eluard. Paris: Les Editions Premières, 1949. © ADAGP, Paris; VAGA, New York, 1985.

PLATE 8. Photograph by Hans Bellmer from *Les Jeux de la poupée.* © ADAGP, Paris; VAGA, New York, 1985.

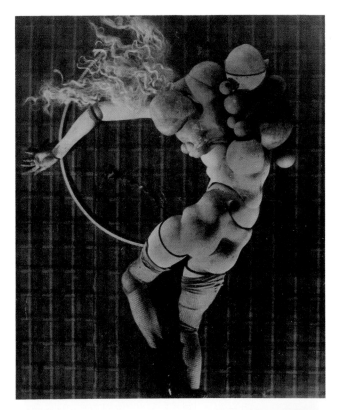

PLATE 9. Photograph
by Hans Bellmer from
Les Jeux de la poupée.
© ADAGP, Paris; VAGA,
New York, 1985.

PLATE 10. Photograph
by Hans Bellmer from
Les Jeux de la poupée.
© ADAGP, Paris; VAGA,
New York, 1985.

PLATE 11. Photograph by Hans Bellmer from *Les Jeux de la poupée*. © ADAGP, Paris; VAGA, New York, 1985.

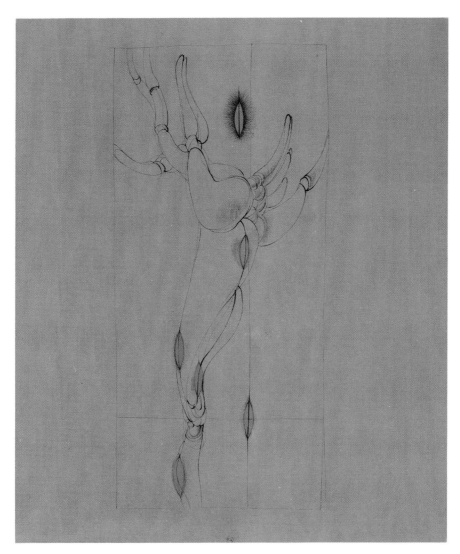

PLATE 12. Etching by Hans Bellmer from Heinrich von Kleist, *Les Marionnettes*. Paris: Georges Visat, 1969. © ADAGP, Paris; VAGA, New York, 1985. Photograph courtesy of the Bibliothèque Nationale, Paris.

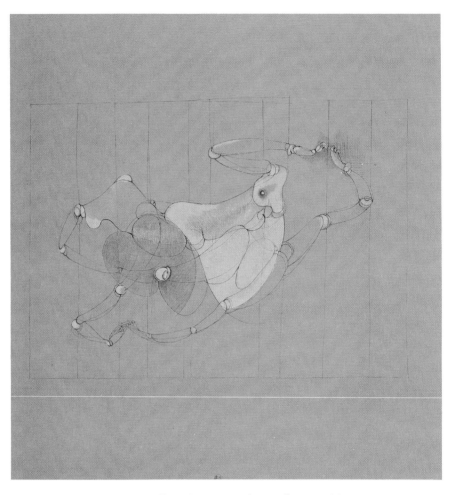

PLATE 13. Etching by Hans Bellmer from Heinrich von Kleist, *Les Marionnettes.* Photograph courtesy of the Bibliothèque Nationale, Paris.

PLATE 14. Painting by Max Ernst, *Quasi feu le romantisme* (Almost Late Romanticism), 1960. © SPADEM, Paris; VAGA, New York, 1985.

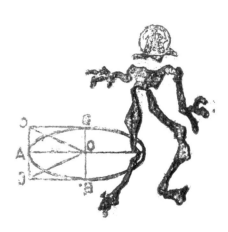

PLATE 15. Lithograph by Max Ernst from *Lewis Carroll's Wunderhorn*. Stuttgart: Manus Presse, 1970. © SPADEM, Paris; VAGA, New York, 1985.

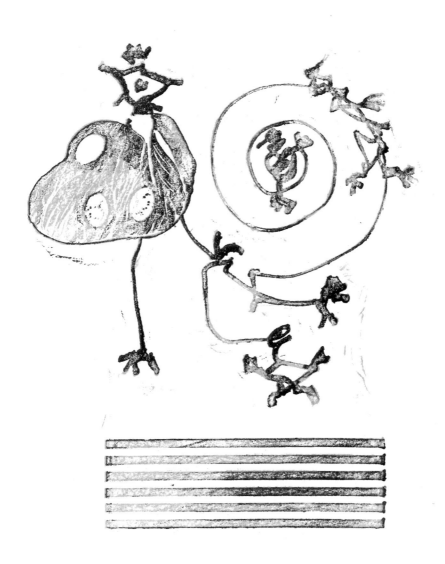

PLATE 16. Lithograph by Max Ernst from *Lewis Carroll's Wunderhorn*.

PLATE 17. Woodcut by Salvador Dalí from Lewis Carroll, *Alice in Wonderland.* New York: Maecenas Press/Random House, 1969. © Random House, 1986.

PLATE 18. Woodcut by Salvador Dalí from Lewis Carroll, *Alice in Wonderland*. © Random House, 1986.

PLATE 19. Woodcut by Salvador Dalí from Lewis Carroll, *Alice in Wonderland*. © Random House, 1986.

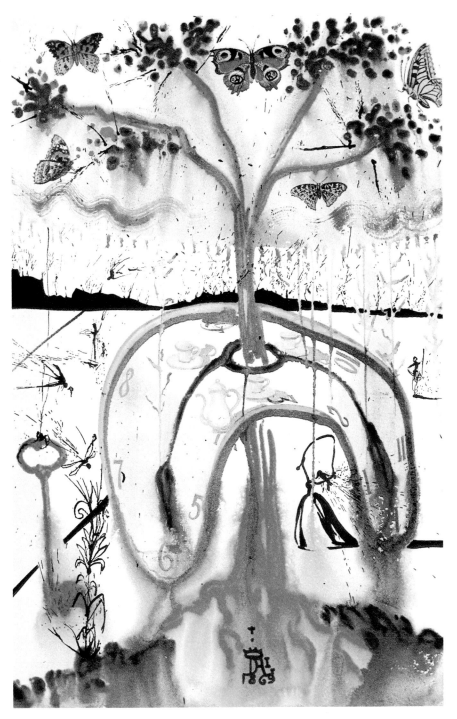

PLATE 20. Woodcut by Salvador Dalí from Lewis Carroll, *Alice in Wonderland*. © Random House, 1986.

PLATE 21. Woodcut by Salvador Dalí from Lewis Carroll, *Alice in Wonderland*. © Random House, 1986.

PLATE 22. Woodcut by Salvador Dalí from Lewis Carroll, *Alice in Wonderland*. © Random House, 1986.

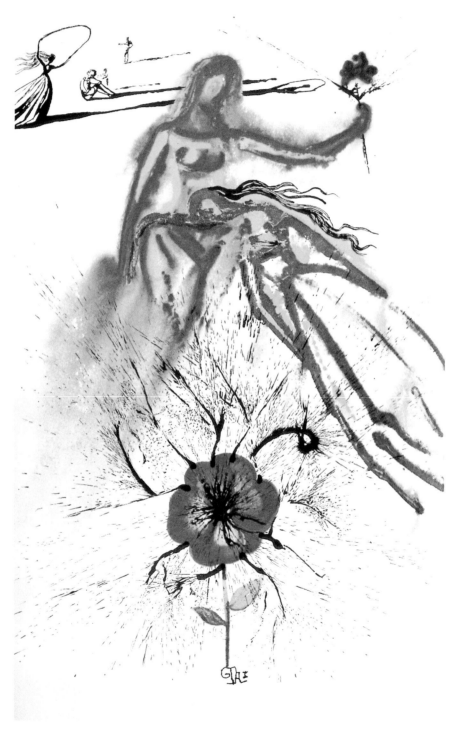

PLATE 23. Woodcut by Salvador Dalí from Lewis Carroll, *Alice in Wonderland*. © Random House, 1986.

PLATE 24. Etching by André Masson from opening section of Arthur Rimbaud, *Une Saison en enfer* (A Season in Hell). Paris: Les Cent-Une, Société de Femmes Bibliophiles, 1961. © SPADEM, Paris; VAGA, New York, 1985.

PLATE 25. Etching by André Masson, "Mauvais Sang" (Bad Blood), from Arthur Rimbaud, *Une Saison en enfer*. © SPADEM, Paris; VAGA, New York, 1985.

PLATE 26. Etching by André Masson, "Impossible," from Arthur Rimbaud, *Une Saison en enfer*. Paris; VAGA, New York, 1985. © SPADEM,

PLATE 27. Etching by Sebastian Matta, "Je fixe les vertiges" (I Arrested Turmoils), from Arthur Rimbaud, *Une Saison en enfer*. Barcelona: Ediciones Poligrafa, 1979. © ADAGP, Paris; VAGA, New York, 1985. Photograph courtesy of Les Editions Georges Visat, Paris.

PLATE 28. Etching by Sebastian Matta, "Je suis intact" (I Am Intact) from Arthur Rimbaud, *Une Saison en enfer.* © Courtesy Les Éditions Georges Visat, Paris.

Le feu vêtu de deuil jaillit par tous ses pores
La poussière de sperme et de sang voile sa
face tatouée de lave
Son cri retentit dans la nuit comme l'annonce
de la fin des temps
Le frisson qui se hâte sur sa peau d'épines
court depuis que le maïs se lisse dans le
vent
Son geste de cœur brandi à bout de bras
s'achève en cinquante-deux ans dans un
brasier d'allégresse

PLATE 31. Lithograph by Rufino Tamayo from Benjamin Péret, *Air mexicain*. Reprinted by permission of the artist.

PLATE 32. Woodcut by Joan Miró from Paul Eluard, A *toute épreuve* (Proof against Anything). Geneva: Gérald Cramer, 1958. © ADAGP, Paris; VAGA, New York, 1985.

Il fait clair je me suis couvert
Comme pour sortir du jour

Colère sous le signe atroce
De la jalousie l'injustice
La plus savante

Fais fuir ce ciel sombre
Casse ses vitres
Donne-les à manger aux pierres

Ce faux ciel sombre
Impur et lourd

PLATE 33. Woodcut by Joan Miró from Paul Eluard, A *toute épreuve*. © ADAGP, Paris; VAGA, New York, 1985.

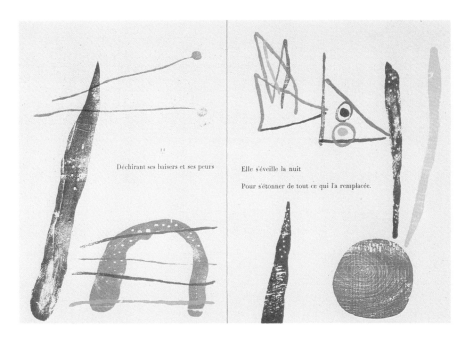

PLATE 34. Woodcut by Joan Miró from Paul Eluard, *A toute épreuve*. © ADAGP, Paris; VAGA, New York, 1985.

PLATE 35. Lithograph from Robert Desnos, *Les Pénalités de l'enfer ou les Nouvelles Hébrides* (The Penalties of Hell or the New Hebrides). Paris: Maeght, 1974. © ADAGP, Paris; VAGA, New York, 1985.

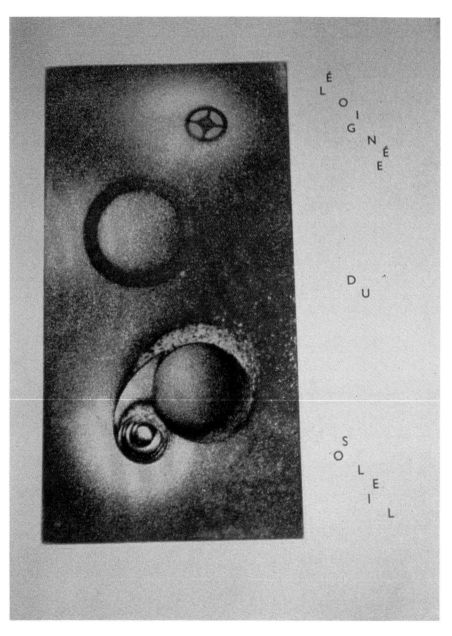

PLATE 36. Etching by Max Ernst from Iliazd and Max Ernst, *Maximiliana*. Paris: Le Degré 41, 1964. © SPADEM, Paris; VAGA, New York, 1985.

PLATE 37. Painting by René Magritte, *The Domain of Arnheim*, 1949. © Georgette Magritte, 1985.

PLATE 38. Painting by René Magritte, *The Domain of Arnheim*, 1938. © Georgette Magritte, 1985. Photograph courtesy of Acquavella Galleries, New York.

CHAPTER SIX

ILLUSTRATING THE PRECURSORS

LES CHANTS DE MALDOROR

SURREALIST writers and painters unqualifiedly endorsed the nineteenth-century poet Lautréamont, repeatedly illustrating, editing, and writing prefaces for *Les Chants de Maldoror*. André Breton praised Lautréamont for his lucid and prophetic statement of a deep cultural, social, and esthetic crisis and credited him with radical ideas that could lead to a new start.[1] Lautréamont's message touched on science, art, literature, religion, and ethics. In his preface to *Les Chants de Maldoror* Breton, who was ardently committed to extending the surrealist revolution to the word itself, stressed the presence of a special verbal liberation: "That puts an end to the imposition of limitations in relating words to words."[2] He trusted that the granting of freedom to the word ultimately would bring about that of mankind.

Breton's persistent preoccupation with a certain type of imagery and metaphor, even if no direct statement to this effect appears in his essays on Lautréamont, establishes a strong link between the two poets. In the surrealist manifestos Breton modifies Reverdy's well-known definition: "The image is a pure creation of the mind. It cannot arise from a comparison, but from bringing together two more or less distant realities. The more remote and accurate the relationships, the stronger the image will be."[3] In other words, the effec-

---

[1] André Breton, *Les Pas perdus* (Lost Steps) (Paris: N.R.F., 1924), pp. 79–85; *Anthologie de l'humour noir* (Paris: Sagittaire, 1940), pp. 227–46; "Les Chants de Maldoror," *Nouvelle Revue Française* (June 1920): 917–20; Comte de Lautréamont, *Oeuvres complètes* (Paris: G.L.M., 1938), pp. ix–xiv of Preface. This edition includes illustrations by Victor Brauner, Oscar Dominguez, Max Ernst, Agustin Espinosa, René Magritte, André Masson, Sebastian Matta Echaurren, Joan Miró, Wolfgang Paalen, Man Ray, Kurt Seligmann, and Yves Tanguy. See the bibliography in *Lautréamont: Entretiens* (Rodez: Subervie, 1971), pp. 216–17.
[2] *Oeuvres complètes* (Paris: G.L.M., 1938), p. xi.
[3] Pierre Reverdy, "L'Image," *Nord-Sud* (Paris: Flammarion, 1975), p. 73.

tiveness of the image and its beauty stem from the distance and difference between the two realities in question, from the gap that has to be filled in order to bring them together. Breton accuses Reverdy of taking an a posteriori position irrelevant to the creative act. As he draws away from Reverdy and his claim that the poet deliberately joins distant realities, Breton draws nearer to Lautréamont, whose theories he extracted from *Les Chants de Maldoror*. Breton insists on chance encounter, on the fortuitous nature of the two realities; the terms *chance* and, importantly, *fortuitous* appear in this context in Lautréamont's text. As Breton empties Reverdy's definition of rationalism, of reference to cause and effect, he stresses the necessity of the active participation, if not the interference, of chance. Lautréamont, who advocated many forms of perversion—linguistic as well as moral—and put great value on the arbitrary, becomes Breton's implicit ally as the latter formulates his theory of automatism and its implications. Such theories will above all be instrumental in revolutionizing standard and even, to a certain extent, modernistic concepts of beauty. It becomes necessary now to consider Lautréamont's famous metaphor, not as a detached fragment but within the framework of the entire sentence to which it belongs in Song Six:

Il est beau comme la rétractilité des serres des oiseaux rapaces, ou encore, comme l'incertitude des mouvements musculaires dans les plaies des parties molles de la région cervicale postérieure ou plutôt, comme ce piège à rats perpétuel, toujours retendu par l'animal pris, qui peut prendre seul des rongeurs indéfiniment, et fonctionner même caché sous la paille; et surtout comme la rencontre fortuite sur une table de dissection d'une machine à coudre et d'un parapluie.

He is as handsome as the retractility of the claws of birds of prey; or again as the uncertainty of the muscular movements of wounds in the soft parts of the posterior cervical region; or rather, as the perpetual rat-trap, reset each time by the trapped animal, that can catch rodents indefinitely and works even when hidden beneath straw; and especially as the fortuitous encounter upon a dissecting table of a sewing-machine and an umbrella.[4]

Lautréamont simultaneously challenges the literary tradition of comparison, the standard definitions of beauty, the acceptance of codes, and the belief in

[4]Comte de Lautréamont, *Les Chants de Maldoror*, dessins de René Magritte (Brussels: Editions de la Boétie, 1948). Isidore Ducasse, *Oeuvres complètes* (Paris: Poésie Gallimard, 1973), p. 233, trans. Guy Wernham (New York: New Directions, 1943), p. 263; subsequent quotations are from these editions. Cf. Ora Avni, "Breton et l'idéologie machine à coudre et parapluie," *Littérature* 57 (1983): 15–26. Cf. also Michel Deguy's lucid comment in *Figurations* (Paris: Gallimard, 1969), p. 237, on this metaphor: "The displacement of the comparison makes it an *index sui*. We are continually incited to take hold of ourselves as subjects of *that* French language."

fixed and, even more, lasting measures or laws. As he parodies description, he implicitly supplies a more dynamic, daring, and flexible criterion for beauty and he forces us to reassess its value. Breton's famous conclusion to *Nadja* can be construed as the ultimate summation of this new esthetics, partially derived from Lautréamont: "Beauty will be convulsive or it will not be."

Before discussing the illustrations by Magritte and Dalí, the most complete graphic "readings" of Lautréamont's text, I shall briefly comment on two works by the surrealist artist Man Ray: a mixed-media object and a photograph, both referring to Isidore Ducasse, Lautréamont's real name. Critics have not considered the pseudonym to be a simple matter of convenience or preference. Ducasse "created" Lautréamont, who created "Maldoror"; we are plunged into a fiction where mirroring techniques fail to lead to self-recognition, where constant shifts produce the unreliability of doubles.[5] Moreover, by functioning both as writer and reader Lautréamont bears witness to the constant denial of both the subject and the process of writing.

Man Ray's object entitled *L'Enigme d'Isidore Ducasse* (1920) (Fig. 63) has been destroyed and thus, like *L'Image d'Isidore Ducasse*, survives only as a photograph. In the mixed-media object he displayed a sack and some string holding together the "enigmatic" content. Were we to view this content, we would destroy the art work made of very ordinary material. Man Ray refers to the paradoxical nature of Lautréamont's work, which keeps the viewer at a distance while provoking him; Lautréamont's reader is at once dragged into and alerted by the *Chants*.

L'Enigme d'Isidore Ducasse also radically challenges the value of art and all concepts of esthetics. Nevertheless, it vaguely resembles a statue that, instead of exposing, hides; instead of displaying marble or bronze, flaunts sackcloth; instead of holding together, has to be trussed; instead of suggesting permanence and perfection, strikes us as unfinished or ephemeral—the whole object being convulsive in the sense that Breton attributed to that term. Just as the creatures to which Lautréamont refers are always amphibious or ambiguous, varying their shapes and never situated in the appropriate context, *L'Enigme* has the characteristics of a statue while remaining a somewhat redoubtable wrapped package too bulky to fit anywhere, holding in check its rebellious and dubious contents. This double inappropriateness creates tensions and alienation, but the work of art cannot be truly appraised from without. Ducasse presents an enigma, so Man Ray suggests; can the viewer or reader join and connive with Lautréamont?

[5] For further discussion of the relation of Lautréamont and Ducasse, see Marcellin Pleynet, *Lautréamont par lui-même* (Paris: Seuil, 1974).

FIG. 63. Object by Man Ray, *The Enigma of Isidore Ducasse*, 1920 (destroyed). © ADAGP, Paris; VAGA, New York, 1985.

Both William Rubin and Uwe Schneede claim that the object wrapped in the cloth is a sewing machine, relating *L'Enigme d'Isidore Ducasse* to the famous metaphor.[6] That relation is overtly represented in *L'Image d'Isidore Ducasse* (Fig. 64). The surrealist image of Ducasse is equivalent to a literal representation of the metaphor. Man Ray undoubtedly assembled the appropriate objects—dissecting table, umbrella, and sewing machine; he made them "pose" in order to photograph them. Let us remember that he was not only a daring experimenter in the art of photography but also the faithful chronicler of the surrealists. He presents us with the portrait of the metaphor, ironically using a realist's approach to interpret an author whose work is an assault upon realism. In his 1944 auto-portrait, through mirroring images, Man Ray cast doubt on imitation, on repetition, on the model as well as on the copy in relation to art, thus undermining the basic assumptions of portraiture. He presents the image of Isidore Ducasse, a paradox all the more

[6]William Rubin, *Dada and Surrealist Art* (New York: Abrams, 1969), p. 62; Uwe Schneede, *Surrealism* (New York: Abrams, 1972), p. 47.

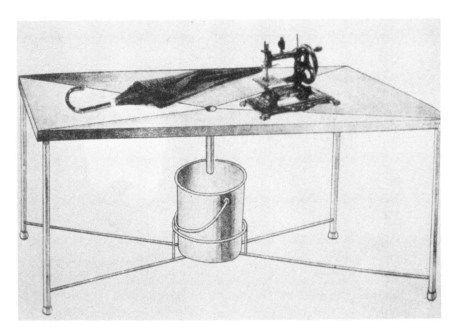

FIG. 64. Reproduction of Man Ray, *The Image of Isidore Ducasse.* © ADAGP, Paris; VAGA, New York, 1985.

striking since photographic or painted portraits of Lautréamont do not exist, aside from imaginary likenesses by Dalí and Félix Valloton. Irony exists not only in regard to photographic technique but also in regard to the replacement of the absent likeness of the author by the outrageous attempt to photograph his famous metaphor, the very metaphor that epitomizes Lautréamont's defiance of literary tradition, his simultaneous attack on form and on aspiration, his ridiculing of mimesis. Finally it seems that Man Ray, by his equation Ducasse = sewing machine + dissecting table + umbrella, parodies the syntactic structure of the metaphor, which stresses again and again the *comme*, giving explicit signs for the recognition of its identity.

If we look at Man Ray's transformed still life, the flowers, fruits, and other natural objects related by centuries of tradition, we realize that he has replaced them with modern ready-made objects, according to the dictates of the poet. These objects are provocative not by their relations or interactions, but because they appear as substitutions for former arrangements that we are no longer capable of restoring or, rather, that we as readers no longer dare to restore. Man Ray does not impose incongruity upon the viewer by means of distortion; he appears to refuse interpretation. His matter-of-fact presentation shifts this task to the viewer. He does not create the image of an encounter, the humanization suggested by the literary terminology. Thus as he under-cuts the poetic dimension, implicit as it may be, by the ambiguity of the lan-guage, he makes the bourgeois name of Isidore Ducasse more suitable than the poetic "Le Comte de Lautréamont." By his "simplistic" image of the met-aphor, Man Ray clearly warns us that we cannot approach the book by seek-ing the image of either author or hero.

.   .   .

Magritte's seventy-five drawings, including full-size plates, illustrations within the text, tail-pieces, and vignettes, constitute the most ample surreal-ist illustration of the *Chants*. The fact that Magritte should have illustrated a book may seem surprising, for several of his best-known paintings reveal the incompatibility of word and image. In his *L'Usage de la parole* (1928) he shows a pipe accompanied by the words "this is not a pipe." Comments on this painting and its variations are numerous, including an essay by Michel Foucault.[7] What the painter simultaneously says and shows seems at first sight paradoxical. He represents an image, but the image must not be taken for the object it supposedly represents, a pipe. Words, which normally denote objects, here refuse to label them. They deny the expected identification. The viewer is warned against associations to which he is accustomed: the word, the object, the image no longer correspond, so Magritte suggests. Real-ity, visual and verbal, as representation is no longer molded into a reliable system. As Magritte insists on these discrepancies, he shakes our beliefs, our conventions. Words betray the image instead of rendering it in a different language or code, just as images betray words.

In view of this readily decipherable message, it seems that Magritte would not aim at any standard method of illustration, based on verbal and visual correspondences. The discrepancy conveyed by a single sentence and a single image would be infinitely multiplied in conjunction with a complete literary text. Magritte's titles, verbal units accompanying graphic units, might possi-bly refer to the paintings but they by no means describe them or make the scene represented more recognizable. As in *L'Usage de la parole*, they address obliquely an intellectual problem which seems to emanate from the canvas. Several of Magritte's paintings show, without any context, six or eight imme-

[7]Michel Foucault, "Ceci n'est pas une pipe," *Les Cahiers du Chemin* 2 (Jan. 1968): 79–108; Michel Foucault, *This Is Not a Pipe* (Berkeley and Los Angeles: University of California Press, 1982).

diately recognizable ordinary objects—shoes, keys, hats—neatly drawn, painted, and framed. Each one is accompanied by a word that names a different object, either absent from or present elsewhere on the canvas. Magritte implies that we may view a key or shoe differently in painting from what it is in ordinary life. He does not copy what his senses perceive, for a key in a painting ceases to be a useful object. The painter is not bound to produce a fixed, preestablished image when he refers to certain words. He proclaims by these banal representations the artist's freedom in regard to vision and creation, in regard to the relationship of the two languages juxtaposed on his canvases.

FIG. 65. Drawing by René Magritte from Comte de Lautréamont, *Les Chants de Maldoror*. Brussels: Editions de la Boétie, 1948. © Georgette Magritte, 1985.

Magritte's seventy-five illustrations do not all maintain the same distance from the text or fulfill similar roles in regard to the entire series. In some cases it may appear that the illustrations assume a decorative role—for example, two small drawings, of a vase containing flowers and of a head smoking a pipe (Fig. 65). Although they cannot be related to specific passages, they are by no means dissonant with the spirit of the text, for they record or echo reversals and trangressions of the accepted order. Two usually unrelated objects are fused here. The outlines of the vase correspond to a face, a bouquet shows a sprouting imagination which cannot be contained within the limits of a skull. Magritte expresses the irony of a text that undermines conventions by showing these personifying transformations of a still life. The pipe-smoker's nose, plunging deeply into the cup of the pipe, prevents the air from drawing into the pipe. The tail-pieces form a series of images in which human anatomy is transformed and distorted, the erotic dimensions of dream and desire becoming cruelly solidified as they assume grotesque shapes.

Images of isolated parts of the body—a hand or an eye—repeatedly appear in the text, where they introduce both a division and a link (Fig. 66). They constitute a break in the page while establishing relations with several passages and several illustrations. The picture of an eye torn from the face, dripping blood, relates to the poem metaphorically, where it recurs as an autonomous object: "Donc Lohengrin, fais ce que tu voudras, agis comme il te plaira, enferme-moi toute la vie dans une prison obscure avec des scorpions pour compagnons de ma captivité, ou arrache-moi un oeil jusqu'à ce qu'il tombe par terre, je ne te ferai jamais le moindre reproche, je suis à toi, je t'appartiens, je ne vis plus pour moi" (p. 65) ("And so, Lohengrin, do what you will, act as you please, shut me up for the rest of my life in a gloomy prison with scorpions for company, or tear out one of my eyes and fling it upon the ground, I shall never reproach you. I am yours, I belong to you, I live no longer for myself") (p. 57).

FIG. 66. Drawing by René Magritte from Comte de Lautréamont, *Les Chants de Maldoror*. © Georgette Magritte, 1985.

This text alludes to more than one transgression and aggression linking the self to others. Magritte's image of the eye dripping blood, a self-sufficient entity, turns cruelty into a force not produced by specific circumstances. At the same time, especially through the recurrence of this illustration, the eye no longer embedded and sheltered, no longer reducible to standard proportions, refers to the new vision verbally and visually created in the *Chants*. The eye dripping blood thus links cruelty to creation, a postulate of the Ducassian poem that can even be related to the famous metaphor.

If illustrations within the text reveal links between text and image, the vignettes framing the initials play another role. In the first one a curtain opens on both the poet's and the painter's performance (Fig. 67). The *P* stands erect in front of the light, at once a letter and the representation of an animated

CHANT PREMIER

lût au ciel que le lecteur, enhardi et devenu momentanément féroce comme ce qu'il lit, trouve, sans se désorienter, son chemin abrupt et sauvage, à travers les marécages désolés de ces pages sombres et pleines de poison; car, à moins qu'il n'apporte dans sa lecture une logique rigoureuse et une tension d'esprit égale au moins à sa défiance, les émanations mortelles de ce livre imbiberont son âme, comme l'eau le sucre. Il n'est pas bon que tout le monde lise les pages qui vont suivre; quelques-uns seuls savoureront ce fruit amer sans danger. Par conséquent, âme timide, avant de pénétrer plus loin dans de pareilles landes inexplorées, dirige tes talons en arrière et non en avant, comme les yeux d'un fils qui se détourne respectueusement de la contemplation auguste de la face maternelle; ou plutôt comme un angle à perte de vue de grues frileuses méditant beaucoup, qui, pendant l'hiver, volent puissamment à travers le silence, toutes voiles tendues, vers un point

7

FIG. 67. Drawing by René Magritte from Comte de Lautréamont, *Les Chants de Maldoror*. © Georgette Magritte, 1985.

FIG. 68. Drawing by René Magritte from Comte de Lautréamont, *Les Chants de Maldoror.*
© Georgette Magritte, 1985.

object: Magritte effects, in an almost natural manner, the transformation from sign to visual image, a transformation which happens simultaneously in the text. Other initial letters become the exponents of textual ambiguities or a preview of forthcoming scenes (Fig. 68). The initial as actor never renounces its characteristics as letter, even if as image it adds another duality to the ambiguity inherent in Lautréamont's text. In Song Three the two-legged *R* (Fig. 69) features a bird claw and a human hand, thus repeating in graphic terms the dual characteristics of bestial and human so frequent in the poetic text. By simultaneously resetting the body in contrasting shapes, Magritte alludes to the poet's infinite exchanges between small and large, material and spiritual, scientific and poetic.

The viewer of the full-size plates quickly recognizes the painter's iconography: bilboquets (Fig. 70), mermaids with fish heads and human legs, apples wearing masks, the head of a woman whose face is replaced by the anatomy of a torso (Fig. 71). Contrary to what we shall see in Dalí, the painter's repetitions do not express personal obsessions but show paradox and ambiguity functioning as the generating principle of thought. The painter, like the

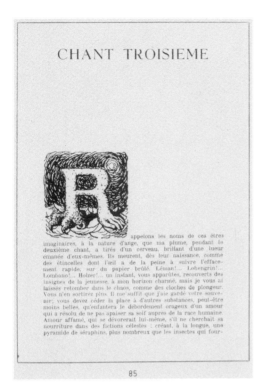

FIG. 69. Drawing by René Magritte from Comte de Lautréamont, *Les Chants de Maldoror*. © Georgette Magritte, 1985.

poet, refers to objects which, although separated from their usual surroundings and their familiar functions, maintain a recognizable identity. Magritte abstracts from the text surprising juxtapositions emerging in unexpected situations, thus fulfilling, at least on the surface, the conditions of Lautréamont's metaphor.

Magritte tends to juxtapose or to represent the encounter of two objects— a face and a house, a head and a sky—in terms of a single dislocation rather than the double one proposed by Lautréamont's metaphor. Even if the junction of disparate objects in an unrelated context appears more limited than the multiple juxtapositions and dislocations of the text, some effects seem similar: discovery of unheard-of qualities, radical metamorphoses. The reader/viewer has to admit that creatures with specific features do not necessarily belong to fixed categories and are not mutually exclusive.

In some illustrations of the *Chants* Magritte follows narrative or descriptive passages. The painter sticks to the text in representing a madwoman, brandishing a stick, who is wearing a shoe on one foot, leaving the other bare (Fig. 72). The woman, with her bewildering facial expression and her corroded, skeletal body, has obviously departed from our everyday world. The

FIG. 70. Drawing by René Magritte from Comte de Lautréamont, *Les Chants de Maldoror.* © Georgette Magritte, 1985.

landscape penetrates and goes beyond the fragmentary, fluctuating outlines of this shadowy, nightmarish phantom. In the background, a tower fallen into ruins belongs to the same shaky, vulnerable universe as the woman. Both are surrounded by a dynamically animated line, and the whole tableau shows nothing but decaying faces. The poet has produced associations on several levels, including that of language, with the appearance of the madwoman: "Elle laisse échapper des lambeaux de phrases dans lesquels, en les recousant, très peu trouveraient une signification claire") (p. 128) ("She lets fall rags of phrases of which, if they were knit together, very few would have any clear significance") (p. 133). Lautréamont's woman is a figment of the imagination, bearer of a secret message which she will drop while performing her dance. Everything expresses the corrosion of her physical being: her smell of decay, the endless pursuit by the children, her loss of human qualities, her hyena-like grin, her weightless dance. As mediator, she channels the oft-repeated enigma which the reader is compelled to pursue but will never overtake. It thus appears that Magritte has faithfully represented dissolution, thereby imposing the realm of imagination.

Another illustration, unrelated to the narrative as such, corresponds to the following two lines:

> A *quoi pensais-tu enfant?*
> *Je pensai au ciel.*
>
> [p. 50]
>
> What did you think of my child?
> I thought of the sky.

Magritte represents a boy's large head split open so that the outer world penetrates in triangulated form (Fig. 73). As in the portrayal of the madwoman (see Fig. 72), the borderline between the object and its surroundings is disrupted; whereas dissolution of reality, the crossing into the realm of shadow, belongs to both text and image in the first plate, here text and image go their separate ways, for the former points to spiritual aspirations which the latter reduces to materiality. Magritte suggests that thinking is essentially a physical activity. The sky in all its concreteness enters the brain, which nonetheless continues to aspire to it ethereally. The sky occupies not only the brain but even the mouth, taking full possession of language. The functions accorded

FIG. 72. Drawing by René
Magritte from Comte de
Lautréamont, *Les Chants de
Maldoror*. © Georgette
Magritte, 1985.

to creation—seeing, thinking, dreaming, writing—are thus interrelated.
The objective referent of thought, the subject of writing and the subject who
writes, will both fuse and fission. Lautréamont's text constantly alludes to creation as a process, to the inseparability of object and subject in such a materialized process.

Magritte, in showing spirituality reverting to materiality, resumes his usual
practice as painter of concretizing not only memories but the act of remembering. This practice coincides with Lautréamont's irony, paradoxically interrelating the failure of justice on a terrestrial level and man's confrontation
with the clouds. In the two examples so far discussed, that of the head split
open and that of the madwoman, interpenetration of incompatible elements
rather than juxtaposition predominates. In both cases Magritte's point of departure is a precise passage, a sentence which he reads literally while adapting
it to the ironical and paradoxical vein of the songs. As a result, the painter
does not fully operate on a metaphysical level either by transforming images
as they occur in the text or by using the famous metaphor of the umbrella,
sewing machine, and dissecting table as a model. Indeed, he rarely, if ever,

FIG. 73. Drawing by René Magritte from Comte de Lautréamont, *Les Chants de Maldoror.* © Georgette Magritte, 1985.

produces clashes between disparate objects in unexpected situations or transforms conventional objects by unleashing their hidden power.

Maldoror is a hero or nonhero with a thousand faces, assuming many disguises—for example, a pelican (Fig. 74) and a rhinoceros—and many roles—narrator, creator, actor and, subversively, even reader.[8] From page to page, from scene to scene, we shift between mystery and revelation. The painter, however, makes the pelican and the rhinoceros perfectly recognizable. Thus, the metamorphosis has already taken place, and the ambiguity of the various shapes assumed by Maldoror is not detectable in any single plate. Still, Magritte's pelican is hardly a replica of the bird we encounter in nature, but is simultaneously a pelican and a sprig of foliage. Wings and leaves show analogous decorative contours, in a manner reminiscent of traditional flora and fauna ornamental designs. However, the foliage displays highly visible arteries coinciding, we may presume, with the bloodstream of the bird. As a result, the pelican is, by the sprouting of its wings, permanently grounded.

[8]Suzi Gablik, *Magritte* (Greenwich: New York Graphic Society, 1970), p. 46. Cf. also Harry Torczyner, *René Magritte: Signes et images* (Paris: Draeger, 1977).

FIG. 74. Drawing by René Magritte from Comte de Lautréamont, *Les Chants de Maldoror*. © Georgette Magritte, 1985.

Magritte had applied the same principle in a 1942 painting entitled *Les Compagnons de la peur* in which several owlplants inhabit a terrestrial landscape. By situating his bound pelican within a seascape, the painter adds still another paradox. Thus this illustration brings us nearer not only to Magritte's paintings but, implicitly, to Lautréamont's metaphor, for the entrapping encounter of the seabird and terrestrial plant takes place in a setting that cries out for mobility.

The poet compares the pelican to a lighthouse standing on an almost nonexistent islet in the middle of the sea. In the text as well as in the illustration, the pelican functions as a protean being, casting a revelatory eye on obscure or hidden zones. For the writer, the pelican takes its place among the many images clearly labeled as arbitrary—a new set of words—discarded before they can be fully replaced. Once more Magritte remains faithful to a passage of the text. By inserting a figure, the plant, among those mentioned by the poet, he restores the basic situation required by the metaphor. In supplementing the poet's imagery the painter does not betray the text, but recreates the metaphor. However, Magritte has either overlooked or bypassed the implicit element of aggression, of incompatibility.

Although the painter's interpretation verges on the purely mimetic, he persistently adapts to Lautréamont's poem his own iconography, rich in paradox and ambiguity, in identity and metamorphosis. Even the narrative problem of continuity and discontinuity finds an echo in the illustration. The cover page clearly shows that Magritte remembered that Maldoror is a vampire story, a fact which adds to those we have already given still another interpretation of the bloody eye. On the cover, from black to white printed words of the title, streams of red blood turn the letters into flesh. Below, a skull crowns a building reminiscent of the Brussels Palais de Justice, proclaiming the violent death of many a legal institution. Magritte has not omitted the polemical aspects of the *Chants* even if the hidden bourgeois lurks everywhere in the drawings.

· · ·

Dalí's forty-one plates devoted to Maldoror, his "portrait paranoiaque-critique" of the poet, and his brief chapter devoted to the poem in *Le Mythe tragique de l'Angélus* indicate that the painter associated his own method with the nineteenth-century text.[9] Repeatedly Dalí presented double images: Alice, a figure accompanied by her own shadow (see Plate 17); Lenine, a multiple appearance of the same figure; Don Quixote and his windmills; the imaginary portrait, divided into a shadowy and a sharply focused part.[10] By means of this portrait Dalí intimates that Lautréamont's reader moves from the tangible to the limitless without having to abolish barriers. The etchings of the *Chants* constitute an act leading from provocation to hallucination. Dalí considered Lautréamont's text particularly well suited to his paranoiac-critical method—the devaluation of outer reality for the benefit of vision and hallucination. The poet had certainly asserted the presence of dream and fantastic visions to the detriment of strictly rational functionings, but without completely submerging his readers in a system of hallucination divorced from reality.

In spite of Dalí's deeply felt affinity for Lautréamont, his viewer experi-

[9]Comte de Lautréamont, *Les Chants de Maldoror*, with forty-four etchings by Dalí (Paris: Skira, 1933); Salvador Dalí, *Le Mythe tragique de l'Angélus de Millet* (Paris: Pauvert, 1963).
[10]Miguel de Cervantes, *Don Quixote de la Mancha*, illustrated by Salvador Dalí (New York: Modern Library, 1946).

FIG. 75. Etching by Salvador
Dalí from Comte de
Lautréamont, *Les Chants de
Maldoror*. Paris: Skira, 1933.
© Courtesy Albert Skira
Editeur, 1986. Photograph
courtesy of the Bibliothèque
Nationale, Paris.

ences a sense of disorientation, as plates rarely refer to the text in a recognizable manner. Some three or four illustrations, representing a spectacular gesture or a statue, can be viewed as monuments to Maldoror, whose face
remains invisible. Many plates map out an assemblage, partial or completed,
precarious or stable (Fig. 75). Some of these structures include more or less
uniform pieces; others contain shapes ranging from geometrical to organic,
giving the impression of stages in a metamorphosis. They emerge in a landscape consisting of receding lines lending depth and perspective to a scene
repeatedly transformed by the suggestive shapes of clouds (Fig. 76). The recurrent image of Maldoror reestablishes at various stages a perceptible contact with the poem, though not with specific passages, and thus prevents a
completely autonomous evolution of the graphic sequence.

We can assess neither the structure nor the representations of this graphic
sequence without taking cognizance of references to other paintings, notably
Dalí's own. The painter's constant parodies of earlier art forms repeat his own
iconography. In his "Hommage à Meissonier" he makes the following com-

FIG. 76. Etching by Salvador Dalí from Comte de Lautréamont, *Les Chants de Maldoror*. Photograph courtesy Dalí Foundation, St. Petersburg, Florida.

ment: "My metamorphosis is tradition, for tradition is precisely change and reinvention of another skin. It does not involve plastic surgery or mutilation, but rebirth. I do not give up anything, I carry on."[11]

A peasant woman, drawn in small scale, her back turned to the viewer, appears not only in *Les Chants de Maldoror* but also in Dalí's *L'Esclave de Michelange* (1966), his *L'Enigme de Guillaume Tell* (1934), and his *Premonition of the Spanish Civil War* (1936). However, only *L'Enigme de Guillaume Tell* appears to be thematically related to the sequence, for the child Tell experiences an erection in the presence of his infanticidal father. By his inventory of recurrent images Dalí ostentatiously establishes the continuity of his delirious activity (Fig. 77).

Dalí introduces other motifs from his William Tell into the Lautréamont suite. The father and son image appears frequently, composed of both figures and shadows, a double image with reference to Dalí's fear of sexual impotence. The piano, undergoing several transformations throughout the sequence, becomes more centrally woven into the fabric of the illustrations

[11]*Oui* (Paris: Gonthier, 1971), p. 132.

FIG. 77. Etching by Salvador
Dalí from Comte de
Lautréamont, *Les Chants de
Maldoror*. Photograph
courtesy Dalí Foundation,
St. Petersburg, Florida.

(Fig. 78). By its weightlessness, its distortions, "cette apparition aérodyna-
mique" suggests an animal with raised rear legs of which the keyboard,
changed into a jaw, constitutes the front. The ambiguity of the shape of the
piano concerns the painter less than does the unveiling of the obsessive qualities hidden beyond the outer appearances and beyond a reality which is abolished stage by stage. The viewer confronting "cette apparition aérodyna-
mique" associates it with the horse ridden by Maldoror and with the many
animal skulls endowed with strong sets of teeth, all of them magnified versions of the keyboard.

All these images exemplify Dalí's notion of cannibalism: jaws appear to
provide a means of gaining awareness of the real. Jaws, teeth, and food
abound in Dalí's art and in particular in the Maldoror illustrations (Fig. 79).
Chops or cutlets undergo multiple variations in the presence or absence of
forks; spoons and knives, defunctionalized in relation to the act of eating, appear repeatedly. An assemblage of two spoons, two chops, two roses, and a
bone, a replica of an earlier engraving, produces the illusion of a face (Fig.
80). Pinned to it is an apple, borrowed from the William Tell myth. Dalí "de-

FIG. 78. Etching by Salvador Dalí from Comte de Lautréamont, *Les Chants de Maldoror*. Photograph courtesy Dalí Foundation, St. Petersburg, Florida.

vours" past art works, including his own: by assembling and disassembling their images he brings his hallucinations into perspective.

Dalí also used the illustrations to assure the continuity of his phantasm rather than to give a convincing translation of the text. Similarly, he introduces Gala's portrait into the sequence in order to link it to other representations of his wife (Fig. 81). Gala's image in the *Chants* focuses on pubic and vaginal areas. It multiplies associations, a key function of the paranoiac-critical method; above all, it establishes relations with Millet's *L'Angélus*. Gala occupies the foreground; the shapes of the peasants are outlined in the clouds. The Millet figures, relegated to the background, the places of the male and of the female inverted, undergo transformations in forming part of a sunset. They become enthroned gods of a hallucinatory world through which Lautréamont's poem is filtered.

Millet in his painting represents a moment of religious contemplation combined with a feeling for nature. Two peasants, after a day's work, piously celebrate the setting of the sun. The depiction of humble people in their relation to God and the soil evokes an annunciation, the mysterious promise of

FIG. 79. Etching by Salvador Dalí from Comte de Lautréamont, *Les Chants de Maldoror*. Photograph courtesy Dalí Foundation, St. Petersburg, Florida.

things to come—of birth and regeneration. Dalí radically transformed the accepted meaning of the painting. He provoked his spectator by showing both in his illustrations and in *Le Mythe tragique de l'Angélus* the "true" meaning of the painting, changing the piano into a sexual message. Dalí claimed that proof of his hypothesis was revealed through an X-ray of the painting: Millet had originally represented the peasants bent over the coffin of their unwanted child. Dalí asserts that the peasant holds his hat so as to hide an erection.[12] Once the viewer accepts this assumption, everything falls into place: the hay-fork stuck into the ground becomes another image of sexual activity; the objects on the cart assume the characteristics of female organs, whereas the handles outline male potency.

In his *Mythe tragique de L'Angélus* Dalí explains that the painting makes a decisive move away from the restrictions imposed by religious forces and the bourgeois code. Through the illuminations derived from *L'Angélus* he was able to multiply his associations, to return to a vision neither timebound nor

[12] *Le Mythe tragique*, p. 7. Subsequent quotations are from this edition.

FIG. 80. Etching by Salvador Dalí from Comte de Lautréamont, *Les Chants de Maldoror*. Photograph courtesy Dalí Foundation, St. Petersburg, Florida.

deterministic. The liberating and seminal process of the Millet painting was central to his activities. In his essay the painter shows how disturbing experiences always led him back to *L'Angélus*.

In the Lautréamont series, the first overt appearance of the Millet peasants, their shapes identical to those of the clouds, introduces the evolutionary, fluctuating oneiric quality that Dalí lends to the painting. In a later plate the peasants, an assemblage of heterogeneous pieces, emphasize sexuality. The woman, with protruding womb and buttocks, is barely covered by a ragged sheet surrounding her loins and legs (Fig. 82). She somewhat resembles the praying mantis to which Dalí compares her in *Le Mythe tragique*. The male figure is composed of two unequal femurs and a distorted penis surmounted by a sack, a copy of the one in the wheelbarrow of Millet's *Angélus*. (As their human characteristics diminish, these figures remain recognizable in relation to the nineteenth-century painting only by gestures and spatial organization.) These two elongated monuments stand on a pedestal in front of a cloud outlining Ernest Meissonier's *Napoleon and His Soldiers, Parading in a Sunset*, which unexpectedly substitutes for Millet's peasants. The dark

FIG. 81. Etching by Salvador
Dalí from Comte de
Lautréamont, *Les Chants de
Maldoror.* Photograph courtesy
Dalí Foundation,
St. Petersburg, Florida.

shadows of William Tell and his son, coupled with the shadows of their shadows, constitute reflections or transformations of paintings, differing only in
their degree of realism. Converging lines, moving from the front to the back
so as to give a sense of depth, but crowned and countered by the rays emanating from the sunset, turn space itself into a double image and enhance the
dispersion of reality.

Characters (for example, the figure we associate with Maldoror) and the
landscape participate in the same process, a process frequently manifested in
Lautréamont's text. Distorted gestures of bent knees and praying hands subsist throughout these often highly stylized displacements. The sack on Millet's wheelbarrow replaces alternately part of the male and part of the female
anatomy. In place of the peasant's heart appears a jaw surrounded by hollowness. As cyclic phenomena follow a prescribed course, jaws, bones, and skulls
denote the acts of eating and gnawing as much as they express dying or death
(Figs. 83, 84). Chops appearing everywhere, even sometimes on the praying
man's head, supply further signs of hunger and cannibalism. Sexual exhibitionism and atavistic aggression belong to both the male and the female. Dalí

FIG. 82. Etching by Salvador Dalí from Comte de Lautréamont, *Les Chants de Maldoror*. Photograph courtesy Dalí Foundation, St. Petersburg, Florida.

considered his phantasm reversible, especially when accompanied by a strong suggestion of anxiety. Eating and being eaten are opposite directions on the same soft dial. In an etching located near the end of the book, the image of the Napoleonic march appears with more pronounced outlines in the clouds, where its cannibalistic and sexual features emerge. There the distance between the peasant figures, which Dalí has maintained all along, is filled by the outlines of another Millet painting, *Les Glaneuses* (1857) (Fig. 85). Dalí explains its presence in *Le Mythe tragique*: "It is certain that behind the two figures of the Angelus, that is, behind the sewing machine and the umbrella, the gleaners can only continue to gather indifferently, conventionally, eggs sunny-side-up (without the dish), inkwells, spoons, and all the silverware that the last gleamings of sunset can lend to that sparkling hour" (p. 97). The gleaners do not merely gather the fruits of the earth, but all objects temporarily solidified and refertilized by Dalí's desires and imagination. Displacements, distortions, metamorphoses defy the notion of denouement. And the final appearance of the Millet peasants occurs in a luminous "exhibitionist" context.

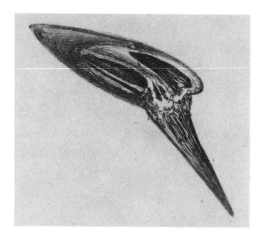

FIG. 83. Etching by Salvador Dalí from Comte de Lautréamont, *Les Chants de Maldoror*. Photograph courtesy of the Bibliothèque Nationale, Paris.

If we have investigated the presence of other paintings in the Lautréamont illustrations and pursued the issue of the coherence of Dalí's delirious activity rather than considering the relation of text to image in a more direct manner, it is because the painter did not use the text as a selecting filter. This role he attributed to the Millet painting and thus distanced himself from the poetic text. In the final chapter of *Le Mythe tragique* he provides the clue to the real link between Lautréamont and Millet: Dalí equates the poet's opus with his famous metaphor. Millet's painting, which constitutes, so to speak, the first illustration for it, reveals the meaning and function of the umbrella and sew-

FIG. 84. Etching by
Salvador Dalí from Comte
de Lautréamont, *Les
Chants de Maldoror.*
Photograph courtesy of the
Bibliothèque Nationale,
Paris.

ing machine having an encounter on a dissecting table. The metaphor becomes the central unifying and structuring device of the poem and art work,
namely, Millet's *Angélus.* Dalí, in using the images provided by other artists,
establishes a sequence that corresponds to various signifiers in the literary text
while obliterating its signified. Dalí may have accepted, in regard to the Lautréamont metaphor, theories propagated by other surrealists who emphasized
chance, who insisted on *hasard objectif,* that is, deliberate absence of motivation, in removing the metaphor from any system of continuity.

Lautréamont subverted what could be called metaphorical traditions and
concepts of beauty. He revealed, so the surrealists believed, the creative value
of the metaphor, which generates its own standards. Its three elements are
man-made. Dalí, in his "assembled" head, replaces the eyes by roses, the
very flower that Maldoror, transformed into a skeleton, holds up in triumph.
He substitutes the seen for the act of seeing, because the old system of beauty
can only block vision. Dalí shows its frailty: the petals, threatened by disintegration, begin to detach themselves and to turn into worms. In Dalí's iconography, where the rose is as edible as the rest, beauty is linked to cannibalism.

FIG. 85. Etching by Salvador Dalí from Comte de Lautréamont, *Les Chants de Maldoror*. Photograph courtesy of the Bibliothèque Nationale, Paris.

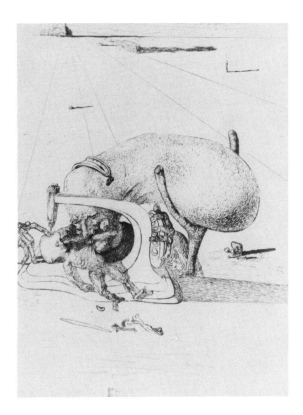

FIG. 86. Etching by Salvador Dalí from Comte de Lautréamont, *Les Chants de Maldoror*. Photograph courtesy of the Bibliothèque Nationale, Paris.

"Beauty shall be edible or it will not be. Eating is a lot of dying": so Dalí parodies both Breton's and Romantic concepts of beauty.[13]

In *Le Mythe tragique de l'Angélus* Dalí discusses the sexual connotations of Lautréamont's metaphor. The umbrella represents the phallic element, the sewing machine the distaff side, the dissecting table the place of the tryst. Dalí's interpretation associates the metaphor with a conscious choice when he discusses Millet: "If, as we claim, plowed ground is the most literal and advantageous of all known dissecting tables, the umbrella and the sewing machine will be transposed in the *Angelus* to a male and a female figure" (p. 97). Dalí stresses the metaphor's potential for violence, the functioning of which is made visible in the Millet painting. Although he claims that Millet provides the key exemplification of the metaphor, an exemplification which he showed in the framework of his illustrations, Dalí nevertheless gives a somewhat literal representation of it in one of his plates (Fig. 86). A small stretched-out body is the victim simultaneously of the cannibalistic aggres-

[13]*Oui*, p. 165.

sion of an old man—a god or father figure (Saturn)—and of the stitching of a sewing machine. Here again, male and female sexual actions are interchangeable. The painter intimately sews his own inventory—soft watches, crutches, overgrown organs—onto Lautréamont's metaphor. This violence directed against what appears to be a child (reminiscent of Dalí's interpretation of Millet's original version of *L'Angélus*) had been prepared all along by the recurrent presence of spoons, knives, and forks, which are but innocent-looking versions of swords, butcher knives, and hay forks ready for acts of mutilation and dissection. The piece of meat, at once part of a skeleton and a live organism, here a soft, flabby tissue, there a hard-edged object, reveals dramatic tensions and dialectics with which the metaphor interweaves throughout, making every moment reversible—with construction and triumph on one side, dispersion and destruction on the other. The act of prayer, consistently represented throughout the sequence, corresponds both to victimization and to exhibitionism.

Dalí reduces the poet to the creation of a fertile metaphor on which he can graphically gloss at will without showing its functioning in the text. The painter's interpretation of the metaphor certainly gives coherence to his own series but provides a highly unreliable method for understanding the text. However, certain not always easily perceptible analogies exist between the poem and the illustrations. Lautréamont's cantos abound in comparisons and metaphors, used in a parodic manner, for they establish strings of paradoxes rather than cohesion and coherence. The poet reveals the structure, if not always the mechanism, of standard rhetorical devices, and he makes their recurrence visible by the use of distortions and inversions. He made his borrowings quite obvious in order to introduce contrapuntally his own peculiar use of language, imagery, and metaphors. The ocean, the dominant element in his poem, absent from Dalí's illustrations, is alternately endowed with material and spiritual, maternal and "bachelor" qualities. By this method the poet abolishes the standard characteristics of comparison and metaphor; he does not show the common denominator among objects or indicate similarities. He suggests tensions and countertensions, while merging and making interchangeable contrasting elements, a method which, in a different context, we detected in Dalí's plates. Both the poet and the painter strive to open up and multiply linking associations within their own productions.

Dalí claims that he approaches the Lautréamont text by what seems a literary bias—the metaphor. As we have indicated, however, he strips the metaphor of its essential poetic function, for he restricts it to a specific, obsessive meaning rather than sounding its creative depths or using it to explore the unknown. He recognized the nature of *Les Chants de Maldoror* as a document of protest acting as a liberating force in the mind of the assaulted reader and propagating tensions and paradoxes. Dalí's illustrations present at once an extension and a reduction of Lautréamont's text: an extension, since they encompass Dalí's former artistic activity, which he thoroughly deconstructs; a reduction, since he only sporadically establishes connections with the Lautréamont series.

Dalí uses Millet's painting as a screen. This permits him to illustrate *Les Chants de Maldoror* without devouring or being devoured by them; he remains at a distance and leaves the literary work essentially intact. As he approached the poem, according to his writings, from a metaphorical angle to which he added an occasional ambiguous and fragmented monument to Maldoror (which he also linked to other figures in his plates not connected with Lautréamont's protagonist), he undoubtedly posited a system of cohesion underlying the text. Yet the fundamental challenge to language, the contestation that questions the acquired meaning of the word, the problem of the polyphonous narrative voice, the act of communication and writing: these were not Dalí's concern and were bound to be obliterated by the mere fact that he used a painting as an act of mediation. Although in both cases we may find a *mise-en-abîme*, Dalí does not delve into the fundamental issue of the creative gesture or raise the questions of origin and future. In Lautréamont's case, reader, narrator, and creator become interwoven in a ceaseless labyrinthine projection. Dalí's labyrinth attains its own order and imposes its own limitations; one could even claim that desire ultimately achieves satisfaction.

UNE SAISON EN ENFER

Surrealist writers have usually appropriated Rimbaud by admiringly quoting one of his sayings or verses. The pamphlet entitled *Permettez*, printed on the occasion of the inauguration of the second Rimbaud monument in the Ardennes and addressed to "Representatives of the Ardennes, President of the Society of Poets from the Ardennes," expresses the surrealist attitude on the twenty-third of October, 1927, that is, in the early stages of their activities: "Priests, professors, pundits, you are making a mistake in handing me over to justice. I have never been a Christian, I do not belong to the race that sang of torture, I do not understand the law. I did not institute moral sense. I am a brute: you are in error." The surrealists did not devote to Rimbaud a true apologia or turn him, as they did Lautréamont, into a full-fledged pre-surrealist model. Masson and Matta focused on Rimbaud as writer rather than symbol.[14] Lucien Coutaud's and Mario Prassinos's interpretations, too, are well worth mentioning.[15]

Masson produced some of the earliest surrealist books. Initially he interpreted contemporaries such as Bataille, Leiris, and Georges Limbour, or, rather, he collaborated with them to create illustrated books. In illustrating *The Rime of the Ancient Mariner*, he ventured for the first time outside his own epoch or indeed his own circle; he chose a poem in ballad form, with a narrative.[16] Instead of forming bridges between physical and psychological elements, he underplayed individual moments and strove for stylization. Although he undoubtedly selected *The Ancient Mariner* because of its fantastic and nightmarish qualities, the lithographs are too reductive and sometimes too mimetic to bring the Romantic poem into the orbit of surrealism. The etchings of Coutaud, who remained on the fringes of surrealism, show scenes, characters, and a narrative characterized by a fair degree of estrangement (Fig. 87), but Masson's nine double-page colored etchings underplay narrative and autobiographical elements. They do not allude to immediately recognizable scenes, but mainly focus on poetic qualities.[17] The occult is overdetermined at the expense of tangible experience.

According to Roger Passeron, the painter selected from each section of *Une Saison en enfer* a specific sentence.[18] This statement, confirmed by Masson, does not necessarily invalidate our attempt to establish the relevance of each plate to the section. In addition the same single page precedes, each time in a different color, each section. It seems that Masson viewed the poem as a series of nine variations and that he sought to register their flux and counterflux while attempting to unify their elements. These single-page etchings indicate the duality that characterizes Masson's illustrations. In a typically surrealist manner they serve as commentaries on a poem without representing any aspect of "its" literature. They include signs of stellar and terrestrial regions, which overlap to a large degree. These signs affirm the creative or-

---

[14]Arthur Rimbaud, *Une Saison en enfer*, with ten etchings by André Masson (Paris: Les Cent-Une, Société de Femmes Bibliophiles, 1961); *Une Saison en enfer*, text by A. Rimbaud, ten original colored etchings by Sebastian Matta (Barcelona: Ediciones Poligrafa, 1979).

[15]Arthur Rimbaud, *Une Saison en enfer*, with eighteen colored etchings by Mario Prassinos (n.p.: Les Bibliophiles Comtois, 1966); *Une Saison en enfer*, etchings by Lucien Coutaud (Paris: Aux Dépens des Bibliophiles de France, 1940).

[16]Samuel Taylor Coleridge, *Le Dit du vieux marin*, with twelve lithographs by André Masson (Paris: Collection Vrille, 1949).

[17]By *poetic*, we refer both to their almost universal surrealist quality and to the specifics of Rimbaud's poetics.

[18]Roger Passeron, *André Masson* (Fribourg: Office du Livre, 1973), p. 162.

FIG. 87. Etching by Lucien Coutaud from Arthur Rimbaud, *Une Saison en enfer* (A Season in Hell). Paris: Aux Dépens des Bibliophiles de France, 1950. © ADAGP, Paris; VAGA, New York, 1985.

der, while the brush-stroke–like lines paradoxically provide the mark of the pen. Prassinos's vigorous, rather abstract, and ornate plates have more affinities with the single plate etchings than the bolder full-sized illustrations of Masson's series.

The vigorous colors of the nine full-sized plates and their never-repeated combinations endow this *livre de peintre* with violence, intensity, and immediacy corresponding to the poetic text. The color system tends to reject shading just as Rimbaud's prose, in its pursuit of immediacy, rejects transition and syntactic coordination. Rimbaud's repeated *voici* should be pointed out in this connection. Masson's color scheme, although reminiscent of "Voyelles," does not establish correspondences among space, form, sound, and human aspirations, but puts into play autonomous dynamic forces. Simulated brush-strokes enhance the impact of immediacy, giving the illustrations the appearance of paintings rather than etchings. Lines and brushstrokes, in denying the idea of completion, function as vectors or vehicles of power.

Masson's powerful strokes and color zones underline the guilt, suffering, and aspiration to purification in the text. Rimbaud's poem, as viewed by Masson, is not ordered by an a posteriori system. Forces and counterforces, hope and despair, constellation and explosion follow one another in a succession so rapid that it tends toward simultaneity. Within a single etching, shapes refer to different stages of a given power. In both text and image the role played by immediacy and by simultaneity reflects the inevitable fusion of subject and object.

Time creates the central problematics of *Une Saison en enfer*. The title itself suggests the paradox of cyclic time of seasons as opposed to the eternity of hell in religion or metaphysics—progression as opposed to accumulation. According to C. A. Hackett, *Une Saison en enfer* encompasses the passage of the human life from spring to summer, to autumn, to winter.[19] Yet the poet does not accept the conventions pertaining to the seasons, whether relevant to humans or to hell. Far from describing a cycle, he undermines all temporal ordering systems. Returning repeatedly to what might pass for a beginning, he stresses the struggle of a language and gestures to relate and overhaul his experience. In the pattern emerging from the illustrations, no simple direction dominates. One may even wonder whether time is signaled by changes within the structure of recurrent contours. Organic and geometrical forms alternate from one plate to the next as well as within the framework of a single movement. Patterns of continuity and fragmentation, marked by ruptures of lines, create tensions that alternately increase and abate.

The first plate, which borders on abstraction, has no apparent link to the text, although the dark background reminds the viewer that the poet writes "mon carnet de damné" (my notebook of damnation) (Plate 24). Demonic forces are emerging, as gray, green, and white strokes propose dispersion rather than consolidation, as though to reflect the search for a past so distant that it can hardly be recovered. From the first to the second plate, density increases. Energy absorbs the entire space and lightens the nocturnal colors. As this energy unleashes new forces, tensions multiply at a feverish pace. Contrary to the dispersive trend of the first plate, shapes emerge in "Mauvais Sang" (Bad Blood), though they are not yet fully identifiable (Plate 25). The brush-strokes of the first plate provide the initial gesture or impulse, while in the second plate the same colors suggest, by different shadings, a reversal of relationships. Margaret Davies points to the subjacent dialogue opposing in-

---

[19]"*Une Saison en enfer*, frénésie et structure," R.L.M. (1973), p. 366.

terdependent voices, which do not necessarily assure continuity in the text.[20] The multiple lines of the etching form a design that echoes both suspense and progression. The text alludes intermittently to lands and quests. Literary critics have referred to a dance or infernal ballet. In the etchings red signs, rhythmic qualities, and variations on shapes open or closed, solitary or interlaced, suggest choreography. Red, brown, and white lines chart unknown continents or races.

The geometric forms of the second illustration and the emerging brush-strokes retreat in the etching accompanying "Nuit de l'enfer" (Night of hell), to be replaced by elements of nightmares. Physical and mental contortions become simultaneous for the poet, who intensely struggles to discard past illusions, who suffers from present damnation. The hallucinatory quality that prevails in the text surfaces in the etching, which is framed by a bright red margin. Narrow and dark lines project movement with relative intensity; heavier olive, red, and blue curves intermingle more closely. A luminous explosion at the right, instead of dominating, frees other forces. In a two-dimensional space Masson evokes several levels of depth, all participating in labyrinthean itineraries, in organic germinations, in feverish crises. Apart from the obvious identification of red with blood, hell, and fever, of white with purity, the colors do not allude to any tangible reality. Since the poet aspires to unspoilt or archetypal originating forces, the colors at best obliquely refer to specific elements—blue suggests fluidity rather than water itself. The use of colors as well as the presence of signs, especially in "Nuit de l'enfer," assumes Chinese characteristics, thereby equating text and image in another way: "the painter moves between two texts (at the very least), first his own (let's say, that of painting, of its practices, of its gestures, of its instruments) and second that of Chinese ideography (that is, of a localized culture)."[21]

Margaret Davies and Monique Jutrin have insisted on the inherent dialogue, the narrative and confessional characteristics of "Délires I," stressing the ambiguity in the identity of "vierge folle" and "époux infernal."[22] They suggest a *mise-en-abîme* ultimately applicable to the etching. "La vierge folle" and "l'époux infernal" are presented on a dark background, the former

---

[20] Margaret Davies, *Une Saison en enfer* (Paris: Minard, Les Lettres Modernes, 1975), passim.

[21] Roland Barthes, "Sémiographie d'André Masson," p. 143 in *L'Obvie et l'obtus* (Paris: Seuil, 1982); cf. André Masson, *Ville de Vénissieux* (Lyons: Galerie Verrière, 1983).

[22] Monique Jutrin, "Parole et silence dans *Une Saison en enfer*" (Paris: Revue des Lettres Modernes, 1976), pp. 445–49.

a golden head turned upward, detached from a body—a suspended dream image. The shadow-like face of the infernal husband "as hideous as a Mongol" is linked to this vision by a meandering black line, already present in the second engraving. As the features of the infernal husband bear a slight likeness to Verlaine, it seems that Masson takes biographical elements into account in this etching. The dialogue between the male and the female, dark and light, continues a dialectic, a tension, inscribed by interrelated color lines and strokes.

"Délires II" reevaluates the poet's past as well as presenting the final evocation of the vision produced by the alchemical method. Masson's plate, divided diagonally into three sections, embodies the visionary process as well as the visions themselves; the light and its refraction, a medieval city on the lower left, a bird in flight on the upper right dislocate time, disturb unity. A blade crescent asserts the forces of fragmentation. Intensity is heightened by a yellow octagonal form, at once a stellar body and a gigantic lens, a human eye trying to seize and transgress the ephemeral landscape. Although fire and delirium have attained this most powerful stage, nonetheless escape remains possible.

The plate accompanying "L'Impossible" further insists on the dialectic of the text as a clear division separates light from darkness, dream from awakening, angel from devil (Plate 26). Neither of the two corresponding figures reaches a stage of arrest or completion. Their outlines emerge from a red sprinkled background producing an intense effect of vibration, of agitation. Angel and devil, forces distinguished by recognizable wings and horns, flaunt their inner labyrinthean landscape and mythology. The struggle of good and evil, of body and soul, central to this prophetic section, refers to the Christian ideology and upbringing against which Rimbaud struggled. Masson's etching includes in its configuration variations on Oriental calligraphy and thus bypasses Christian ideology and textuality.

"L'Eclair" records the slow approach to death, where procrastination alternates with velocity tailed by an aspiration toward a stable future. Suzanne Bernard suggests that the text of "L'Eclair" (Lightning) is characterized by a great number of reversals, of exclamations. These verbal gestures express revolt, rejection of the past, disbelief in the communard ideology which briefly attracted Rimbaud in 1870.[23] Tensions present in former sections take a different direction and have a different emphasis. By representing a single figure and further reducing the color scheme, the illustrator suggests a significant

[23] Suzanne Bernard, *Le Poème en prose de Baudelaire jusqu'à nos jours* (Paris: Nizet, 1959).

step toward unification. No forces can oppose the dissonant red tones expressing fire, hellish torture, convulsion, eroticism. The figure implies a continuous osmosis from which no escape is possible. An eye and a mouth isolated from the main figure allude to inner vision, self-knowledge, self-evaluation, and thus reintroduce autobiographical elements. The intertwining of various parts of the body, the torso bent forward, simultaneously suggesting guilt, prayer, and sexual experience, repeat the dialectic movements of the previous plate: a glorious sunrise and hellish suffering. Thus Masson embodied his own myth, without violating the poet's words.

In the metapoetic "Matin" (Morning) a vigorous past contrasts with an anemic present. The poet, in attempting to account for his life, tends initially to formulate a song for the future as a reversal of Christian ideology. The text ends on a note of harmony which is echoed in the etching. Violence has subsided. Two figures, drawn in white, sketch the itinerary to the future. Blue, yellow, and black strokes chase gray zones while mysterious graphic signs make visible a new realm of alchemy. The final poem replaces the unnecessary past with a vision of things to come: "C'est l'heure nouvelle, c'est la veille, splendides villes, posséder la vérité dans une âme et dans un corps" (It's the new hour, it's the eve, splendid cities, to possess truth in a mind and a body). These assertive words lead to a synthesis. The writer revises his poetic career by reducing his past ambitions to fictions. In accepting his limitations and his errors he expresses his search for truth and justice. In the final plate, accompanying "Adieu," the constellations assume greater intimacy as forms encountered in the course of the suite dynamically reemerge. Masson opens up a nocturnal world whose initial vigor has by no means dissipated. He traces the flight of the birds, their rapid movement through time, as well as the forces of attraction that stellar illuminations exert upon each other. A yellow starlike figure summarizes the fertility of the future world. The painter's primeval forces are upheld, like a splendid city, embodying the union of creator and creation, body and soul.

Une Saison en enfer offered to Masson the challenge of penetrating the structural and textual complexities of the poem. He discovered an echo of his own myths and thematics: modern man's physical and mental struggle to return to an original strength and to reinvent a new language for a radically new experience. His quest was unencumbered by Christianity or traditional notions of good and evil. In a way he began where Rimbaud left off. From the beginning he rejected categories and made deconstruction and regeneration almost simultaneous. His dynamic scribal constellations make viewer and reader inseparable, for, as Françoise Will-Levaillant has pointed out in regard to *écriture*: "[Writing] links up, not the closed system of a language, but the unutterable of a phantasm."[24]

To a certain extent Masson salvages the poet's task by often imposing on pages colorfully framed groups of signs whose motions exceed their meaning, much in the manner of his abstract expressionist followers.

· · ·

Sebastian Matta has in recent years become a prolific book illustrator. Since he had close ties with such surrealists as Breton and Dalí as early as the thirties and forties, his illustrations of *Une Saison en enfer*, *Ubu roi*, *Hom'mère*, *Garganta tua*, and other works in the late seventies and early eighties testify to the continuing life of major surrealist illustration.[25] *Une Saison en enfer* is one of the most complex works jointly created by an artist and his printer. Matta, a careful reader, had repeatedly discovered the disquieting side of literary works from a surrealist as well as a political perspective. In addition to ten aquatints, the book includes two double foliosheets reproducing Rimbaud's text in eight columns. Between the columns and in the margins Matta provides an abundance of annotations and sketches. On this worksheet he evolved and reveals his creative method, a method whereby he sometimes traps his reader.

He hardly proposes parallel reading, for the annotated folio page is separated from the engravings, whose titles correspond to brief textual quotations. Unlike illustrators who try to establish a one-to-one relationship between text and image, Matta transforms the text into an image by a partially destructive gesture, as is stated on the title page: "Une Saison en enfer; dix gravures originales, cessons l'enfer de Sebastian Matta" (Let us put an end to the hell of Sebastian Matta). The painter indicates his plan of action, as one would expect from a politically committed artist whose paintings and engravings assert freedom, revolt, liberation. He becomes at once Rimbaud's accomplice, his rival, and even his opponent. This ambiguous relationship is fostered partly by Rimbaud's title, where the temporal and timeless are paradoxically juxtaposed, and by the poet's frequent undermining of conventional attitudes toward the seasons. Matta's handwritten words make the painter present within the text and thus stress his active relationship with Rimbaud's lively literary adventure. Approaching the text through selection, Matta signals the pres-

[24]"Catalogue des ouvrages illustrés par André Masson," p. 9 in *Ville de Vénisseux*.
[25]Sebastian Matta, *Hom'mère*, texts and colored etchings (Paris: Visat, 1974–77, 3 vols.); Alfred Jarry, *Ubu roi*, with eight colored etchings by Matta (Paris: Dupont-Visat, 1982); Sebastian Matta, *Garganta tua* (Florence: Edizione della Bezuga, 1981).

ence of Rimbaud. However, from the inception of his work Matta subordinates fidelity and admiration to a thrust forward. The annotating *figures*, no less than the *discours*, serve as a filter enabling the painter to translate Rimbaud's words into his own language in order to generate a new opus. Rimbaud's text, dismantled if not deconstructed by Matta, provides a new form of emphasis and stress.

Words in the margin and between the lines assert and, so to speak, stand in the painter's own space. He composes a transitional, incipiently illustrated text, partly colored, partly uncolored, but always embossed in the paper. At this stage the reader-viewer, peering through a mirror, is able to look both backward and forward to Rimbaud, as well as to Matta's forthcoming *Saison*. By prefacing his aquatints with clarifications that proclaim, or at the very least disclose, stages or even hesitation in the genesis of the work of art, Matta deviates from the usual surrealist practice. Since the handwritten words constitute a reservoir containing, among other things, the titles of the plates, it seems that Matta literally and pictorially adapted the message of "L'Alchimie du verbe." The plates that dissociate the sequence of *Une Saison* hardly coincide with the structure and poetic order of the text. The ten titles are gleaned from "Mauvais Sang" (2), "Vierge folle" (Foolish Virgin) (2), "L'Alchimie du verbe" (The Alchemy of Language) (5), and "L'Eclair" (1). According to the order of the poem, "Je suis intact" (I am intact) should title the first plate, and not, as is the case, the last one. After the experience of the inferno, after its fires and explosions—"Feu, feu sur moi" (Fire, fire on me)—Matta's self survives: "Je suis intact." Rimbaud tends, on the contrary, to assert a precarious freedom and immunity rather than declare the total survival of his self: "Les criminels degoûtent comme les châtrés, moi, je suis intact et ça m'est égal" (Criminals are as disgusting as eunuchs, as for me, I am intact and couldn't care less). The painter has thus transcended in his denouement the paradoxes to which the poet repeatedly alluded.

"Je fixais les vertiges" (I arrested turmoils) introduces the first plate, a paradoxical universe consisting of a sort of whirling stability (Plate 27). As in many of his canvases, Matta does not represent space as geometrical but, rather, as visceral, thereby suggesting the depth of the sea or the atmosphere, and undoubtedly pertaining to the inner world; it provides an inscape with cosmic dimensions where the two worlds become indistinguishable. The poet alludes to what words cannot express, to what lies beyond silence and immobility. Matta readily recognizes the paradox of an expression in which movement and immobility enter into prolonged tensions. The interference of outer space, which had so critically threatened the self, ends with Matta's reassuring "Je suis intact" (Plate 28), whereas for Rimbaud the conclusion remains open-ended, as it allows, perhaps ironically, for the possibility of a new experience: "Il me sera possible de posséder la vérité dans une âme et dans un corps" (It will be possible for me to possess the truth in a mind and in a body).

The colored sketches accompanying the text do not provide a reservoir of outlines or shapes for the engravings, and only an occasional mimetic allusion can be detected—for example, three musicians accompany the words "Je suis un opéra fabuleux" (I am a fabulous opera). Rather, most of the figures express destruction and defiance, often directed at the text. The past, the historical and mythological references, fragmented and intermittent in Rimbaud's text, are dramatically reversed in the painter's world so as to point to the future. A statement made by Matta in 1938 has considerable relevance in this connection: "Let us overthrow all the displays of history with their styles and elegant wafers so that rays of dust, whose pyrotechnics must create space, will stream forth.[26]

Matta radically transforms Rimbaud's many-faceted persona, in its suffering capable of being simultaneously absent and present. The painter, who has no use for a central persona, sets up the space of hell by the explicit presence of flame-colored surfaces and figures, which produce a stormy intensity. He evokes atmospheres of varying tonalities and moods while rejecting contemplation in favor of passion and spectacle. Matta relies on radical experiences beginning on the perceptual level, whereas Rimbaud concerns himself with the process of provocation more than with its sustained or tangible manifestations. The persona, however, ironically seeks to locate a fragmented self and tormenting experiences in a spatial order: "Je ne suis plus au monde. La théologie est sérieuse, l'enfer est certainement *en bas* et le ciel *en haut*. Extase, cauchemar, sommeil dans un nid de flammes" (I am no longer in the world. Theology means business, hell is certainly down under and heaven up above. Ecstasy, nightmare, slumber in a nest of flames). Such spaces depend on the poet's ability to push aside, for instance, the azure of the sky, and thus remove or receive established or establishable boundaries. As a result, his space appears hardly compatible with the placing of objects or entities on a painter's canvas.

Matta shows, however, the keenest awareness of Rimbaud's revolutionary concept of space. In the engravings, movement or, rather, extraordinary mobility leads to decentralization while generating energies that cannot be tied to a situational source. Such forces scarcely require the orchestration so

[26]"Mathématique sensible, architecture du temps," *Minotaure* 11 (1938): 43.

prominent in Masson's interpretations. In Matta's universe the viewer, assaulted by multiple impulses, realizes that color, lines, and surfaces evolve in a continuous flux, open-ended and unrepeatable. Rimbaud, as we have suggested, often insists on a disproportion between the container and the contained, on the pursuit and disappearance of lines of demarcation. In Matta's all-pervasive dynamism, the distinction between the container and the contained becomes irrelevant. Rather, a fugal interplay of lines sets up a pervasive vibration. In the absence of containment, movement emerges as invasion and escape, occasionally corresponding to certain forms of Rimbaud's refusal.

Color zones, color lines, and color flux generate abstraction and retraction, dispersion and reduction to particles. Specks, spots, and discontinuous streaks suggest painterly brush-strokes or even fingerprints and frequently appear as independent elements within the plates. In the first aquatint (see Plate 27), characterized by upward motion, arches soar above a central red figure propagating vortices. Its intertwining branches produce contrapuntal movements eschewing closure. Floating green shapes to the left of the treelike figure add still another arch; they are topped by small semicircular transparent figures that seem to follow their own laws of motion and not to show subservience to the green vortices. A transparent cylindrical screen provides a relatively fixed plane from which spring rays forming an additional cycle. Finally, white, gray, and yellow lines, singly and in groups, curved and in knots, add to the multifarious motions illustrating "Je fixais les vertiges." Here and in other illustrations the painter's conception relies, not on a homogeneous field, but on a variety of fields making their own laws of generation and propagation. Certain elements recur from plate to plate: shapes floating or even propelled through space, vibrating shaded surfaces, dynamic lines whirling into knobs or balls. In addition to red constellations, transparent or translucent screens not only establish relations among the plates but concentrate or disperse light and color. The variable scale of the colors, their dotted or sparkling quality, discourages any attempt to pinpoint energy and movement in a specific context.

In Matta's *Une Saison en enfer*, fire, water, and air function as dynamic, transformative presences. In certain plates—for instance, "Attire le gai venin" (Attracts the joyous venom)—the deadly shades of rainbow and fire successively produce dispersion and concentration. In "Je fixe les vertiges" (see Plate 27), "Nous ne sommes pas au monde," "Feu, feu sur moi," "L'Explosion qui éclaire mon abîme" (The explosion illuminating my abyss), "Je suis intact" (see plate 28), and "L'Ame est une couronne" (The soul is a crown) a red figure or a group of figures dominates the scene. The identity of such figures remains enigmatic; one is tempted to call them otherworldly or extraterrestrial. They offer partial resemblances to trees, gadgets, fauna. Such figures suggest the difficulty of separating the self from the world, the creator from the created, the actor from the scene. Hell, a persona, embodies a dynamically changeable atmosphere. The painter has not only pictorialized the language of his titles but has graphically reinvented "L'Alchimie du verbe." Matta thus responds to an alchemical experiment without having to rely on contrasts or compensation, an experiment in which fire and blood are transmuted into radiance and explosion without offering a glimpse of the alternative spectacle of darkness or eclipse. Whereas Rimbaud ironically aspires to revelation, Matta boldly and unhesitatingly produces it.

"Feu, feu sur moi" forms a complex system of rectangular shapes, delineated by red lines reverberating with the impact of fire and explosion, where reference to nature is almost completely eliminated. Yellow surfaces and lines suggest the violet projection or radiation of beams and compose a contrapuntal network so complexly patterned that it defies both solution and dissolution. The central figure would make it impossible to separate creative action from passive victimization, escape from concepts which in Rimbaud's world alternate and never become simultaneous.

In some plates emerge beams of light not usually integrated into the patterns of luminous vibration. Their lines, which transmit vitality with great immediacy, tend to form spiral clusters. They simulate signs of magnetic and electrical activity, occasionally taking the shape of arrows; they indicate the direction of an irresistible trajectory. Here and there a set of lines reminiscent of handwriting echoes the painter's exchanges with the poet while forming secret codes hovering in space and enacting changes in the world. They fabricate unencumbered networks, whereas "Feu, feu sur moi" responds mainly to a poetry in search of itself as a means to a radical transformation. "Des secrets pour changer la vie" (Secrets to change life) insistently recalls Matta's version of inscape and provides a glimpse of the "enchantements assemblés sur mon cerveau" (enchantments assembled on my brain). "Une morphologie psychologique" (a psychological morphology) suddenly made wide open to the cosmos, is Matta's response to and refutation of a poet whose inner hell originates in the poison he has consumed.

Since for Matta time can only be linked to prophecy and must project into the future, since the hell and suffering speak only of immediacy, eschewing contemplation, the series should end with explosive figures inscribing in the sky the shaped infinity of a rainbow, which definitely replaces the abyss in a final telescoping of spatial landscape and inner vision.[27] Matta has enacted both *Une Saison en enfer* and "Cessons l'enfer." Rimbaud's final "Il me sera loisible de posséder la vérité dans une âme et dans un corps" (I'll be free to possess truth in a soul and in a body) suggests that after the experience of mutilation, the aspiration toward unity was of minor concern to him.

In the eyes of the painters, so it seems, *Une Saison en enfer* presented a more challenging text than *Les Illuminations*. Masson, closely associated with Bataille and Leiris as well as with the more orthodox surrealists, rejected illustration based on overt affinity with literary concerns. He attempted to show the passage of Rimbaud's visions, the itinerary of his dynamic transformations. Matta, who put a greater emphasis on action, power, and modernity as threats of total alienation and uprooting, saw above all the need to move forward toward a more harmonious future.

The Lautréamont illustrations belong to an earlier period. They attempt to reconcile a revolutionary book with the painter's iconography. Masson and especially Matta envisioned the *livre de peintre* as a sort of transcendent object, capable of revolutionizing their own art. As a result, they showed far less concern for subject matter than Magritte or even Dalí did. Masson and Matta introduced bolder experiments with space and color and often decreed the exclusion of closure and immobility. They proclaimed themselves surrealists just as much as Dalí (in 1936) and Magritte, while employing engraving techniques so much more innovative that these artists are occasionally included among the abstractionists.

Moreover, Masson's dynamic antitheses and Matta's vibrating inner space come to terms with a nuclear age that has relegated even such revolutionary artists as Rimbaud, Lautréamont, and the early Dalí to a dead past.

[27] Cf. a passage from Italo Calvino's text on Matta entitled "L'Altra Euridice": "Freeing her became my sole preoccupation: breaking down the doors to the outside, invading the external with the internal, joining Eurydice once again to terrestrial matter, building over her a new vault, a new mineral sky, saving her from the hell of that vibrating air, of that sound, of that song" (p. 7 in Germana Ferrari, *Matta: Index dell'opera grafica dal 1969 al 1980* [Viterbo: Amministrazione Provinciale, 1980]).

CHAPTER SEVEN

ILLUSTRATION
AND COMMITMENT

CAHIER D'UN RETOUR AU PAYS NATAL

IN THE CHAPTERS DEVOTED to the nineteenth century and pre-surrealist texts, the problematics raised by the book itself, such as the nature of collaboration and experimentation with text and image, played only a minor part. By selecting such texts as *Alice in Wonderland* and *Une Saison en enfer*, we examined various transformations and interpretations of nineteenth-century works. In the present chapter, our choice of books is again determined by the nature of the texts. Both *Cahier d'un retour au pays natal* and *Air mexicain* belong to the literature of commitment: both openly advocate and appeal for political action.[1] The illustrators are known for their engagement or even militancy. Painters and poets, whatever the nature of their personal contacts or encounters, engaged in the same or similar political pursuits and became de jure collaborators. The poets speak for downtrodden peoples—Péret for Indians, Césaire for Blacks—and so their texts assume an epic quality quite different from the lyric and polemic explosions of the texts examined so far. The two writers formulated a plea for the liberation of peoples outside Europe, a liberation, both political and social, to lead from repression and slavery to spiritual awakening, identity, and plenitude. A statement made by Leiris in his book on Lam is pertinent here: "Not long before World War II, two of the most influential surrealist writers, though dissident, were still searching for horizons wider than those of our mechanized culture."[2] Potential and promise, in both the present and the future, can only be achieved by

---

[1] Aimé Césaire, *Retorno al país natal* (La Habana: Colección de Textos Poéticos, Molina y Cia, n.d.); Benjamin Péret, *Air mexicain* (Paris: Librairie Arcanes, 1952).
[2] Michel Leiris, *Wifredo Lam* (New York: Abrams, 1970), no page numbers.

the rediscovery or redefinition of a past, by the revelation of the true meaning of its myths and legends.[3]

The surrealism of *Cahier d'un retour* has been challenged. The majority of his critics claim Aimé Césaire as above all a Black poet, as a spokesman for the downtrodden: the Blacks of the Caribbean, the Blacks of Africa, the Blacks of all nations. Surrealism as a way of life, as an artistic movement, belonged, so these critics suggest, to Europe during a specific period. More than Césaire's poetry such as *Les Armes miraculeuses* (1946) and *Ferrements* (1960), *Cahier*, with its lyric thrusts and its discursive rhetoric, is a call to arms for a Caribbean awakening, if not revolt. Césaire's exposure to surrealism during his sojourn in Paris has never been doubted. It undoubtedly contributed to the discovery of his true identity and will to action. Of greater concern to us is the resemblance of his explosive images to those of Breton's *Révolver à cheveux blancs*. Such images occur when Césaire plunges into the oneiric experiences belonging to Caribbean myths and beliefs. His verbal and poetic techniques are grounded in surrealism even if the anthropological and social functions of his thought originate in a mixture of rational reconstruction and personal experience.

According to several critics, Lam as a painter, although to a lesser degree, has raised ethnic issues similar to Césaire's concerns. Lam is a Cuban of Black and Chinese origin. Culturally he belongs to Africa, Europe, and the Caribbean. Dominique Le Bahau states: "Indeed, in his art several traditions combine. . . . He has us read a vast assembly of metamorphoses in the depths of a turbulent night."[4] *Cahier d'un retour*, translated into Spanish, illustrated by Lam, and published in Cuba, was aimed at a different public than most of the books discussed in previous chapters. This publication, modest in its appearance and meagerly illustrated with reproduced drawings, may be compared to early plaquettes such as *Dormir, dormir*. In both books the cover illustration is emphasized by color; two vignettes are in black-and-white, and the typography tends to be conventional. Such minimal illustration was not uncommon; many books can boast only a frontispiece, though for others such as Char's *Le Rempart des brindilles*, Lam provided a substantial number of colored engravings.[5]

A biographical or ethnic affinity that gives priority to experience rather

---

[3] Matta was perhaps more concerned with obliterating the European past than with rediscovering a set of Chilean myths.

[4] *Hommage à Wifredo Lam, XXème Siècle* 44 (June 1975): 41.

[5] René Char, *Le Rempart de brindilles* (Paris: Broder, 1963).

than to a common conception of art or an identification with surrealism provides the basis of Lam's illustration. However, the impact of surrealism cannot be discounted altogether. Various versions of the text have been given prefaces either by Benjamin Péret or André Breton, poets who have been instrumental in extending the domain of surrealism beyond the continent and the cultures of Europe. Péret stayed several years in more than one Latin American country. Breton visited the Caribbean, where he "discovered" Césaire. He describes his meeting with Césaire in his article "Un Grand Poète noir," in which he speaks of *Cahier d'un retour* as the greatest lyrical poem of its time.[6] Escaping the German invasion of France, Breton and Péret visited lands that, according to them, kept alive values forsaken by bourgeois capitalism. In his *Anthologie des mythes, légendes et contes populaires d'Amérique*, Péret reveals the authenticity of myths in which the oneiric plays a significant role.[7] Breton wrote prefaces for a volume on "art magique" and one on the art of the Aborigines.[8] In "Un Grand Poète noir," which also served as preface to a bilingual edition of *Cahier d'un retour* published in New York, Breton turned the Caribbean poet into an exemplary hero whose illuminations coincide with surrealist aspirations.[9] He cites Césaire's originality, his ability to venture onto uncharted roads: "And it is a Black man who today wields the French language as no white man is able to wield it. And it is a Black man who guides us today to unexplored territory, progressively and with ease establishing the contacts that enable us to advance across the sparks."[10] The poet does not attempt an objective reading, as he searches above all for solidarity and communion: "J'eprouvai tout le prix de me sentir en si étroite communion avec l'un d'eux, de le savoir entre tous un être de volonté et de ne pas distinguer, en essence, sa volonté de la mienne" (I knew all the worth of feeling in such complete communion with such a poet, of seeing him to be a man of will and of not distinguishing in essence his will from mine).[11] Breton's recognition of the poet suggests at once an inclusion of Césaire among the surrealists and an invitation to take his work as an example of militant writing.

A similar approach characterizes Breton's writings on Lam. In his 1941 es-

---

[6] In *Hémisphères* 2–3 (Autumn–Winter 1943).

[7] *Anthologie des mythes, légendes et contes populaires* (Paris: Albin Michel, 1960).

[8] André Breton, *L'Art magique* (Paris: Club Français du Livre, 1957); *L'Art à l'état brut: Peintures et sculptures des aborigènes* (Lausanne: La Guilde du Livre, 1962).

[9] *Cahier d'un retour au pays natal/Memorandum on My Martinique*, trans. Lionel Abel and Yvan Goll (New York: Brentano, 1947).

[10] Ibid. Our translation.

[11] Ibid., trans. Abel and Goll.

say devoted to the painter, the poet again establishes a form of communion by abolishing the separation between art and the artist, between art and nature. In the cases of both Lam and Césaire, Breton suggests leadership in poetic terms by metaphors of light: "Lam, l'étoile de la liane au front et tout ce qu'il touche brûlant de lucioles" (Lam, the star of the liana on his forehead and everything he touches glowing with fireflies).[12] He endows painter and writer simultaneously with visionary qualities: their contact with the primitive and savage offers, according to Breton, always in search of the fundamental, a golden age, effectiveness in the present, and the acute awareness so vital at a time when the upheavals of World War II had frustrated dreams and aspirations.

In his long prose poem Césaire narrates incidents from his childhood in Martinique, his trip to Paris, and his return to his native land. As he gains awareness, his experiences become meaningful and he discovers an identity, first personal, then more broadly humanistic in scope. At first the poet recapitulates, for he has still to learn a language capable of expressing his protest and faith.[13] Through his powerful formulations he frees himself from patterns of repetition and subjection; he establishes contact with his own authentic being, with that of the Black man of his island and throughout the world. At times the work achieves a metaphoric intensity equivalent to passages from Rimbaud, Breton, or Péret. In its polemic sections with seemingly straightforward narrative, however, it is less comparable to surrealist manifestos: "Et ni l'instituteur dans sa classe, ni le prêtre au catéchisme ne pourront tirer un mot de ce négrillon somnolent, malgré leur manière si énergique, à tous deux de tambouriner son crâne tondu." (And neither the teacher in his classroom nor the priest at catechism will be able to get a word out of this sleepy little nigger, no matter how energetically they drum on his shorn skull).[14] Ironically the poet shows the misguided whites transforming the Black boy into an African drum. Passages such as this one bear little relation not only to surrealist outbursts but also to Wifredo Lam's highly stylized, nonmimetic illustration, exemplified by the figure on the title page (Fig. 88). By comparing Lam's art to stained glass, Breton introduced him as a painter

[12] André Breton, *Le Surréalisme et la peinture* (Paris: Gallimard, 1965), p. 171; trans. Taylor, *Surrealism and Painting*, p. 170.

[13] In regard to linguistic awareness, cf. the introduction to Aimé Césaire, *The Collected Poetry*, trans. Clayton Eshleman and Annette Smith (Berkeley: University of California Press, 1981). All translations below of *Cahier d'un retour* are from this edition. Cf. also Aliko Songolo's perceptive discussion of Césaire's poetry in *Aimé Césaire: Une Poétique de la découverte* (Paris: Edition de l'Harmattan, 1985).

[14] *Collected Poetry*, p. 36. Subsequent quotations are from this edition.

AIME CESAIRE

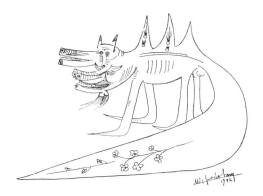

RETORNO
AL PAIS NATAL

PREFACIO DE BENJAMIN PERET
ILUSTRACIONES DE WIFREDO LAM
TRADUCCION DE LYDIA CABRERA

COLECCION DE TEXTOS POETICOS

FIG. 88. Drawing by Wifredo Lam from Aimé Césaire, *Retorno al país natal* (Return to the Native Country). La Habana: Colección de Textos Poéticos, n.d. © SPADEM, Paris; VAGA, New York, 1985.

FIG. 89. Drawing by Wifredo Lam from Aimé Césaire, *Retorno al país natal*. © SPADEM, Paris; VAGA, New York, 1985.

who actualizes god. More importantly, the image of the filtering glass suggests that Lam transforms the raw data provided by nature or sight:

C'est à leur pied que Wifredo Lam installe son 'vêver,' c'est-à-dire la merveilleuse et toujours changeante lueur tombant des vitraux invraisemblablement ouvragés de la nature tropicale sur un esprit libéré de toute influence et prédestiné à faire surgir de cette lueur les images des dieux.

It is at their feet that Wifredo Lam sets his *vêver*, that is to say the marvelous, ever-changing rays of light from the delicately worked stained-glass windows of tropical nature that fall upon a mind freed from all influences and predestined to make the images of gods rise up out of these gleams of light.[15]

Lam's full-page drawing consists of a single constellated figure (Fig. 89). The basic elements of this composition can of course be found in many of his other works, but he has avoided the depth and perspective achieved, in many of his paintings, by multiplication of color planes as well as recurring patterns. Compared to *Peinture* (1950–55) or the well-known *Jungle* (1942), both reproduced in *Le Surréalisme et la peinture*, fetishes, symbols, flora, and fauna represented in the illustration present a similar ambiguity without even aiming at the same plenitude or complexity. The viewer is struck by the absence of geometric lines and of any form of angularity, by the almost exclusive presence of round, recognizable shapes. Lam's obvious references to organic forms enable us to relate his illustration to the text: "Et ce ne sont pas seulement les bouches qui chantent, mais les mains, mais les pieds, mais les fesses, mais les sexes, et la créature tout entière qui se liquéfie en sons, voix et rythme." (And not only do the mouths sing, but the hands, the feet, the buttocks, the genitals, and your entire being liquefies into sounds, voices, and rhythm) (p. 41). Césaire, here and in other passages, is less intent on decomposing and deconstructing so as to attain the fundamental of the organic order than on stating the autonomy of the parts without mutilating the unity of the whole. As mouth, sex, hands, and buttocks participate in the song they undergo a metamorphosis, and barriers between spiritual and physical worlds are abolished. Language, at once spiritual and physical, becomes universal. In the drawing by Lam we can discover similar features. His constellated figure, which bears no resemblance to any single ritual or live creature, includes the outlined parts of a body, made autonomous by separation from the natural order and from each other.

Ambiguity plays a less significant role in the painter's drawing than in the poet's words. Contours abounding in arches and curves signal the process of

[15]*Le Surréalisme et la peinture*, p. 172; trans. Taylor, *Surrealism and Painting*, p. 172.

transformation at the expense of a static or fixed world. From Césaire's universe, encompassing past, present, and future, Lam has abstracted a moment rich in potential and concentration. He refers at times to Césaire's dynamic, explosive lyricism, expressing rediscovered and revitalized links between man and nature. He becomes the catalyst of forces operating in the text. He emphasizes the fluctuations of time, the liberation of the poet, the appeal for a general human and social awakening, for communion with the physical and cosmic world:

> A force de regarder les arbres je suis
> devenu un arbre et mes longs pieds
> d'arbre ont creusé dans le sol de larges
> sacs à venin de hautes villes d'ossements
> à force de penser au Congo
> je suis devenu un Congo bruissant de
> forêts et de fleuves.
>
> [p. 51]

> From staring too long at trees I have
> become a tree and my long tree
> feet have dug in the ground large
> venom sacs high cities of bone
> from brooding too long on the Congo
> I have become a Congo resounding with
> forests and rivers.

Césaire renders the process of metamorphosis explicit; he outlines its origin and its direction. This type of metamorphosis occurs in Lam's drawing through the overlapping of forms and meaning: the human and the vegetable order exchange and combine their characteristics. Leaves with constellated veins resemble wings or raised arms; the fruit they bear takes on the shape of breasts. As Lam's transformations tend to be two-directional, metamorphosis becomes reversible. He shows a universal becoming or unfolding. Metamorphosis does not constitute an isolated phenomenon of limited scope, for it puts an end to immobility, to the sedentary, fragmented, diseased state evoked in the early part of the poem.

> Au bout du petit matin le soleil qui
> toussote
> et crache ses poumons
>
> [p. 51]

> At the end of the wee hours the sun which
> hacks and spits up its lungs

Here the sun betrays its nature, forsakes its identity, which later, thanks to the vigor of metamorphosis and the poet's regained strength, will be restored.

Blood can be termed the central metaphor of the poem. The violence of the color and the implications of fertility further the relations already outlined and extend its network:

> *Ma mémoire est entourée de sang. Ma mémoire a sa ceinture de cadavres!*
> [p. 59]
>
> My memory is encircled with blood. My memory has a belt of corpses!

The poet alludes to exchanges between the spiritual and the physical, which further enhance the process of reinvigoration. A similar exchange is described in poetic terms by René Char: "Le radium même, dans une telle réunion, serait le grand scarabée de l'humus fiévreux, beau joueur cuivré et inoffensif. La réplique à l'imagination chez un peintre est confondante puisque la faulx parvient à donner la vie au lieu de la prendre." (Radium itself, in such a gathering, would be the great scarab of the feverish humus, a good sport and quite innocuous. The painter's retort to the imagination is confusing, for the scythe succeeds in giving life instead of taking it away.)[16] Although organisms are disturbingly present in both the painter's and the poet's world, the former refrains from linking the abstract to the organically concrete, but attains unison by means of an imposing figure in which the spiritual and the physical are tensely combined. Lam does not reflect Césaire's theoretical polarities. This may be one reason why the metaphor of blood finds no direct equivalent in the illustration:

> *Je force la membrane vitelline qui me sépare de moi-même.*
> [p. 57]
>
> I am forcing the vitelline membrane that separates me from myself.

On more than one occasion the poet mentions belts and chains, all forming obstacles that are not necessarily insurmountable. The movement of revolt assumes organic characteristics; it becomes associated with birth, with identity. The poet conjures the central face of liberation and restores a natural order. He becomes an omnipresent mediator, reasserting his identity in the broadest human sense. This return to the autobiographical side of the poem marks a fundamental difference between poet and painter. For Césaire the mediating role of the poet cannot be discounted. His ventures soon exceed

---

[16]René Char, "De la sainte famille au droit à la paresse," p. 114 in *Wifredo Lam* (Madrid: Museo Nacional de Arte Contemporáneo, 1982), also published as a separate text (Paris: Le Point Cardinal, 1976).

the personal and lead to the discovery of a new humanity, through a process that offers unexpected analogies with Cartesian methodology.[17] Humanism, fostered by artistic mediation, has no equivalent in the drawings.

Lam and Césaire met in 1942 in Havana, barely a year before publication of the Cuban edition. Three years later Césaire wrote an article for *Les Cahiers d'art* on Lam's recent paintings. These paintings are far different from the illustrations and the canvases of 1941–42. Lam's art had evolved after his return to his island, just as Césaire's return to Martinique stimulated a new awareness. The poet's commentary is revealing, even if only obliquely relevant to the drawings we have examined. He insists on the revolutionary nature of Lam's art, on his relationship to the Caribbean islands:

Et la peinture de Wifredo Lam roule bord sur bord sa cargaison de révolte: hommes pleins de feuilles, sexes germés, poussés à contre-sens, hiératiques et tropicaux: des dieux.

Dans une société où la machine et l'argent ont démesurément agrandi la distance de l'homme aux choses, Wifredo Lam fixe sur une toile la cérémonie pour laquelle toutes existent: la cérémonie de l'union physique de l'homme et du monde.[18]

And Wifredo Lam's painting rolls on and on with its cargo of revolt: men full of leaves, sprouted genitals, pushing in the wrong direction, hieratic and tropical: gods.

In a society where machinery and money have increased beyond all measure the distance between man and objects, Wifredo Lam sets on canvas the ceremony for which all things exist: the ceremony of the physical union of man and the world.

In referring to Wifredo Lam's typical representations, Césaire succeeds in bringing the painter as much as possible into his own orbit. He sees in him the exponent of revolt against capitalism, responsible for a false modernization in which the links between the individual and mankind and between mankind and nature have been severed. But the pictorial world of Lam does not show forces of opposition, a cleavage or even a polarization as clearly as Césaire claims in his article and manifests in the *Cahier*. Lam's *Jungle* is an awe-inspiring vision of an alien world. As Leiris has pointed out, when Lam returned to Cuba after an extended stay in Europe he became fascinated with the otherness of the jungle: "It incited him to reevaluate everything, so that painting became a means not only of affirming himself, but of formulating by brilliant, suggestive images what it is to be a man among men and a living being within the cosmic immensity."[19] Lam participated in the Spanish war,

---

[17] Such similarities have also been noted between Descartes's *Le discours de la méthode* and Breton's *Le Manifeste du surréalisme*.

[18] Aimé Césaire, "Wifredo Lam," *Cahiers d'art* 20–21 (1945–46): 357.

[19] Leiris, *Wifredo Lam*.

but we cannot determine the exact nature of the painter's conscious opposition to and defiance of other specific events and institutions, whether we examine the *Jungle* or the illustrations of *Un Cahier*. His drawings never allude in any overt way to any cultural institution attacked in the *Cahier* (see Fig. 89). A subsequent statement may help to clarify Leiris's position: "[Lam] was also concerned with the fate of mankind as it undergoes a series of incessant mutations and catastrophes, affecting animals and plants, which it has no more right to consider as inferiors than any race is entitled to place itself above another."[20]

In his essay on Lam Césaire uses the same metaphoric language as in his poem. The jungle is not a spectacle to be viewed or described; it forces an encounter between man and nature wherein sap and blood merge and become indistinguishable from one another. Lam's references to nature include sky, earth, water, stars, fauna, and flora but, as Césaire rightly states, they are free of any concern for documentation.[21] Without using, as Breton does, terms of communion, Césaire in a way identifies with Lam, insofar as his iconography evolves toward defiance instead of simply paying homage to Caribbean myths or Cuban landscapes. His art, so Césaire believes, becomes a warning, a search for self-possession, a prophecy. Péret, more than Césaire, probes deeply into the religious and poetic forces at work in Lam, for he alludes to an exorcism capable of freeing man from impurity and encroachment upon his freedom, without seeking its models in Western revolt.

The interpretations that Césaire, Breton, Péret, and Leiris give of Lam's art differ only in degree; all see him as an artist committed to their common cause. Although they may hold various positions regarding surrealism, their fundamental allegiance to that movement outweighs their differences.

In terms of the surrealist book, the collaboration between Césaire and Lam appears radically different from the teamwork in *Les Malheurs des immortels* or *Facile*. Ernst and Eluard, as well as Man Ray and Eluard, pooled their efforts in producing a new type of book, inventing novel ways of relating text and image, notably by the introduction of the collage and photography. The 1943 edition of the *Cahier* illustrated by Lam and with a preface by Péret, and, for that matter, the bilingual edition, without illustrations, published in 1947 in New York, soon followed by the first Paris edition, both with a preface by Breton, show partnership of a different kind.[22] Displaying a closer involve-

[20] Ibid.

[21] By insisting on the rituals of nature, on its vitality and promise, Lam has excluded the modern crowded metropolis, which subjugates mankind.

[22] *Cahier d'un retour au pays natal* (Paris: Bordas, 1947).

ment with ideology than with art, the *Cahier* advocates disturbance; it subordinates concern for art forms to the defiance of an entire culture.

If Césaire, Breton, and Lam predispose the viewer to disruption or alienation, it is always in the name of higher aspirations. It would be more questionable to consider the Cuban edition of the *Cahier* in isolation than, say, the ironic and hermetic *Les Malheurs des immortels*, which requires intellectual detachment on the part of the reader-viewer.

Breton's trip to Martinique, his subsequent shift to a more epic form of poetry as exemplified in his *Ode to Charles Fourier* (1948), and his article on Lam published in *Le Surréalisme et la peinture* all have some pertinence to our discussion. In the 1924 manifesto, Breton had stated the need for a new man. With the contact of the *barbare* in Rimbaud's sense of the marvellous, the *ailleurs*, a new form of transcendence emerged in which Césaire and Lam could gradually assume a central position. However, the painter may not have reduced Césaire's world as radically as we suggested, to an intimate correspondence between the human and the cosmic, the ritual and the organic. Lam's drawing suggests simultaneously an upward and a downward direction: totemic animal heads with horns and threatening fangs hang or are bent downward, while partly visible, large hands grip the earth (see Fig. 89). The drawing suggests the duality of an inclination toward the earth and a leap upward speaking of fertility, luminosity, proliferation. The figure culminates in a starlike explosion in which metamorphoses participate. By this dual direction the spatial context is created through a contrasting dynamic surging beyond good and evil. By this structure Lam denies that Césaire's text is only a litany, prayer, or prophecy, exclusively written in the future tense.

AIR MEXICAIN

In 1952 the Librairie Arcanes published a slim volume entitled *Air mexicain*: the names of both the surrealist poet Benjamin Péret and the Mexican painter Rufino Tamayo appeared on the title page. As early as 1929, Péret participated actively in political and revolutionary movements in Latin America as well as Spain. He visited the Canary Islands, Brazil, and Mexico, and he lived among the Indians of the Amazon. He also displayed his opposition to the values and institutions of the Third Republic and Western culture by militant intervention and self-imposed exile. At the time he wrote *Air mexicain* he had lived for nine years in Mexico.[23]

[23]For a detailed account of Péret's interest in Mexican culture see "Péret et le Mexique" in *Benjamin Péret*, edited by Jean-Michel Goutier (Paris: Editions Veyrier, 1982).

The title suggests that Péret is singing about Mexican life and poetry, that he owes both rhythm and inspiration to them, and he asserts that his text will bear the imprint of a Mexican face. Jean-Marc Debenetti closely examines the role of myths in the poem: "Thus, most of the images encountered in *Mexican Air* stem either from the literal translation of Nahuatl metaphors or from the evocation of one or another aspect of Nahua symbolic mythology. This applies in particular to colors and numbers."[24] By referring frequently to sound, music, and rhythm, the poem recaptures and transmits natural and mythical forces. Words referring to face, skin, and appearance convey an interplay between features revealed and features hidden.

Tensions between or successions of divergent forces characterize the surrealist poem. Péret creates an "air," an atmosphere of tension; the volcano with its eruptions acts as the image of time past, present, and future. Continual shifts occur from one level to another. The past, long buried, erupts from subterranean layers: "Son cri retentit dans la nuit comme l'annonce de la fin des temps" (His cry reverberates in the night as though to announce the end of time).[25] Nonetheless, direct prophecies of an apocalypse can raise hopes. The present moment consists of successions of spectacles, rituals, and gestures which can neither be conceived as a unity nor focused by a single word: "et des paroles noyées dont le corps momifié flotte flotte et s'envole d'un coup d'aile dans un rais de lumière qui s'éteignant les rejettera sur la terre pour qu'elles donnent des fruits d'obsidienne" (and drowned speech whose mummified body floats floats and takes wing in a ray of light which, when it dies out, will throw them back on the ground to have them produce obsidian fruits) (p. 217). Grammatical tenses change rapidly. Allusions to seasons, especially spring, suggest new beginnings and a purification expressed by running water, by storms and fire rituals. Such returns bring with them gusts of energy, recrudescences of natural resources and fertility, alternating and even mingling with forces of degeneration and decline.

> *tu n'auras plus que mon souffle pour t'endormir*
> *sur les vagues furieuses de la terre*
> *comme une algue agonisante avec son corail captif.*
> [p. 255]

> You will have only my breath to put you to sleep
> on the raging waves of the earth
> like an agonizing alga with its captive coral.

[24]Jean-Marc Debenetti, "A propos d'*Air mexicain*," in Goutier, *Benjamin Péret*.
[25]Benjamin Péret, *Oeuvres complètes*, vol. II (Paris: Losfeld, 1971), p. 215. All quotations are from this edition.

In the introduction to his *Anthologie des mythes, légendes et contes populaires*, Péret states: "Le pas qu'il a fait la veille ne le dispense nullement du pas du lendemain puisque tout est à recommencer tous les jours et ce qu'il a acquis à l'heure du sommeil est tombé en poussière à son réveil" (The step he has taken the day before in no way exempts him from the step he will take on the morrow, because everything must begin once again every day, and whatever he acquires during moments of sleep falls to dust upon his awakening).[26] Thus movement is continuous; a complete halt never occurs.

Time, which does not follow a linear pattern, cannot be measured. As forgetfulness is reversible, memory, contrary to Breton's postulates, does not produce division. Time pulsates, beats a rhythm, bursts into action; it assimilates years to a single moment while avoiding meditation and speculation; time spans transform into a conscious presence or awareness. As Péret says, "Ils arrivent du berceau des hérons d'aurore et marchent pendant que les années se nouent d'elles-mêmes en deux bottes d'asperges décapitées" (They arrive from the cradle of the herons of dawn and advance while the years get themselves knotted into two bunches of decapitated asparagus) (p. 226).

These opposing forces, these crescendos and diminuendos engage the fundamental elements of nature: air, fire, water, earth. Fire, the foremost element, and air emerge in fertilizing and sterilizing cycles as they erupt in incendiary power or the gusts of tornados; healing rains may succeed wild torrents; earth can take the shape of a steep mountain or of dispersing dust. Motion through space ranges from stellar heights to underground caves, from vast elevations to narrow, dark gorges. Engaged in either quest or conquest, all creatures cross vast domains to spur further encounters: "Nul doute que le grand serpent à plumes las d'une migration sans espoir ne revienne vers son peuple aux yeux de cratère" (No doubt whatever that the great plumed serpent, tired of a hopeless migration, will return to its crater-eyed people) (p. 227). Rapid flights, sudden drownings, unexpected leaps, and explosively rising temperatures move north, south, east, and west. Presumably these movements relate to the four suns that preceded the sun of the Aztec world: the northern sun, sun of darkness; the southern sun, sun of fire; the eastern sun, sun of water; and the western sun, sun of magic. The dark, northern direction is repeatedly invoked:

Il écoute et n'entend couler que le torrent de sa sueur d'or avalée par le Nord noir.

[p. 215]

It listens and hears only the torrential flow of its golden sweat swallowed by the black North.

[26] *Anthologie*, p. 30.

Le Nord en deuil perpétuel déjà rejetait ses vagues d'êtres.

[p. 223]

The North in perpetual mourning was already rejecting its waves of beings.

The north represents the bleakness which must be overcome; it also points in the direction of barbarians who have not adopted the cult of the corn god.

In the powerful interactions of nature's forces, sky, sun, and moon undergo violent metamorphoses. Isolation of individual contours becomes impossible, for they reveal unexpected affinities through their encounters or clashes. By means of dynamic transformations the deeply buried secret turns into revelation, without abolishing the mysterious forces that inscribe enigmatic numbers and codes. Allusions to death and oblivion—"forêt pétrifiée" (petrified forest), "soleil d'oubli" (sun of forgetfulness), "des échos calcinés" (calcinated echoes)—produce cumulative effects leading not to final burials but to reversals. Hatred, rage, hostility, however destructive they may seem, generate forces indispensable to a struggle for liberation. The irrational asserts itself incessantly; delirium, hallucination, and intoxication predominate, heightening the impact of sacrificial rites, eliminating calculations and interest: "vers les étendues de viande bouillante dont l'effarement imite le galop de l'ombre s'avançant l'éclair à la main vers le délire des branches" (toward the expanses of boiling flesh whose fright imitates the shadow's gallop as it advances, with lightning in its hand, toward the ravings of branches) (p. 219).

Air mexicain, like many another surrealist text, bursts out, unleashing physical forces and denying all forms of stability. More indeed than pre–World War II surrealist texts, it refers to warfare and conquests, violent actions which add to the calamities produced by natural forces, calamities which are by no means episodic: "l'enfant que nous édifierons au bord du lac où nous a chassé la grande marée de son ennemi tantôt vainqueur tantôt vaincu" (the child that we shall establish on the shores of the lake where we were driven by the great tide of his sometimes triumphant, sometimes vanquished enemy) (p. 218). Moreover, lions, eagles, tigers, serpents, and scorpions, intimately linked to Aztec myths, enhance, for the French reader, the presence of violence and threat. *Air mexicain*, like Breton's *Martinique, charmeuse de serpents* (1948) or *Ode à Charles Fourier* (1947), evokes an uncontaminated world free from bourgeois customs and industrial domination. Péret uses surrealist imagery in conjunction with Aztec myths to celebrate in his verse the rise and fall of mysterious deities. The past survives in subconscious forces of dream; when it emerges in the present, it encounters modern forces hostile to both nature and man. Survival can be assured only by repeated or continuous rituals and ceremonies as mankind, by gestures, appeases offended gods. Restriction and liberation create reversible tensions. Thus rituals, although enactments of past moments, become timeless manifestations of desire and imagination; they reiterate the rejection of Christian suffering and distortion.

As the poem progresses, Mexican, especially Aztec, allusions multiply. The sun and animals such as the jaguar and the eagle, all incarnations of Mexican divinities, recur throughout the poem, acting in conformity with the myth as mediators and participating as gods in man's world.[27] Such myths blend into the poetic text without creating discordances, without disturbing Péret's usual surrealist strategies. The plumed serpent cannot be isolated or delineated as a force, for by its dual nature—it is a reptile with a bird's plumage—it has the ambiguity of a surrealist motif. Rampant movements and eclosion of venomousness become ubiquitous—a radiating, contagious presence clearly corresponding to the Aztec tradition: "En fait tout est serpent: les traces de pas humain, les rubans qui flottent, les rivières, la pluie, les éclairs, les processions, etc. La mer qui entoure le monde est le plus grand serpent" (In fact everything is serpentine: the traces of human steps, floating ribbons, streams, rain, lightning, processions, etc. The sea that encircles the world is the largest serpent).[28] Péret's outspoken hostility toward Catholicism and its clergy plays a role very subsidiary to that of ceremonies and sacrifices relating to primitive gods. The most violent flow of blood becomes a manifestation of life's cycles: its power of regeneration through death, of liberation through imprisonment.

Air mexicain, in its length, its scope, and its thematics, is epic poetry. Its very form—its long sentences, abuse of rhetoric, rhythmic patterns, and all-encompassing movement—distinguishes it from surrealist lyric texts. Péret not only welds natural, timeless forces to Aztec myths but brings to bear the social and political forces of modern Mexican history. The poem, by stressing the alternation of strength and weakness, of rise and decline, endorses the Aztec belief in episodes and cycles.

The poem does not gloss over the ultimate pessimism in Aztec mythology, which predicts a final cataclysm.

Les Voilà qui reviennent les ombres barbares à face de dollar numéroté. Regardez-les ronger les pierres qui portent la honte au front ronger la terre qui les voudrait dissoudre ronger les hommes jusqu'au coeur qu'elles empestent. [p. 232]

---

[27]Cf. the section on "Les Aztèques" in Pierre Grimal, ed., *Mythologie des peuples lointains* (Paris: Larousse, 1963), p. 196.
[28]Ibid., p. 195.

Here they are back again, these barbarian shadows faced like a numbered dollar. See them gnawing stones bearing shame on their brow, gnawing the earth which is eager to dissolve them, gnawing and infecting men to their very core.

Here pessimism pertains not only to a natural cataclysm, as in mythological prophecies, but also to more recent events in Mexican history, to Zapata and Juarez. Aztec culture becomes almost simultaneous with recent threats and invasions. Natural cataclysm and myth are finally overshadowed by historic events which presently threaten and will ultimately crush civilization's most dynamic forces. As metaphors of compression, corruption, disease, perversion, imprisonment, and lack of light creep into the poem, they gradually obliterate the sun cults:

Rien n'y fait. L'homme qui vit du soleil battant la charge est devenu un champion de cave pour les rats de la terre et la terre meurt de faim tandis qu'un crapaud enfle jusqu'à se croire général de ses pustules. [p. 231]

Nothing doing. Man who lives on the sun beating a charge has become a cellar champion for earth rats and earth dies of hunger while a toad swells until it fancies itself the general of its pimples.

As in the quotation above—"son cri retentit dans la nuit . . ."—Péret denounces the decline of a world in which unadulterated vigor made the reverberations of song and the shout almost identical, in which dream and revolt, arising from the earth or the sea, overlapped. As long as caves explode and lava gushes forth, hell, doubling as a sun cult, is reversed in an upward aspiration.

In the final stanza the poet indicts modern bourgeois values and culture, which the surrealists strove to undermine. *Air mexicain* is a surrealist poem with a strong anti-colonialist message; it may almost be labeled a manifesto. It "rises" against the conqueror who builds societies on the destruction of entire peoples and, above all, of their beliefs. Even if the poem ends on a pessimistic note, it leaves open the possibility of liberating forces yet triumphing. Toward the end, terms implying slavery alternate with those designating liberation. Prophecy leads to revolution; the imperative need for action threatens the existence of the white conquest not only in Mexico but also in the United States. And Jean-Marc Debenetti convincingly relates the poem to the French context: "It is not a question of Péret exalting a poetic theme hitherto unknown in French literature; this long poem should also be understood as a war cry denouncing infamy (past, present, and future) and has its only echo in revolt."[29]

Blocks of centuries, nightless years testify to the powers of the cosmos and of history, functioning not as memory but as experience. The poem shows the oneiric imagination of the Aztec culture as it merges with surrealism. By cross-fertilization the poem not only echoes or reflects creation but becomes its incarnation. In his introduction Péret asks: "Si l'homme d'hier ne connaissant d'autres limites à sa pensée que celles de son désir, a pu dans sa lutte *contre* la nature, produire ces merveilleuses légendes, que ne pourra pas créer l'homme de demain *conscient* de sa nature et dominant de plus en plus le monde d'un esprit libéré de toute entrave?" (If men of the past, knowing no other limits to their power than those of desire, could in their struggle *against* nature produce these marvellous legends, what cannot be done by the men of tomorrow, *aware* of their nature and more and more dominating the world with a mind freed of all impediments?)[30] Even as he reveals his own defeats the poet raises the hopes of his readers.

. . .

In spite of his long friendship with Octavio Paz, Rufino Tamayo did not have very pronounced literary interests and, consequently, in his rare statements about painting he primarily stressed its plastic qualities. Tamayo illustrated three books, *Aztlan: Songes mexicains*, published the same year as *Air mexicain*, and in 1959 *L'Apocalypse de Saint Jean*. (Although the New Testament text and Péret's poem seem to have little in common, the former could be described as epic and the latter as apocalyptic.) Octavio Paz clearly distinguished Tamayo's conception of illustration from that of the surrealists: "The canvas became the plastic counterpart of the poetic image. Not the visual translation of the verbal poem, as for several surrealists, but a plastic metaphor, nearer Miró than Max Ernst."[31] Tamayo's book illustrations show French influence, insofar as the *livre de peintre* never really tempted the major artists of the Mexican League of Revolutionary Painters—Diego Rivera, Jose Clemente Orozco, David Alfaro Siqueiros, and Tamayo himself. Mural paintings afforded them a more appropriate mode of conveying their art than the expensive intimacy and possessiveness of limited editions.

Tamayo's canvases appear simple and streamlined compared to surrealist

---

[29] "A propos d'*Air mexicain*," p. 142.
[30] *Anthologie*, p. 28.
[31] *Rufino Tamayo: Myth and Magic* (New York: Guggenheim Museum, 1979), p. 11.

imagery with its web of expanding analogies and its multiple hybrid forms. Tamayo's two-toned and two-dimensional representations form colorful constellations and can be called illuminations. In the Mexican painter's world, a slice of watermelon acts like a sun without adopting its shape and thus creates a truly plastic ambiguity. Often he represents figures in motion, stretching out their arms or dancing rhapsodically. Yet they always seem self-contained, as though the purely plastic order imposed upon them intensified movement without producing a metamorphosis or suggesting a transgression. Through his figures Tamayo implies curtailment of distances. In his pictorial space, sky and earth become very close. Like Péret and other surrealists who bring distant objects within immediate reach, Tamayo's spatial explorations are revealed by titles such as *Terror cósmico (Cosmic Terror)* (1954), *Avión más rápido que el sonido (Supersonic Plane)* (1954), and *El astrónomo (The Astronomer)* (1954), for in each case the human and the cosmic events are marked on the same scale. This produces an effect of extreme density and compactness, where a vector functions not only linearly but also dynamically, suggesting concentration or dispersal of forces. These general characteristics of Tamayo's art appear in both his canvases and his lithographs.

Although André Breton includes an article on Tamayo in his 1965 edition of *Le Surréalisme et la peinture*, he makes no explicit association between the painter and surrealism. Indeed, he endorses Tamayo's own statement that he tried above all to create a Mexican art and to rediscover its lost purity. The quality that Breton most admired in Tamayo, the poetic language that fosters a return to a fundamental unity, is a quality that he perceived in surrealist artists such as Ernst and, above all, Miró. By his art Tamayo succeeded in bridging the gap between man and outer space:

Monde moins policé que le nôtre, et d'autant mieux pris dans l'engrenage lyrique, où tout trouve sa réponse de haut en bas de la création et où, comme Tamayo le montre aussi, les nerfs de l'homme tendus à se rompre, prêtent toute résonance aux cordes des constellations.

A world less organized than our own and for that very reason caught all the more tightly in the mesh of lyricism, a world in which everything, from the top to the bottom of creation, finds its particular echo, a world where, as Tamayo also shows, man's nerves are stretched to breaking-point and so lend a marvellous resonance to the strings of the constellations. [32]

Tamayo's art, linked to the Mexican soil and coming after the Mexican revolution, rediscovers the Eternal Mexico and thus speaks the universal lan-

---

[32]*Le Surréalisme et la peinture*, p. 234; trans. Taylor, *Surrealism and Painting*, p. 234.

FIG. 90. Colored title page by Rufino Tamayo from Benjamin Péret, *Air mexicain*. Paris: Librairie Arcanes, 1952. Reprinted by permission of the artist.

guage that Breton discovered in surrealism. Tamayo's indebtedness to pre-Columbian art and culture was exemplified in the 1979 retrospective exhibit in the Guggenheim Museum. By juxtaposition of his art with pre-Columbian works Tamayo's association with this remote past emerged most dramatically. In *Air mexicain* Tamayo's adherence not to surrealism but to the Mexican past, to its art and culture, is made apparent in two figures inscribed on each page. The first, an emblem of a corn god, and the second, an unidentified figure, are slightly modified copies of glyphs (Plate 29). Thus every page, by doubling as old manuscript inscription and modern printing, combines reduction with expansion. From the paper emerges the encounter of past and present, of image and text, of repetition and proliferation. In the very act of endorsing Péret's text Tamayo discreetly modifies and strengthens its ties to the past.

The lettering of the book cover is interwoven with ears of corn, representing the basic agricultural product of the country, dating back at least to the Mayas (Fig. 90). Pre-Columbian Indians believed that maize, with its sun-colored glow, was a gift of the gods. The eleven ears of corn adorning the eleven letters of the cover are all different: they float like open flowers or birds with unopened wings; they suggest a stellar constellation without relinquishing their vegetable identity. They announce the richness of Péret's transformational imagery by recalling Mexican myths. These myths are not only suggested by Tamayo's decoration of the words, which are thus, from the very inception, endowed with ritual powers, but they correspond to the reverberations of the poem:

Le frisson qui se hâte sur sa peau d'épines court depuis que le maïs se lisse dans le vent. [p. 215]

The shiver that hurries along its skin of thorns has run ever since the corn's soft unfolding in the wind.

Here the corn creates a link; it becomes an agent of propagation, a movement of transformation, as depicted on the cover:

Mais voici qu'il entraîne dans son sillage de maïs en fleur des silhouettes vaporeuses de visages blancs à barbe de caverne abritant mille scorpions au dard dressé. [p. 227]

But presently it sweeps along in its wake of flowering corn vaporous outlines of white faces with cavern beards sheltering a thousand scorpions ready to sting.

In the second quotation the personified corn becomes even more obviously an agent of transformation, as threatening manifestations displace orderly, blooming fields; in this capacity, it marks a stage in the intensification of the hero's quest.

In the third lithograph, where the yellow, flowering surface is surrounded and compressed from all sides, Tamayo orders the temporal sequence of the poem into a scene of spatial simultaneity, yet without suggesting the propulsion characteristic of the poetic text. The first plate, representing visually all the objects named in the text (Plate 30), corresponds to the dramatization of specific images such as:

De l'oeil qui éveille pour mieux endormir était descendu le serpent à plumes blanc et barbu offrant comme jadis au sommet des monts d'adoration à la lumière et à l'ombre. [p. 223]

From the eye that awakens so as all the better to put to sleep had descended the serpent, white-plumed and bearded, offering as before on mountaintops adoration to light and shadow.

By the spatial arrangement Tamayo suggests interrelationships, perhaps even causality. However, he does not allude in a single plate to recurrent contrasts, increasing tensions, temporal references, including the promise of a return so central to Péret's poem. In Tamayo's lithograph the ritual is represented by a luminous constellation giving cosmic expression to the Aztec myth, not by explosive clashes as in the poem. But the first plate, illustrating a specific passage or image, also takes into account the narrative sequence of the text. The plumed serpent, white in color and impressive in size, its folded wings partially overlapping the white arabesque of the sky, contrasts with the pattern formed by two towering black mountains, volcanoes or pyramids, phallic shapes stained by red streaks. Suggesting forces of death and evil, the mountains complement the image of the plumed serpent, savior of mankind but, like all gods, demanding sacrifices. Serpent and volcanoes come closest to an encounter in a yellow zone uniting diffuse sunlight with golden corn, both reminders of divine intervention. A huge, open eye, closer to surrealist iconography than any other image here, enhances the visionary and moral aspects of the first plate. The overwhelming proportions of the eye, with its unadulterated blue and black and the intrusion of gray, stormy forces unrelieved by smoothly colored surfaces or straight lines, underscore the resurgence of a threatening nature and impending transformations. Like Péret, Tamayo represents forces in a state of confrontation on each plate, but he usually understates their aggression, their cataclysmic effects.

If the first plate introduces opposing forces, the last one reveals the direct results of their antagonism. The power of light has diminished; sun and corn have shrunk almost to the vanishing point. The serpent coils over vast surfaces, while the volcano is reduced to a single bloodstained tower. The serpent, who in the first plate speaks for a divine presence, is metamorphosed into a black, all-embracing spiral. The Aztec culture loses its status, surviving only as a feeble echo of its former prestige. Tamayo responds to the narrative course of the poem in its broad outlines; he recognizes its epic qualities by accounting for the emergence and decline of Aztec culture and by stressing Mexican myths rather than by rendering the text's surrealist imagery or the complexity of its webs.

The second and third lithographs include almost no recognizable allusions to the serpent and the volcanoes. The second plate, similar to one of the illustrations of the apocalypse, displays constellated forces that do not really evoke an eventual confrontation. Its latent energy radiates in all sectors while maintaining an extraordinary equilibrium. An almost completely black sun surmounts a dark net covering most of the surface. Its combined upward and downward movements amid curved and straight lines appear essentially as variations in black of dislocated sunrays: "la pyramide que caressera le soleil arrêté pour ronronner au-dessus de nous" (the pyramid that the sun will caress stopping to purr above us) (p. 219), "de l'ombre qui étrangle avec le délire de ses vols noirs" (of the shadow that strangles with the delirium of its black flights) (p. 218). The black birds in their downward flight relinquish their divine origins.

In the third lithograph white masks spotted with red surrounding a golden circle produce almost formless contrasts and dashes (Plate 31). In parodying our modern, shadow-like civilization with its crushing power, Tamayo may even overstate the pessimism of the text. The yellow surface, referring once more to germinating forces contained in the sunny expanses of golden corn, is repulsed and cornered by four scorpion-like forms. So strong a threat of extinction by violence, poison, and imprisonment, so powerful an alliance of negative forces is never expressed with such concentration by Péret. The poet does not dichotomize opposing forces, good or bad, black or white, but points to their inevitability in a cosmic material and spiritual struggle for survival. For Péret all forces participate in a vast struggle in which their potential metamorphosis, their fluctuating dynamism may prove to be beneficial. Tamayo selects stages in an epic movement representing the rise and fall of the Aztec civilization, but he omits the call to revolution, which extends to all continents and people. Tamayo does not join Péret's appeal linking surrealism and revolution, but chronicles in apocalyptic terms the myth that is embedded in the poem and surfaces in various ways in so many of his paintings. Tamayo's illustrations offer little promise for the future but greatly enhance the present.

· · ·

Whether we compare Péret and Césaire from the point of view of their philosophical or poetical stances (not our prime concern in these pages) or whether we examine mainly the relation of the illustrators to the poets, we cannot overlook the discrepancies between their commitments just because they all were at different moments linked to surrealism. From the writers' point of view, experimental poetic technique was at the service of the message and the cause. Whereas Péret, to incite anti-capitalist action, principally speaks of Indian and Mexican revolts which had already taken place or would soon take place, Césaire achieves personal awareness in a poetic discourse that can be considered almost equivalent to Descartes's methodical pursuit of logical truth. He finds himself caught between surrealism and the search for Black origins, a dichotomy which cannot be completely resolved.

For Tamayo, himself of Indian origin, the illustrations did not require the same type of adjustment. The Mexican myths remained his first allegiance, and this may explain why he did not accompany the poet in his more utopian formulations and prophecies. For Lam the discovery of origin linked to the jungle, rather than the clash between social classes and civilizations, could lead to plenitude and purity. Awareness for him meant a return to hauntingly familiar signs rather than the elaboration of new methods and new rhetorics, verbal or plastic.

CHAPTER EIGHT

DISPLACEMENT OF NARRATIVE

SURREALIST ILLUSTRATORS, as we have repeatedly stated, shunned mimesis no less than the cubists who preceded them; they did not wish, in the manner of their nineteenth-century predecessors, to supply a graphic paraphrase of the text. This refusal to imitate persists even when the pictures, as in Breton's *Nadja*, appear to provide reliable documentation or when a sequence of images purports to function as a continuous narrative even to the extent of substituting for words, as is the case in Ernst's *Une Semaine de bonté*. In both of these thoroughly surrealistic works, narrative continuity is totally subverted for the sake of perilous forays from the banality and corruption of everyday existence into the world of the marvellous.

In order to achieve their subversive tasks, both Breton and Ernst ground their works as convincingly as possible in everyday experience, the former by multiplying his so-called documents, the latter by referring in his title to a well-intentioned but silly institution of the Third Republic, "la semaine de bonté." Ernst of course uses the title ironically, for he shows a spreading of evil deeds during every day in the week and, unlike Franz Masereel, who created the genre of the graphic novel, he offers little hope for future goodness.[1]

NADJA

Nadja has provoked debates concerning the literary genre, if any, to which it belongs, its reliability as autobiography, its psychological value, and the nature of its narrative.[2] We focus our discussion on the problematics of *Nadja*

[1] Cf. Franz Masereel, *Das Werk* (Munich: Kurt Wolff, 1928); *Die Idee* (Paris: Ollendorff, 1920).
[2] See Renée Riese Hubert, "*Nadja* depuis la mort de Breton," *Oeuvres et Critiques* II, 1, *Prose romanesque du XXème siècle* (Spring 1977): 93–103; Marc Bertrand, "*Nadja*, un secret de fabrication surréaliste," *L'Information Littéraire* 31 (1980): 82–90, 125–30; Lawrence D. Kritzman, "For Structural Analysis of *Nadja*: A Scientific Experiment," *Racksham Literary Studies* 4 (1973): 9–23.

as an illustrated book, for, unlike others we have examined, it does not rely on the participation or partnership of a visual artist. Breton himself by no means put the image in painting on an equal footing with the photographic image. Differing from those in *Facile*, *Nadja's* seventy-five photographs serve as adjuncts to the written word. While Breton refers to the accompanying photographs in *L'Amour fou* and *Les Vases communicants* as *figures*, he defines those in *Nadja* as *illustration photographique*. Judith Preckshot clearly explains that different concepts of photography prevail: "We should note that *L'Amour fou* was published nine years after [1937] *Nadja* and evinces an evolution in Breton's concept of photographic illustration in the shifting of the lens from the object in reality to the object as imagined, or as placed in a network of imagined relations."[3] Breton indicates that on several occasions he used available photographs; others were specially made, not for artistic purposes, but to preserve faithfulness and authenticity. Even Man Ray's portraits have no more than an ancillary function in Breton's daring interpretations. From the very start, the reader-spectator guesses that the visual and verbal interrelations, from a spatial as well as a textual point of view, have subtly been rendered enigmatic by Breton.

Critics tend to suggest that the photographs have essentially documentary functions, that at least some of them replace descriptions deliberately omitted from the text. The author himself, in his 1962 *Avant-dire*, states that he used photography in order to eliminate description. In *Le Manifeste* Breton had launched an attack on the realism and mimesis still prevalent in fiction at the time. In *Nadja* he reminds the reader of what the Place du Panthéon looks like: he makes it visible but refrains from providing an intellectual and subjective verbal description.

Although photography plays a substantial role in this text which moves further and further away from persuasion and objective perception, Breton himself expresses doubts, on more than one occasion, concerning his photographic venture:

je tenais en effet, tout comme de quelques personnes et de quelques objets, à en donner une image photographique qui fût prise sous l'angle spécial dont je les avais moi-même considérés. A cette occasion, j'ai constaté qu'à quelques exceptions près ils se défendaient plus ou moins contre mon entreprise, de sorte, selon moi, que la partie illustrée de Nadja *fût à mon gré insuffisante.*

[3] Judith Preckshot, "Breton's *Nadja*, a Family Album," unpublished paper. Preckshot insists on the different statuses of photographic illustrations and of those that appear in the *livre de peintre*, as the former resembles the unordered collection of mementos that characterizes a family album.

I wanted in fact—with some of the people and some of the objects—to provide a photographic image of them taken at the special angle from which I myself had looked at them. On this occasion, I realized that most of the places more or less resisted my venture, so that, as I see it, the illustrated part of *Nadja* is quite inadequate.[4]

According to Breton, photography should be highly subjective, strictly immediate or instantaneous, a style not normally associated with documentation. Breton chose the reproductions and made known his assessment of them only at the end of his quest. His intent would not be incompatible with Johannes Molzahn's rather bold assessment of photography and its functioning: "Photography will be one of the most effective weapons against intellectualization, against mechanization of the spirit."[5] In other words, it may count as an active agent in the surrealist war against bourgeois domination. At the end of *Nadja* the reader understands that Breton has subverted the photographs in all their banality and metamorphosed them into the marvellous.[6] The photographic project evolved with the writing of the text. The distance between the verbal and the visual varies throughout, so that the "illustrations" never function simply as an addition to a completed text.

In the beginning the photographs operate less as substitutes for more complete verbal descriptions than as frames of reference, situating places where Breton's itinerary originated. As the author's material transformed itself by stages into a *récit*, he realized that the photographic image had become incompatible with his writing. "Objects" had become convulsive and shied away from the lens. His basis for rejecting mimesis had widened. Early in the book, when he speaks of Giorgio de Chirico's art, Breton makes a statement which, if applied to the photographs, reveals that they do not really facilitate the process of recognition:

Certes l'oeuvre qui en résultait restait "liée d'un lien étroit avec ce qui avait provoqué sa naissance," mais ne lui ressemblait qu'à la façon étrange dont se ressemblent deux frères, ou plutôt l'image en rêve d'une personne déterminée et cette personne réelle.

[p. 15]

---

[4]*Nadja* (Paris: Gallimard, 1964), p. 199; trans. Richard Howard (New York: Grove Press, 1977), pp. 151–52. All quotations are from these editions.
[5]Quoted in Rosalind Krauss, "When Words Fail," *October* 22 (Fall 1982): 91. See also *L'Amour fou: Photography and Surrealism*, ed. Rosalind Krauss and Jane Livingston (New York: Abbeville Press, 1985).
[6]Lollie Groth has shown that, in *Nadja*, banal photographs are turned into manifestations of the marvellous: "Photographs in *Nadja*," unpublished.

Certainly the resulting work remained "closely linked with what had provoked its birth," but resembled it only in the strange way two brothers resemble each other, or rather as a dream about someone resembles that person in reality.   [p. 15]

Breton's remark about the inadequacy of the photographs comments primarily on the nature of the text, on its genesis, rather than on the reliability of the photographs as faithful illustrations of his *récit* or as "witnesses." Taken by themselves the photographs, whether we look at them singly or as a series, do not move the viewer; they are divorced from what Barthes would call adventure. The following comment from *La Chambre claire* would apply to Breton's "visual" documentation if we disregarded *Nadja* as text: "Photography is vaguely established as object while the characters appearing in it are clearly set up as characters, but only because of their resemblance to human beings, without any particular intentionality. They float in between the shores of perception, of sign, and of image, without ever reaching any of them."[7] Whether we refer to Roland Barthes's statement or to Breton's self-judgment, the introduction of photography raises the question of resemblance and identity, of reality versus shadow, the liberation of which the surrealists practiced in their literature and art. Breton uses photography in *Nadja* as a distorting echo, a practice somewhat similar to Dalí's in his illustrations of *Alice in Wonderland*. In a more general context, Breton said, "Subjectivité et objectivité se livrent au cours d'une vie humaine une série d'assauts" (p. 6) (subjectivity and objectivity in the course of a human existence engage one another in a series of assaults). The photographic illustrations, "vaste dossier saisi sur le vif" (vast true-to-life file), situated among pages of text cannot be considered static, unchangeable, reliable, easily accessible, for they collide here and there with the text or set up a tension with it. In short, they foster *hasard objectif* at the expense of mimesis.

Gilbert Lascault shows that indeed the photographs, instead of enhancing, undermine the objective and realistic dimensions of the *récit*.[8] Breton includes the photograph of La Place du Panthéon with L'Hôtel des Grands Hommes seemingly to provide the point of departure of his peregrinations. However, the function of the "true-to-life" photograph remains ambiguous. In omitting verbal description from the text in order to reintroduce it by means of "reproductions," Breton reveals the banality of description in the

[7]Roland Barthes, *La Chambre claire* (Paris: Seuil, 1980), p. 39.
[8]"L'Illustration surréaliste de l'égarement quotidien," *XXᵉᵐᵉ Siècle: Le Surréalisme* XLII (1974): 117–21.

ordinary literary work while leaving his own text intact. Lascault discusses the nonlinear characteristics of the *récit*, the difference between chronological time and autobiographical notation, as distances vary between protagonist, narrator, and author, between experience and its transformation into *écriture*. He claims that these nonlinear systems break our linear progression in reading. We are forced to trace some of our steps backward or skip forward when we encounter photographs which, with one or two exceptions, refer to specific passages in the text: both a relevant page and a quotation are provided. The illustrations impose upon the reader a rereading of a certain passage. Such rereadings, far from establishing parallelisms between text and image, produce a corrosive effect and tend to put into question the apparent clarity of meaning. The photographs, as we have stated in a different context, do not assume the function one might expect in illustrations—that is, of commentary or expansion of the text. Even if we were to consider the photographic material as realistic expansion, by substitution, of the text, the confrontation of text and image mainly brings to the surface the reductive and retrograde nature of the visual material as compared to the daring, exploratory text.

As Jacqueline Chénieux suggests, not all the photographs have the same function.[9] They occur with greatest frequency at the beginning of the *récit*, before Nadja enters the scene but at the time that Breton formulates in his autobiographical project his concern with errors and omissions. He claims to give points of reference but in reality he marks moments of disquieting interference with the ordinary functionings of life. The photographs decrease in number when the narrator and Nadja see each other most frequently and when the precise dates of their encounters are recorded. Temporal precision in a sense replaces the initial photographic realism but proves to be just as ineffective a prop for the *récit*. Photographs become more numerous after Nadja's disappearance; they tend to reproduce drawings and paintings while providing an accompaniment to Nadja's reactions. In the final section, when Nadja has irrevocably disappeared as a person and Breton reviews his experience and channels it into a mode of writing, visual materials once again occur less frequently.

Whatever the evolution of the photographs, Breton's illustrations must, of course, be seen in a verbal or even literary perspective, all the more because two-thirds of them include—aside from the captions—written or printed let-

---

[9] "Le Surréalisme et le roman: 1922–50," Thèse de Doctorat d'Etat présentée à la Sorbonne, 1979, vol. II, p. 304. This commentary has been partially reproduced in her book: *Le Surréalisme et le roman* (Lausanne: L'Age d'Homme, 1983).

ters, more or less fragmentary portions of the text. They entice the viewer to identify the images by deciphering the words: names on buildings, comments accompanying drawings, reproductions of pages from books. Even without reproduced words, the viewer will establish verbal links, for portraits represent writers, scenes from plays depend on texts, and paintings always bear titles. In *Nadja*, the pictures thus appear to function intertextually, in the critical as well as the etymological sense of the term.

Three photographs taken by Man Ray introduce Eluard, Péret, and Desnos, the first two in the attire of ordinary middle-class citizens. These photographs, as a means of assessing identity, hardly differ from the snapshot of the physician of Ste. Anne taken by Henri Manuel, who also took Breton's portrait. Desnos appears in a double pose recording his sleeping and waking exercises. The text supplies little information about Eluard's or Péret's identity. The impact of their encounter with the poet exceeds in importance their actual presence. Péret makes his influence felt in an occult manner even before he has a chance to appear, while Eluard's presence passes almost unnoticed and unidentified. Their portraits seem incommensurate with the mystery that surrounds their interferences.[10]

The reader, returning to the text after having glanced at the photograph of Blanche Derval, may very well find that her presence, if not her credibility, has been seriously undermined (Fig. 91). An actress at the Théâtre des Deux Masques, she performs the role of Solange, "personnage trop tenant pour être vrai" (too consistent a character to be true) and then is removed from the play, as though to announce, by an evanescent performance, the spectacular emergence and subsequent disappearance of Nadja. Breton includes at least two photographs of Parisian landmarks such as sites and statues without reference to the text (Fig. 92), as though to heighten the conflict between absence and presence. The statues of Etienne Dolet and Henri Becq do not function as stone portraits asserting an identity, but as strange, almost absurd, sources capable of exerting strong influences, the first on Nadja, the second on Breton. These cumbersome, ornate masses of stone paradoxically undermine our sense of stability and thrust us onto a road where attraction or repulsion acts as a stimulant making us aware of the absurdity of solid, recog-

---

[10]Gloria Feman Orenstein, "*Nadja* Revisited: A Feminist Approach," *Dada/Surrealism* (1978): 92, maintaining that the true meaning of Nadja's revelations are not disclosed, makes the following comments relating to the photographs: "Nadja's use of language corresponds more exactly to Breton's use of photography. Her questions are signals, denoting the identity of those charged objects, places and sensations or topics that point to the existence of the 'other' level of experience on which her own psychic life is lived."

FIG. 91. Photograph by
Henri Manuel, "Blanche
Derval," from André
Breton, *Nadja*. Paris:
Gallimard, 1964.

nizable landmarks. Whereas the photographs of Eluard and Péret conclude
the incidents, implying that they retrospectively furnish visible proof of the
influence of the occult, the statues serve as points of departure. In either case,
the photographic evidence fails to persuade the reader or viewer. The imita-
tive process falls short of its mark even at that level. Moreover, persuasion
would not be considered, from the surrealist point of view, as an acceptable
approach.

The photographs of the "Librairie de l'Humanité" and the café "A la
France Nouvelle" (Fig. 93) show quite ordinary buildings, whereas their
names express an optimistic view of the world in general and France in particular. But how can rejuvenation take place, considering the total absence of
clients from both the bookstore and the café? The café, selected as a meeting-
place by Breton and Nadja, never becomes the scene of their encounter. Absence and presence are reversed so as to cause confusion. Words no longer
carry a direct or accessible message, while the protagonists' encounters become separated from the kind of physical environment that counted so heav-

FIG. 92. Photograph, "La Statue d'Etienne Dolet," from André Breton, *Nadja*.

ily in the realist novel. The illustrations give the viewer disconcerting signals, reminiscent of the oracles of old.

Portraits, buildings, landmarks so evidently reminiscent of realism and so broadly selected in the early stages of the text constitute only a small part of the photographic dossier. More than one of Breton's photographs show printed or written documents: a page from the Dialogue between Hylas and Pilonous, of the History of France, the handwritten letter of an actor of the Théâtre Moderne, the printed program of *L'Etreinte de la pieuvre*. The latter two texts, in tiny indecipherable lettering, disturb the reader who looks eagerly for relevant information. From the point of view of pre-surrealist fiction the actor's letter is as useless to the narrator as to the reader. The printed program of the film refers to a serial of fifteen episodes and gives a partial account of the fifth, yet the text speaks of the eighth and final episode. The *récit* often changes direction; its enigmatic accountability is no more attenuated by the playbill than by the narrative, all the more because the ambiguous title heightens (but in no way explains) the author's fascination with the playbill.

FIG. 93. Photograph, "A la Nouvelle France," from André Breton, *Nadja*.

Breton does not succeed in centering or bolstering his fleeting identity in the context of a decrepit theater and a mediocre performance. And as only the bill or title of a movie is offered us, we suspect even more strongly that the illustrations share in the process of dissolving and depreciating established fictional techniques. By his oblique or devious use of photographed material Breton implies that both words and images fail as representations.

The photographic illustrations we have discussed so far, "copies" of people or objects taken from ordinary life, lose their "meaning," for they rarely create any context from one page to the next and do not "fit" into the text as enticement or explanation. Breton also includes images of what can be defined as surrealist objects—for example, the strange object found at the flea market, or one of the erotic figures or maps which Breton himself labels as perversions. Here mystery and desire arise from the photograph itself and hardly require the corroboration of the text.

Breton also includes a single glove, bent in the middle like a soft fabric that has hardened into metal, and related metonymically to the hand and metaphorically to the heart. In the text the narrator refers to two gloves, one sky blue and weightless, the other made of bronze. Each glove, deprived of both a function and an owner, stands as the metamorphosis of the other. Text and

FIG. 94. Drawing and cut-out by "Nadja" from André Breton, *Nadja*. Courtesy Gallimard, 1986.

image compound their ambiguities. Rosalind Krauss has discussed the dominant role of the hand in photographs from the nineteen-twenties.[11] She also mentions André Breton's self-portrait, a 1938 photomontage entitled "Automatic Writing," which refers to the relationship he had established between photography and automatism as early as 1920. Read in the context of Krauss's article, the allusions to the hand in *Nadja*, perhaps more visual than verbal, connect a number of incidents: the palmistry of Madame Sacco, Nadja's portraits, handwritten and hand-drawn documents. Not only does the empty or full glove add one more absence or presence, in a sense interchangeably, but also it clearly alludes to the hand that writes and clicks the camera, the hand that draws, that creates "sur le vif." Text and images represent themselves through the hand in whose palm a hidden inscription is enclosed. The image of the glove obliquely prognosticates the still unwritten text, the book that is "like a book."

Reproductions of drawings by Nadja and the art that provoked her intense

[11] "When Words Fail," pp. 91–103.

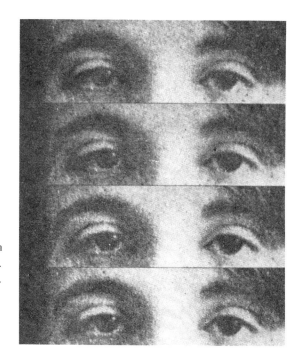

FIG. 95. Photograph from
André Breton, *Nadja*.
Courtesy Gallimard, 1986.

reactions function as a narrative in quite a different way (Fig. 94). Her draw-ings accompany her words and Breton comments on both.[12] The drawings originate in the domain of the imaginary without direct reference to everyday reality. They are made at a time when Nadja and Breton no longer see each other, when the protagonists' physical interactions play a steadily decreasing role. Thus the drawings participate in the creation of her physical image. Her imaginary museum consists of Braque, Ernst, de Chirico, a mask, and an Easter Island statue, to which she adds now and again her frequent signa-tures, enigmatic exclamations, as well as repeated references to herself and the narrator. Within the frame of the drawings she provides a new facet of her missing portrait, which indeed could never be represented in a single snap-shot, any more than her irrational behavior can be accounted for and fixed by any form of discourse. The portrait cannot say the unsayable; it cannot represent the unrepresentable. It remains for the writer and also the reader to assemble and to create.

[12]Both Preckshot and Orenstein, though from different perspectives, comment on the "pauci-ty" of Breton's remarks on the drawings. For a detailed commentary on the photographic series see Colette Guedj, "*Nadja* d'André Breton, ou l'exaltation réciproque du texte et de la photo-graphie," *Les Mots, la vie* (Nice: Publications du Groupe Eluard, 1984), pp. 91–131.

FIG. 96. Drawing and cut-out by "Nadja" from André Breton, *Nadja*. Courtesy Gallimard, 1986.

Three illustrations provide visual traces of the protagonist as adjunct to her drawings. Her eyes—the expression "yeux de fougères" (fernlike eyes) is repeated four times—isolated from the rest of the face, bring us to the threshold of the dream world (Fig. 95). A cut-out showing head and hand juxtaposed includes two of Nadja's signatures (Fig. 96). Whereas the first "portrait" abolishes the distinction between the viewer and the viewed, the second casts the protagonist in the double role of subject and object, artist and model. The cut-out does not present a portrait with tangible features, but "translates" Nadja's occult power. Her face, half hidden, is invaded by heart shapes. It becomes almost indistinguishable from the mask (like the glove from the hand). Heart shapes, the number 13 in the very center of the face, and her eyes all reveal the mysterious powers of interference. Shapes, numbers, and words all play a role. Nadja with her signature nestled in her lovelock can rightly be labeled a heart-catcher: "Découpage également, mais en deux parties de manière à pouvoir varier l'inclinaison de la tête, l'ensemble constitué par un visage de femme et une main" (p. 141) (likewise a cut-out, but in two parts, so as to vary the tilting of the head, the whole consisting of a woman's face and a hand; p. 121, translation emended). The cut-out with its ambigu-

FIG. 97. Photograph by
Pablo Volta from André
Breton, *Nadja*.

ous and mobile hand emphasizes the intangibility of the protagonist, for she
will not face the viewer from a stable, circumscribable perspective.

Shortly after Breton's statement concerning the problematics built into illustration, he refers to a "statue" of the Musée Grévin, the reproduction of
which would constitute an act of aggression (Fig. 97). In the 1959 edition, a
photo by Pablo Volta was added. The Musée Grévin, in 1928 a wax museum
housing the likenesses of great men, primarily those loyal to the Republic and
its institutions, held great appeal for the surrealists. Breton's wax figure represents a woman adjusting her garter. The poet completely subverted the
code of the museum; he rejected its conventionality and bourgeois hierarchy.
Breton says in the text that this statue, "dans sa pose immuable, est la seule
statue que je sache à avoir des 'yeux'" (p. 175) (in its immutable pose, is the
only statue I know of with 'eyes') (p. 152). An intimate gesture subversively
displaces a public pose. The poet endows his wax figure with vision while
conversely implying the blindness of all other museum worthies or celebrities
as well as of such characters as the psychiatrist of Ste. Anne, who is responsible for Nadja's internment.

Breton's text reveals the ambiguity of the wax figure without making the reproduction superfluous. The "portrait" focuses exclusively on legs and gloved hands; bust, feet, and head are absent. Sexual overdetermination prevails: the lifted skirt provokes the potential viewer, whose eyes willy-nilly meet the clearly outlined "eye" of the female genitals. Intrusion cannot be avoided. We are reminded of the rubber gloves depicted in the earlier photo and of the "yeux de fougères." The black-and-white contrast gives to this statue in its "immobile" pose a powerful luminosity like Nadja's own, soon to be eclipsed. Text and image engage in an interplay between withdrawal and revelation as well as in a game of substitutions among the various parts of the body, substitutions essential to surrealist liberation as practiced by Magritte, Ernst, and Bellmer. But the photograph has little to do with the Musée Grévin; caption, reproduction, and textual comments form a triangle in which the relative proximity of two elements seems to determine the greater distance of the third, as in Lautréamont's famous metaphor.

The photograph of Breton, placed just before the Musée Grévin photograph, toward the end of the book, may in the context of our discussion seem curiously misplaced. We may wonder both in relation to the text and to the photographic sequence what distinguishes it from the portraits of Desnos and Eluard, placed at the beginning. What counts is, of course, not so much the nature of the photograph as its relation to the text. Our classification according to the subject matter of the photographs may in this instance be misleading. Accompanying Breton's portrait are the words "J'envie tout homme qui a le temps de préparer quelque chose comme un livre" (p. 170) (I envy any man who has the time to prepare something like a book) (p. 149). The caption by Breton is on Breton. It is not an ironic and belated introduction or encounter. The portrait introduces Breton as writer at the very moment when both protagonist and narrator finally recede into the background.

UNE SEMAINE DE BONTÉ

La Femme 100 têtes, Une Semaine de bonté, and *Le Rêve d'une jeune fille qui voulut entrer au Carmel*, which Max Ernst calls novels,[13] are composed of collages accompanied by brief texts. A novel, however, by rights belongs to

---

[13] Max Ernst, *La Femme 100 têtes* (Paris: Carrefour, 1929); American edition: *The 100 Headless Woman* (New York: Dover). *Une Semaine de bonté* (Paris: Editions Jeanne Bucher, 1934); trans. J. J. Pauvert with the French title (New York: Dover, 1963). *Rêve d'une petite fille qui voulut entrer au Carmel* (Paris: Carrefour, 1930); American edition: *A Little Girl Dreams of Taking the Veil*, trans. Dorothea Tanning (New York: George Brazillier, 1982).

language, which in these works plays a role very subsidiary to the collages. *La Femme 100 têtes* and *Le Rêve d'une jeune fille* have captions for each plate. *Une Semaine de bonté*, composed of 180 collages, includes only a few words—titles, subtitles, quotations. It could be considered as an illustrated book for which Ernst created the collages and wrote the minimal text, but the very existence of a "text" remains questionable and its relevance to the collages by no means is evident. In view of the precarious situation of the text *Une Semaine de bonté* raises problems concerning its genre, both as novel and as illustrated book.

The title of the work and its subdivisions emphasize organization: one week subdivided into seven booklets corresponding to the days of the week. This apparently rigorous chronological order is not really carried through, however. After the fourth *cahier*, devoted to Wednesday, a final section covers Thursday, Friday, and Saturday. In his monumental study of Max Ernst's collages Werner Spies shows that the painter, inspired by Rimbaud's *Voyelles*, wrapped each *cahier* in a different color: "Max Ernst has confirmed in conversation that the different colors for the individual sections of *Une Semaine de bonté*, even if they are not equivalents, suggest Rimbaud's 'Voyelles.'"[14] This reference in *Une Semaine de bonté* to literature does not suggest a novel, nor does it directly relate to Ernst's text. The painter submits neither to his own plan of organization nor to Rimbaud's colors. And how could the poet's vowels introduce Ernst's days of the week? We clearly face several displacements or substitutions. Both the shift involving the numbers and the simultaneous, albeit dual, scheme of arranging the days should alert the viewer or reader. We might construe the use of Rimbaud by Ernst as an absolutely minimal quotation in a subversive text, according to Antoine Compagnon: "Quotation is a privileged element of the adaptation, for it is a locus of recognition, a guide in reading. It is perhaps for this reason that no text, however subversive it attempts to be, completely renounces all manner of quotation. Subversion displaces all competences, confuses their typology, but does not abolish them in principle, which would be tantamount to cutting oneself off from all reading." He relates quotation to collage: *les ciseaux* (scissors) and *le pot à colle* (paste pot), reading and writing, being merely a more adult version of collage.[15] We shall see that Ernst's minimal text, including the words naming the days of the week, relies heavily, if not exclusively, on quotation. Indeed, both Ernst's collages and his text in *Une Semaine de bonté*, incom-

[14] *Max Ernst—Collagen* (Cologne: DuMont-Schauberg, 1974), p. 195.
[15] *La Seconde Main* (Paris: Seuil, 1979), pp. 23, 15.

patible as they may seem, can be considered as quotations, with minimal creation or transition.

The five colored envelopes were discarded in subsequent editions. They did not establish affinities among color, form, and sound as in the famous sonnet, nor was Ernst's book with its sociopolitical overtones compatible with the spiritual elevation which ultimately resulted from a secret order of linguistic signs. According to Spies, the color wrappers were to express the political aspects of *Une Semaine de bonté*. Rimbaud merely provided the clue that the 180 collages had a revolutionary intent. Purple is the color of the clergy, whose powers are displayed best on Sunday; Monday's green pertains to water; the perpetual presence of the fire-spitting dragon accounts for the redness of Tuesday. Oedipus in bequeathing his royal blood inaugurates a blue Wednesday; the cock prolongs the dark night, hence the blackness of Thursday. Spies's explanations reveal the complexity of the table of contents and demonstrate the unlikelihood of a coherent system dominating Ernst's so-called novel. The division of time according to days of the week seems barely valid, for reasons stated earlier. The blue and the purple have sociopolitical implications, redness can be equated with the adventures of revolutionary activity, but the green color standing for water fails to fit the scheme. Moreover, the mythical dragon, the legendary Oedipus, and the contemporary clergy cannot be situated in the same chronological system or have similar implications for the Third Republic.

Ernst introduces the days of the week not only by color but also by one or another of the four elements and by "examples." In the first four *cahiers* the element mainly provides a spatial context, but this system breaks down long before we reach the end of the week. On Thursday, not only the color but also the element is black. It follows mud, water, fire, and blood, which, in addition to spatial connotations, introduce the concept of cleansing. The blackness of Thursday refers to spiritual blindness; it now becomes difficult to separate space from time. Friday represents sight, and Saturday represents the unknown promise of a new world or at least a new departure.

In his choice of titles, subtitles, and announced categories, Ernst appears to remain faithful to the code of the classical novel: color equates with time, element with space, example with hero and action. In his use of examples, however, Ernst may have raised our expectations of a rational coherence only to destroy them at the first opportunity. Actually, his system breaks down as early as Monday, a day when water plays the dual role of element and example, of place and protagonist, while the lion, the cock, and the dragon are mythical, imaginary, or symbolic characters, capable of serving as exemplary models. Thursday suddenly provides two examples: the Easter Islands emerge after the cock. Such irregularities, which constantly circumvent and pervert the announced order, are further compounded by the inner contradiction featured in each *cahier* (on which we comment below). On the last two days the announced fictional pattern breaks down completely. Ernst leads or shunts his viewer/reader toward poetry. Friday's "Trois poèmes visibles" shift us from outer to inner vision. Saturday thrusts us into the unknown where songs of freedom prevail. In general, the surrealist prose narrative substitutes inner coherence, analogy, and other poetic devices for a discursive structure. We do not really suggest that Ernst has written a surrealist novel, but that he uses words in order to provoke an irresistible shift in that direction. As Sylwia Gibs says of *Etes-vous fous?*: "Thus, by a continual transgression of the categories of traditional narrative, the dialects of history and discourse give rise to a new kind of narrative whose 'upside down' operation may establish the sur-reality of the narrative text."[16] Simultaneously with Ernst's gradual liberation from conventionality in *Une Semaine de bonté*, the sociopolitical concerns decline: disguises, lions or dragons drowned in floods or tempted by fire, are singularly absent from the final *cahiers*.

In addition to the ironical, subversive titles and subtitles that do not represent the book, we must mention the quotations, each of which serves to introduce a *cahier*. These quotations function, we presume, as intertexts for the collages. In his article "Intertextualité surréaliste" Michael Riffaterre considers the surrealist text as a special case: "As there is no reason why surrealist writing should not answer to the same laws as the other kinds of literary discourse, the production of obscure meaning, of difficult interpretation, even of nonsense can only be a particular case of intertextuality."[17] If the quotations, with or without continuity, constitute a surrealist text, the fact that these texts have to be read primarily as intertextual in relation to the collages makes them even more special and perhaps exceptional.

Ernst's quotations are attributed either to authors directly associated with the surrealist movement, such as Eluard, Breton, and Péret, or to writers acceptable to surrealists, such as Jarry and Pétrus Borel. He also invents apocryphal names—one a scientist, another a storyteller. The painter sometimes introduces exact quotations, but more often gives spurious attributions, in addition to the occasional texts from nonexistent authors. Two exact quotations from Marcel Schwob's *L'Anarchie* and *Le Rire* become disconcerting in

---

[16] Sylwia Gibs, "L'Analyse structurale du récit surréaliste," *Mélusine* 1 (1979): 116.
[17] *Mélusine* 1 (1979): 28.

FIG. 98. Collage by Max Ernst from *Une Semaine de bonté* (Goodness Week). Paris: Pauvert, 1963. © SPADEM, Paris; VAGA, New York, 1985.

FIG. 99. Collage by Max Ernst from *Une Semaine de bonté*. © SPADEM, Paris; VAGA, New York, 1985.

274

this context. Nonetheless it is by no means impossible to relate them to the "Rire du coq" *cahier* they introduce. In *L'Anarchie* Schwob evokes a completely imaginary anarchistic society, whereas in *Le Rire* he speaks of the threat of too much law and order. These antithetical ideas complement and complete one another. Ernst, in his collages, shows constant disorder invading churches, bedrooms, theater loges, railroads, until, on the roofs of Paris, the cock puts up the tricolor. The *coq gaulois* with his questionable individualism becomes an accomplice of the Third Republic (Fig. 98). Ernst once again proclaims that authority may be good for the Republic but not for people, whereas the second quotation, "Le Rire est destiné à disparaître" (Laughter is fated to disappear) announces an ambiguous prophecy. Their juxtaposition corresponds to two incompatible aspects of the collage where the cock refrains for a long time from interfering in the disorderly scenes he witnesses.

In the Tuesday section, which introduces the dragon and fire, Ernst tells a tale by the Comte de Permission, an early seventeenth-century "fou littéraire" (literary madman), followed by a plausible quotation from Tzara's *Où boivent les loups* (Where the Wolves Drink, 1932). The tale follows a fable-like pattern in which human and animal protagonists intermingle; it also serves as a fairy tale, since magical objects produce metamorphoses. Gold may embellish, but above all it represents buying power. The Comte de Permission's tale shows man's desire to possess, to subjugate others, and, in particular, to reduce women permanently to a state of meek acceptance. Not only in "La Cour du dragon" but throughout *Une Semaine de bonté*, all participants become partners, whether they have wings, tails, or beaks (Fig. 99). Scenes of subjugation and humiliation recur in the collages: kneeling down, praying, bending one's head, even being overcome by smoke. Ernst shows the dichotomy between strong males and intimidated females, especially in "Le Rire du coq" and "Le Lion de Belfort." Both tale and collages contain curious disguises, so that the surface and the depth do not seem to pertain to the same or to expected patterns.

The discrepancy between form and fiction, reality and appearances is further strengthened by the added quotation from Tzara's *Où boivent les loups*. The obvious is told by means of surprises, and the surprises repeat the obvious; the reader or spectator, amid reiterated discontinuities, does not always gain full awareness. Whereas the tale points to Ernst's plates in the context of a narrative sequence or disruption, the poetic line duplicates the method of the collage: the everyday phrases "Entrez, dit-il" (Come in, he said) and

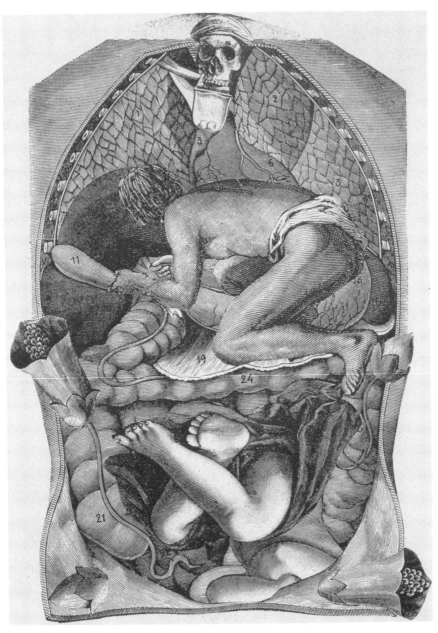

FIG. 100. Collage by Max Ernst from *Une Semaine de bonté.* © SPADEM, Paris; VAGA, New York, 1985.

"Personne n'avait frappé" (Nobody had knocked) are linked by a quotation from Genesis, "et la lumière se fit" (then there was light), which can hardly serve as transition. "Entrez, dit-il" followed by "personne n'avait frappé" accumulates surprise, logic, and contradiction that cancel each other out. In his collage Ernst shows a woman praying under a crucifix (see Fig. 99), next to a gigantic dragon of which she seems totally unaware. The dragon behaves like an intruder, whose presence is "improper" in every sense of the word. The confining surroundings where the woman prays become at once a middle-class bedroom and a dragon's cavern.

Arp's brief and probably apocryphal exclamation establishes relations with the use of metaphors in the collage novel, a use which tends to increase in the course of the work: "Les pierres sont remplies d'entrailles. Bravo. Bravo" (The stones are filled with entrails). Arp presents a paradox: stones are not stones throughout, but are filled with live organs. The organic and inorganic are united by being container and contained, an almost conventional relation, as well as by chance encounter. The first collage of the series seems to give a faithful mimetic representation of Arp's metaphor (Fig. 100). Ernst displays the inner walls of a container where serpentine intestines and other organ-like elements form a labyrinth. A skull crowns the womb-like opening explored by two human beings. Could Arp's "bravo" relate perhaps to these explorers of a hidden world? Their adventures assume sexual characteristics through the intertwining of their members and the shapes of the objects they manipulate. The metaphor of the collage is enhanced by the pseudo-scientific, map-like aspect of this purely imaginary landscape. In his strange statues Ernst presents other visions of Arp's stones filled with brains and intestines, live statues, stone-like masks.

"Un homme et une femme absolument blancs" (A man and a woman absolutely white): this brief line from *Le Revolver à cheveux blancs* prefacing Ernst's second "poème visible" sends us to a poetic text which we can decipher simultaneously with the painter's poem. Breton speaks of the transformation, if not purification, of everyday existence by the marvellous, of a sun-like luminosity emerging from the dark night peopled with prostitutes. Ernst's poem moves from religious, mystical, but conventional allusions to the marvellous. In the final collage he assembles boots, objects borrowed from various "models" depicted in the catalogs of a "magasin de nouveautés" (a fashion boutique). As he stacks these boots, he composes a rather fantastic many-footed leg. Both Ernst and Breton introduce eroticism as they deconstruct spatial contexts and their continuity.

We have seen that the table of contents announces a deconstruction of a traditional novel, and the quotations provide another device to stress the disruptive nature of Ernst's fictions. Each quotation in some ways fits and in others misfits, thus dissolving the last remnants of mimetic concordance in this novel. The many mini-texts ultimately become meaningless statements, surviving as enigmas and queries. They parody epigraphs which would veil or reveal the nucleus or ultimate truth of a book. Thus, while he disentangles the sociopolitical problems Ernst simultaneously undermines some of the literary and verbal practices of the Third Republic.

Critics who have written on *Une Semaine de bonté* have paid little, if any, attention to the mini-texts, so that questions such as, Does the text illustrate the collage or the collage the text, would be considered irrelevant, if not absurd.[18] Once Ernst himself has undercut the autonomy of these texts, they become fragments from dubious wholes or fabricated bits of nonexistent works.

Ernst's collages are borrowed from literary and scientific works; however oblique they may be, such relations cannot be overlooked. John Russell provides a list of journals in which the works were published.[19] Werner Spies gives further documentation and includes in the appendix of his study some pages of the scientific and fictional works that Ernst used in his collages: *Le Magasin pittoresque*, *La Nature*, *Catalogue du grand magasin du Louvre*, and *Magasin des nouveautés*, as well as two novels by Jules Mary, *Les Damnés de Paris* and *Les Aventures de Monsieur Claude*. Ernst, disregarding the text, selected various elements from the pictures, which he deliberately combined with extraneous material: "A perusal of the material presented leads us to assert that, with ready-mades, you cannot take over something that already exists without making changes."[20]

We assume of course that in these materials used by Ernst—*faits divers*, scientific vulgarizations, political harangues, and, above all, popular novels—text and illustration ran a parallel course. In the novels, the engravings

---

[18]Cf. John Russell, *Max Ernst* (New York: Abrams, 1967); Renée Riese Hubert, "The Fabulous Fiction of Two Surrealist Artists: Giorgio de Chirico and Max Ernst," *New Literary History* 4 (1972–73): 151–66; Margot Norris, "Deconstruction in the Works of Max Ernst," *Structuralist Review* 1 (1979): 3–29. Our book was already in press at the time of publication of Evan M. Maurer, "Images of Dream and Desire: The Prints and Collage Novels of Max Ernst," in *Max Ernst: Beyond Surrealism* (New York: New York Public Library and Oxford University Press, 1986), p. 37–94.

[19]*Max Ernst*, p. 188.

[20]*Max Ernst—Collagen*, p. 449.

FIG. 101. Collage by Max Ernst from *Une Semaine de bonté*. © SPADEM, Paris; VAGA, New York, 1985.

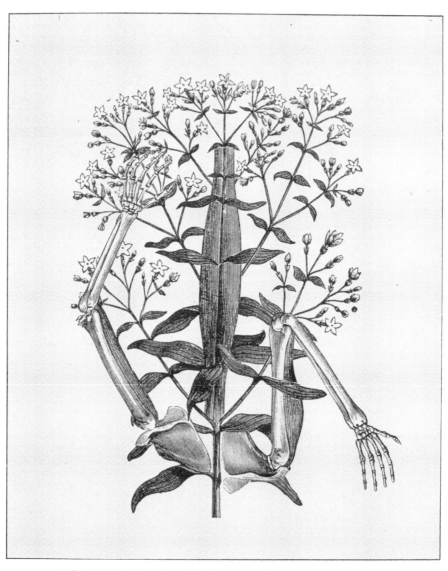

FIG. 102. Collage by Max Ernst from *Une Semaine de bonté*. © SPADEM, Paris; VAGA, New York, 1985.

give a faithful image of the characters, their adventures, and the setting. Ernst's collages, all of them transformations of nineteenth-century illustrations, are conditioned by the text he eliminated or did not select. The viewer is tempted to reconstruct the original plates, the banal stories, through his own knowledge of potboilers. The kind of fiction from which Ernst derived his collage series—none of the painter's novels originate in a single text—is highly melodramatic, full of violent action and moral indignation, describing both regular and irregular family affairs, shifting between the sordid and the sentimental. In *Les Damnés de Paris* and *Les Aventures de Monsieur Claude*, intense relations between male and female occur frequently; romantic embraces alternate with licentious seductions and promiscuous displays between prostitutes and elderly "gentlemen." They show a succession of climaxes and crises undoubtedly keeping pace with the literary text. According to Margot Norris, these novels consist of "bourgeois melodrama, pulp adventure, or old-fashioned pornography—[all of which] suffer from insufficient signification."[21] The pages of these two popular novels exemplify the need for sensation and indignation, the insatiable desire for the seamy side of life.

In the sections preceding the "poèmes visibles," Ernst maintains the atmosphere of the popular novel, moving from climax to climax. Paradoxically, he asserts, as a true surrealist should, a pure present by destroying the continuity of the shoddy and outmoded novel on which he depends. He rarely borrows two sequential plates in a book. Hence, Ernst's sequence of episodes does not produce the same effect or sensation as the original, for the surrealist painter relies on shock and surprise, and his discontinuities avoid subordination. There is no standard way by which Ernst transforms nineteenth-century melodrama into modern absurdity.

Examples or specimens taken from catalogs or inventories tend at times to divert the course of the "narrative," acquiring through their transformation the semblance of magical power. Usually, however, they function in the same way as the other borrowed materials. Doré's illustrations to *Paradise Lost* may be an exception, as they curiously "intrude" into Ernst's "Cour du dragon" (Fig. 101). The epic and cosmic dimensions, the supernatural aspects, of the nineteenth-century plates become unrecognizable in *Une Semaine de bonté*. Contrary to the illustrations from the popular novels, Gustave Doré's engravings lose their original qualities. Only readers acquainted with the nineteenth-century woodcuts will be tempted to restore Milton's

---

[21]"Deconstruction in the Works of Max Ernst," p. 16. See also Margot Norris, *The Beasts of the Modern Imagination* (Baltimore: Johns Hopkins, 1983).

FIG. 103. Collage by Max Ernst from *Une Semaine de bonté*. © SPADEM, Paris; VAGA, New York, 1985.

text. Satan, deprived of his wings, separated from the majestic forces of nature, is squeezed between a middle-class woman and her servant. Instead of confronting chaos as a metaphysical force, he participates in the creation of more disorder in a living room where multiple interferences contrive to compound the irrational. By combining Doré's illustration with that of a popular novel, Ernst suggests an affinity between the collage and the surrealist metaphor as first formulated by Lautréamont. Ernst avoids transitions wherein borrowed elements might appear to be so compatible that they would lose all trace of their original identity. Spies feels that the presence of borrowed graphic elements enhances the tensions of the collages. Doré's illustrations merely introduce details, not scenes.

We have so far discounted any form of repetition underlying *Une Semaine de bonté*. All our examples have shown individual subversions and transformations. In the Sunday series entitled "Le Lion de Belfort," practically all the male characters wear lion's heads; in the Monday series entitled "L'Eau," rising waters and splashing waves invade rooms, streets, cemeteries. In the third *cahier*, large and small dragons and other reptiles intrude into the scenes represented by the nineteenth-century plates. In the Oedipus series, a bird-headed person appears in each scene, and many males of the Ile de Pâques section have stone heads borrowed from mythical figures. The change brought about by adding lion, bird, cock, and stone heads, rushing water, and dragons amounts to a persistent undercutting of the mimetic banality of the original scene. Incredible acts insert into the melodramatic scenes characteristics of the supernatural, the mythical, the gigantic. The protagonists, who barely modify their initial dramatic poses, are totally unaware of these new threats and intrusions. From situation to situation, from character to character, the protagonists in their endless disguises pertain to a structure which does not correspond to its promised plan.

Ernst tells a tale in which different manifestations belie one another. The viewer, as he moves from collage to collage, cannot find any significance in the presence of extraneous material. The quotation "Was ist das," humorously attributed to Pétrus Borel in the Saturday section, pertains to Ernst's novel as a whole. The three "poèmes visibles" bring to an end parodies or distortions of narrative forms. The protagonist is absent both in his identity and by his actions. The juxtaposition of divergent material does not produce a rift as in the previous sections, but attains poetic integration (Fig. 102). The majority of the collages belonging to the "poèmes visibles" section derive from scientific drawings and display a high degree of stylization rather than

FIG. 104. Collage by Max Ernst from *Une Semaine de bonté*. © SPADEM, Paris; VAGA, New York, 1985.

pictorial representation. Eluard's introductory statement to the "Premier poème visible":

> *Et j'oppose à l'amour*
> *Des images toutes faites*
> *Au lieu d'images à faire*
>
> And to love I oppose
> Ready-made pictures
> Instead of images to be made

seems to raise in an oblique fashion the paradox of the ready-made and the created image, upon which Ernst seems to insist. Throughout *Une Semaine de bonté* the painter plays with the problem of the borrowed image versus creation or even the creative process. He thus compounds the literary problematics of intertextuality.

In the "poèmes visibles" the images are fitted together like constellations, like an artistic construction. The first plate shows a plant represented with scientific rigor (see Fig. 102); its leaves are composed of parts of a human skeleton and both blend perfectly into a constellation. Later, the body of a naked woman is surrounded by a dense cluster of cactus leaves, variations on her sexual anatomy (Fig. 103). Form, affinity, repetition, and variation dominate the collages of the "poèmes visibles" until we reach the final poem with its endless repetition of cyclopic eyes confronting each other and of stone-like hands interlaced. Spatial limitations and cluttered scenes bereft of reciprocity have disappeared. Repetition without relation to mimesis leads to infinity, second sight, communication, creation symbolized by a single egg in a cup (Fig. 104). The visible poem stands as a monument.

In the final, Saturday series, Ernst, without relinquishing the poetic vein, returns to a heroine whom, unexpectedly, as an ironic gesture, he thrusts into dreamland. Yet *Une Semaine de bonté* with its telling subtitle "les sept péchés capitaux" (the seven deadly sins) remains an institution of the Third Republic, where visiting dragons display the hidden obsessions of citizens rather than their transgressions. It is not so much on that level that Ernst advocates change. As we have shown, popular literature and surrealist poetry are both present in the novel; the former is misused as documentation, the latter provides parallels to the practice of collage. The interplay of the absence and presence of literature enables Ernst to produce an illustrated book consisting almost exclusively of visual elements and to embody the central problem of book illustration: the model versus the imagination. The sheer originality of

Nadja and *Une Semaine de bonté* suggests that already in the twenties and early thirties, a fair degree of consciousness concerning the book had existed among the surrealists, above the usual preoccupation of relating image to text. This incipient awareness became far more pronounced after World War II, when a few enterprising publishers eagerly exploited the potential of books wherein writing, graphics, and typography combine in a single work of art.

CHAPTER NINE
POSTWAR ACHIEVEMENTS

LONG AFTER THE DADAIST REBELLION and the surrealist revolution had abated, many years, according to purists, after surrealism had ceased to exist as a viable movement, the surrealist book, aided and abetted by dadaist inventiveness, came into its own and triumphed as a fully integrated work of art. None of the volumes so far discussed would qualify in this respect, though both Masson's and Matta's *Une Saison en enfer* come close. Unfortunately, the typography of the Masson volume, beautiful though it is, can hardly be described as inventive and would just as well suit many another literary text. Matta's *Saison* could better be classified as an album than as a book. The printed text, a facsimile of the 1873 edition reproduced in two folio sheets, precedes the ten plates. Matta's graphic in-text commentaries transform it, as we have shown, into a sort of *poème-objet* separated from the full-page aquatints. Other books by Matta, however, would easily fit into this chapter, notably his outstanding illustrated *Ubu roi*.[1]

The belated triumph of the surrealist book has its paradoxes and ironies, mainly resulting from financial considerations. Instead of making surrealist ideas and practices beneficial to everyone, these *livres de peintre* can belong only to wealthy collectors and, unlike paintings, can never be admired in museums and only rarely as reproductions. In a way these expensive volumes betray both dadaism and surrealism by selling out, in both senses of the phrase, to a class that these two subversive movements had done their utmost to destroy.

All four works to be discussed result from close collaboration between a painter and a publisher. In all four of these lavish books, there occur strangely original interplays between word and image, between typography and illus-

---

[1] Alfred Jarry, *Ubu roi*, with eight colored etchings by Matta (Paris: Atelier Dupont-Visat, 1982).

tration, interplays reminiscent of early surrealist games and, like them, making good use of *hasard objectif* and automatism. In some respects, these belated volumes are the only genuine surrealist *livres de peintre*. Although the genre as such has not said its last word or shown its last image, fewer and fewer are being produced.

PARLER SEUL *and* À TOUTE ÉPREUVE

Miró showed a marked, though not exclusive, preference for writers such as René Char, René Crevel, Paul Eluard, Robert Desnos, and Michel Leiris. For each volume that he illustrated, he made totally new demands on himself without in any sense attempting to find mimetic equivalents for poetic texts primarily based on imagery and verbal puns.

Tristan Tzara had written his text for *Parler seul* by 1945; Miró's lithographs, printed by Mourlot, were not completed until 1950. By rapid successions of absence and presence Tzara evokes confrontations of man with man and of man with the world. Movement, trajectories, and swift passages represent human existence. Since only violence and tension can regenerate vital forms, repose and equilibrium appear to be at best transitory states. The universe remains at a constant stage of dissolution, which paradoxically preserves it from complete collapse. Tzara multiplies paradoxes and antitheses in order to abolish categories and distinctions. As liberation and restriction alternate, the poet retains and repeats the same signs for all confrontations, whether physical or spiritual. The verbal flow, never interrupted by the intrusion of capital letters and punctuation, impels the reader toward transgressions, toward the unknown. Miró's lithographs amplify a text barely thirty pages long: every printed page is decorated, framed, and extended by an illustration, and even more numerous are the pages covered by lively constellations of color without benefit of a text (see Figs. 7,8).

On the box, a torn piece of paper is decorated with a black sign forming a double loop. The title of the book and the names of the two collaborators appear on a little yellow surface with irregular borders. The shapes of the lettering had to be modified in order to be squeezed into this inadequate, awkwardly shaped space. The black, dynamic sign that occupies the central position is surrounded by a little red-spotted sun and a black star superimposed on an uneven azure cloud that has somehow managed to spill down from the sky. The cover thus includes the entire repertory, from blackness to bright color, from fragmentation to completion, from the readable to the indecipherable. All proportions are reversed: the azure cloud in the lower left corner, representing the sky, has only limited contact with the red sun. What counts is the potential of the various elements to regenerate.

Inside the book, lines, spots, and stars regroup. According to the code inscribed on the box, black, irregular brush-strokes are the gesture and seal of the painter. The dynamism of a single black, vertical stroke at times suffices to animate the text. Other black lines form networks halfway between drawing and writing, evoking the passage from scriptural gesture to plastic language. Forms gradually assume greater complexity; even traces of a landscape emerge. Red, blue, and yellow circles, recalling stars and flowers in a landscape reduced to a minimum of signs, enliven the text (see Fig. 7). Each form with its ramifications lends itself to metamorphosis and amplification while avoiding closure or even definition (see Fig. 8). Toward the end of the book, the color spectrum becomes even richer, while some contours, without losing any of their ambiguity, suggest the human figure. Lines create networks that resemble the patterns of handwriting without ever duplicating them. It would not be meaningful to discuss single illustrations and consider them as comments on specific passages. In this connection, it is interesting to note the profusely illustrated table of contents. Miró illustrated a book as a whole, not lines of poetry or single poems. In short, we cannot take any given page as a focal point in establishing relationships between text and image.

Tzara, in his poetry, debunks many of the conventions of language. Whereas in the poetic text verbal dynamism dominates, its visual equivalent, the irruption of the line, becomes manifest in the lithographs. We considered the text a focal point of tension and vibration where paradox becomes a rejuvenating force. Miró's characteristic shapes force the printed page to shun all repose and equilibrium; thus they make the dynamism of the text visible by transgressing the expected orderliness of graphic representation.

The text provides plenty of stimulation, but without ever providing models as in traditional illustration. Tzara's post-dadaist adventure is extended by Miró; both refuse to accept the imprisonment of page, punctuation, or frame. Neither Tzara nor Miró grants the reader/viewer the reassurance of recognition or familiarity. On the contrary, text and image, by their intransigent reciprocation, seem to form an alliance against him. The text animates the painter's gesture which, by its use of scribal signs, gravitates toward literature. Thus the painter maintains close contact with poetry while fully developing the plastic rhythms indispensable to art.

A *toute épreuve* is rightly considered one of the major achievements of the surrealist book.[2] Ten years elapsed between its conception and publication.

[2]Paul Eluard, A *toute épreuve*, with eighty woodcuts by Miró (Geneva: Gérald Cramer, 1958).

Eluard wrote his poems in the late twenties; in 1948, the Swiss publisher and book designer Gérald Cramer chose as particularly suitable to his own remarkable talents a text that had first appeared in 1930. Since Eluard wished to revise his poem, Miró did not begin until the final version was completed. He prepared 233 woodblocks for some 78 illustrations in order, as Douglas Cooper says, "to give full expression to a simultaneously poetic and decorative conception."[3] Anne Greet's searching study on this book provides detailed commentaries on the genesis of A *toute épreuve*, especially on the creative role played by Gérald Cramer.[4] After a brief description of the book, she reads the text and the image simultaneously to show their fusion and also, in more than one case, to record their differences. Throughout her study she keeps in mind the conventions of bookmaking in order to show the innovative practices of Cramer, Eluard, Miró, and the printer, Jacques Frélaut. The title A *toute épreuve*, which refers to the hardships of experience while retaining the meaning "foolproof," seems to have suggested to Miró the proofs and trials of print-making. In any case, poet, painter, and publisher produced a masterpiece in keeping with still another meaning of the title, "invulnerable," "indestructible."

According to Greet, "The lapse in time between 1930, when Eluard published his poem sequence, and the 1950s, when Miró designed his woodcuts, was not detrimental to the book's aesthetic unity. Miró's style and mood vividly recall those attributes which Eluard first expressed in his poem 'Joan Miró' of 1926."[5] Miró conceived of illustration as an attempt to bridge the gap between two complementary realms kept separate by custom but closely related on the level of the creator and the created: "Je ne fais aucune différence entre peinture et poésie. . . . Il m'arrive d'illustrer mes toiles de phrases poétiques et vice versa" (I make no distinction between painting and poetry. . . . It happens that I illustrate my canvases with poetic sentences and vice versa).[6] Anne Greet's article corroborates this theory by showing that the woodcuts are responses to specific sections of the poetic text. She demonstrates that they reflect changes in the poet's mood, and she turns Miró into a very close reader who in his woodcuts "followed" the poem stage by stage while remaining faithful to his own talent and manner. But she also recognizes the poet's

[3] *Joan Miró: Bois gravés pour un poème de Paul Eluard* (Paris: Bergruen, n.d.) (no page numbers). "The printing of the 80 woodcuts took more than a year and required more than 42,000 impressions."
[4] Paul Eluard, A *toute épreuve* (New York: Braziller, 1984).
[5] Ibid., p. 11.
[6] *Joan Miró: Bois gravés.*

contribution to this *livre de peintre*, for he helped to plan the typography and "the shade of the ink" while Miró controlled the makeup of the page.

Although the same type font is used throughout A *toute épreuve*, it varies in size, sometimes on a single page. Repeatedly the final lines are less tightly spaced and larger print is used, emphasizing the conclusion. Some of the poetic texts thus acquire greater distance, others greater proximity, so the printed text does not produce the usual impression of mechanical repetition. Repetition is also avoided by placing the text sometimes on the left, sometimes on the right, but very rarely on both sides, or by leaving two completely printless pages, while "inset plates," confronting one another from opposite sides, transpose and extend the poetic and graphic continuity previously established (Plate 32). In *Parler seul*, the text appears on various sections of the page, as if the accompanying lithographs had driven it into a corner (see Fig. 8). Often the page on the right, completely appropriated by a lithograph, provides a visual and paroxysmal prolongation of the confrontations between text and image on the left, where the illustration is usually characterized by a simpler, linear design. Often in A *toute épreuve* the text, framed by a woodcut, must be read through a sort of window. The text also seems to respond by visual signals to the graphic proliferation that surrounds it. Paradoxically, the wood engravings seize the initiative (Plate 33) and emerge before the text, even though the poem had chronological priority.

Although Eluard's poem remains faithful to his major themes of dream and love, he displays greater range than usual in imagery. The poet establishes intimate relations between the presence of the beloved and an ever-changing still life derived from everyday objects and reflecting their various relationships:

> *Une chanson de porcelaine bat des mains*
> *Puis en morceaux mendie et meurt*
> *Tu te souviendras d'elle pauvre et nue*
> *Matin des loups et leur morsure est un tunnel*
> *D'où tu sors en robe de sang*
> *A rougir de la nuit*
> *Que de vivants à retrouver*
> *Que de lumières à éteindre*
> *Je t'appelerai visuelle*
> *Et multiplierai ton image.*[7]

[7] Paul Eluard, *Oeuvres complètes* (Paris: Gallimard, 1968), vol. I, p. 293. All quotations are from this edition.

A porcelain song claps its hands
Then in pieces begs and dies
You will remember her poor and naked
Morning of wolves and their bite is a tunnel
Whence you exit in a dress of blood
That makes one blush about the night
How many of the living must we meet again
How many lights extinguish
I shall call you visual
And multiply your image.

This poem, like others in the collection, almost appears to have been composed in the presence of Miró's works. It shares his humor, his colorful vision, and his propensity to personify and thus would easily fit in *Donner à voir*, where Eluard's affinity with painters results in poems providing verbal renditions of purely plastic worlds as visionary as his own.[8] Eluard celebrates the poetic act where he simultaneously sings, names, and makes visible the beloved and the world in an all-encompassing gesture that comprises repeated passages from darkness to color or light, from eclipse to fragmentation, from fragmentation back to unity, from loss to recovery and rediscovery, until the poet reaches the final eclosion of recurrent dream imagery.

Repeatedly the poet alludes to the simultaneous presence and absence of the beloved: "Fantôme de ta nudité" (Phantom of your nakedness). The woman becomes a nocturnal being who, instead of mediating, overshadows poetic creation and spurns the poet. Eluard repeatedly transgresses and obliterates ordinary contours and borderlines. Far from relying on description and providing definitions, he immediately transforms surface appearances into ambiguous allusions:

> *Plume d'eau claire, pluie fragile*
> *Fraîcheur voilée de caresses*
> *De regards et de paroles*
> *Amour qui voile ce que j'aime.*
> [p. 293]

> Clear water feather, frail rain
> Veiled freshness of caresses
> Of glances and of words
> Love that veils what I love

[8]*Donner à voir* (Paris: N.R.F., 1939).

The repetition of the word *voiler* seems as significant as the repetition of *fantôme* in the previous section. The poet evokes a world of fluidity, mobility, reflection where elements recreated through love and communications become interchangeable. No element exists in isolation; each permeates and is permeated by another. Together they assume unexpected characteristics, multiply paradoxes, enhance mystery, and remove the reader several steps further from the everyday. Miró's graphically impressive use of woodcuts does full justice to Eluard's creative process, perhaps because neither the poet nor the painter resorts to recognizable fixed images. On the contrary, they both encourage the viewer to seek, beneath the surface, unheard-of transformations and revelations.

Miró's illustrations are so abundant that they simply overwhelm the text. It seems as though in order to emerge at all Eluard's poems must seize whatever typographical characters happen to be available, while the woodcuts, almost denying spatial limitations, paradoxically express the lightness of touch so characteristic of Eluard's verse. Miró's ornamentation somehow lifts the words into another space (see Plate 33): through his graphic manipulations "le poème prend le large" (the poem puts out to sea), which shows that the text, however exiguous, is nonetheless the center from which all the ornamentation emanates. The woodcuts, like much of Miró's art, attain immediacy by the use of five basic colors and recurrent shapes—arches, sickle forms, circles, bending lines. Colors become, to a certain degree, objects. The pure spectrum remains unchanged even when one colored spot overlaps with another. Surfaces often attain a true monochrome, but even more frequently reveal the fibers of the wood. Miró avoids angular lines, which might curtail mobility and animation. In his woodcuts he evokes a world in a state of transformation: the haphazardness of their shapes and structures counteracts any kind of stability, equilibrium, or permanence. He responds faithfully to Eluard's own unstable universe by overdetermining a multiplicity of entangling lines at the expense of clearly defined shapes. These lines bend, twist, form spirals and, by the complex web thus produced, bridge the gap between drawing and writing. Much in the manner of the illustrations in *Parler seul*, they often suggest a network capable not only of reducing the distance between the many bouquets or constellations, but also between the regular-shaped letters and the dancing, starlike images.

The most important innovation that Miró made in *A toute épreuve* was by experimentation to reveal visually as well as poetically the potential of the woodcut. He insists on making the grain of the wood fully visible (Plate 34). In thus revealing a formerly hidden presence and establishing immediacy, he undercuts representation by refusing to reduce the wood to pure instrumentality. He simultaneously inscribes color-shapes on the page and brings the fiber to the surface, instead of merely using the wood to apply a layer of color. Some monochrome pages serve primarily to reveal in red, yellow, or gray the design of the fiber. The sizes of the fibers and the complexity of their designs vary. Some plates show vertical cuts; others, horizontal sections. The textures of the wood seem unlimited. The two collages in the book (as well as the torn pieces of wrapping paper) introduce an additional texture and a new juxtaposition (Fig. 105). Functioning simultaneously as finished and as raw material, they represent the various stages in the making of a book, stages which through unexpected alternations set up a dialectical relationship between matter and function.

Miró undercuts the representational function of the collages by partially covering them with a layer of color and by not respecting the margin which ordinarily delineates one piece of paper superimposed on another. His interference changes the collages into new forms. In searching for immediacy, in revealing hidden qualities, in reducing art to craft, Miró rejects mimetism in all its forms. The image that Miró, in his collages, superimposed as one piece of paper on another or one image on another seems to deny or belie their initial pictorial status. This nonmimetic approach is also noticeable in the color scheme, for "suns" and "moons," which never appear in their expected colors, are repeatedly divided horizontally into red and blue hemispheres. Miró thus implicitly treated his work as illustrator as calling for a return to origins, to fundamentals. The poem served as a mediator, for the poet identified himself as an image maker who transmits indefinitely his gift of seeing and revealing. For the painter the wooden block he engraves promises a wealth of scenes and landscapes. Miró, as we have stated, recognized the intimate link between writer and painter. In his illustrations he literally objectifies the affinity between the paper on which the poem is printed and the woodblock on which the engraving is inscribed. Moreover, he alludes to the various media used by both poet and painter by multiplying lines and strokes, by simulating the glow of wet ink and oil.

Miró chose to experiment with wood engraving because he realized that the potential of this art was much greater than that of metal. Greet has studied the results of Miró's combined use of metal and wood: thin lines joined, shaded colors. In A *toute épreuve*, iron wire, shaped by Miró, is introduced at least three times. Wire is softer than wood in the sense that it gives under pressure from the press or the hand. According to Cramer, it leaves a "softer

FIG. 105. Woodcut by Joan Miró from Paul Eluard, A *toute épreuve* (Proof against Anything). Geneva: Gérald Cramer, 1958. © ADAGP, Paris; VAGA, New York, 1985.

impression, both literally and figuratively, than does wood."[9] Several pages reveal the inner landscape of the wood—for instance, a vertical black line topped by a yellow circle presents the surface of a wooden stem crowned by a sunlike flower. There is no need to cover the large surface with azure blue to speak of a limitless sky, for a blue star showing the wooden texture summarizes in a single "word" all the skyscapes and seascapes. It corresponds in depth to Eluard's lines, "Je t'appelle visuelle / Et multiplierai ton image" (p. 293). Within a single woodcut absence and presence, immediacy and distanciation combine. Vertical and horizontal curves, framed and unframed contours open wide-ranging patterns as they merge with the circular shapes of violent red balls or with a scaffold of lines ascending to endless metamorphoses.

Miró's introduction of collages in more than one form reveals the range of transformation from wood to paper and paper to wood, from nature to artistic proliferation. Eluard's poem alludes to the recapturing of what had become invisible or eclipsed: "Que de vivants à retrouver" (so many living people to recover). The poem and the illustrations reveal that creation encompasses both a return to that past and a leap into the future. Miró's woodcuts make simultaneous various stages of his efforts. Sun and stars may emerge together, a circle may be divided into contrastingly colored hemispheres, just as Eluard's "Que de lumières à éteindre" (So many lights to extinguish) plunges the reader into ambiguity about day and night. The insert on one of the collages is upside down, with the signature of the unknown artist from which it was borrowed reversed on the top left corner (see Fig. 105). Moreover, in this as in the other collage, wood is transformed into images or simulacra of wood; by reversing the borrowed picture, Miró seems to shun the obvious implications of intertextu(r)ality. Lines and texture thus take on new depth, while repetition is avoided. The sea with its ripples replaces the sky crowned by luminous circles which lie outside the confines of the insertion. The limits of this picture are thus extended like the space of the poem, so that Miró's creatures as well as his scaffolds can move according to their own laws rather than to the already established order.

Miró's seemingly spontaneous lines and shapes appear to have arisen from some kind of gestural drawing: spiral, snake-like curves and uneven circles abound, as though to suggest their own extensibility. Moreover, the colored surfaces and the translucent texture of the wood set up contrasting systems of vibration. Spontaneity is further brought out by *papiers déchirés* (torn-up pa-

[9]*A toute épreuve*, p. 9.

pers) used as collages and by specks of movement-producing color. Although Miró generates a world where everything is marked by a potential for growth and proliferation of natural movements, nowhere can we find a replica of anything organic. Thus both the artist and the poet assembled images bordering on nonfiguration but always true to the basic cycles of nature.

LES PÉNALITÉS DE L'ENFER

Les Pénalités had been a joint project of Miró and Desnos in 1925.[10] The book that appeared in 1974, long after the poet's death, undoubtedly bears little relation to the initial plan. It is presented in a box covered in natural-colored linen and lined with a paper printed with a highly colored, multi-figured design accompanied by dancing letters (Plate 35). Two dissimilar eyes, which the viewer may take for stars or breasts, introduce an illustrated book that defies the usual parallelism between text and image in order, by its sheer lopsidedness, to establish unexpected affinities between typography and painting. The box turns the book into an object, a treasure house temptingly dangerous by reason of its title, which ironically warns of eternal retribution.

This *livre de peintre* shares its box with a smaller volume, entitled *Documents*, that gives the archives and an historical account of *Les Pénalités de l'enfer*. Desnos and Miró had planned a full collaboration but ran afoul of a series of political catastrophes. Years after Desnos's death, his widow, Youki, made public the unpublished manuscript and Miró's sketches, which Maeght added as documentation to authenticate the joint conception of the book and the painter's loyalty to the writer. The inclusion of *Documents* side by side with the main volume, which consists of numerous lithographs by Miró and an incomplete text (part of the poem included in *Nouvelles Hébrides*), transforms the whole work into an object while recapitulating the complex process of its elaboration.[11] Interesting as this ensemble may be in regard to the conception of an illustrated book involving two major surrealists, considerable doubt has been cast by Marie-Claire Dumas on the relevance of the sketches to *Les Pénalités de l'enfer*. It is likely that they were meant for an entirely different collaborative effort.[12]

This sumptuous Maeght edition lacks any perceptible unity. The text be-

---

[10] Robert Desnos, *Les Pénalités de l'enfer ou les Nouvelles Hébrides*, with colored lithographs by Miró (Paris: Maeght, 1974).
[11] Robert Desnos, *Nouvelles Hébrides et autres textes* (Paris: Gallimard, 1978). Page numbers refer to this edition, edited by Marie-Claire Dumas.
[12] Marie-Claire Dumas, *Robert Desnos ou l'exploration des limites* (Paris: Klincksieck, 1980).

gins with random episodes, deviations or detachments from tales; then poetry takes the upper hand; finally, songs and quatrains lead to surprising "maximes," "proverbs," "prières." The typography created by Michel Otthoffer effectively displays all these generic displacements. Robert Desnos wrote to Jacques Doucet: "C'est en effet ma première oeuvre en prose que j'ai écrite sans autre désir que de m'amuser et de combler à tout prix le vide dans lequel je me suis trouvé au début de cette année" (It is indeed my first work in prose, written without any preoccupation but my own amusement and to be rid at any cost of the emptiness I experienced at the beginning of the year).[13] This "prose work," which Desnos sometimes calls a novel, contains many songs and poems recited by various characters. No poem except "Chanson du Trappeur" (The Trapper's Song), "Bois brûlé attaché au poteau de torture par les Indiens Sioux et Comanches" (Burnt wood fastened to the torture stake by Sioux and Comanche Indians), and "Nous voulons" occupies more than a single page of widely spaced lettering, and several texts are merely sections of longer versions later published in *Les Nouvelles Hébrides*. For this reason each text appears to be autonomous, and the typographical inventiveness only enhances this impression.

Since humor and parody characterize the poetic text, it seems only natural that Miró chose to illustrate it. Desnos turns the wisdom revealed by the proverbs upside down, without destroying their syntax and form:

> *Si tu plantes l'ivraie, tu récolteras les coquelicots*
>
> [p. 92]
>
> Plant cockles and you will harvest poppies
>
> —*Un bienfait est parfois utile à quelqu'un*
>
> [p. 92]
>
> —One good turn sometimes turns out well for somebody
>
> —*A père avare grand-père paralysé*
>
> [p. 92]
>
> —From the skinflint father comes the palsied grandfather

Proverbs and maxims in their customary formulation rely on a central chain, on certain beliefs about behavior and ethics. The first proverb prepares us for the "knowledge" that hard labor will yield flowery, if not fruitful, results. But in reality it states a relation between the nature of the seed and the produce and not between labor and harvest. The second shows a more clear-cut type of subversion: the exception takes the place of the universal and substi-

---

[13] *Nouvelles Hébrides*, p. 500.

tutes the haphazard for logical rules. The third example proposes a chrono-logical reversal of the influence of paternal sin. Here the heritage passes from father to grandfather, rather than to son as in the original proverb, "A père avare fils prodigue" (From the miserly father comes the prodigal son). The replacement of son by grandfather, of generosity by paralysis, casts doubts on moral decrees often repeated but never questioned. By these types of subver-sion—chronological, logical, moral—Desnos suggests new associations and transgressions capable of exploding old molds. He introduces verbal fantasy in a seemingly innocent fashion: "Si tu plantes l'ivraie, tu récolteras les coquelicots" proposes a surrealistic encouragement to practice the irrational. Poppies produce sleep, hence dreams; *ivraie* has the same origin as *ivre*, "drunk." Although the maxims and proverbs, far from following each other, are dispersed throughout the book, alternating with other types of sayings and with rhymed verse, the reader becomes aware of the transformation of the known into the unfamiliar. The "organized" wisdom of proverbs becomes a surrealist game, the best-known example being Péret and Eluard's 152 *Prov-erbes mis au goût du jour*.[14] Surrealist proverbs advocate freedom instead of restrictions. In *Les Pénalités*, maxims and proverbs also encourage substitu-tion of a new form of language for an old one.

In addition to proverbs and maxims relating to human behavior in a more or less oblique fashion, Desnos included nonsense and non sequiturs, once more mocking traditions that find it necessary at each stage to proclaim gen-eral truths:

> *Le coeur est un oiseau comestible*
> *en silence arithmétique*
> [p. 93]
> The heart is an edible bird
> in arithmetical silence

This slogan, which by means of its syntax and its formulation makes us be-lieve that we have entered familiar territory, belongs to a group of texts in which words referring to food or consumption abound. The association of the heart with an edible bird and with silence implicitly equates *battement d'ailes* (beating of wings) with *battement de coeur* (heartbeat), an association in which the quantitative science replaces organic rhythm. The heart is de-fined not by its capacity to feel, but by its timebound vulnerability. Apparent nonsense leads to surprising but relevant associations.

[14]Paul Eluard, 152 *Proverbes mis au goût du jour*, en collaboration avec Benjamin Péret (Paris: La Révolution Surréaliste, 1925).

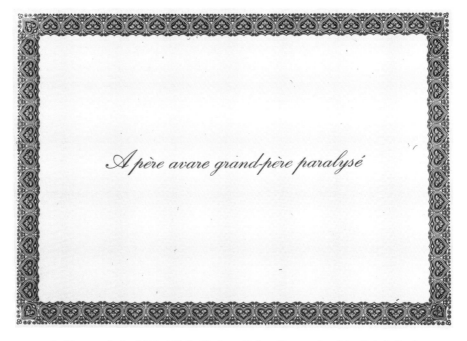

FIG. 106. Typography by Michel Otthoffer from Robert Desnos, *Les Pénalités de l'enfer ou les Nouvelles Hébrides* (The Penalties of Hell or the New Hebrides). Paris: Maeght, 1974. Courtesy of Fequet and Baudier.

The truncated poetic texts, far from being self-sufficient, require all the help that typography and spatial arrangement can provide to assert their meanings. As typography makes use of the widest possible range of characters, the text is not merely printed but is literally translated into visible language.[15] Let us reexamine in this context certain proverbs: "Un bienfait est parfois utile à quelqu'un," and "A père avare grand-père paralysé" (Fig. 106). Both proverbs are printed in italic, a font not used for the rhymed texts. Each one occupies an entire folio page, surrounded by an open or closed frame consisting of a decorated pattern. This rather simple, repetitious design, borrowed rather than invented, adds to the highly stylized manner of printing. The act of reading has apparently been simplified; the reader confronts a single message in very large lettering that suggests no secrecy or mystery. The page and its ornaments belong to a pictorial order. The frame transforms certain pages into a keepsake, an embroidered doily, even a drawer. The order

[15]Visible language does not primarily lead to transparency, but becomes an object that retains opacity.

and regularity of the design and the pattern, the symmetry, the perfection, far from corresponding to the key characteristics of the text, merely echo surface conventionalities. They do not give away Desnos's subversion or even contradict it, but translate its underlying paradox into visible language, as though no passive way of viewing a page would be viable.

As we suggested earlier, the text of the Maeght *Pénalités de l'enfer* is varied in style and form. The typographer did not reduce the freedom of the poetic text to the uniformity and standardization usually imposed by the printed page. Framing rectangles of different sizes occur on different areas of the page and thus provide different kinds of *mise-en-abîme*, like windows with varying perspectives. Vertical juxtapositions of right and left pages alternate with horizontal ones. Types and sizes of letters change from one page to the next. Here capital letters are emphasized by size, there by decorations. The compactness or condensation of the text as a whole as well as of individual letters introduces further variety. As the relative affinity of the letter to drawing or handwriting or printing varies considerably, the implied presence or absence of the artist or poet seems to play an intrusive role in the composition.

The first text, entitled "Le Robinet lyrique" (The Lyrical Tap), consists of a rhymed quatrain. The title occupies the larger portion of the page, composed of a heavy black center surrounded by a white frame. Three words, on different levels, suggest the outlines of a faucet (Fig. 107). The letter R is replaced by the schematized representation of the tap. Since the rest of the word has not been obliterated, the tap functions simultaneously as letter and image. The surrounding letters propose a literal reading of the title. The faucet, a piece of plumbing detached from fixtures that would make of it a useful object, is represented as a defunctionalized object capable only of asserting itself as an esthetic signifier. The zigzag line of the text, which cannot possibly correspond to the natural flow of water or lyricism, suggests the disruptive, subversive quality of Desnos's poetry, just as the word *robinet*, associated both with the poetry and with the diminutive of Desnos's given name, Robert, dislocates the normal context of lyrical poetry in the direction of the simple mechanics of turning on a tap. The presence of the tap as visual image fosters duality rather than entailing a complete overlap.

> *Le Robinet lyrique*
> *On assassine une assiette creuse en vol de gypaète*
> *qui passe le bras autour d'une caille*
> *je n'aurai donc jamais de plomb dans la tête*
> *la fenêtre est ouverte et le thermomètre chante sa taille*
>
> [p. 53]

On assassine une assiette creuse en vol de gypaète
qui passe le bras autour d'une caille
je n'aurai donc jamais de plomb dans la tête
la fenêtre est ouverte et le thermomètre chante sa taille

FIG. 107. Typography by Michel Otthoffer from Robert Desnos, *Les Pénalités de l'enfer*. Courtesy of Fequet and Baudier.

They murder a hollow saucer taking flight like a gypaetus
which puts its arms around a quail
thus I shall never have lead in my head
the window's open and the thermometer sings its size

This logically patterned sequence presents explosive images to the reader. Eroticism, violence, and liberation emerge from displaced words. *Caille* and *taille* may well be reversed, for the arm surrounds the waist and the singing comes from the bird. The poem magically establishes new adventures and relations, here and there undercutting each other: an attack directed against a flying saucer has been diverted; the bullet leaves the poet unharmed; faucet and bullets are made of the same base metal. Such accidents and coincidences will make it possible for the "lyrical tap" to flow. A similar principle recurs in "Chant de R. Desnos regardant, transformée en sextant de marine, la pièce de monnaie qu'il avait jetée en l'air pour tirer à pile ou face" (Song of R. Desnos Watching, Transformed into a Sextant, the Coin He Had Tossed Up in the Air for Heads or Tails). The typographer replaces part of the *p* and part of the *a* with the two sides of a coin, faithfully reproduced. As the tail of the coin covers the loop of the *p* belonging to the word *pile*, the head covers the loop of the *a* of the word *face*. By replacing the hole in the letter, the hole

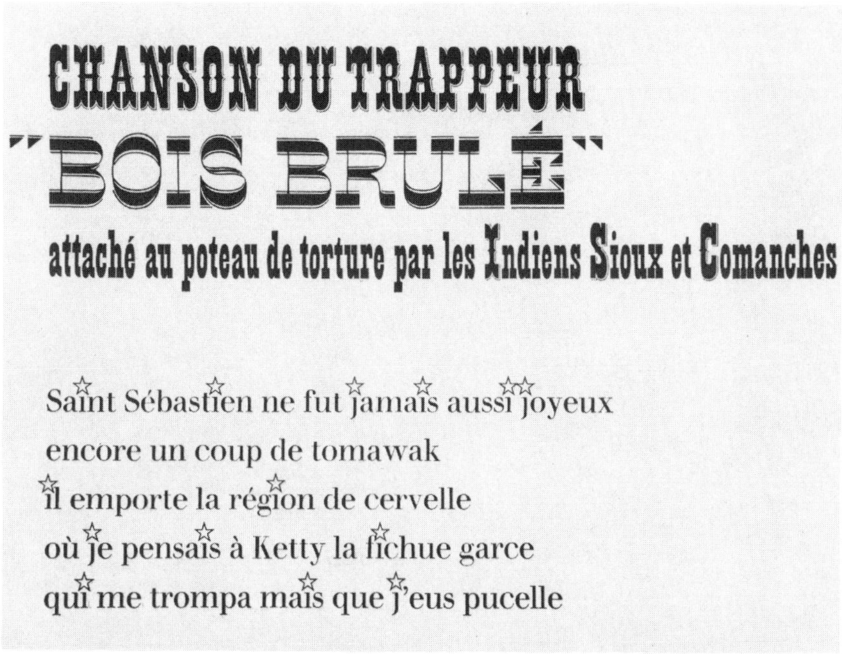

CHANSON DU TRAPPEUR
"BOIS BRULÉ"
attaché au poteau de torture par les Indiens Sioux et Comanches

Saint Sébastien ne fut jamais aussi joyeux
encore un coup de tomawak
il emporte la région de cervelle
où je pensais à Ketty la fichue garce
qui me trompa mais que j'eus pucelle

FIG. 108. Typography by Michel Otthoffer from Robert Desnos, *Les Pénalités de l'enfer*. Courtesy of Fequet and Baudier.

in the coin produces an even greater effect of trompe l'oeil, of manipulation, because of the constant interplay between the visual and the verbal, between presence and absence.

The process takes still another twist in the typography of the sentence "St. Sébastien ne fut jamais aussi joyeux" (St. Sebastian was never so joyful). The dots over the *i*'s and the *j* are replaced by stars (Fig. 108). Thus a mere typographical embellishment, by establishing St. Sébastien's direct contact with the stars, authenticates his happiness. In each of the preceding examples we could claim that language was objectified. The word was personified as object without losing its ordinary semantic function, and we realize that here at least the printed text is much more than a mere transcription of the poet's words.

The playful antagonism between the orderly, often deliberately old-fashioned, always rigorous lettering and the lithographs filled with free-floating ambiguous creatures belonging simultaneously to flora and fauna, to sky and earth accounts for and reconciles the reversals and transgressions in the text. The black color of the lettering and the whiteness of the page are

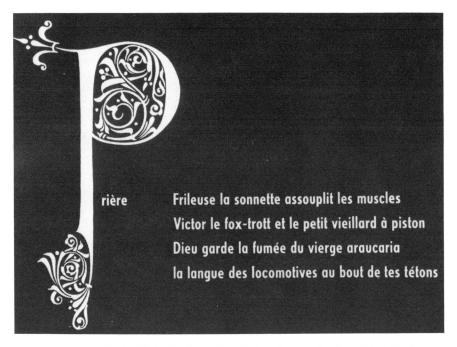

rière

Frileuse la sonnette assouplit les muscles
Victor le fox-trott et le petit vieillard à piston
Dieu garde la fumée du vierge araucaria
la langue des locomotives au bout de tes tétons

FIG. 109. Typography by Michel Otthoffer from Robert Desnos, *Les Pénalités de l'enfer.*
Courtesy of Fequet and Baudier.

reversed on two occasions. One page in particular, far from being an unrelieved black surface, stands out as a canvas entirely covered with brown and black brush-strokes. As such it makes still another shift between text and image, with painting suddenly invading the territory reserved for printing. Conversely, the paper itself can play an active role by its resistance to an absorption of color. It serves alternately if not simultaneously as surface, substance, and window. Miró can establish continuity merely by juxtaposing two black-brown pages where graphic representation faces printing. The silver used in printing the lower parts of some of the letters reappears in the lithograph as a star.

The continuity of the two other black pages confronting one another is more paradoxical. In the word "Prière" the *P* is decorated almost as richly as in a medieval manuscript, "suitably" preparing the reader for religious words (Fig. 109). As soon as the reader turns into a viewer he will notice the pointed arrow on the top section, recognize the phallic sign prolonging a curve, and detect multiple interwoven lines. The initial, a calculated distortion of the conventions used in religious books and a trap to lure the viewer into entanglements, illustrates the following four lines:

Frileuse la sonnette assouplit les muscles
Victor le fox-trott et le petit vieillard à piston
Dieu garde la fumée du vierge araucaria
les langues des locomotives au bout de tes tétons

[p. 53]

The chilly bell limbers its muscles
Victor the foxtrot and the little old piston man
God protects the smoke of the virgin auricaria
the tongues of the locomotives at the tip of your nipples.

The poem seems at first to consist entirely of non sequiturs, but eventually the reader discovers that it combines a sequence of actions or gestures no less erotic than poetic. Incongruous elements are constantly juxtaposed, normal functions constantly bypassed: God participates in erotic desires, while man becomes a mechanical contrivance and objects are personified. "Prière" does not, however, parody a particular type of prayer in alluding to God's questionable protection of virgin trees. Syntactical devices turn adjectives into proper nouns and create characters. Victor is both a man and a victrola; Frileuse is a woman. The ringing of the bell arouses sexual responses: loosening of muscles, rubbing action, kissing, until such activity encompasses everything named by the poet.

Once again, Desnos establishes links by substitutions: the smoke that should come from the engine surrounds the trees; pistons belong not to engines but to old men, while the tongue belongs to an engine. Ultimately in this multiplication of false contacts, gestures, and relations, God is transformed into a woman and becomes an actor in a universal lovemaking. Desnos has subverted prayer instead of discouraging illicit love. The word *langue* bridges the gap between eroticism and verbalism. The prayer, in true surrealist fashion, has been transformed into desire and wish fulfillment. Since a return to innocence has been made impossible in a world of black pages, the irony of the title *Les Pénalités de l'enfer* becomes clear. The large initial P of the word *prayer* with its labyrinthian design suggests ironic and even erotic variations on patterns used for earlier book illumination. The convoluted leaf and flower motif, characterized by multiple crossings and interlacings of lines, heightens various analogies obliquely proposed by the text. Ultimately we realize that the initial pushes us toward liberation. The lithograph on the opposite side is composed of a convoluted line "quickly drawn" in black pencil, contrasting with a carefully worked-out floral pattern. Although the autonomy of the poem, the typographic design, and the lithographs is firmly maintained, all three engage the reader in a free-for-all full of playful reverberations.

In silvery script appear the words: "ce qui serait extraordinaire, c'est que l'extraordinaire n'arrivât point" (What would be extraordinary is that the extraordinary should not happen). This sentence seems to formulate common wisdom and express faith in the marvellous. The ten words arranged in four lines could serve as a model for young students. On the opposite page appears a figure, a streamlined form composed of a trunk and a face. Bright red shapes suggest eroticism and voyeurism. Two smallish figures, one a green, distorted sickle, the other a star drawn in silver pencil, merge into a constellation—forms within forms, emerging from black zones and suggesting endless transformations and improvisations. As the "handwritten" text combines short and long lines, so the lithograph combines painted, drawn, enamelled, and cut-out elements in circular and triangular shapes. Both sides stress creation and craftsmanship, while the poem itself severs all contact with everyday reality. Juxtaposed to the dark web of the lithograph, it consists of a conditional sentence that includes an imperfect subjunctive.

The most systematic exploitation of text and typography occurs in the poem "Nous voulons" (We want). The text, composed of fewer than ten lines occupying two pages, appears to be more openly programmatic than the others. It formulates desires and proposes action. "Nous voulons" is both the title and the first line of the poem. As title, it is printed in three-dimensional tilted letters, composed of strong black and white contrasts, of ribbons and blocks floating in space. The lines are tilted as though some mysterious power had forced the typographer's hand. The words of the quatrain are carefully separated, more in tribute to linear straightness than in respect to linguistic unity, and thus they move as directly as possible toward the fulfillment of desire. One may claim that the poem is an invocation ultimately echoed by the typography. The poem moves in an upward, heavenly direction: "Cheminée, fusée, appel du matin, clair soleil" (Chimney, rocket, call of morning, clear sun). It formulates a gradual transgression of obstacles, a soaring to wider spaces, an uplifting progression that the syntactic simplicity makes immediately detectable.

The text, printed first in small and then in progressively larger letters, breaks typographical continuity in following the trajectory of desire which increases until, ultimately, it transforms itself into a call to action. The final word, "Les Portes," strategically singled out, is printed in large block letters at the bottom of the page. The poet no longer refers to the tiny key that opens the door leading to the street, but to forceful gestures that push open all doors. The poem can be read as a manifesto, a call for liberation; the message and its movement are rendered more dramatic, more accessible by the typography and spatial arrangement of the page. Different again is the relation of text to typography in "Testament pour mes amis." The title word is surrounded by a wreath of flowers and leaves. Below these regular, undisturbed patterns appears a four-line poem. The page's resemblance to a tombstone is belied by the vitality of the text.

Let us consider for a moment not the entire text of a page but the varied functions of initials. Capital letters, which often appear to have a life of their own, introduce disorientation and increase complexity. The N initial of Nicolas II belongs to two different types of printing, the two different styles opposing one another; naturally contradiction emerges as a third dimension. The very simple name Nicolas becomes ambiguous by reason of typographical conflict and fantasy. Capitals are not merely bigger letters, but here and there acquire strange reliefs, as though to indicate their eagerness to leave the page of the poet for that of the painter. They become compelling images rather than merely an emphatic way of printing. The M of *Marquis* looks like a well-starched dickey; in relation to the streamlined modern lettering used for the rest of the word, this creates an anachronistic pattern and can thus be considered a typographical cadenza based on the title "marquis."

Les Pénalités de l'enfer includes a wide variety of texts whose differences, as we have shown, are considerably increased by typography. Each page has its own style, its unique composition, its particular conception of space. Each page transforms the text into a never-duplicated plastic work. Since repetitiousness in the text is reduced to a minimum and uniformity of printing has been avoided at all costs, each page asserts itself as an independent work of art. This situation appears highly paradoxical since stylization, order, and symmetry dominate the printed page and leave little room for improvisation. Typography, far from making the text available by means of a universal code, generally imposes an order entirely its own. Miró, by frequently introducing colored and linear signs that evoke writing and printing together with a multiplicity of gestures suggesting creative improvisation, also imposes an order of his own making. The typography clashes with the lithographs insofar as regular shapes, indispensable to printing, are avoided. Nonetheless, the typography is no less playfully subversive than the lithographs themselves; all kinds of lettering are introduced: calligraphy, gothic types, geometric forms, all conveying the diversity of the poetic language while functioning in a referential semantic system. This range and variety somehow match the concatenation of pencil sketches, fingerprints, shiny oil painting, frottages, and collages of the lithographs, where all possible means are used to avoid homogeneity and repetition and to display difference.

The book is presented in a linen box, a luxurious container enclosing hell (see Plate 35). The letters, irregular but readable ink-shapes, dance freely on the page. As container and contained merge, thanks to the superposition of their identical designs, so image and text, writing and painting form a common web, capable of entrapping and even relating contradictory assertions of affinity and difference: the words within the text, the words as images, and all their pictorial counterparts. This Pandora's box becomes a container of multiple expressions and manifestations in both art and literature. Within its boundaries messages countermand themselves: every letter assumes its own direction and releases its energy without truly submitting to the continuity of the line or any other recognizable order. Desnos's "message" cannot fit into a linear system made up of words with fixed meanings or artificially pushed into a semblance of unity.

A chest of drawers is outlined toward the end; it has been emptied—"Les boîtes à cigarettes sont toujours vides" (Cigarette packages are always empty). Desnos not only refers to the absence of cigarettes, but links the recurrent desire to imagination, transgression, poetry. The lithographs have all along emphasized the vigor of colors unwilling to submit to contours, but not nearly as opposed as we had first thought to the rigors of printing, to the framing or laurel-wreathed surfaces, to the useless, empty drawers. *Les Pénalités de l'enfer* exemplifies the struggle between a fixed and spontaneous creativity, the struggle for a liberation which has to be renewed time after time, for constraints and obstacles will always be with us. The book presented in a box, the lining of which shows letters, figures, colors so lively that they jump out at us, exemplifies the highly original conception of illustration that Miró, prompted by Desnos, so successfully elaborated.

MAXIMILIANA

In 1964 in Paris Le Degré Quarante et Un published *Maximiliana ou l'exercice illégal de l'astronomie*: "Pour commenter et illustrer les données de Ernest Guillaume Tempel mises en lumière par Iliazd" (To comment on and illustrate the data of Ernest William Tempel, brought to light by Iliazd).[16] The volume, a joint homage by Max Ernst and Iliazd to the unknown astronomer Tempel, is generally considered one of the major achievements of

---

[16] *Maximiliana or the Illegal Practice of Astronomy*, script and etchings by Max Ernst.

twentieth-century book art. It deserves special attention in Max Ernst's long career as a book illustrator, for here at least the painter does not have to respond to a literary text but to the trials, tribulations, and discoveries of a late-nineteenth-century German astronomer who would not or could not conform to the scientific establishment of his day. Ernst, who tends to neglect Tempel as an author, limits his endeavor to a commentary and an illustration of the astronomer's "verbal data," which provided the basis for both *gravures* and *écritures*. Ernst, in collaboration with Iliazd, acts as intermediary for an obscure astronomer whose raw data he expands and transforms into an illustrated book. From Tempel's words and charts will be wrought the *livre de peintre*'s indissociable texts and images.

The title page, in addition to naming Ernst's dual role, informs us that Iliazd the editor brought *Maximiliana* to light. By his discovery of Tempel, his search for relevant documents, and the artistic presentation of the book, Iliazd makes permanently visible the planet discovered by the astronomer. The name Maximiliana, bequeathed by its discoverer, was quickly replaced by its official name Cybèle, and Tempel fell into an almost brutal oblivion. In 1878 he had himself compared "la perte de la mémoire" (loss of memory) to "la perte de l'art de voir" (loss of the art of seeing). Ernst's and Iliazd's contributions, termed "illustrer" and "mises en lumière," are destined to end, by the creation of the book, the physical and spiritual eclipse of an astronomer and a planet. As Tempel dies before the book's close, as his discovery is superseded, Ernst and Iliazd complete their journey alone; Tempel, Iliazd's discovery, stays behind.

Ernst and Tempel can be intricately linked. Peter Schamoni includes in his *Max Ernst Maximiliana* a photomontage composed of two portraits representing Ernst surrounding one of Tempel, both men wearing the same clothes, thus suggesting that one was the other's alter ego.[17] Maximiliana begins with "Max"; Tempel's given name is Ernst. Indeed, the painter makes use of word-games in *Maximiliana* as he had in illustrating the Mad Hatter's Tea Party and in *Paramyths*. Nothing appears more basic in a linguistic game than the act of naming. Through the visual representation of the bird and the verbal designation of Loplop, Ernst pointed not only to the problem of identity, analyzed in detail in *Au-delà de la peinture* (*Beyond Painting*), but also questioned the relationship between the signifier and the signified.[18] Tempel himself was preoccupied with a system of designation. Thus the substitution of Cybèle for his own Maximiliana stripped him of his identity and reduced

---

[17]Peter Schamoni, *Max Ernst Maximiliana* (Munich: Brückemann, 1974), p. 79.
[18]In Max Ernst, "Oeuvres de 1919–39," *Cahiers d'Art* (1937): no page numbers.

the significance of his name. Ernst had introduced Maximiliana into the skies and vision as early as 1931 in a collage accompanying *Poèmes visibles* and again in 1948, in a drawing in *A l'intérieur de la vue*.[19] His fascination with the planet and the astronomer goes beyond the coincidence created by the identity of names. He saw, perhaps under the influence of Iliazd, in the nineteeneth-century astronomer a subverter of official standards. The fact that Tempel practiced astronomy illegally and entered into conflict with the authorities appealed to the author of *Une Semaine de bonté*, which reveals the "hidden" vices of the Third Republic. From Ernst's perspective, Tempel, misunderstood and threatened, becomes the revolutionary artist willfully deprived of appropriate channels of communication: "L'art de voir est en train de se perdre par suite de l'invention de toutes sortes d'instruments optiques" (The art of seeing is disappearing because of the invention of all sorts of optical instruments, 1878), "Je crois qu'un peintre paysagiste se rangerait de mon côté" (I believe that a landscape artist would be on my side, 1882).[20] Tempel implicitly advocates artistic as opposed to technological tendencies in his search for vision, particularly inner vision.

In this respect Ernst would naturally recognize in him an ally who, some eighty years earlier, had faced the same problems. Indeed, the painter had on numerous occasions sought new ways to represent domains inaccessible to normal perception. On numerous occasions he had painted, etched, or drawn the sky, its constellations, their myths and mystery. In the very year of publication of *Maximiliana* Ernst stated: "The firmament is no longer the thurible it was a thousand years ago, and in another thousand years' time, no one will be entitled anymore to address it by its given name."[21] In 1933 he painted his famous *La Foresta imbalsata*, on which he made the following comment: "Forests swallow the horizon. They take over the sun, having sometimes nothing but an aureole without rays."[22] In many of his paintings and engravings Ernst, far from revealing the infinite distance to stars and planets, gives the impression of bringing the sky into close proximity to the viewer.[23] By dividing his paintings horizontally into two parallel sections, by reducing the landscape to its essentials, by making land and water inter-

---

[19] Max Ernst and Paul Eluard, *A l'intérieur de la vue, 8 poèmes visibles* (Paris: Seghers, 1948).
[20] Quoted in *L'Art de voir de Guillaume Tempel*, catalog (Paris: Le Point Cardinal, 1964), no page number.
[21] Quoted in Schamoni, *Max Ernst Maximiliana*, p. 88.
[22] Ibid., p. 36.
[23] *Pour une école de hareng* (For a School of Herring) (1965); *L'Air lavé à l'eau* (Air Washed with Water) (1969).

changeable and the sky polyvalent, Ernst abolishes the spatial dimension linked to perspective. He created more than one work where the cosmic space and the confines of a room overlap, for instance, *La mer, le soleil et le tremblement de terre*, 1931, and the collage "A la recherche de l'innocence" (see Fig. 19). In "Mon Petit Mont Blanc," a collage from *Les Malheurs des immortels*, a woman's buttocks and Saturn so completely overlap that microcosm and macrocosm seem to match without incongruities. In the upper part of several paintings Ernst includes a circle summarizing the sun or a window looking onto the sky (see Fig. 53).[24] The latter reveals a slanted view, signaling that the world is in motion. In lieu of a fragment of the phenomenological world, Ernst provides the viewer with a perception of a work of art. In such canvases the painter refers both to the relation between nature and art and to different modes and styles of painting.

Before *Maximiliana*, he had alluded to long-distance vision by the inclusion of eyeglasses, lenses, and telescopes. The constellations in his skies, differing in texture, pattern, and structure, are "seen" through various optical instruments. Ernst, who throughout his career attempted to translate the invisible cosmos into visibility, stated in 1926 that the sun and moon, which play such an important part in human consciousness, would recur as images in his subsequent work. It is by no means surprising that in *Maximiliana* he gave both commentary and an illustration concerning Tempel, who, according to Iliazd, "était poussé à chercher l'arbitrage du peintre. Ayant mesuré l'influence de ces inventions sur le sort de la peinture, désormais asile de l'oeil" (was pushed to seek the painter's arbitration. After he had measured the influence of these inventions on the fate of painting, henceforth the sanctuary of the eye).[25]

The reader does not immediately encounter Tempel's data as transmitted by Iliazd and translated by Ernst. From the vellum cover through layers of empty sheets of paper varying in texture, grain, and shade, the reader/viewer journeys through space before he even sees writing and etching. In ever-changing patterns of text and design, verticality gradually prevails over horizontality. Ernst and Iliazd have studiously avoided the usual parallel black lines of ordinary letterpress on white paper; they have transformed each page, as Greet has shown, into a crafted three-dimensional space: "[Iliazd] chose as his schema a geometric form and outlined it in small squares. The schema is

---

[24] *Ici meurent les cardinaux* (Here Die the Cardinals) (1962); *Le Mariage du ciel et de la terre* (The Marriage of Heaven and Earth) (1964).
[25] In *L'Art de voir*, preface.

recurrent, and it is not centered on the page. Instead, shapes are tilted and the design is off-center; part of a rectangle or spiral is missing, as if it sloped off into the void."[26]

Iliazd arranged fragments of Tempel's official statements and his letters into a confession both personal and scientific, which includes passages in French, German, and Italian that refer to Tempel's voyages, his search for a more congenial climate. One after another follow pages of poetry, of sensitive observations, of maxims, of declarations concerning human existence. The text constitutes Iliazd's re-creation of Tempel's journals and sayings as well as the editor's personal, ironic intervention after Tempel's death. These various types of discourse are printed in always different spatial arrangements and typographical characters. Most pages are broken up into several juxtaposed sections—typography and etching, typography and collage, or two differing kinds of typography, including printed characters, mysterious figures, and "hand-drawn" letters. The pages suggest graphic images even when they are primarily composed of a printed text.

One of the simplest designs consists of a few words scattered on the page (Fig. 110). Each word, read in a zigzagging but clearly descending movement never forming a straight or repetitive line, resembles a constellation in which individual letters mirror the passage of shooting stars. The meaning of the text, always concerned with distance, clearly relates to the etching (Plate 36). Two pages facing each other frame the image. The eye moves across the picture of Maximiliana in a pigmented sky, perhaps referring to the Milky Way. The planet, invisible to the naked eye, surrounded by a sun and a moon, is personified in the text insofar as it is integrated into or belongs to a family. Ernst's sky views, which include heavenly bodies with similarities to spirals and clockworks, combine the natural with the mechanical, the mechanical with the invisible, a combination Ernst had introduced as early as 1920 with his *La Petite Fistule lacrymale qui dit tic-tac* (The Little Tear-Gland That Says Tick-Tock). The clockwork wheel and the unwinding spiral situate Maximiliana in a paradoxical time-span where immobility and rotation are suggested simultaneously. On the title page appear the dark outlines, enlarged in dimmer shades, of an anthropomorphic figure, thus introducing at the outset the paradox of double vision.

We have mentioned that a mysterious writing covers various pages in con-

---

[26] Anne Greet, "Iliazd and Max Ernst: 65 Maximiliana or the Illegal Practice of Astronomy," *World Literature Today* 56 (Winter 1982): 10. The following appeared when our book was already in press: Anne Hyde Greet, "Max Ernst and the Artist's Book: From Fiat Modes to Maximiliana," in *Max Ernst: Beyond Surrealism*.

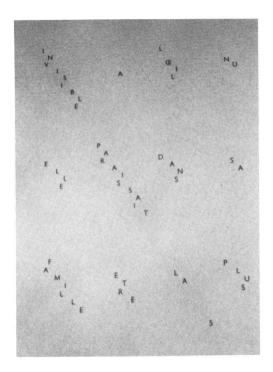

FIG. 110. Typography by Iliazd and Max Ernst from Iliazd and Max Ernst, *Maximiliana*. Paris: Le Degré Quarante et Un, 1964. © SPADEM, Paris; VAGA, New York, 1985.

junction with ordinary typography, collage, or etching (Fig. 111). The invented characters and the conventional typography confront each other on most pages. Werner Spies calls the ciphers *Geheimschrift*: "Max Ernst developed for this book a secret writing, which did not contain a single recognizable letter and had to be read in the same way as the heavenly bodies. . . . The blocks of writing do not only serve as formal matter. Max Ernst juxtaposed in this book the Milky Way with messages scattered in illegible signs."[27] Ernst may have invented the secret writing for *Maximiliana* but he did not use it exclusively in this book.[28] He created an "alphabet" that is infinitely expandable as well as adaptable to varying spatial conditions. His system imposes no limits on what signs can be made available. The secret writing bridges the gap between a familiar and an unfamiliar world, between the visible and the invisible, composed as it is of signs that belong simultaneously to visual and to verbal codes. The writing, which functions throughout as a visual sign, creates the momentary illusion that it is decipherable, that the letters or shapes may somehow yield a meaning. On densely covered pages this

[27]Werner Spies, *Die Rückkehr der schönen Gärtnerin* (Cologne: DuMont-Schauberg, 1971), p. 100.
[28]Cf. *Le Monde des naïfs* (1965).

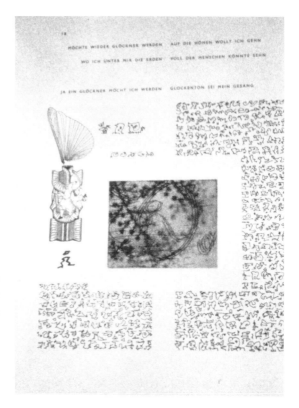

FIG. 111. Mixed media by
Iliazd and Max Ernst for
Maximiliana. © SPADEM, Paris;
VAGA, New York, 1985.

visible language seems to withhold its message with even greater stubbornness. This *écriture* transmits the language of the unknown without in any way
sacrificing its mystery.

The secret language does not assume a single format. The parallelism of
its lines is at best of secondary importance. At times the ciphers form a solid
wall whose impenetrability we strive to challenge (Fig. 112); at others, it is
reduced to marginal strips of varying sizes where verticality tends to dominate, as though to withdraw part of its visibility from the reader. Each of its
signs suggests a vitality or dynamic shape, capable of expansion and above all
of metamorphosis, defying the notion of finality. Repeatedly the secret wall
multiplies circular or hexagonal shapes, pieces broken loose or made autonomous. Larger figures, resembling—momentarily, at least—birds and other
creatures, promising to become shapes in a continuous process, belong to a
field of vision corresponding to Tempel's central preoccupation. On sparsely
covered pages the signs tend to show greater fluidity and more closely approximate ideograms. On several pages the secret writing acts as a frame surrounding a central section neatly delineated and teeming with drawings of

FIG. 112. Mixed media by Iliazd and Max Ernst for *Maximiliana*. © SPADEM, Paris; VAGA, New York, 1985.

figures, themselves variations of writing (see Fig. 111). This simultaneous projection, on each page, of close and distant visions reflects Tempel's attempt to make stars visible by magnifying them. Because the secret writing can turn both the center and the frame of the page into spatial entities, it not only bridges the gap between verbal and graphic but becomes *écriture* in the strong sense. Void and plenitude are no longer contradictions. These figures in the center, by evoking the viewer surrounded by the view, create, as it were, a semiotic portrait of Tempel, stressing his upward-turned glance, his aspirations.

Such processes at the very least disturb habitual reading habits. As we read, decode, decipher, we deviate from the accustomed manner of reading, abandon all parallelism and change our course. We read as we journey through space. Within the space of the page appear not only variations and expansions of the mysterious code, but drawings and etchings. Repeatedly, pronounced rectangular and spiral shapes, even "diagrams," emerge in the etchings. These reduced and stylized forms speak of the swiftness of celestial movements and inscribe the evanescent traces of planets. These in-text etch-

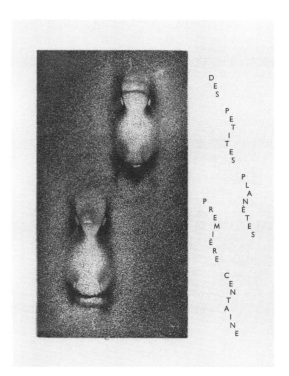

FIG. 113. Etching by Max Ernst
for *Maximiliana*. © SPADEM,
Paris; VAGA, New York, 1985.

ings introduce still another perspective of the skyscape. In relation to the secret writing and to the larger, almost full-sized plates, they present different
degrees of immediacy, different forms of reduction, different ways of conveying the distant world. They provide references to Tempel's observations, to
his theories, which Ernst transmits, all the while establishing exchange and
even reversibility between comment and illustration. The book, a prophecy
composed of collected data, embraces a wide range of "written" or "scribal"
art forms which invite the viewer to create other combinations.

In Ernst's etchings subdued blue- and red-shaded clouds emerge. Solar
and stellar shapes combine recognizable signs both from maps and from otherworldly visions (Fig. 113). Amid these dispersions and condensations the
planet "unfolds" like a cell, spelling out the promise of the future, of new
birth. These maps, making visual Tempel's sayings and sometimes inspired
by the astronomer's own lithographs, offer surprising variations on Ernst's
own work.[29] The painter also repeatedly includes figures of a distorted over-

[29]Cf. *La Lune est un rossignol muet* (The Moon Is a Mute Nightingale) (1963) and *La Terre
vue de . . .* (The Earth Seen from . . .) (1963).

grown net or grid in which organic and geometrical forms merge. A black tree pressing against a leaf-colored net creates a new set of signs. The gigantic flower, a reduction of the sun with its multiple lines and loops, resembles nonlinear handwriting.

As we mentioned earlier, the legible pages of *Maximiliana* vary considerably, not only in their spatial arrangement and typography but also textually. In addition to an account of Tempel's planetary discovery and subsequent persecution, Iliazd includes a poem, a continuous narration spread over four pages. It confronts and crowns the mysterious writing arranged in variously shaped blocks as well as more or less recognizably outlined figures suggesting mobility and fluctuation. The secret writing with its emancipated, autonomous figures functions as an illustration for the regularly printed text, suspended in the upper regions of the page and "singing" the epic existence of Tempel:

> *Möchte wieder Glöckner werden, auf die Höhe wollt ich gehen*
> *Wo ich unter mir die Erden voll der Menschen könnte sehen*
> *Ja ein Glöckner möcht ich werden, Glockenton sei mein*
> > *Gesang*
>
> I would like to become a bell-ringer again, I would like to climb heights
> Where I can see below me the earth full of men
> Yes, I would like to become a bell-ringer again, let the sound of the bells be my
> > song

This man who longs for the height of the bell tower, who seeks to extend his vision, who subordinates his personal life to the discovery of new perspectives, strongly resembles the astronomer. The bell resounding across great distances corresponds to the planets that Tempel wished to make visible. The text, alternating between sensuous vision and conceptual language, includes proverbial statements which, unlike the poem, do not provide an image of the astronomer's career. They seem to convey with brevity the wisdom acquired and transmitted by Tempel.

"Ce ne sont pas les grandes lunettes qui font les grands astronomes" (it is not great telescopes that make great astronomers): this proverb refers to Tempel's fundamental opposition to mechanization and his assertion of inner vision. We hear at the end of the book that the astronomer's method will not stand the test of time, for those who follow Tempel will make their discovery by instruments, without benefit of poetic vision. Thus the proverb becomes paradoxical. Strangely enough, Ernst seems to parody his own notorious phrase from *Au-delà de la peinture*: "Ce n'est pas la colle qui fait le collage"

(It is not the paste that makes the collage). Our interpretation is based both on Ernst's love for verbal puns and on the presence of collages in *Maximiliana*. On the two pages that include the above statements, the painter introduces cut-out sections, collages alluding to his earlier works (see Figs. 111, 112). These borrowed images are by no means mere repetitions, for they are swiftly transformed under the viewer's eyes—a shell into a skirt, a medal into a star, a bodice into a book. By adding zigzag lines to a plain seashell he evokes a dancing figure—the rim of the shell becomes the pleats of the skirt, thus suggesting the impact of movement undercutting the solid, material aspects of the shell, so that hypothetically it can be projected into space. As we leaf through the book we also see repeatedly that as soon as letters are enlarged they tend to free themselves from the two-dimensional surface of the page and emerge as figures.

The shell and the bodice are inscribed in the margins of two facing pages, where etchings framed by secret writing reveal the center (see Fig. 111). Spatial display on the page exposes separate but autonomous parts producing interrelations rather than interference, comparable to a flash of poetry. We have maintained that on most pages we are drawn into the "orbit" of writing as a visual and plastic entity. The orbit as a space, as a traceless trajectory described by a body, refers to both visibility and invisibility. The ambiguous role of "Ce ne sont pas les grandes lunettes qui font les grands astronomes" stresses once again the importance of semantics, which will soon be challenged on pages where the encroachment of the purely visual manifests itself too strongly. The representation of a distant stellar landscape is juxtaposed with the phrase "Télescope à vendre" (Telescope for sale). In *L'Art de voir* we find that statement—supposedly made by Tempel for purely economic reasons, but its ideological overtones are inescapable. The accompanying vision of the landscape is far, not close, distinct, not blurred; thus, the verbal statement multiplies meanings and levels of interrelationship. Ernst's contribution to the book never parallels in a simplistic manner Tempel's sayings or Iliazd's arrangements. Tensions, remarkable changes in distance, occur throughout.

Maximiliana truly represents the book as object. The paper supplies substance and texture, the typography plays a prominent creative part, the folio pages have been folded into double pages. Greet points out that "in their ensemble the 30 leaves compose a triptych whose three sections of eight, fourteen and eight pages are closely and logically linked."[30] To us the word *triptych* has additional implications, for the book includes three types of

---

[30] "Iliazd and Max Ernst: 65 Maximiliana or the Illegal Practice of Astronomy," p. 12.

printing, the alphabet, the ideograms, and graphic representations; and three types of discourse, the personal, the literary, and the scientific. Three men, scientist, editor, and painter, were involved in the fabrication of the book. The editor contributes to the visibility of Maximiliana by writing a preface, a eulogy of Tempel; the scientist, alienated from his time, opposed the commonly accepted ideas of progress. Tempel himself becomes an artist whose observations led to vision, who drew maps and made lithographs. Ernst, the creator of many a *machine célibataire*, has emulated and parodied, graphically and poetically, certain scientific pursuits. By his *écriture* and *eau-forte* he became the accomplice of Tempel, whose ventures, revealed to him by Iliazd, he made visible and therefore known. *Maximiliana* constitutes a manifesto engaging reader and viewer in Ernst's and Tempel's fight against the loss of inner vision. Ernst strove to show the full range of language as visual and conceptual entities. When images reflect each other, when words illustrate representations which are mirrored in both text and image, the illustrated book abolishes the distinction between verbal and visual.

CHAPTER TEN

BEYOND THE BOOK

IN THE PAST THE WESTERN WORLD derived its subject matter from texts, and until the Renaissance, the text considered most worthy of representation was of course the Bible—the Book. A medieval church with its stained-glass windows, its statuary, decorated columns, and frescoes functioned in part as an enormous volume where the faithful, most of them unlettered, could *read* all they needed to know about their status in this world and their chances in the next. It was only with the waning of the Middle Ages that artists illustrated mythological, historical, and literary writings. In seventeenth-century France painters were considered far superior to artisans only because their art could have intellectual, even literary, merit. Their primary task was to represent to perfection whatever sacred, historical, or even mythological events their patrons might require them to paint.

Since the middle of the nineteenth century, painters have generally freed themselves from texts, particularly sacred ones. Even Millet's *Angélus*, in spite of a religiosity that only Dalí would deny, owes nothing to books, but only to a ritual. And it conveys feelings, mostly esthetic, rather than ideas. In a sense, the canvas in all its opacity has already taken over.

Unlike other modern painters, surrealist artists frequently derive their subject matter from texts of all sorts, and not only when they illustrate books. Even then, as we have seen, they do not respect the kind of mimetic approach that painters of the past would have considered indispensable. The one exception to this rule is René Magritte, that most literary of all surrealist artists, whose illustrations for *Maldoror* did now and again descend to the level of graphic paraphrase. Indeed, many of his famous works, no less than those of, let us say, Philippe de Champaigne, illustrate an idea. Not surprisingly, several of his canvases bear literary titles derived mainly from Edgar Allan Poe, judged by the French to be not only an incomparable writer of fantastic fiction but a major poet and a theorist whose ideas must be taken with utter seriousness.

Magritte's paintings based on three of Poe's tales mark in a sense a return to artistic practices of the past while suggesting a step forward, a way to go beyond the book. There are, as we shall see, other successful ways of going beyond the book or, rather, sidestepping it—for example, Cornell's transformation of a volume into a box and, more recently, the displacement of the book into various kinds of art objects.

THE HOUSE OF USHER *and* THE DOMAIN OF ARNHEIM

In several letters Magritte touches on the subject of illustration:

I shall add . . . a reminder concerning the lack of interest of illustrations (illustrations in the usual sense). Instead of the idea of illustration, I would prefer that images accompany a text. Thus images would not be "commanded" or "inspired" by the text, but could *felicitously encounter it.*—Illustration implies labor applied to . . . whose simple or complex mechanism can be dismantled. The reunion or encounter of a text and an image is foreseeable.[1]

Magritte illustrated several texts, two of which were published in book form: Eluard's *Les Nécessités de la vie et les conséquences des rêves, précédés d'exemples* and of course Lautréamont's *Les Chants de Maldoror.*[2] Yet in his Maldoror illustrations, discussed in an earlier chapter, Magritte seems to deny his own theories, probably because he accepted Lautréamont's insistence on the term *rencontre* in his metaphor. The painter gives his readers every inducement to remember the text, without presenting them with potentially fruitful juxtapositions of unrelated materials. Elsewhere Magritte always strove to free the surrealist painter from the burdens of the past and the mimetic constraints of the present. A painter who remembers or pays homage to another creation, visual or verbal, prolongs, we believe, an imaginary world, but does not subject himself to it or make literal use of it. It is in this sense that we have to interpret Magritte's statement on one of his paintings devoted to Poe's "Domain of Arnheim": "*The Domain of Arnheim* brings into being a vision that Edgar Poe would have greatly appreciated: an enormous mountain whose

---

[1] René Magritte, *Ecrits complets* (Paris: Flammarion, 1979), pp. 485–86.
[2] Paul Eluard, *Les Nécessités de la vie et les conséquences des rêves, précédés d'exemples* (Necessities of Life and the Consequences of Dreams, Preceded by Examples) with illustrations by Magritte (Brussels: Lumière, 1946).

form exactly corresponds to that of a bird with its wings outspread. One can see it from an open bay window on whose edge two eggs are placed."[3]

Magritte named many paintings after literary works, for example, *Les Fleurs du Mal* (1946), *Les Affinités électives* (1933), *Les Liaisons dangereuses* (1935), *La Géante* (1935), and *Les Bijoux indiscrets* (1963). To Edgar Allan Poe alone he devoted five paintings: *The Fall of the House of Usher* (1949), *The Imp of the Perverse* (1927), and three different paintings all entitled *The Domain of Arnheim.*[4] For several reasons it may be paradoxical to include these in a study devoted to illustration. The first reason is Magritte's own reservations about the term, even when applied to a continuous sequence. Second, a single painting referring to a text has limitations and consequently imposes from the start a great deal of reduction, and in any case it is not presented to the viewer as, for instance, in *Les Chants de Maldoror*, "physically" in a juxtaposition of text and image—it does not provide the viewer with a simultaneous experience. Third, we should take Magritte's general theory in "Les Mots et les images" seriously: "An object is not so closely linked to its name that it is not possible to find a better one."[5] The name of a literary work would, according to Magritte, necessarily come to mean something else by the very act of denoting the painting. Magritte undoubtedly used the literary titles to create another dimension rather than to establish a similarity between his own painting and the literary work. Since the titles of his paintings are by no means descriptive, but enigmatic and deliberately unpredictable, the relationship between his paintings and the literary work will necessarily tend to entrap rather than enlighten the viewer.

. . .

In "The Fall of the House of Usher" Poe establishes great cohesion between the physical and the moral universes of the protagonist, whose abode collapses when the last Usher goes to his doom. The inbreeding of the family, whose last offspring, brother and sister, are barely distinguishable, corresponds to the enclosure of their domain, from which nobody has departed and into which nobody enters, a decaying domain that survives as a mere phantom. Not only does the physical decadence of the domain and its enclosure correspond to moral isolation and disease, but the spiritual activity of Roderick—his dreams and hallucinations—shows the same pattern as the

[3] *Ecrits complets*, p. 111.
[4] Cf. William Goldhurst, "Literary Images Adapted by the Artist: The Case of Edgar Allan Poe and René Magritte," *The Comparatist* 3 (May 1979): 3–15.
[5] *Ecrits complets*, p. 60.

tunnels and vaults, images of death, of burial, of darkness, of imprisonment that haunt him. Dream and outer world, almost identical, are mirrored in the reading and music upon which Roderick feeds his imagination. The accumulation of these activities further accentuates the artificiality of his existence, which is cut off from life-giving forces.

The tale is rich in scenes and images, sights, open and closed vistas which amplify the narrative account. The narrator sees, for instance, the image of the house in the pool as clearly as he sees the house itself, and with an even greater shudder. Later, in the absence of the moon, he notices that "the undersurfaces of the huge masses of agitated vapor were glowing in the unnatural light of a faintly luminous exhalation."[6] Appearance, hallucinatory images, and shadows haunt the viewer's sight, blocking out everyday experience.

René Magritte's painting, with its streamlined simplicity, omits the psychological dimensions of the narrative, the spiritual disease coupled with physical decline, the contagious effect that the atmosphere has on the narrator, who cannot remain a mere witness. Magritte omits all descriptive details concerning the sinister domain: its forbidding approach, its dreary rooms, culminating in images of the crypt and tomb. The painter shows a scene without human protagonists. The curtain, the small, artificial-looking moon, the painted backdrop owe far more to theatricality than to nature (Fig. 114). The curtain opens onto space which becomes part of the spectacle of death. The painter shows the void on both sides of the drapes. Because the curtains are only half-open, they conceal as much as they reveal to the viewer, who witnesses a spectacle at its denouement.

In front of the curtain, the arboreal protagonist performs simultaneously as actor/spectator irremediably locked into a situation that makes any future encounter impossible. By this theatrical device Magritte not only represents by a series of analogies the merging of brother and sister and even the narrator, but he also indicates that the protagonist/spectator has gained awareness of the actor's fatal performance.

The Ushers have mysterious affinities with plants. A single overgrown leaf which has sprung from a tree trunk serves as a metaphor for their family lineage. Here Poe's text provided the lead, for when the narrator, prior to reaching the Ushers' house, considers the family's history, he says, "The *stem* of the Usher race, all time honored as it was had put forth at no period any enduring or collateral *branch* in the direct line of descent, and had always, with

6Edgar Allan Poe, *Complete Stories and Poems* (Garden City, New York: Doubleday, 1966), p. 188. All quotations are from this edition.

FIG. 114. Painting by René Magritte, *The Fall of the House of Usher*, 1949. © Georgette Magritte, 1985. Photograph courtesy of the Menil Foundation, London.

very trifling and very temporary variation, so *lain*" (p. 178). In other words, we can claim that Magritte did not invent a metaphor to illustrate the tale but that he deciphered it in the text itself. The central image, borrowed from Poe, depicts a distorted, even thwarted, tree. The image of the verbal expression also provides a diagram. Poe's metaphor of the genealogical tree is allusory rather than precise, permitting the integration of the physical with the moral domain. As Joseph Riddel states: "This 'deficiency' as the narrator twice calls it, signifies the end of both the family and history, and reveals that both are problematical metaphors based on a questionable analogy between a biological and genealogical order."[7] In Poe's text, the metaphor of the branchless tree is preceded by the narrator's noticing "inverted images of the gray sedge, and ghastly tree stems, and the vacant eye-like windows" (p. 178). Vision as well as what is seen is distorted. Images pertaining to nature, which introduce the family and its decline, produce effects on all aspects of their lives.

Crowned by a leaf, Magritte's tree trunk takes on the identity of a stem. As a trunk it lacks the necessary length; as a stem its wooden fiber and its thick-

[7]Joseph Riddel, "The Crypt of Edgar Poe," *Boundary* II, 7 (1979):126.

ness are incongruous. Rootless, it stands on a ground without depth. This position refers to the lack of a solid past, to the absence of life-giving forces from an underground network. The short stem bearing a huge leaf increases the sense of disproportion. The green foliage full of traceries reminiscent of blood-filled veins and arteries, contradicts and displaces the desiccated appearance of the wood. The anemic Usher family hardly seems compatible with these vigorous arteries. As the leaf is broken and death imminent, the "fall" of the leaf becomes a theatrical revelation of a foregone but unstated conclusion. The leaf alludes ironically to the Ushers' false concern with aristocratic superiority and singularity, with their "overblown" self-concern. The texture and veins of the leaf seem to echo the brain's convolutions. Magritte points to the fabrication of the family's own myth. The impotent Usher family generates the myth of its own power; it performs in the presence of the friend, in reality inevitably a stranger, rituals derived from a meaningless past and from esoteric works of art, rituals to which the friend is invited as to a theatrical presentation. Magritte's translation of Poe's narrative into theater appears all the more convincing since the fall takes place in a void, in an empty space symbolic at once of the present and the future of the family.

In front of the curtain, which is probably in the process of dropping, two stones lie next to the tip of the leaf. They seem unrelated to the barren soil and to the leaf. Yet, they too have fallen: of the vast house, after its collapse, only two insignificant pebbles remain, alluding to the last, thoroughly inbred Ushers, dead as stone. To a certain extent the painter undercuts the coherence of Poe's presentation wherein all elements mirror each other, a tale in which shadow, copy, reflection, and fiction abound. Magritte, in his eagerness not to be seduced by false legends, interrelated all aspects of his paintings; the curtain, far too long, appears to form its own fibers and vessels in creating its own reflection. Curtain, tree and leaf, moon and stone are variations on the same model, devalued from the beginning.

· · ·

Magritte's art has been termed literary because of his apparent lack of preoccupation with technical innovations, a shortcoming which the painter's own statements seem to confirm: "In the art of painting as I conceive it, technique plays only an episodic part. Its interest is purely professional, incapable of satisfying anything but idle curiosity."[8] The literary quality of Magritte's art may also derive from his awareness of language, revealed above all in his use of

[8]Marcel Lecomte, *L'Oeuvre de René Magritte*, catalog of Knokke exhibit, July-August 1962, p. 5.

enigmatic, punning titles. Instead of giving a direct explanation or description, they relate obliquely to the work by providing a verbal juxtaposition to the drawn and colored assemblage. Magritte's paintings appear to provide an example of encounters of two unrelated objects in an unexpected spatial setting. The language of the titles extends this chance encounter in another direction. Therefore, the viewer cannot expect that the painter will merely make visible, on a two-dimensional canvas, the entire domain of Arnheim, the paradise that Poe evoked.

The Belgian painter entitled three somewhat different paintings *Le Domaine d'Arnheim*; an interval of twenty-five years elapsed between the first and the last version. As the basic landscape structure remains unaltered, the difference between them should perhaps be explained in terms of conception rather than imagination. The second painting (1949) stresses the separation between reality and image; the first (1938) and third (1962)—which are very similar—nature versus artifice.

The first part of Poe's tale focuses on an esthetic discussion culminating in the formulation of an ideal, while the second recounts the pursuits and realization of this ideal, or, in other words, the transformation of a concept of beauty into a poetic vision. The fundamental question raised in the theoretical pages bears on the relative superiority of art to nature, on the perfectibility of both, and on the possible correctives that art can make to flaws that mar nature's harmony. Poe applies to nature a terminology usually more relevant to art: "No pictorial or sculptural combinations of points of human loveliness do more than approach the living and breathing beauty. In landscape alone is the principle of the critic true, and, having felt its truth there, it is but the head-long spirit of generalization which has led him to pronounce it true throughout all the domains of art" (p. 575). Ellison, a poet in the broad sense of the term, probably an idealized version of the author and his dreams, defines the landscape garden as the sole domain where nature and artifice can be fused. Through effort, the artist using nature as raw material overcomes its inherent imperfections, however great, whereas mere words or brush-strokes cannot make up for the deficiencies of a nature irredeemably lacking in esthetic qualities.

The superiority of art and its god-like attributes or associations are implicit in Poe's theory of the ideal creation in which the man-made and the natural—as their differences and rivalries have been transcended—unite and blend their essences. Although a god is mentioned in Poe's universe, the landscape garden is not so much the product of divine intervention as of angelic mediation. Poe employs irony, for Ellison's spiritual attainment depends on material wealth well invested; a chain of superlatives enumerates the extraordinary wealth and possessions that unexpectedly fall into his hands. Spiritual accomplishment is connected in more than one way to material objects. The landscape garden, in order to become a tangible reality, necessitates the lifelong dedication of its creator and the investment of his inheritance, even if all traces of labor, effort, and expense ultimately have to be erased. The spiritual values of the domain remain inseparable from its physical reality, from its spatial expansion. The landscape garden belongs to the realm of poetry, according to Poe the highest of the arts.

The 1949 version of *Le Domaine d'Arnheim* does not represent the paradise that Poe evokes. Perceptions sublimated by synesthesia and the interplay between water and other elements, so important in Poe, play at best an insignificant role in the painting (Plate 37). The mountain rocks with their bluish hues and their white crevasses have some correspondence with the changing map of the sky. A dual vision confronts the spectator: one whole, the other fragmented; one a configuration of reality, the other a reflection. However, since the skyscape is separated from the landscape by a wooden bar and can thus be viewed as a separate picture, Magritte introduces a further ambiguity. As the painter presents a view neatly framed by a broken window, he introduces a second frame offering an ironic counterpart to the first. The irregular broken outlines of the inner frame make the regular outlines of the rectangle, which indicates the limits of visible nature, appear artificial. Nature rarely provides the regular geometric lines often favored by the artist.

As the outside landscape and its image on the window are identical, the absence or presence of glass becomes meaningless. The transparency of the pane accounts for this sameness: Magritte shows that nature and its reflection are equally visible since the problematics of distance has been overlooked. Now one more incongruity strikes the viewer: the broken pieces of glass lack transparency. Many of the painted pieces are stood up: odd-shaped canvases reproducing sections of the landscape. We wonder whether Magritte does not present his viewer with the two possibilities that Poe's narrator, after some hesitancy, weighed before giving his account of the domain of Arnheim— detail, and general vision. The writer had pointed out a flaw in both alternatives: neither one, if used mimetically, could offer a valid representation of a firsthand experience. In Magritte's painting, the colors, relief, and outlines of the fragments differ from the larger landscape; as they become autonomous they take on a new intensity, with deeper gorges and more threatening avalanches. The spectator realizes that he tends to perceive or to preserve fragments of a unity either lost or totally artificial.

The 1949 version of *Le Domaine d'Arnheim* raises rather obliquely the very problem that sets Ellison on his quest: the fusion of nature and artifice in the creation of the landscape garden. In Magritte's universe, art and nature tend to form a reciprocal system of reduction and subservience rather than combine in mutual exaltation or idealization. The two versions of *Le Domaine d'Arnheim*, which do not include references to human beings, propose not, as in Poe's tale, the perspective of the creator or superior being, but that of the humble spectator, even the bourgeois consumer. The ironic, basically negative twist Magritte gives to Poe's hopeful idealism echoes the surrealists' accusation that their contemporaries suffered from a cautiously limited perception and an inability to enter the realm of imagination.

Poe, who focuses primarily on the artist's aspiration, is, however, not unconcerned with the observer or reader. In the latter part of the tale Ellison no longer functions as commentator and exponent of a theory of esthetics. The author evokes the domain from the point of view of a visitor who approaches it gradually instead of giving a global reconstruction by an all-seeing author. The reader is confronted with a voyage by stages each of which is characterized by new and ever-changing vistas. Seeming to reflect Poe's Romanticism, Ellison asserts that the superior response of the reader or spectator manifests itself emotionally, whereas the creative act has primarily intellectual implications. Penetration into the domain brings about changes in the traveller; he will eventually participate in the work of art and even, once his spiritual forces are aroused, contribute to the idea of art. Magritte, on the contrary, undercuts the spectator's realm of imagination by the mirroring technique which often occurs in his works and which makes landscapes indistinguishable from representations of them. He thrusts at the spectators the images most likely to satisfy them or the only ones that their rigidity, their vested interests, and their lack of critical sophistication will allow them to recognize.

In assuming the point of view of the traveller who approaches and enters the domain, Poe uncovers discoveries unfolding in time. This evolutionary dimension of the narrative has no equivalent in Magritte's paintings. Poe's traveller experiences novelty but never repetition or prolonged exposure to a single sight. All along, the poet stresses the presence of both natural and artificial elements, as well as their interrelationship. By using nature as its material, the work of art assumes the power of a landscape with unlimited spatial expansion. The simultaneity of art and nature, rather than their rivalry or the transformation of the latter by the former, offers the supreme esthetic experience. The author describes in rational progression the scenes of the unfold-

FIG. 115. Painting by René Magritte, *The Domain of Arnheim*, 1962. © Georgette Magritte, 1985. Photograph courtesy of the Menil Foundation, London.

ing landscape. In the progression of the boat the traveller captures vibrant configurations brought forth by and appealing to all his senses.

The basic principle of Poe's fusion of the visible and the invisible, the gradual penetration into the domain, the transformation of the spectator, who no longer feels the impact of the outer world, are totally absent from Magritte's second *Domaine d'Arnheim*. In the 1949 version Magritte raises the question of the distance between landscape and representation, while in the 1938 (Plate 38) and 1962 (Fig. 115) versions he is concerned with the problem of the distance between landscape and spectators. As a wall (horizontal and vertical in the 1939 version and horizontal only in the 1962 version) separates the scene from us, we will always be outsiders: the landscape will remain on the other side; we may view it but will be excluded from all participation in it.[9]

The scene of the third version of *Le Domaine d'Arnheim* is bathed in

[9]Similar walls rising before the bourgeois observer appear in several Magritte paintings; for example, in *La Carte postale* (1960), an observer in black coat and hat turns his back on viewers of the canvas.

darker blue shades, whereas by its coloring the first accentuates the snow. In both these paintings, however, the forbidding mountain, with its meandering valleys and protruding rocks culminating in the head of an eagle, offers a more pronounced and slanting perspective than in the second version. The separation made by the wall is counterbalanced by the extended and dramatic mass of rocks (horizontally curtailed and in every respect more subdued in the 1949 version). The darker blues of the sky (here no longer separated from the mountains by a wooden panel) echo the mountains but also strongly suggest water, a key element in Poe's tale, the fluid course of which plays an essential part in the perfectly timed penetration of the domain. *Le Domaine d'Arnheim* 1962 represents a different moment of day, to judge by the significantly darker hues and the moon crescent. Yet the light tone of the sky, compared to the coloring of the mountains and the rest of the scene, by introducing a certain degree of paradox makes the reference to time of day perplexing, as is so often the case in Magritte.

Whenever Magritte shows "beautiful" scenery—worthy of a nineteenth-century landscape artist such as Caspar David Friedrich—there is an ironic counterpart. Irony in *Le Domaine d'Arnheim* centers on the eagle and its nest or, in the earlier version, the two eggs resting on the wall. On the one hand, Magritte raises the paradox of fresh "shell" eggs and a stately eagle; on the other, he introduces into the "seductive" azure-hued nature a hierarchical, figurative if not pseudo-allegorical, dimension, which relates to the spectator's impulse to give meaning to and discover recognizable shapes, to transform living impulses into monuments. The landscape with its snowy or azure overtones consists primarily of a pair of spread-eagle peaks.

Magritte has objectified literary ambiguity and polyvalence in this and other paintings. He has referred to Poe's metaphors of fluidity versus rigidity as well as his paradox between detail and vision. He has also parodied artistic creations that take nature as subject matter. Poe insisted on the incompatibility of rigidity and artistic creation, while Magritte has transformed many of his figures, including the eagle of *Le Domaine d'Arnheim*, into petrified shapes.[10]

Bird and stone having become synonymous, is true life lacking? The organic and inorganic are equated. Opposed to the petrified eagle, reminiscent of past existence, are the small eggs (especially in the later version), promising future life, at once belonging yet totally unrelated to the gigantic bird. This strange severing is further dramatized by the separation of the nest from na-

---

[10] In *La Fontaine de Jouvence* (1958), the bird's outspread wings double as a tombstone or funeral plaque.

ture and its mysterious placement on the wall. Its closeness to the hypothetical viewer turns the landscape into fiction: it suppresses any belief in its possible powers of transcendence. It undercuts Poe's vague dream of a new race, a new birth; it erases all trace of utopian thought underlying spiritual or esthetic idealism. (It is true that Ellison's domain remains the creation of an individual and that the narrator only leads the visitor to the door.) The nest deepens the notion of separation that Foucault has revealed in his analysis of "La Trahison des images."[11] Discontinuity and rupture dominate this apparently highly unified and harmonious landscape.

Magritte's technique of surrealist juxtaposition does not correspond to Poe's search for integration. The American writer gradually loosens the grip of rationality as his hero announces the attainment of a new inner order and forms of beauty. It is likely, however, that Poe mentions perfectionism with tongue in cheek. But even if the voyage to Arnheim resembles, here and there, a descent into hell, in an intense moment of vision the narrator asserts: "Not a dead branch—not a withered leaf—not a stray pebble—not a patch of the brown earth was anywhere visible. The crystal water welled up against the clean granite, or the unblemished moss, with a sharpness of outline that delighted while it bewildered the eye" (p. 579). Magritte believes neither in coherence nor in the encounter of the genuinely new—unless we take too seriously his bold proclamation that the impossible is possible, that castles float in the air. Whatever the limitations and restrictions on which the Belgian painter insisted, before or after his confrontation with the fantastic world of Edgar Allan Poe, he linked them to the bowler-hatted bourgeois whose disguise he often wore. Tales such as "The Imp of the Perverse" and "The Domain of Arnheim" undoubtedly made him realize that, like Ellison, he used landscapes not as a set of convincing images but as the substance of his artistic inventions and structures.

JOSEPH CORNELL'S BOXES AND COLLAGES

In his boxes and collages Cornell persistently borrows from works of art and literature. He makes ample use of objects combining verbal and visual elements (such as maps and posters), reduced to fragments by erosion and segmentation. Cornell, whose range of literary allusions is extensive, usually reduces a work to its title, a key quotation, or random sentences. Both Dore Ashton and Diane Waldman have demonstrated that Romantic and surreal-

[11]Michel Foucault, "Ceci n'est pas une pipe," *Les Cahiers du Chemin* (January 1968): 79–108.

FIG. 116. Collage by Joseph
Cornell, *Vierge vivace*, 1970.
© Estate of Joseph Cornell, Pace
Gallery, 1985. Photograph
courtesy of Castelli Feigen
Corcoran, New York.

ist writers play a significant role throughout.[12] Cornell often turns the title or
quotation into a relic, illustrating an absent text. He stores words, like recollections, in containers where they shed their familiar meanings, to live again
in strange surroundings. The artist combines verbal and plastic elements that
in their mutual fragmentation often assume analogous roles and become almost interchangeable.

In 1971, Cornell entitled a collage *Vierge vivace*, words from the first line
of Mallarmé's sonnet (Fig. 116).[13] Although the collage is clearly related to

---

[12]Dore Ashton, *A Joseph Cornell Album* (New York: Viking, 1974); Diane Waldman, *Joseph
Cornell* (New York: George Braziller, 1977).

[13]The prose translation of Stéphane Mallarmé's poem "Le Vierge, le vivace et le bel aujour-
d'hui" transcribed by Joseph Cornell is: "The virginal, vigorous and beautiful today, will it tear
for us with a / blow of its drunken wing this hard, forgotten lake haunted under the / frost by
the transparent glacier of flights that have not flown! A swan / of former days remembers that it
is he who magnificent but without / hope frees himself because he did not sing of the country
in which to / live when the tedium of the sterile winter shone. His whole neck will shake / off
the white agony inflicted by space on the bird that denies it, but not / the horror of the soil in
which his feathers are caught. A phantom whose / pure brilliance relegates to this place, he
remains immobile in the cold / dream of scorn that in his useless exile dons the swan."

the text, we may wonder whether it stands as a visual equivalent or whether Cornell has merely indicated his poetic source. The artist's signature appears as a mirror image. Cornell avoids a side-by-side display of the visual and the textual, the conventional pattern of illustration; he thereby refrains from reducing the *Vierge vivace* to the status of a mimetic representation of "Le Vierge, le vivace et le bel aujourd'hui." Mallarmé's sonnet does not become a quotation or fragment in Cornell's art work. The American artist even shelters the poem from the reader's possible reconstruction.

In a blue space the luminous image of the pure white swan with its large wings and elegant neck occupies the center of the collage. The swan's central position coincides with the strongest photographic precision. Contrasting with the dark background, the white swan casts luminous reflections that scatter like ripples on the water. Further reflections, ambiguous due to their cloudiness, form a somewhat irregular circle on the periphery.

From the precision of the swan image, to the semi-vagueness of its reflection, to the scattered reverberations on the outside, we detect a clear progression. Nonetheless, this apparent unity suffers from more than gradual dispersion. The clearly delineated swan image casts reflections that disintegrate the photographic clarity. We may say that this belongs to the nature of reflection. Yet when we turn our attention to the outer reverberations we can no longer account for their source with any certainty: we may associate them with the shadows of foliage, with clouds, without, however, completely forgetting the central image of the swan. The image appears more and more out of focus as our eye moves from the center to the periphery. More important still, the nature of representation becomes discontinuous: from a snapshot we move to a sort of rayogram; the surrealist technique is undeniable.

By his central figure Cornell refers directly to Mallarmé's white swan, to the hypothetical movements of its wings:

> *Va-t-il nous déchirer avec un coup d'aile ivre*
> Will it tear for us with a blow of its drunken wing
>
> *Tout son col secouera cette blanche agonie.*
> Its whole neck will shake off the white agony.

Mallarmé proposes a possible future that will eventually turn once more into negation of poetic action and liberation. This failure serves to prolong a limitless past, because day after day the flight has not materialized. Mallarmé combines a shadow-like existence with pure whiteness: "Fantome qu'à ce lieu son pur éclat assigne" (Phantom who to this place his pure brilliance relegates him). The poet's white swan remains inseparable from the white landscape. Cornell, on the other hand, in spite of the pronounced contrast of blue and white, makes swan and landsape echo each other, as we have suggested. But the cold winter day, the icy lake, the layers of frozen water set up no reverberations in the collage. In the sonnet the poet establishes correspondences between the inner and outer world—the immobility of the lake, the paralysis of the swan, the psychological stagnation of boredom, the futility of the poet's existence.

Cornell, without translating the unity created by Mallarmé's correspondences, metaphors, and symbols, implies by the gradual dispersion of the central image toward the periphery that this dissolution parallels the swan's vain efforts. Robert Greer Cohn in his analysis of the sonnet states: "And although the words, in a linear progression, tell a story on the basis of their ordinary meaning, they also, like the star-words of the *Coup de Dés*, radiate among each other—in a crystal-like or constellar pattern—to create a vibrant atmosphere well beyond that rather commonplace message."[14] The structure of Cornell's collage may reflect the transformation of the words within the poem from their ordinary referential function, appropriately represented by a photographic image, to their overdetermination in a poetic framework. Cornell implies a separation, if not a rift, between the two types of language; in this way he goes beyond the surrealist illustration. As we intimated, the American artist left the symbolist poem intact, yet in his collage he clearly adopted only one level of the sonnet's multiple layers. Whereas Mallarmé evokes dramatic tension between dream and reality, potential and defeat, Cornell addresses himself merely to the dream, a concentrated image which necessarily moves into zones of greater fluidity and undergoes simultaneously the cycle of repetition, variation, and loss of autonomy. His collage does not show the image of the frozen swan; in fact, one may claim the absence of the poet's swan but the presence of its speculations, deriving from the presence of the swan in the poetic text.

Cornell's title *Vierge vivace*, separated from "le bel aujourd'hui," the reference to the winter morning, alludes merely to the swan, thus destroying the ambiguity based on time. He must substitute spatial embellishments for verbal splendor. As usual, these embellishments display marks of an unfinished, uneven execution. The description of the work reads: "Collage of reproduction, paper, with pencil and stain." Irregularity characterizes the square containing the swan image. In addition to photographic precision, Cornell has

[14]Robert Greer Cohn, *Toward the Poems of Mallarmé* (Berkeley: University of California Press, 1965), p. 125.

traced geometric lines to emphasize imperfection. Moreover, the black back-ground on one side oversteps expected boundaries, partly eclipsing the swan's luminous shadow as well as some cloud-like forms. A similar interplay be-tween perfection and incompleteness characterizes the outer rectangular frame. It comprises geometric figures—circles, arches, and straight lines—endowed with a conceptual rigor pertinent to Mallarmé. Inscribed on a stained surface, it bears signs of erosion. Impeccability and precision belong to both the photographic reproduction and the mathematical contours; both are based on the circle. But distance from the centered image of the swan and the globe increases fragmentation and corrosion. Cornell reduces to a single level thematic and structural repercussions, but, again like Mallarmé, he re-stores duality, division, in the realm of esthetics. He accomplishes the seem-ingly impossible task of treating in a collage, based by definition on fragmen-tation, the sonnet that best exemplifies the creation of harmony through multi-leveled structures.[15]

The various functions and manifestations in collage that we attributed to fragmentation also operate in some of Cornell's boxes, which can be consid-ered three-dimensional collages or subverted books. The round cardboard box, according to its title, *Mémoires inédits de Madame la Comtesse de G . . .* (Fig. 117), printed on top of the lid, presents an unpublished version of a nineteenth-century book. The date of publication and name of the editor are furnished at the bottom. All these data correspond precisely to the memoirs of Madame de Genlis published in 1825; Cornell has, then, adopted an ex-isting paradox and put it in a new context. His box, housing words, papers, and souvenirs, becomes indeed a new version—unique, therefore unpub-lished—of the eight volumes of Madame de Genlis's memoirs, strikingly re-duced and fragmented. The box contains two different texts: one, inscribed in the lid, is a letter from Auguste to Eugène dated 15 April 1820; the other, in the interior, contains sand, a ball, and a ribbon, in addition to loose strips on which words, partly hidden by the sand, are printed. Amid these yet unauthored words, one detects the name or potential signature G. . . .

In their present form these recollections and inventories of words lack unity, coherence, and continuity. Badly cut-up name tags, randomly thrown on top of each other, defying all our reading habits, are objects rather than

---

[15]Time, suppressed in the title, returns in the form of erosion or duration made tangible. Compare the definition of the collage formulated by the "Groupe *Mu*": "The technique of collage consists in appropriating a certain number of elements from works, objects, messages already in existence, and integrating them into a new creation so as to produce an original whole where ruptures of various kinds are disclosed": "Douze bribes pour décoller en 40 000 signes," *Collages, Revue d'Esthétique* 3/4 (1978): 13.

FIG. 117. Box construction by Joseph Cornell, *Mémoires inédits de Madame la Comtesse de G.*, 1939. © Estate of Joseph Cornell. Photograph courtesy of Castelli Feigen Corcoran, New York.

words. The lid or functional lining presents a legible text, not devoid of meaning, taken from an unknown French epistolary novel of the period. This quotation is truncated, for the circumference of the round box cuts the edges of the rectangular shape of the printed page. The passage, predating Madame de Genlis's *Mémoires inédits*, serves as a sort of commentary on the new "mémoires" inédits.

The relation between the two texts is one not only of elaboration versus raw material but also of word versus image, for the text in the lid constitutes a segment of discourse, that in the box shows an assemblage of disconnected words and letters—a heteroclite collection of *objets trouvés* (found objects).[16] Illustration, as in *Vierge vivace*, does not depend primarily on the visualization of the finished text, but on a process of consolidation and dispersion. Each text shows up by comparison the incompleteness of the other. As a quotation, the text in the lid becomes a potential intertext and, as such, is threat-

[16]We have repeatedly stated or implied that there is a connection between quotations and collages. Cf. in this context Jean-Yves Bosseur, "Le Collage, No Man's Land," in *Collages*, p. 291.

ened by further curtailment. Their juncture proposes a critical dimension similar to the one we discovered in other chapters.

The letter from Auguste to Eugène constitutes another double in the complex series we have detected so far. It contains, printed in italics, a hypothetical letter that Eugène would have written in response to Auguste's and the latter's justification, printed in roman characters, regarding Eugène's forestalled reproaches. Cornell adds another dimension to the reverberating interplay of published versus unpublished material. Eugène's unwritten letter, another intertext, postulates chance, lack of motivation; the reprinted letter by Auguste states belief in reason and practicality as a principle of behavior. However moral in appearance, such reflections are merely metacritical here, since the later stages of artistic creation curtail the artist's freedom by their overdetermination. The strips of words in the box permit every possible chance and rearrangement.

The title page of Madame de Genlis's memoirs, reprinted on the lid's exterior, promises a historical or political account from the eighteenth century to the present; the words in the letter put at the viewer's disposal merely reiterate banalities. Nevertheless, the book is a magic container lined with velvet and bearing a glass seal. An object of contemplation rather than participation, it is in dire need of mediation as the written, unwritten, and rewritten fragments attain practically the same status. Cornell shows Mallarmé's sonnet as a relic that impelled him to create an imperfect object. In *Mémoires inédits de Madame la Comtesse de G. . .* , he again suggests the treasure of a book that houses objects and words, incapable, in spite of renewed efforts, of constituting a whole.

In at least three works, *Nouveaux Contes des fées*, *Les Trois Mousquetaires*, and Untitled (*Paul and Virginia*) (Fig. 118), Cornell represents famous works of fiction by a set of identical empty boxes, a fragmentation that makes the parts appear totally indistinguishable. *Paul and Virginia* is made up of a mirrored door lined with cut-up sections of an illustrated edition of the eighteenth-century novel and a cabinet shelving a number of smaller boxes and framing two sealed compartments containing objects. Cornell used some woodcuts from the profusely illustrated Curmer edition (discussed in the Introduction, above) and fragments from an English translation of the novel to compose his single-page, duly signed collage. This collage door, made of paper from the same literary source, possesses unity on a certain level. The famous illustration celebrating the romantic union of Paul and Virginia amid the harmonies of nature occupies the central position (see Figs. 2, 3, 4, 5). Devoid of any direct bearing on this illustration, the surrounding passages of text become merely a frame of printed words pasted together.[17] They do not even provide the continuity of the white paper margins they replace. Irregularities and imperfections mar these cut-out sections, which do not contain a single complete sentence. In spite of the disintegration of the original book and the fragmentation of the collaged page, which Cornell presents as his own work, the new relations created by text and image, frame and center, bring out key tensions in Bernardin de St. Pierre's novel, *Paul et Virginie*; thus the fragmented sections indeed constitute an illustration.

The idyll portrayed in the center stresses the notion of protection—Paul shelters Virginia and both are sheltered by nature—whereas the surrounding text speaks of tension and upheaval. Hints of family feelings emerge from one fragment, of the opposition between solitude and usefulness from another, of storminess and shipwreck from a third. Contrary to the illustrated edition, where the plates reflect on or mirror the text, Cornell's collage brings out a relation totally dependent on conflict. The sequential order of the text is broken down by spatialization, for juxtapositions on the semantic level result in a non sequitur, while bringing out contradictions postponed in the text to specific later sections. Cornell's signed page includes pieces of other illustrations. Detached from the text to which they belonged, in which they were embedded as vignettes, they have thus undergone a double fragmentation. The truncated image transforms the other elements of the collage as it injects a creative force into Cornell's new story. The rift that emerges between the text and the central illustration is still further widened by other fragmented woodcuts. For Bernardin de St. Pierre's concern with man's relation to nature, Cornell substitutes the problem of representation in art and literature.

Book pages line shelves and as boxes, functioning as chapters, hide their emptiness.[18] The discontinuous text on the door gives hints of meaning; the infinitely fragmented, indecipherable strips on the shelves are reduced to texture. As our eye passes from the mirror to the collage, it encounters reversals and dislocations even before it can reach the little boxes. Identical in size, they are stacked in a slightly irregular, somewhat disturbing manner; as their blueness reveals alluring variations, they seem to be exposed to changes of light. Are these boxes made of fragments cut from a sky represented in painting? Has Cornell transformed the painter's perspective into sixteen separate three-dimensional objects, as he has replaced the three-dimensional book by the surface of the collage and its multiple pieces?

[17]Cf. Laurent Jenny, "Sémiotique du collage intertextuel ou la littérature à coups de ciseaux," *Collages*, p. 165.
[18]Edwin A. Bergman has given us a detailed description of this box.

FIG. 118. Box construction by Joseph Cornell, untitled (subtitled *Paul and Virginia*), 1946. Private collection. Photograph courtesy of Castelli Feigen Corcoran, New York.

The boxes plus the sealed compartments epitomize Cornell's repeated mirroring of open and closed containers, secrets and disclosure. By more than one device and, as we have seen, in more than one work Cornell has obliterated the difference between the raw material and the created artwork. The partly blue windows refer obliquely to empty boxes. Although not mentioned in the single-page collage, eggs and nests recur frequently in Curmer's plates, preparing step by step for the key illustration. Cornell's landscape diverges from it, as he shows threat, storminess, and eggs abandoned in sharp-edged straw.

Cornell transforms Bernardin de St. Pierre's narration into a simultaneity, that of the collage and the windows, from which we start rereading, reviewing, and reconstructing the fragmented book; simultaneity is a characteristic aim of the surrealist book, as we have repeatedly noted. And the reading that Cornell proposes by pasting together fragments of a book is not unlike those required by surrealist writers and painters. In Cornell's work the author has vanished and the text is revamped so that it becomes illustration without being related to iconography and invention.

We have discussed collages and boxes by Cornell in order to establish their link with the verbal arts and their derivation from literature, hence from books. Among Cornell's many untitled works are fabricated "book constructions," which can be related to surrealist objects, especially modified, perturbed, or interpreted objects.[19] In other words, "book constructions" are modified objects in which the point of departure coincides with a specific object: a book. As the emphasis falls on the fabrication of the object, not on the text, Cornell, who might have appeared marginal to our purpose, is seen as a forerunner of recent experimentation in book art. In "book construction," Cornell adds to or subtracts from an existing book. He almost invariably introduces a volume from an earlier period, as though to undercut obvious features of modernity. The volume represents a document of the past. The text in question is often a scientific treatise: *Bibliothèque de médecin-practicien*, *Précis de physique*, by M. Privat Deschanel, *Recherches sur les accumulateurs électriques*, by R. Tamine.[20] Cornell modifies these scientific texts by adding, in some cases, images borrowed from other volumes or paper cut-outs manufactured for children. In *Object—A Right System of Teaching French*, by E. C. Dubois, he introduces a luscious-looking palm tree growing over a luxuriant fern with a fashionably dressed woman sprouting butterfly wings. Cornell ironically implies that nature and artifice may harmonize as they clash with a text they partially cover up.[21] This French teaching manual, displaying conjugations of the verbs *to have* and *to be*, belongs as much to the child's world as the papercuts do. Here unadorned morphology juxtaposed with picturesque disguise forms a collage no less disruptive than some of Max Ernst's. Cornell, even more than Ernst, turns us away from the act of reading by the minuteness of the printed characters, segmentation, erosion of old documents, upside-down lettering, brush-strokes covering up printing. His texts tend to function as souvenirs, as partial survivors, as textuality that defies illustration and lends itself neither to enrichment nor interpretation.

In more than one of his "book constructions" Cornell has inserted a square hole in the center of the page, partially filling the empty space with tiny objects such as a window, a spiral, or pieces of marble as well as marbles.[22] In focusing on the center of the page the viewer shifts from a two-dimensional to a three-dimensional space, which thus becomes the emplacement of illustration. The destruction of the integrity of the book and the unity of the page results in a volume, in both senses of the word. It is not a specific text but

[19]Cf. Joseph Cornell, Museum of Modern Art nos. 58 to 63.
[20]Both at The Art Institute of Chicago, n.d.
[21]At The Art Institute of Chicago.
[22]E.g., *Object, Recherches sur les accumulateurs électriques*, and *Untitled (Rosalba, Book with Marble)*.

FIG. 119. Book-object by Helmut Löhr, 1984. © Galerie Caroline Corre.

textuality itself that is illustrated, for the page becomes a fragment of a volume made visible from the inside rather than the outside. At the same time, by means of his usual peepshows, Cornell diverts us from the act of reading.

Cornell, perhaps a more thorough Romantic than most surrealists, has made a strong impact on recent *livres d'artiste* exhibited in 1985 at the Centre Georges Pompidou and in 1984 at the Galerie Caroline Corre.[23] The work of Jan Kristofori is particularly interesting here, for it permits us to point out how the surrealist book underwent modifications. Kristofori often assembles old books in his constructions, almost in the manner of a still-life. Kristofori shares Cornell's respect for "the original," which he often improves by "antiquing." Karel Trinkewitz has compared Kristofori's boxes to astronomers' libraries and alchemists' kitchens.[24]

It is not so much the poetics of these boxes as their relationship to surrealist books that preoccupies us. Everything in the construct is simultaneously exposure and hiding of writing or printing. Every line is displaced. Printed lines cover shelves; other printed lines cover margins, while pages are folded over.

[23] *Le Livre d'artiste*, Paris, Centre Georges Pompidou, 1985 and *Livres-objets, exposition réalisée par Caroline Corre*, Paris, Bibliothèque-Discothèque Faidherbe, March 1983.
[24] *Livres-objets*, p. 32.

Pieces of printed paper overshadow others and often obliterate each other. Writing, printing everywhere and not a line to read! The image of printing replaces the text; visibility makes legibility futile. Or, rather, text and image problematize each other, as they simultaneously attract and repulse the reader. Cornell and Kristofori have opened the way to the deviant books of Helmut Löhr and others. Löhr's *livre-objet* suggests a piece of sculpture wrought not in brass or marble but in paper.[25] Pages are bent, twisted, forced to overlap; and Löhr comments on our culture by putting reading, made forever inaccessible, on a pedestal (Fig. 119). It also appears that illustration has finally devoured and absorbed its other, the text. The tension between word and image, always latent in the surrealist works surveyed, has thrust us beyond the illustrated book.

[25] Ibid., p. 34, and *Livres-objets*, Galerie du centre d'action culturelle Pablo Neruda, Corbeil, 1984, p. 26.

SPECIFICITY OF
THE SURREALIST BOOK

WE HAVE STRESSED THROUGHOUT THIS STUDY a number of anti-mimetic characteristics which the surrealist book shares not only with other surrealist artifacts and activities but with modernist works in general. In keeping with the principles formulated by Breton in his *Manifestes*, the surrealist work of art, whether verbal or visual, is marked by a peculiar kind of (self)referentiality. In their relentless pursuit of another world, the surrealists carefully avoid traditional forms of representation that in one way or another favor a mechanical adherence to the tangible world of experience. In elaborating their own referentiality, they appear to follow basic tenets and even techniques equally pertinent to verbal and to visual language, which they alternately combine and differentiate. Artistic manipulation and dream activity provide necessary mediations that encourage them to transform recognizable or descriptive reality into otherness. This does not mean that allusions to everyday existence cannot be traced in surrealist works in general and books in particular. Our discussion of illustrations in *Nadja, Une Semaine de bonté*, and Magritte's *Les Chants de Maldoror* touches on the presence of commonplace reality lurking within the contexts of metamorphosis, juxtaposition, and assemblage. In most instances, the point of departure or token origin and, quite frequently, other salient moments, standing exposed within the field of observation of the ordinary, invite both text and image to disrupt and subvert them, usually by displacement. The reader experiences pleasurable if disquieting surprises at the repeated dismantling of all mimetic representations and, indeed, of all reassuring relationships.

We can even claim that this anti-mimetic pursuit reaches its greatest intensity in the surrealist book, where verbal and visual elements converge and combine in order to fulfill the surrealist ambition of revolutionizing rather than restating and of reversing accepted values instead of merely analyzing or restoring them. In keeping with the movement's anti-mimetic stance, the illustrator, far from considering the text a model for which he must provide a graphic equivalent, treats it as a stimulus for his imagination capable of putting him in close contact with his own redoubtable cerebrations. The reader is more than once torn from a comfortable adherence, if not to reality, at least to a monolithic form of representation. The interacting presences of verbal and visual texts inimical to all overt parallelism or analogy give the star role to paradox and force the reader through a series of repeated disturbances, each of which may lead to the esthetic delight of decoding a forbidden artifact—forbidden insofar as it withholds the secret of its multiple interactions from the noninitiate.

Since we have implied that the creation of art objects whose elaboration belies and bypasses all mimetic intent characterizes most modernist art and literature from Joyce to Picasso, from Breton to Ernst, from Woolf to Nolde, our commentary must, if only to do justice to the surrealist book, reach beyond its confines. We therefore propose to stress its divergences and determine its originality by comparing it to the expressionist book, a highly prolific and in many ways innovative genre, whose manifestations extend beyond the years 1907–27, which are generally assigned to expressionism in Central Europe even though such major artists as Max Beckmann, Ernst Kirchner, Oskar Kokoschka, Emil Nolde, and Max Pechstein produced masterpieces for decades after the supposed demise of the movement. There exist, as we have shown, even more cogent reasons for not confining the surrealist book to the period of *Nadja*, *Le Paysan de Paris*, and *Le Grand Masturbateur*. Such chronologically framed views undoubtedly serve the purpose of historians, but they may hinder attempts at esthetic definition and interpretation. We do not consider the surrealist book a mere side effect of more important manifestations, whether polemic, critical, ideological, or creative, but a genre which broadened and diversified over a long period and remains very much alive in the 1980s, as Matta's remarkable *Ubu roi* (1982) so brilliantly demonstrates. Similarly, expressionism had ramifications outside Central Europe—for example, in Edouard Goerg's *L'Ange du bizarre*, with twenty-eight etchings (Paris: Sautier, 1947), and Mario Prassinos's *La Ballade du vieux marin* (Paris: G.L.M., 1946). Thus it appears to extend far beyond 1927, the date Lothar Lang chose as the cut-off for his study, and even beyond World War Two. Lang has shown the opposition that the expressionist book encountered, primarily from historians and bibliophiles.[1] Surprisingly, hostility to-

[1]Lothar Lang, *Expressionist Book Illustration* (Boston: New York Graphic Society, 1976), p. 15.

ward the surrealist book arose far less frequently and in quite different quarters. In fact, late productions, such as Masson's *Une Saison en enfer,* were even commissioned by decorous societies of bibliophiles. The early surrealist book remained to a large extent a confidential and almost private endeavor, as far removed as possible from the marketplace. Printed in small editions, it was circulated almost exclusively among friends and thus could hardly produce a disruptive stir in a public unaware of its very existence. The extreme example of such privacy is of course Eluard and Ernst's secretive *Au défaut du silence,* but even polemical works such as *Les Malheurs des immortels,* for want of a proper arena, found few, if any, challengers.

The attack against the expressionist book was directed first of all against the publisher, who somehow became identified with and shared responsibility with the writers and artists he discovered.[2] The same fate or glory did not befall Parisian publishers. Even if the majority of Jean Hugues's books pertain in one way or another to surrealism, bibliophiles never seem to take offense at his productions. Although Dalí's *Chants de Maldoror* provides an undeniable example of a shockingly disturbing illustration going far beyond the poet's provocative text, the Swiss publisher, Skira, succeeded in lending an aura of respectability to the entire enterprise. Enemies of the expressionist book, which they viewed as an abominable distortion of a traditional and hence untouchable object, repeatedly took aim at what appeared to them violations of the sacrosanct act of reading.[3] This objection may to a certain extent apply to the work of the surrealists. Patrons and critics have every right to expect that a proper book, whatever its nationality, should conform to and enhance universal bourgeois taste, particularly if it must double as an art object—as a personal possession, as a manageable, marketable, competitive investment, displaying the cultural prestige of wealthy families. The expressionist book, according to its detractors, violated all such norms of good taste, beginning with the esthetic unity of the page. In spite of the daring use of photography with its erotic "exposure," Man Ray's *Facile,* published in Paris, does not appear to have disturbed the bibliophilic establishment, even though critics often inveighed against surrealist painters and film directors for their indecency and lack of taste.

We do not mean to deny that such books as *Facile, Les Malheurs des immortels,* and *Les Chants de Maldoror* fully exemplify the revolt with which

[2] Ibid.; cf. Orrel Reed, Jr., *German Expressionist Art,* (Los Angeles: Frederick S. Wight Art Gallery, University of California, 1977), p. 267.
[3] Lang, *Expressionist Book Illustration,* p. 15. Cf. *L'Expressionisme à travers la gravure allemande, Cahiers de l'image* 2 (Paris)(1982): 4–5.

everyone associates the movement. After all, they present suspicious views of a nude torso, a baby's legs struggling out of a glass bowl, a face that is a simulacrum composed of edibles and kitchen utensils. But expressionist book illustration may have aroused the ire of the reading public not only by the disturbing nature of its subject matter, by inveterately offensive imagery, but perhaps principally by its bold if questionable techniques. The widespread use of woodcuts by expressionist artists is well known, as is their emulation of late medieval and sixteenth-century prints. They attempted to adapt their landscapes, their perspectives, and even their typography to an earlier, and by some deemed inferior, state of the art. True, Ernst in his use of collage clearly alludes to earlier art, but he does so with total lack of respect, in order to chastise the reading public's outmoded taste and adherence to superannuated models. And even when the surrealists do use wood engraving, for instance in A *toute épreuve*, where the wood fiber shows through the design, they attempt to establish immediacy between the artist and the medium rather than incorporate into modern creativity a practice better suited, in the eyes of hostile critics, to a bygone age. Comparisons among a number of plates engraved in wood, created by surrealist and expressionist artists, would show that the space of the German woodcut tends to be representational and relies on closure, whereas the surrealist woodcut opens up space and, by this device, liberates the unconscious.

The expressionists used woodcuts because they provided a natural medium to stress disproportion by means of the wood grain, though not the pattern of the fibers. In emphasizing distortion, they relied to a greater extent than the surrealists on their readers' propensity to recognize a world that they would pull out of shape. This could serve to undermine notions of stability and was made all the more disturbing by the use of spatial reduction, which reinforced the distortions of the world therein depicted. The surrealist book, instead of presenting to its readers a universe featuring disproportion, exploits more pronounced forms of surprise, disruption, and alienation. It tends to deny the traces and marginal referentiality of a recognizable world. It opens up instead of confining, be it spatially or through detailed representation. It brings out as many conflicting aspects as possible, by juxtaposition instead of distortion. It seems that the expressionist book focuses on a tragic vision, whereas the surrealist book tries to lead its readers toward visionary participation in another world. In this connection, surrealist illustrators, notably Dalí and Masson, exploit not simply the technique of collage but its very principle, particularly by introducing materials that do not harmonize in an expected manner. In the expressionist book, one text, either readable or visible, can still be construed as accompanying another or at least as providing the other with a suitable frame or color. Such reassuring characteristics do not apply to surrealism. There one text catapults the other onto a new territory and precipitates its latent potentials, as in *Les Marionnettes, Alice in Wonderland,* and *Une Saison en enfer.* Consequently, the expressionist book owes its structure to a certain degree to formats and patterns that recur and unify while avoiding digression and redundant ornamentation. The surrealist book in most instances eludes the limitations of scale and repetitions, which do not extend, except in Ernst's "poèmes visibles," to poetic indefiniteness.

"Le peintre ne tâche pas de reconstituer une anecdote, mais de constituer un fait pictural" (The painter does not attempt to reconstruct an anecdote, but to establish a pictorial fact).[4] It seems that Braque the cubist here expresses in different terms the anti-mimetic stance on which we have so often insisted and which appears to distinguish the surrealist from the expressionist book. An anecdote, a story would necessarily introduce referentiality, but Braque's rejection aims primarily at formulating a perhaps biased distinction between modern painting and what preceded. True artists must distinguish themselves from those who, in his opinion, do not paint but narrate. Braque seeks to protect the integrity of his art from the constant intrusions of literature. Now, surrealist art has been criticized far more frequently than other forms of modernism just because of the presence of the anecdotal. The painters were thus accused of being more literary than painterly; the writers, of committing the opposite sin of merely stringing images together. Braque, on the contrary, was praised for reconstructing the phenomenological world, after reducing it to its essentials and denying it its privileged position. If the surrealists do at times tell a tale, they place it in a disquieting landscape where new elements emerge, where sea and earth coincide, where constellations multiply. Contours and colors cannot be circumscribed by lines; the entire palette has to be reinvented.

Kahnweiler, an editor intimately associated with the initial thrust of cubism, strongly supported the early efforts of the surrealists in spite of the fact that the analytical approach and search for essentials so characteristic of the former have little in common with the latter's exploitation of the irrational and the unconscious in their ventures beyond the known and the familiar.

[4]Braque, quoted in *Lettres et manuscrits autographes,* Hôtel Drouot, Room 3, 12 December 1985, no. 22.

The publisher's inventive skills somehow establish a common bond between works as different as André Derain's *L'Enchanteur pourrissant* and André Masson's *Simulacre*, where the painter perpetuates Michel Leiris's militancy against the appearances of the real. Actually, Masson's engravings have all the linear simplicity that a cubist graphic artist could wish, even though they differ considerably in their manner of assembling lines and planes. And this resemblance goes beyond the anti-mimetic stance common to the two schools.

The publication of *Simulacre* almost exactly coincided with the official proclamation of surrealist allegiance to automatism. In his *Manifeste*, Breton had obligingly provided directions for the production of genuine automatic texts and drawings. The gestural quality of certain illustrations, notably those composed by Masson for *Une Saison en enfer*, do relate to automatic practices, which the artist eagerly substitutes for self-conscious or already codified forms of representation. There of course exist various ways whereby automatism can impinge on the viewer. Péret in *Dormir, dormir dans les pierres* spontaneously sets off an irresistible flow of imagery. The poems of *Les Malheurs des immortels* may well have resulted from words initially ejaculated without benefit of reason and which generated verbal collages. Nevertheless, automatism, however widespread it may have been in surrealist practice, tends to undermine our assertion that the illustrator functions as a reader, a viewer, and an interpreter whose translation of the text into another language is generally subversive and projective. Automatism as such may not suffice to project the subversive potential of the text. Dalí manipulated Lautréamont's text until he could read into it his own obsessive iconography, which shows that we should beware of minimizing a painter's role as reader. But automatism, a cerebral exercise, lends itself to misinterpretation. Initially it served as a means to break down existing barriers, and, by requiring a focus on the present strong enough to alienate the past, it succeeded in dividing the self. But such an operation, however sophisticated it may appear, can hardly elaborate artifacts involving more than one artist and combining more than one medium. For that reason, the complexities of the surrealist book may serve as a caution to those who would grant too great an importance to automatism in their assessment of the movement.

The subject of automatism came up during a Matta retrospective held at Stockholm in 1959, where he mentioned that Masson's drawings were often produced through automatism.[5] Of course, frottage and sand-painting lend

[5] *Matta*, Centre Georges Pompidou, 3 October–16 December 1985, p. 287.

themselves to automatism far more readily than etchings, woodcuts, or even lithographs, the usual media of book illustrators. Matta, still taking Masson as an example, stated that in the very act of splashing a multiplicity of colors on a white surface, "it [the method] consists in relying on automatism until the moment when the destiny of the work gets the upper hand. The unconscious and willpower bring equal forces to bear in the game."[6] This statement by one of the few survivors among the major surrealists certainly testifies to the persistence as well as the modification of the initial aims of the movement. Even though Breton had pledged that surrealism would never write its own history,[7] Matta, from the vantage point of 1959, addressed, at least implicitly, the question of the changing role of automatism and, more explicitly, the stages through which the artist must pass in the course of artistic creation. Matta's point of view, somewhat at variance with the principles governing the early days of surrealism as well as with our first chapter, appears eminently suited to post-war achievements. In these late works, the artists go beyond mere visual and verbal inventiveness or exchanges of views with collaborators in order to experiment with the book itself, henceforth regarded as an autonomous genre. Matta's statement suggests that the surrealist painter, in becoming progressively more aware of the nature of his art, inevitably shuns the possessiveness of his own creative impulses which, in the manner of a Paul Valéry, he subordinates to the work itself. The ambiguity or paradox of surrealist art, so overt in the illustrated book, centers on the unstable relationship between creative act and artifact, whose status has always remained in question. In the book, artists, often stimulated by book-designing publishers, highlighted artistic potential in waging their war against all possible codifications.

Ernst devoted some of his last illustrations to Beckett's *From an Abandoned Work*.[8] Once more frottage, so close and so analogous, according to *Au-delà de la peinture*, to collage, emerges among other lines in the etching. Not surprisingly, the post-modern Beckett enables Ernst to move further along the path toward discontinuity and deconstruction than any of the surrealist writers or their precursors did. Indeed, Beckett, in subverting lyricism, narrative, and representation, far outstrips Breton and even the most recent of his followers. To be sure, he does not dismiss narrative and anecdote to the same

[6]Ibid.
[7]For that reason he opposed the reprinting of major surrealist journals such as *La Révolution surréaliste*.
[8]Samuel Beckett, *From an Abandoned Work* (Stuttgart: Manus Presse, 1967).

extent as Braque the cubist did. Although Ernst has provided *From an Abandoned Work* with an illustration that does not differ radically from those interacting with surrealist texts, nonetheless he has brought surrealism to the very threshold of post-modernism—which is by no means the threshold to that "other world." He has meticulously confronted the metacritical web of Beckett's text by reducing frottage, itself a vestige or trace of automatism, to the shadow with which nobody can dispense.

Index

Design and Composition: Wilsted & Taylor
Printing: Malloy Lithographing, Inc.
Binding: John H. Dekker & Sons
Paper: 70# Stora Matte
Typeface: Electra